SPIKE LEE

That's My Story and
I'm Sticking to It

SPIKE LEE

That's My Story and I'm Sticking to It

as told to
KALEEM AFTAB

W. W. Norton & Company
New York   London

First published in England 2005 by Faber and Faber Limited
Copyright © 2005 by Kaleem Aftab
First American edition 2005

For information about permission to reproduce selections from this book, write to
Permissions, W. W. Norton & Company, Inc., 500 Fifth Avenue, New York, NY 10110

Manufacturing by R. R. Donnelley, Harrisonburg Division
Production manager: Julia Druskin

Library of Congress Cataloging-in-Publication Data

Aftab, Kaleem.
    Spike Lee : that's my story and I'm sticking to it / as told to Kaleem Aftab.—
1st American ed.
        p. cm.
    Includes index.
    ISBN 0-393-06153-1
    1. Lee, Spike. 2. Motion picture producers and directors—United States—Biography.
3. African American motion picture producers and directors—United States—Biography.
I. Lee, Spike. II. Title.
    PN1998.3.L44A68 2005
    791.43'0233'092—dc22
                                                                2005014211

W. W. Norton & Company, Inc., 500 Fifth Avenue, New York, N.Y. 10110
www.wwnorton.com

W. W. Norton & Company Ltd., Castle House, 75/76 Wells Street, London W1T 3QT

1 2 3 4 5 6 7 8 9 0

Contents

List of Illustrations

SPIKE LEE

That's My Story and I'm Sticking to It

I 40 Acres and a Mule

A wooden boat crosses the Atlantic Ocean. Down in the galleys are women and men squashed together, gagged and bound in chains, ordered not to talk to each other. So they create a rhythmic patois by which to communicate. The names of these people are not recorded — and in any case, their names would soon be changed by their white slave masters as a mark of proprietorship. These black-skinned human cattle were stolen from their families and homes to be exploited across the length of a land itself once roamed by "Native Americans." These "savages and animals" are the ancestors of Frederick Douglass, Booker T. Washington, Marcus Garvey, Mary Bethune, Ella Fitzgerald, Jackie Robinson, Willie Mays, Joe Louis, Muhammad Ali, Adam Clayton Powell Jr., Stokely Carmichael, Martin Luther King Jr., Malcolm X, Jesse Jackson; not to speak of soldiers who fought in the American Revolutionary War, the Civil War, the First and Second World Wars, the Korean War, the Vietnam War, the Persian Gulf War and others.

The vestiges of slavery are still very evident in the United States, where more than one in ten inhabitants call themselves "African-American." To first encounter slavery's appalling history is an experience memorably captured by Malcolm X in his celebrated *Autobiography*: "I will never forget how shocked I was when I began reading about slavery's total horror. It made such an impact upon me. . . . The world's most monstrous crime, the sin and the blood on the white man's hands, are almost impossible to believe."

Shelton Jackson Lee — "Spike" as the world would know him — is also a man who embraced African-American history. Lee's name first erupted into the American popular consciousness with the release of his début feature film, *She's Gotta Have It*, in August 1986. The movie, independently financed on a budget of $175,000, grossed $8 million at the box office. Though such success in itself would normally have been sufficient to garner a certain amount of media attention, it was not this filmmaker's unique selling point. Spike Lee was black, and he had made a film about black people, starring black people, that played for black audiences. From Hollywood's vantage point, that was way too much black in one sentence.

She's Gotta Have It was a production of 40 Acres and a Mule Film-works; and the name Spike Lee bestowed upon his company was the most pertinent signal of his sense of politics and history. "Forty acres and a mule" constituted the first formal efforts of the United States in the wake of the Civil War to make reparation for the treatment of slaves, though the precise origin of the term is contested. Forty-acre allotments of land were offered to freed slaves in Section 4 of the First Freedman's Bureau Act, defeated by Congress in 1866. But General Sherman also sought to allocate forty acres apiece, along with a hardy mule, to the freedmen who marched with him across Georgia — only to see his order rescinded by President Andrew Johnson. The issue of reparation for the iniquity of slavery has never died, and Spike Lee is not of a mind that the debt has been settled.

SPIKE LEE: *We fought for the Union against the Confederacy like we've always fought wars for America, from fighting the British right up to today's war in Iraq. But very few freed slaves got their forty acres and a mule . . . so the name of my company is really a reminder of a broken promise. Many promises have been broken by American governments, such as all the treaties with the Native Americans. They designate a reservation, they say, "Work the land." Then it's, "Oh! We've found some oil there, you guys have gotta go. . . ." How can you call yourself a great democracy and a moral authority when this country was built on the genocide of the Native Americans and on stealing people from their homeland and bringing them here for their free labor?*

I don't think you can ever be taught too much history. Today it seems like young people especially aren't taught enough of it and aren't interested in things that were happening before they were born. If you don't know who you are or where you came from, if you don't acknowledge your ancestral roots, then you really are asleep. When I go to Africa, people there tell me that I look Senegalese.

There has always been a debate about "What is black? Who is black? Who is blacker than black?" I don't really want to get into that; but what I will say is that in America, if you have one drop of black blood, you're considered African-American. There are a lot of people now who choose to check the "biracial" box on the census. And people have to understand that when I started traveling outside of the United States, doing interviews for my films that touch upon racism, it's hard for a lot of the European journalists to understand the films. They cannot get a grasp of racism in America. But race is still a big part of the fabric of America. Until we deal with it — until we deal with slavery—I feel that we are never really going to be as great as we can be as a country.

It's important for all of us to be politically aware. You have to know how politics affects your life: what you become, where your children go to school, what kind of health care you can have, how much money you can make, what potential you have—it's all shaped by politics. If you just look at the 2000 presidential election in America—there was war in Iraq because of what happened on that day, November 2. There would have been no war, I think, if Al Gore had won. In fact, he should have won—that election was rigged.

There are so many questions. And that's something I've been accused of: of raising questions without having answers. But I've never felt it was the filmmaker's job to have all the answers. I think, for the most part, if we choose to do so, we have more of a provocateur role, where we ask these questions and hopefully they will, by the way that they are asked, stimulate and generate some discussion and dialogue. But to find answers for racism and prejudice in films? You can't do that.

To pigeonhole Spike Lee on the grounds of his race would be to inflict a great injustice. This is a man who, over the two decades in which he has been in the public eye, has come to be recognized as a quintessential New Yorker: whether for watching basketball games courtside at Madison Square Garden, employing the city as the primary location for most of his films or providing his oft-reported commentaries on New York politics and daily life. "I'm definitely a product of New York City in my sensibility," says Spike. "At one time there was a campaign to make New York City the fifty-first state of the Union. And New York City is so much different from the rest of the United States that it's frightening at times."

Yet it was in his hometown, amid the commanding heights of the Twin Towers of the World Trade Center, that the defining event of recent American history would take place. The reaction of the man to that atrocious day, in both his personal life and his work, would show that Spike Lee could not be cast simply even as a New Yorker. He may yet be perceived as standing outside the mainstream, but Spike Lee is part of the cultural fabric of America.

There are eight million stories in the Naked City, and this is just one of them. . . .

2 The Early Years

SPIKE LEE: *A lot of things have happened to me in my life. Some higher being looked over me—pushed me in another direction, from the place I wanted to go to where I needed to go. It was just the right time for a young African-American filmmaker to break through. Fate has played a big part in my career, but you must also add talent, hard work, luck and timing. All those things contributed to my success.*

I think that I was born in the right year—1957—and then all I went through growing up in the turbulent sixties in America....

The eldest child of Bill Lee and Jacquelyn Shelton Lee was christened Shelton Jackson. At a young age he acquired the moniker of "Spike" via his mother, who had by then quit her teaching job to rear her five children: Spike, Chris, David, Joie and Cinque, born within an eleven-year span. Jacquelyn quickly grew accustomed to opening the window that faced out onto their tree-lined street in Brooklyn and yelling "Spike!" to call her son away from the street games in which he reveled. The nickname was in honor of the boy's petulant and fiery nature, one that his four younger siblings found considerably irksome.

Spike looks back fondly on his youth. Although he would be outspoken and very opinionated and upon occasion answer his parents back, shirk his chores and tease his youngest siblings, Spike says of his childhood demeanor, "I was not an angry child. I was an obedient child, a happy child. I was the firstborn, and my mother put a lot of responsibility on me." It was behavior that many would later see as being archetypical of an eldest child. Spike would be protective of his family members and in due course provide his father, Bill, sister, Joie, and brothers, David and Cinque, with their first breaks in the movie industry. But it was the more domineering aspect of his childhood character and the side that earned him his nickname that the media would later concentrate on, to such an extent that Spike Lee has grown accustomed and weary of issuing denials that he is an angry man by nature.

Spike's roots, like those of many black families in New York, are to be found in the south. He was born in Atlanta, Georgia, on March 20, 1957, but soon after his birth the family moved to Chicago. At the

time, the Windy City was home to a bustling jazz scene, and Bill Lee—
an upright bassist who would later play with such luminaries as Miles
Davis, Bob Dylan, Judy Collins, Peter, Paul and Mary, and John Lee
Hooker—joined the plethora of musicians hoping to find work in one
of the many jazz clubs. In a turn of events similar to that which saw
Chicago briefly become the home of American movies during the
silent-film era, the city's preeminence as the center of jazz excellence
was short-lived. Just as movie stars headed to Hollywood following
the advent of talkies, musicians struck out for New York once electric
instruments and rock'n'roll took over the music scene. The Lee family
barely caught the end of the jazz wave that swept Chicago, and were
soon on their way to the Big Apple.

Brooklyn, New York, was Spike's playground—and it was a very
different Brooklyn from the black neighborhood he would depict
in his early films. As Spike recalls, "In 1962, when we moved from
Crown Heights to Cobble Hill, an Italian-American neighborhood, we
were the first black family there. But New York City is so diverse that
at that young age I never really thought of myself in terms of color."
As a child, Spike witnessed Brooklyn's transition from majority-white
to majority-black. The Lee family found themselves at the forefront of
a trend that would see ethnic minorities move in large numbers into
homes vacated by white New Yorkers who had left the crime-ridden
inner city for the supposedly idyllic surrounds of suburbia as idealized
in TV shows such as *Father Knows Best*. Between 1950 and 1957
alone, Brooklyn's population dropped by 135,000. Spike would later
boast that his mother showed remarkable foresight in choosing to buy
the family brownstone in Fort Greene, Brooklyn, rather than rent like
the majority of the black and Puerto Rican populace who filled this
newly created housing vacuum.

One might imagine New York was a safe haven for the Lee family: far
removed from the battles of the civil-rights movement then being waged
in Georgia and across the south, from the murders of four little girls in
Birmingham, Alabama, in 1963, from the "Jim Crow" laws and from
police battering African-Americans for the crime of being black. But in
truth the north was no more removed from these battles than Birmingham itself: segregation was just as vicious and carried an insidious de
facto veneer. Northern whites could claim that they were not racist
because they did not have Jim Crow laws; and yet racial tensions were
often higher in tightly packed northern cities such as Chicago, Detroit,
Newark—and New York. As Spike grew older, he was made increasingly aware of the hardships that attended being black in America.
On the day of Dr. Martin Luther King's assassination, April 4, 1968,

Spike and brother Chris (the second eldest child) received the startling news when they saw their mother returning from work, running down the block and screaming, "They killed him, they killed Dr. King!"

For the young Spike, folk seemed to come in all colors, shapes and sizes: he would later describe New York as "the city viewed by most of America as the home of Jews, niggers, spics, and homos." But from his seat at the family dinner table, Spike was left in no doubt about his identity. "From early on," says Spike, "my parents were telling me how it was, all the time. We were always encouraged to question stuff we read in the papers or saw on TV." These dinner-table advice sessions hit home once Spike sampled racism for the first time: "I wanted to join the Boy Scouts in Cobble Hill and they told me that I couldn't join because I wasn't Catholic. But really they just didn't want a black kid in the Scouts. My father sat me down and explained it plain and simple to me."

Every summer the Lee children would be further reminded of their roots when they were packed off to spend part of the summer vacation with their maternal grandparents in Atlanta, and their paternal grandmother in Snow Hill, Alabama. Unsurprisingly, they were warned to tread more warily there than they did in Brooklyn, which, despite developing a bad reputation for rising street crime, seemed a carefree place by comparison to the south. "Like a lot of black people, to get rid of you for a break our parents would ship our asses down south to spend part of the summer vacation," says Spike. "Chris and I, we'd say, 'This stuff is too slow down here.' We liked going down, but after a while we were ready to get back to the energy of New York City."

From an early age Spike was also exposed to the arts. His father, Bill, practiced his music at home, and mother, Jacquelyn, would take Spike to see plays and musicals. (He would always retain a strong recollection of crying at a performance of *The King and I* "because the seats we had were so far up. It scared me sitting that high.") As with most aspects of his upbringing that involve his mother, Spike has fond memories: "I've always been the product of a loving and supporting family. If your family is behind you, that's half the battle. I've always felt that children's dreams are killed by their parents more than anybody else, but my parents were not like that—my *grandparents* weren't like that."

This is a viewpoint shared by David Lee, the middle child and a movie stills photographer who has worked for Jim Jarmusch, Michel Gondry and Whit Stillman, as well as his brother: "Spike is loyal to, number one, the family, and number two, African-Americans. We've always had a great deal of creativity in our family, going back further generations—my dad, of course, and then my grandparents on both sides of the family have been educators and musicians." It is a source of great pride to Spike that his great-grandfather William Edwards Williams, who studied under Booker T. Washington at Tuskegee Institute, started the Snow Hill Institute in Alabama. Nonetheless—and despite the valiant attempts of Spike's parents to expose him to politics, race and the arts—the marches against the Vietnam War and the continued struggle of the civil-rights movement did not feature on Spike's list of priorities during his youth. As he recalls, that list was all about "sports, Motown and the Beatles. Sports was all I did, that's all I cared about. I wanted to be a baseball player."

The shifting state of the music scene would once more have a dramatic effect on the Lee household. Electric instruments became *en vogue*, much to the dismay of Bill Lee, a jazz purist who refused to plug in anything that he was going to play. So, to make ends meet, Jacquelyn returned to teaching English and found a job at St. Ann's School in the plush neighborhood of Brooklyn Heights. Unlike his other siblings, who attended St. Ann's, Spike went to public school and attended John Dewey High in Coney Island, in the south of Brooklyn. Coney Island was (and is) one of New York's poorest neighborhoods, home to the Cyclone, a wooden roller coaster added to the National Register of Historic Places in 1991 that is now little more than a dot in a skyline dominated by row upon row of high-rise, low-cost housing. But having one parent in work and living in a brownstone made Spike well-to-do by comparison with some of his classmates. Earl Smith, who lived in the projects, recalls, "The first time I went into a brownstone was at Spike's. I was shocked at how high the ceilings were. I was like, 'Spike, you can play *basketball* in here. . . .' He would call up sometimes and say, 'Earl, I have tickets for the Knicks, you wanna go?' We were way up there, last row, last seat, but always *happy* to be there." In return Earl—tall, muscular and excellent at basketball—would watch Spike's back in the school playground.

Whenever he could, Spike would go—mainly with brother Chris—to see the New York Mets play baseball at Shea Stadium and the New York Knickerbockers play basketball at Madison Square Garden.[*] The Garden was also the site of many of Muhammad Ali's greatest fights and, at the age of eleven, Spike was dumbstruck at the image of Tommie Smith and John Carlos giving the Black Power salute during the playing of the U.S. national anthem as they collected their 200-meter medals at the 1968 Mexico City Olympics. Spike dreamed of becoming a professional athlete and playing second base at Shea Stadium, but these ambitions are set in stark perspective by classmate

---

[*]Spike's love for watching sports, especially the Knicks, is recounted in great detail in his basketball memoir (written with the late Ralph Wiley), *The Best Seat in the House.*

Earl Smith: "Even in the ninth grade at John Dewey school everything was about sports, baseball and basketball especially. The funny thing is that Spike wasn't the best athlete, but he would always be captain. I guess if you're captain and choosing sides, you're always going to play. So he would grab the ball first." Of course, talent scouts like to see a positive attitude in a young player, but they value athletic talent yet more; and Spike soon realized that his chances of becoming a professional athlete were less than zero.

Nor was he the best possible student: he hated math and science, and generally did just enough to get by. English, the subject his mother taught, was his favorite subject and it was in this class that Spike had a great revelation: "For me, the most influential thing that I ever read was *The Autobiography of Malcolm X,* as told to Alex Haley. I read that in junior high school." But Jacquelyn showed serious concern about the lack of enthusiasm that her son was exhibiting at school, not to say his own apparent satisfaction with grades that were good but not spectacular. At home, Jacquelyn took on the role of "bad cop" to her husband's "good": whenever the kids wanted to do something, they would ask Daddy. But Jacquelyn would lament that young Spike needed to assert himself more. "My mother sent some letters to my grandmother that are now in my possession," says Joie. "In one of them she wrote, 'Oh God, I hope Spike will amount to something, he is so immature. . . .'"

In 1975, following family tradition, Spike left home for the predominantly black Morehouse College in Atlanta, where his father first met his mother. (Jacquelyn had been attending Spelman, Morehouse's sister school, located across the street.) Then, as now, Morehouse placed special emphasis on teaching students about the history and culture of black people. The liberal arts school was founded two years after the Civil War in order to prepare black men for ministry and teaching: Martin Luther King Jr. is just one of the many prominent African-Americans who have passed through its gates.

As Spike began his studies, the mid-seventies were shaping up to be a lively cultural moment. The advent of George Clinton's techno-funk was an indication that black artists were building upon the pioneering work of Motown and Atlantic Records and were now featuring with increasing regularity on the *Billboard* chart. Spike, meanwhile, began writing for the Morehouse student paper, *The Maroon Tiger.* Girlfriendless, he tended toward fellow students who shared his developing interest in the performing arts. One such fellow, Monty Ross, would have a pivotal role in the development of Spike's film career. Ross recollects, "The first time I met Spike was through a mutual friend, George Folkes. Spike remembered a play that I was in, *The Bad Seed*. What I remember most about *him* was that he had a big afro, was careful about what he said, and asked a lot of questions." At the time, the big afro hairstyle was a political statement of black pride linked both to the Black Power ethos and the Black Panther party; as such it immediately forewarned Ross of Spike's political leanings. The Panthers—set up by Bobby Seale and Huey P. Newton to establish revolutionary socialism through mass organization, militant self-defense and community-based programs—had by now acquired an international profile and even captured the imagination of world-famous filmmakers, most notably Michelangelo Antonioni, who cast Panther Kathleen Cleaver in a cameo for the opening reel of his revolutionary fantasia *Zabriskie Point* (1970).

Monty Ross and Spike bonded over black politics and a shared passion for movies. They also shared a regret for the manner in which American movies traditionally played on stereotypical images of black people. The pair spent many a night out on the porch at the house of Spike's grandmother Zimmie Shelton, who lived four blocks from the college and would prepare meals for Spike that were far superior to those offered by the school canteen. She also played a pivotal role in his future development, as Spike is happy to relate: "It was my grandmother who put me through Morehouse, then NYU Film School, plus she gave me additional funds for my films at film school—the aborted *Messenger* and *She's Gotta Have It*. She wasn't rich at all—she just saved all her social security checks and gave it to her struggling first grandchild."

The aforementioned George Folkes, two years ahead of Spike and Ross, took the pair under his wing, and they soon received an opportunity to make a first filmic collaboration. "I was doing an internship with a professor," says Ross, "and she got a letter from the City Bureau of Cultural Arts in Atlanta. It said that they were giving away a $1,000 grant to students to do some art-related activity. George asked Spike to write a screenplay, we shot a twenty-minute movie on campus, and I was the lead actor. The lead actress was Rolanda Watts, who ended up being a top newscaster." Also involved in the making of the film was a classmate of Spike's called Pamm Jackson. Spike remembers this movie, *Black College: The Talented Tenth* * with all the fondness of a claustrophobe recalling a humid summer's day spent on a New York subway train stuck in a tunnel during rush hou

---

*This is a reference to a concept first expounded by W. E. B. Du Bois in 1903, ing the necessity for higher education to develop the leadership capacity among able 10 percent of African-Americans.

day he earnestly hopes that director Folkes has mislaid the only copy known to exist. Monty Ross, too, recollects that Spike was distressed by their first foray into filmmaking but still had other irons in the fire: "I think after we screened the film, Spike came and said, 'I've written another screenplay, called *It's Homecoming.*' That script ended up becoming *School Daze.*"* Spike was now taking his first steps down the career path he had chosen for himself. "I decided I wanted to be a filmmaker between my sophomore and junior years at Morehouse," he states. "Before I left for the summer of 1977, my advisor told me I really had to declare a major when I came back, because I'd used all my electives in my first two years. I went back to New York and I couldn't find a job. There were none to be had. And that previous Christmas someone gave me a Super-8 camera, so I just started to shoot stuff."

In that same summer of 1977 Spike made a call home to be told by his aunt that Jacquelyn Shelton Lee had lost a fight against liver cancer. Spike has described this news as "the worst words a human can hear." And throughout the rest of his college years, he recalls, "I had recurring dreams where I had conversations with my mother—she would come to me and we would talk."

In the midst of this bereavement, Spike was nevertheless alive to what was going on around him, and he began to capture it on film. "The summer of 1977," he remembers, "turned out to be momentous —the heat wave, the blackout† and the first summer of disco." Armed with his Super-8 camera, Spike shot footage of looters running amok in Harlem during the blackout; also of people dancing the hustle— that summer's biggest dance craze—in Brooklyn. He further persuaded his brother Chris to act out stealing a pair of shoes, while his father gave an eyewitness statement arguing that the opportunism exhibited by members of the poor black community during the blackout was the result of four hundred years of subjugation.

"When school started again in September 1977," Spike recalls, "I declared my major in mass communications, which was film, TV production, radio and print journalism. The class was taught at Clark College, now called Clark Atlanta University. I had a great instructor, who still teaches there: Dr. Herb Eichelberger. He pushed me, took a real interest in me—that's when I really decided what I wanted to do." The young Dr. Eichelberger had recently joined the Clark teaching staff, having previously worked for Kodak, and he remembers of

*See Chapter 4.
†On July 13, 1977, New York City was without electricity for twenty-five hours when the national grid failed. The occasion was marked by rioting, looting and 3,800 arrests.

Spike: "He was a hard worker. In fact, I used to correct Spike's exams first and used them as keys, because I knew that if Spike got it, then I was relaying the information well. I've still got his exam papers stashed away in a cabinet." Jacquelyn Lee would have been pleased, and no doubt surprised, by her son's fledgling studiousness.

Dr. Eichelberger further encouraged Spike to edit the footage he had shot over the summer of 1977 into a film. Spike set to work excitedly and added a voice-over narration from classmate Pamm Jackson that described the events during the blackout as "like Christmas in July." The result was a forty-minute slice-of-life short titled *Last Hustle in Brooklyn*. From the get-go Spike was showing a propensity to make use of friends and family, a fascination with New York as a backdrop and a desire to tell stories from a black perspective. His first foray into filmmaking has a loose narrative structure: after showing the looting in Harlem, it ends with those happy people dancing the hustle. (The film has failed to turn up in subsequent Spike Lee retrospectives, in the first instance because its source music was never formally licensed; but this is an excuse that also suits Spike, because he is still embarrassed by the film's rudimentary technique.)

In contrast to his authoritarian manner at home, Spike was shy at school and Dr. Eichelberger remembers that this was a pupil who needed a lot of encouragement: "At first he didn't seem to take a leadership role. I think that film gave him an avenue to express himself—to put his stamp on things, so to speak. Film allowed him to be larger, externally, than he was in the everyday walk of life. He wasn't the most die-hard person to pick up a camera. But he always loved the editing process, and I used to have to kick him out of the editing booth. I told him, though, that a good editor would be a good director."

And so Spike began to see his future in cinema. Actor Bill Nunn, another fellow student at Morehouse, recollects: "I would see him at plays and I would see him with George Folkes and Monty Ross. They were always with their Super-8 cameras. Spike would say, 'I'm going to be a filmmaker.' I encouraged him, but of course I was thinking, 'Yeah *right*, you're going to be a filmmaker. . . .'" Nunn's doubts stemmed from a belief—shared by no shortage of others—that cinema was not a realistic career goal for an African-American. Even Dr. Eichelberger, though tasked with mentoring and encouraging his students toward a vocation, was careful to warn them that their chances of success were slender: "You could only think of a few people who were black filmmakers—Oscar Micheaux, Gordon Parks, Melvin Van Peebles. And such people were not really recognized. Apart from Sidney Poitier, no one loomed on the horizon. But Spike was in a group that said, 'Hey, I want to make some changes.' I was there to support him as much as possible, but I never really dreamed of the level he would ascend to."

In 1971 Melvin Van Peebles had directed and produced *Sweet Sweetback's Baadasssss Song*. Together with Gordon Parks's *Shaft* and Ossie Davis's *Cotton Comes to Harlem*, the picture served to herald the "blaxploitation" genre of gritty urban films in which the black man was more than a mere secondary character: this time, he got the chicks and ruled the roost. These films enjoyed considerable box-office success, not least given their limited budgets, and the Hollywood studios, then struggling to adapt to the methods of the "New Hollywood" directors (Coppola, Friedkin, Bogdanovich, Hopper, Rafelson et al.), were quick to knock out their own imitations. Blaxploitation would in time enjoy a grand revival by way of videocassette and, later, DVD, and it is now credited perhaps above all for inspiring Quentin Tarantino, as well as a subsequent wave of urban black films. Back in 1971, at the time of *Sweetback*'s release, Melvin Van Peebles struggled to find two cinemas in the whole country that were willing to show his film. He finally succeeded in doing so only after he persuaded a white producer to pretend that he had helped to make the film.

A yet more pertinent example to Spike Lee was the struggle fought by Oscar Micheaux to get his films made. In 1918 Micheaux became the first black man to make a feature-length film, by adapting his autobiographical novel *The Homesteader*. Unable to attract interest from Hollywood studios, Micheaux wrote, produced and directed all of his forty-three films, including the first talkie made by a black man, *The Exile*, in 1931. In 1920 he directed *Within Our Gates*, a black response to D. W. Griffith's *Birth of a Nation* that was thought lost for many years, until a copy was recently discovered in Spain. For decades his were the only films that tackled issues of race from a black perspective. Since he was the only widely recognized black director of the time, black talent flocked to his Micheaux Film and Book Company. It was here that talents such as Paul Robeson first appeared.

"People didn't really believe me when I told them that I was going to be a filmmaker," Spike Lee acknowledges. "They probably couldn't name any African-American filmmakers then. The only one working at the time was Michael Schultz." In 1975 Schultz had directed *Cooley High*, which was set in 1964 so as to exploit the nostalgia value of Motown. The picture follows two high-school students in a Chicago project who get caught up in a criminal investigation. Schultz followed up with *Car Wash* (1976), a workplace comedy helped to great box office by its joyful theme song, and *Greased Lightning* (1977), in which Richard Pryor played the groundbreaking stock-car racer Wendell Scott. In 1978 Schultz became the first African-American director to land a Hollywood assignment without a racial theme: unfortunately, this was *Sgt. Pepper's Lonely Hearts Club Band*, a terrible Beatles homage starring the Bee Gees.

Taken together, the precedents for Spike Lee's ambitions were not encouraging. But one person who believed that Spike could surprise everyone and achieve an unlikely breakthrough was Dr. Eichelberger, who continued to push Spike to learn more about the technical aspects of filmmaking: "He did his first 16mm film here, a film called *She Wore Black Shoes*. He'll kill me for talking about this, but it was his first trek into science fiction. It featured a woman with nice legs who wore black stockings and carried slime in her purse. Anybody who got touched by the slime would die instantly. Spike gets embarrassed when I talk about it—I think he probably took the film and destroyed it." But, as we have seen, a hatred of his filmmaking juvenilia would become a confirmed Spike trait.

Spike was still spending his summers in Atlanta, and one year he volunteered to assist high-school kids on a filmmaking program backed by a local cable channel and run by George Folkes. With Folkes was a young white filmmaker, Barry Brown. "I didn't really get to know Spike that summer," says Brown, "and I think everyone was a little suspicious of George bringing me around, because I didn't fit in. But soon I became friends with everybody." Brown made his name shortly thereafter as director of *The War at Home*,[*] a documentary about the protests against the Vietnam War in Madison, Wisconsin, that was nominated for an Academy Award.

It was not only through making shorts that Spike began to hone the skills he would later use to make feature films. In 1978 he directed the Morehouse Homecoming coronations. "It was like a variety show that the college had every year," Spike recalls. "George Folkes had directed it one year; Monty and I assisted him. Then I directed it the following year, and Monty directed one at Clark. We really cut our teeth doing these Homecoming shows—that was where I learned about directing large numbers of people."

Spike also learned that people would not back down easily when he tried to change traditions or rewrite rules. For his show, he decided that since this would be the first coronation in the new Dr. Martin Luther

[*]Co-directed with Glenn Silber.

King Chapel there should be a dress code and females should have their dresses of a proper length. "The girls, especially those belonging to sororities, were *not* happy with the new dress code, and they complained to their frat brothers," says Spike. "A group of frat boys came looking to beat some sense into me." Luckily, one of Spike's assistants, Ivy Butler, managed to alert Monty Ross (himself busily organizing the Clark coronation) to Spike's predicament. As Spike recollects, "He ran all the way to Morehouse to stop me getting my ass whipped."

In the summer following the Homecoming coronation and his own graduation, Spike earned a summer internship at Columbia Pictures in Hollywood. At this time he also had a falling-out with his father. Bill Lee had started to see a woman who didn't meet with Spike's approval, and the eldest son was furious that his father had begun such a relationship so soon after his mother's passing. Spike felt that Susan Kaplan—the white Jewish woman who was to become his stepmother—destroyed the family unit on the day that she moved into the family home. Spike says, "In retrospect, I blame my father. He could have stopped her from systematically kicking all of us out of the house, but he didn't. And one by one we got the boot." This was the first in a series of run-ins that Spike was to have with Bill over the following years. Their relationship was to blow hot and cold even as Bill composed music for Spike's student films and also his first four feature films. There is a tension that remains between them, one that led to Spike not wanting his father to be interviewed for this book.

Post-Morehouse, Spike was determined to attend film school but faced a dilemma over which institution he should target. "I wanted to go to USC or UCLA," he recalls, "but you have to get an astronomical score on the GRE, the standardized postgraduate test. And since I didn't get the necessary score, I didn't apply. I think academic institutions really limit themselves in the way that they choose students. I know there's some need for standardized testing, but it shouldn't be the sole criterion. I wasn't applying to the law or MBA programs: I was trying to get into their graduate film program. How does a standardized test measure an applicant's creativity?" Ultimately it was New York University—which placed a greater emphasis on the individual student's application form and on his or her creative ideas—that accepted Spike into its film course. To his mind this institution had one overriding attraction: "If you look at film schools like USC and UCLA—I don't know if it's still true today—but back then not every student got to make a film. You submitted a script, but the faculty chose which films would get made. At NYU *everybody* got to make a movie."

Of course, New York City was also home, but Spike could not move back into his father's house while another woman was sleeping in his mother's bed. He lacked the funds to move into a place of his own, so he accepted a berth with his Uncle Cliff. Spike's cousin Malcolm Lee recalls: "Spike lived with us from his first year at NYU until he graduated. I knew he was going to school for film, but I didn't really know why. I remember asking him, 'What are you doing this for?' He said, 'I'm going to make movies.' I didn't believe him. It was a preposterous idea, the thought that someone in my family, let alone somebody *black*, would be making movies." This sentiment was by no means parochial, and is echoed by Lisa Jones, daughter of the renowned poet and leading black nationalist LeRoi Jones (who changed his name to Amiri Baraka following his conversion to Islam in 1968). Jones remembers, "I first heard of Spike through his brother David, whom I was at Yale University with. David would say, 'My brother's in film school.' I'd never even *heard* of film school. Who can imagine themselves in such a place—let alone a black person?"

As Spike arrived at NYU, the Sugar Hill Gang's "Rappers Delight" had just introduced the world outside of New York's Club 371 to the beats and rhymes of rap; and Michael Jackson's huge-selling *Off the Wall* album had consolidated the presence of black artists at the apex of the music business. But within the corridors of film academe, Spike discovered that one Ernest Dickerson was the only other black face amid a sea of white. "Naturally we tended to gravitate toward each other," Dickerson recalls. He had much in common with Spike, having attended another historically black school, Howard University, where he studied architecture. Dickerson too was from a family marked by bereavement: his father, also a jazz musician, died when he was eight years old. It was Dickerson's love of photography and architecture that pushed him toward film school.

"Ernest and I were not welcomed with open arms," Spike remembers. "Not by the faculty, nor by the students. A lot of people thought that we were there for the quota, to make up numbers so NYU could get their federal grant money. So we knew that, in order to succeed, we had to be five, even *ten* times better than our white classmates. That's something drilled into every minority child. Your parents will tell you —as their parents have told them—that you can't just be *as* good as your white counterpart. It's not fair, but that's just the way it is. I knew that people were looking at myself and Ernest, thinking, 'What are *you* guys doing here?' But we knew right away that we belonged. All we wanted was the equipment. That's how we saw film school—as a rental house. You had your classmates as crew; you had to feed them but you didn't pay them. And the school had an agreement with SAG [the Screen Actors Guild] so you got your actors for free too. We both understood that having a master's in fine arts from NYU wasn't going to get us jobs. You had to come out of NYU with a thesis film that could demonstrate to agents, producers, the studios that you had skills.'

Remembering what Dr. Eichelberger had taught him at Morehouse, Spike set about using film as a medium to protest against the institutional racism he perceived all around him. His ire reached boiling point when the faculty applauded D. W. Griffith's *Birth of a Nation*. "I mean, it's fine to teach the great cinematic techniques that Griffith came up with," Spike argues. "But let's not also leave out the fact that that film was used as a recruiting tool for the Ku Klux Klan and was directly responsible for hundreds of black men being lynched and/or castrated."

The first year of the NYU film course required students to perform certain technical exercises and to produce one silent film. Spike, conscious that Oscar Micheaux's response to Griffith had been buried along with many of his other films, decided to take his own stance against the so-called "Father of Cinema" and made *The Answer*. This twenty-minute film tells of a black filmmaker being given $50 million to write and direct a remake of *Birth of a Nation*. Spike saw his film as a means both to attack the racism of Griffith's original and to issue a "fuck you" to the NYU faculty for celebrating it. Thereafter Spike had just one problem: at the end of the year, all of the students' silent films would be screened and graded by the faculty, to decide who should and shouldn't remain on the course. "The legend has it," says Spike, "that they didn't like *The Answer* and I got kicked out of school. But before they viewed the films, they'd already given me a job for the next year as a teaching assistant, because I had worked the whole first year in the equipment room and I was a hard worker. So they *wanted* to kick me out, but they couldn't."

In one important aspect—and for a welcome change—being black was advantageous to Spike, because one way for a student to guarantee that his or her film would at the very least be well shot was to enlist Ernest Dickerson as cinematographer. Says Dickerson, "I remember Spike as a quiet guy who would always work on the sound for other people's movies. I was happy to help him, and we first worked together on *Sarah*, which was shot at his uncle's house." Spike readily admits, "One of the most important things that ever happened to me was hooking up with Ernest. I learned so much from him. In film school my visual sense was really lacking, so Ernest was the one that really made the stuff look great. He was the one who was composing the shots, while I was more about the words. So he deserves great credit for my development as a filmmaker."

Sarah was the film Spike made at the end of his second year, in 1981: "My grandmother saw *The Answer* and said, 'When are you going to make a nice little film that *I'm* gonna like?' Realizing that my grandmother put me through Morehouse and NYU, I listened to her and made *Sarah*. I adapted a story about a disastrous Thanksgiving dinner. And that was the last time I ever made a film for somebody else, because I don't get good results when I do a film that's not for me, even for my loving grandmother." On the plus side, Spike had the benefit of working with Dickerson, and he also saw how much his father's music improved his film: "My father is a great musician, and for me it was very natural to have him do the music for my movie." At this time Spike also began to broaden the horizon of his film knowledge: "NYU was really the first time that I was seeing world cinema. Up to that point it was Hollywood stuff. But Kurosawa's *Rashomon* and Godard's *Breathless*, as far as the editing, ended up being big influences on *She's Gotta Have It*."

Shortly after completing *Sarah*, Spike got a call from Barry Brown, now president of First Run Features: "A group of us had founded First Run to distribute American independent movies," says Brown. "Each one of us had a movie, and we basically built the company around those four films. We needed someone to do a part-time job cleaning film prints and rewinding them. I thought this would be a good job for a film student, and I remembered Spike, so I gave him a call. He had done *Sarah*, which I didn't think was so hot. But he took the job, and we got to know each other. We bonded over our point of view on movies. Unlike many people in the independent film scene, I didn't go to the movies because of 'the message'—I liked entertainment. The only other person at the time whom I knew and who I thought understood that was Spike. As a teenager, I appeared in a lot of musicals as an actor, and Spike *loved* musicals. His mother had taken him to a lot of them. And to say 'I love musicals!' at that time in the early eighties did not go down well in the independent film community."

The First Run job placed Spike at the center of the independent film scene in New York, and it was at First Run that he first encountered producer John Pierson. Pierson remembers, "Spike just kept his cap pulled down low and sort of slipped in and out. I don't think it was because he was dealing with me—a whitey. People to this day think that Spike is way too public and way too angry, but one thing that I want to convey to people reading this book is that he is really funny, but fundamentally very shy."

Third-year NYU film students were required to produce a sound film as part of their thesis. Spike wrote *Joe's Bed-Stuy Barbershop: We Cut Heads*, the story of Zachariah Homer, a barbershop owner whose business partner falls foul of a gang running a numbers racket. "It's a billion-dollar industry, always has been and always will be," says Spike. "Every day, you get a figure that is the total amount of money bet at the racetrack that day, and the last three numbers are the winning numbers. Numbers-running has always been a key part of the African-American community, so we wanted to do a semi-gangster film that takes place in a barbershop." In the film the gang want to make use of Homer's shop as a location from which to run their illegal activity, and so he faces a dilemma: should he acquiesce or make a stand?

Joe's cost $10,000 and was backed by Spike's perennial financier, his maternal grandmother, Zimmie. Pamm Jackson, Spike's former classmate and narrator of *Last Hustle in Brooklyn*, signed on as a producer. The lead role of Zach went to Monty Ross, who, after graduating, had stayed in Atlanta and married, but who now responded to a desperate call for help from Spike: "Once I arrived in New York, I was driving around and doing a lot of the PA [production assistant] work too. Spike's and Ernest's whole thing was that they wanted to be the best, they were determined to rise above the crowd. But the number-one thing for Spike was that he had to finish the film, because most of the guys at NYU never did that." The script was intriguing to Ross, but what really struck him was Ernest Dickerson's skill behind the camera: "I realized he had this ability to take Spike's script and create an image, take whatever was on the page and technically manipulate it." Spike would let Dickerson concentrate on the images, while he dealt with the other aspects of the film set. And *Joe's Bed-Stuy Barbershop* was proof of a fruitful collaboration. (Film historians will also want to note that the sound recordist was classmate Ang Lee, later to direct *The Ice Storm* and *Crouching Tiger, Hidden Dragon*.)

Events in the larger U.S. film industry were also giving a fillip to Spike's aspiration that he could become a successful black filmmaker. Indigo was a production company set up by Columbia Pictures and Richard Pryor—the black comic star par excellence prior to Eddie Murphy's meteoric rise—in order to produce films that would star black talent and attract the "black audience" whose existence Hollywood had so long denied. Columbia, recognizing that its organization was as white as snow, decided that Pryor (a phenomenal talent beset by chronic cocaine addiction, which almost claimed his life in 1980) could deliver this black audience for them. They allotted him $40 million and total artistic control to make four films of his choice aimed at an African-American demographic. It was a deal that no African-American filmmaker had enjoyed before, or has enjoyed since.

Even the Academy of Motion Picture Arts and Sciences appeared newly receptive to black talent, as Malcolm Lee recalls: "I remember the night when Lou Gossett Jr. won the Best Actor in a Supporting Role Oscar for *An Officer and a Gentleman*. We were watching the ceremony on TV. Spike went crazy, running around the house, punching his fist into the air." On that night of April 11, 1983, Spike discerned that the Academy—which previously had only bestowed one of its prized Oscars on a black male actor, Sidney Poitier—was slowly but surely accepting more black faces into the club.

Nevertheless, the apparent dawn of a new era in black film quickly turned into an unmitigated disaster. Indigo was racked by mismanagement. Many could scarcely believe that Pryor had appointed ex-football-legend-turned-actor Jim Brown as the company's head: the general feeling was that he got the job simply because Pryor credited Brown with saving his life. Pryor and Brown then fell out in December 1983, and Indigo closed down soon after. The only films to come out under its banner were Pryor's third concert movie, *Richard Pryor Here and Now*, and the autobiographical *Jo Jo Dancer, Your Life Is Calling*, which Pryor directed. Meanwhile, Columbia and the other leading studios noted the contemporaneous failure of *Beat Street* and *Breakin'* —films that tried to exploit the craze for rap and hip-hop, and their associated dances and fashions—and settled on the view that it was specific stars rather than specific subject matter that could draw a black crowd. Spike Lee was himself dumbfounded when the plug was pulled on Indigo: "I don't know how they only made one film. They had a good fund of money to make any film they wanted. Look at the films they passed on—*Purple Rain*, *The Color Purple*, *The Charlie Parker Story*[*] . . . It was a lost, lost opportunity."

Despite this fiasco, Spike had outstanding personal cause to be cheerful when he received news that *Joe's Bed-Stuy Barbershop* had won the Student Academy Award. "I thought I had been delivered," he recalls. All of a sudden he felt the world was at his feet. Author and filmmaker Nelson George—at the time managing editor of music magazine *Billboard*—was one of the many who now started to take note

*Subsequently filmed as *Bird* (1988).

of Spike: "I was at home one night watching PBS and they showed *Joe's Bed-Stuy Barbershop*. I was really impressed by it. It felt like the Brooklyn that I knew. I knew a lot of people in independent film from my job on the *Amsterdam News*, so I arranged to meet Spike. We met in a Chinese restaurant, and he was weird and unusual and had a strange energy—but I liked him. He was smart. I had a film idea, too, but he didn't seem interested."

Nonetheless, Nelson George spread the word about this new young hope for black film. One of the people he called was Lisa Jones: "Nelson said, 'Come with me to the Donell Library and hear this guy, he's a dynamic film student.' I thought, Wow, this is the brother that David used to talk about at Yale. After a screening, Pamm Jackson, Monty Ross and Spike stood up, and it was like some version of the Panthers—a nationalist pose that I connected with from my childhood. I didn't get to meet Spike that night, but a week later I ran into him at this party and said, 'Hey, I want to work with you.'"

Yet the biggest single filmmaking inspiration to Spike at this juncture in his budding career had nothing at all to do with "black film." Rather it was a feature film by an ex-NYU classmate to whom Spike had once checked out equipment and which premièred at the Rotterdam Film Festival in 1983 to widespread acclaim. "For me," Spike asserts, "the defining moment of film school was when Jim Jarmusch's *Stranger than Paradise* became a hit. All of a sudden, we all felt that making films was now doable. When you're studying the masters—Hitchcock or Scorsese or Coppola—film seems remote, distant. But when someone you *know* makes it, it's no longer hocus-pocus."

First Run Features decided to distribute *Joe's Bed-Stuy Barbershop*. The unusual step to release a short was taken not because of the Student Academy Award: "I was still an employee there," Spike points out. "They didn't have much choice." The film quickly received a lot of attention and Spike was invited to several festivals, including Rotterdam, which constituted Spike's first trip overseas. Soon after, he became the first student director to have his film shown at the Museum of Modern Art's New Directors New Films.

Spike's ego was now being stroked from all quarters, and in his eyes this was only the beginning of bigger things. Acting coach Susan Batson recalls, "When Spike graduated from NYU, he wrote to all the black SAG actors, saying that he was showing *Joe's Bed-Stuy Barbershop* and he would like to work with them. And there was a phenomenal interest, because you already felt that something was going to happen with this guy—he knew how to market himself." "You know, I still *got* that damn letter somewhere," says Ossie Davis, actor, director and co-host of the PBS TV show *Ossie and Ruby!* "It said, 'I'm the son of Bill Lee, who's a musician with a group that backed you up in the Village at a poetry show. And one day I want to work with you.' I put the letter aside. But one day I'll find it and I'll answer that man."

Spike had also secured suitable representation for himself: "I got an agent at William Morris and I just thought that I could sit by the phone and I'd get calls from Spielberg, Coppola, Lucas, Warner Bros., Paramount, Columbia, offers to write and direct feature films." But, as it turned out, Spike's telephone proved the least useful of the few items he owned in this period. With hindsight, he is philosophical: "It was naïve for me to think as I did, and I woke up. I don't blame the agent at all." Nevertheless, Spike then decided that he had no need of an agent for the time being and, better still, that the decision would save him surrendering 10 percent of whatever fees would soon be coming his way.

Still certain that he would soon be at the helm of a feature-film project, Spike kept himself permanently on the lookout for artists he could work with. Actor Giancarlo Esposito remembers, "I was doing a play written by Charles Fuller called *Zooman and the Sign*, and I remember one night a little man coming backstage and saying, 'You were good. . . .' It was Spike. He told me that he was interested in my doing a project with him called *Homecoming*, actually the precursor to *School Daze*. It was a wonderful script—like a black *Animal House*." Indeed, Spike was still working on the script that he had first shown Monty Ross and George Folkes at Morehouse. In Washington Square Park, Spike bumped into Larry Fishburne, who had begun to make his name with *Apocalypse Now* and *Rumblefish*: "He was just sitting there," Spike remembers, "and I walked up to him, introduced myself, and I might have invited him to a screening of *Joe's*. He was cool, and we exchanged numbers."

Fishburne even agreed to star in an on-spec promo video for "White Lines," a cut by Grandmaster Flash and the Furious Five that Spike wanted to use as a means to break into the burgeoning music-video market. "Music videos were blowing up," says Spike. "There was a show on Channel 7 in New York called *New York City Hot Tracks*, and it was a way for young filmmakers to get work, by doing videos." Spike's vision of "White Lines" makes Al Pacino's *Scarface* look like no more than a recreational cokehead. Fishburne plays a pimp in a white suit snorting powder off the backs of scantily clad women and strutting around a den of sin. "Those motherfuckers from Sugar Hill Records, they turned the video down," Spike recalls. "But then they ended up using it anyway, despite the fact that it wasn't even finished. Ten years later they put it out on a compilation DVD. I should still sue their ass." By contrast, the official video, directed by Malcolm McLaren offered a PG-rated interpretation of the song, focusing on the white painted lines of a school playground. Grandmaster Flash and the Furious Five subsequently fell out themselves with Sugar Hill Records over creative control and money matters and, following an acrimonious lawsuit, made their way to the Electra label. Sugar Hill's name was dirt; for young up-and-coming rappers, the only safe home seemed to be the small Def Jam label part-owned by entrepreneurial twenty-seven-year-old Russell Simmons, who had been promoting hip-hop shows since his teens and now managed the groundbreaking hip-hop crew Run-DMC, of which his brother Joe was one third.

At the start of 1984, Spike and Ernest Dickerson sent a copy of *Joe's Bed-Stuy* to director Michael Schultz in the hope of getting jobs on a hip-hop picture he was directing entitled *Rap Attack*. Schultz was still the only black director making films that received wide distribution. Dickerson duly picked up his first major gig as a cinematographer, but Spike, who had wanted to work as an assistant director, was turned down. The film eventually appeared as *Krush Groove* (tag line: "It's Chillin'") and is notable for showcasing a who's who of the New York rap scene at the time. The plot was loosely based on the life of Russell Simmons: Blair Underwood plays Russell Walker, manager of Krush Groove records, who runs into trouble when he borrows money from a drug dealer cum loan shark to fund his label. Simmons himself was soon thereafter christened "the mogul of rap" by the *Wall Street Journal*. Rap was as yet something of a niche-market taste in the U.S., but Simmons, as head of RUSH Productions which boasted Run-DMC, the Beastie Boys and LL Cool J, was poised to press home his advantage.

Dickerson and Lee also tried to get jobs on John Sayles's *Brother from Another Planet*. Again, only Dickerson was employed, although Sayles kindly told Spike that there was no point employing him as an assistant because he was a director in his own right. Spike's patience with waiting for others to give him a job ran out: it was time to follow the example of Jim Jarmusch and get his own script made on his own terms. Whatever the setbacks he had had, he still wanted for nothing in the way of confidence. Barry Brown recalls, "We were walking through Fort Greene one day, and Spike would point out buildings and say, 'I want that building one day. I like that one too. I'm gonna own them and I'm going to make a movie every year.' I said, 'Shut up, motherfucker.'" Undeterred, Spike set about preparations for his début feature.

"After Spike showed me the script for *It's Homecoming*, which he knew he couldn't get done at the time," says Giancarlo Esposito, "he gave me another script called *The Messenger*. It was a piece that was really dear to me, because I'm from a mixed racial background and I understood that Spike was living something that *I* was living. That's how we became friends, in a way. I knew that when his mother passed away and his father married a white woman it was hard for him, at that particular time of his life."

The Messenger concerned a young bike-riding delivery boy in New York whose life is turned on its head when his mother dies and his African-American father marries a white woman. The messenger gets entangled in a mess that leads to a series of car chases and helicopter rides, before finally taking retribution against his stepmother. Spike offered the lead role to Esposito and put together a cast that included Larry Fishburne. Esposito says of the film's narrative, "It was definitely autobiographical, in the sense that Spike himself had been a bike messenger for a while; and he was confronting his own racial prejudice. He was really inward-looking at the time, and he was looking at what had formulated his life. He looked at what he felt was adverse about white people, why people always told him 'No.' I was really jazzed because I had the leading-man role—the guy who kicks his mother out of the house. Eventually what happens is that he tells his mother to 'get the fuck out.' Spike loved that moment. And it was well written."

There was a question mark over Ernest Dickerson's availability to shoot *The Messenger*: he had become a father, and he was due to be working with John Sayles on the very dates scheduled for Spike's shoot. Spike had more luck with Monty Ross when he called him again to come up from Atlanta: "I had joined the army. When I got back, I got a call from Spike, and he blasted me out. 'Where have you been? Why did you join the army? Come on, we got work to do. Come to New York and work on *The Messenger*.'"

But if Spike had thought the going was tough for him after graduation, he was ill prepared for the nightmare that was *The Messenger*. Rehearsals had begun and Spike was gearing up for the shoot when disaster struck on several fronts. "Unfortunately that movie never got made, for a number of reasons," says Esposito. "One was that Spike simply couldn't get the union to give him compensation to go ahead and do it on a low-budget-movie scale. I don't know if I ever said this to him, but I thought, I told you so. Months before we were doing that movie, we had to go to the union, because he was dealing with union-scale actors. Larry and I were in the Screen Actors Guild, and I said, 'Spike, you can't do your movie unless the Guild approves; otherwise I'll get fined.' He was young and brash and he said, 'I don't care. I'm going to do it.' Once he didn't get the money, of course, he realized that you had to try and work within the system."

Pre-production on the film had already run to $20,000, bankrolled largely by Spike's trusty sponsor, grandmother Zimmie. In order to move forward, the film needed the next installment of finance, which a family friend of the Lees had promised to deliver. At the last minute Spike and Monty realized that it would not be coming. "We were waiting on this producer at his office, and his office stayed locked all day," remembers Ross. "We sat there the whole day, hoping that he would show up. '*Please* show up. . . .' I felt really down in the dumps because we put a lot of effort into it. The production manager came to Spike and said, 'What are you gonna do about it?' I didn't like the way he was talking to Spike, so I asked him to cool down. Then he left, and I said to Spike, 'Next time you do a project, let me be your production supervisor.'"

To say Spike was downbeat at the turn of events would be a grave understatement of how crushing a blow this was to the twenty-six-year-old who, one year earlier, had been making plans to be the messiah of black cinema. Now it seemed that he would be lucky to earn so much as a footnote in his own family tree. He had pulled out all the stops to assemble a dream cast: "How could I ask people to work on a film again with me? I was marked 'Lousy,' and rightfully so. People were kind and understood the circumstances, probably more than I did. They didn't hold a grudge. They were angry—but they let it go." Esposito says, "I was jazzed. If we'd made the movie, it would have changed my career." Larry Fishburne, who had lived through the experience of Coppola's *Apocalypse Now*, was more understanding, especially as he had met his future wife filming the "White Lines" video.

But Spike was distraught: "Nothing could prepare me for failure. At the time I thought that my career was over. But in retrospect it was the best thing that happened to me, because even if I'd got the money to make *The Messenger*, there was no way I could ever pull it off. I was not ready to do that film. It would have been a disaster, maybe something that I wouldn't have been able to rebound from. My self-confidence and also my ability as a filmmaker would have been shot. It would have been terrible, a debacle, a fiasco, a travesty, a mockery. This is one of many examples where the Spirit looked after me and kept me out of harm's way." Nelson George remembers being given the *Messenger* script, and also his shock at what he read: "There is a lot of shit that is very problematic with *The Messenger*. It wouldn't have been *She's Gotta Have It*. I don't even think it would have been distributed . . . After I knew Spike a bit more, I was like, 'Spike, you're pushing a white woman down a *staircase*. Are you fucking *crazy*?'"

Following the project's collapse, Monty Ross tried his best to keep Spike's spirits aloft: "Spike was like, 'This can't be happening, we've got to get something made.' The funniest thing was that we had a party after we finally pulled the plug, and there was a lot of product-placement merchandise that we had already secured for the picture. One of the items was Jack Daniels. . . . And that night on the smelly New York subway, it was hot and muggy—and we were *ripped*." Spike, who claims to have never drunk whisky in his life, maintains that he was not drunk, although he might have had a couple of beers. Monty, however, was unquestionably inebriated: "I was throwing up. And it was at this point that Spike first started saying, 'I'm going to give people what they want. The next script's gonna have sex in it. I'm going to do something that's gonna be simple but still have integrity. And I'm going to go all the way to Hollywood.'"

3 She's Gotta Have It

Failure in 1984 was to prove a defining moment for the man about to become Brooklyn's most famous son. An unexpected setback was the spur that drove him to the focus of international attention within a further two years. It was a transformation that would surprise everybody within his chosen profession: this young black man tore down the numerous obstacles put before him in relentless pursuit of what he saw as his destiny, his rightful place at the top of the world. This conquering hero, Mike Tyson, told anyone and everyone who would listen that he was "the Baddest Man on the Planet," and by the summer of 1986 there were very few people willing to argue with him. By a strange quirk of fate, Spike Lee, another ambitious Brooklyn boy, was to undertake a similar meteoric rise into the public consciousness.

In the summer of 1984 there was no question as to who was the most famous black man hailing from Brooklyn: *Beverly Hills Cop*, directed by ex–NYU student Martin Brest, established Eddie Murphy as perhaps the biggest box-office draw on the planet. The picture grossed over $200 million in North America alone, and on the heels of his earlier hits *48 Hrs.* and *Trading Places* it cemented the *Saturday Night Live* graduate's place in the pantheon of American celebrity. *Purple Rain*, a movie vehicle for the many gifts of Minneapolis's musical genius Prince, was also a box-office smash—one that had, regrettably, passed through the hands of Richard Pryor's short-lived Indigo. Prince's accompanying soundtrack album flew straight to number one on the charts and stayed in the countdown for six months, spawning numerous hit singles too. Meanwhile, on September 20, 1984, the landscape of U.S. network television was to change utterly with the début of *The Cosby Show*. The brainchild of comedian, actor and educator Bill Cosby, this half-hour show, based in Brooklyn and detailing the travails of a middle-class black family headed by Dr. Cliff Huxtable and his lawyer wife, would become the most-watched sitcom in America over the following four years.

After the last-minute collapse of *The Messenger*, Spike felt somewhat as if he himself had been in the ring with "Iron" Mike Tyson. Thus he took stock of the situation: "I learned my lesson that one must crawl before they can walk. After the debacle of *The Messenger*, I made sure that my next film—if I ever got it made—would be something small, something that was constrained, something that I could *do*." Spike began to mull over how he could write a story about sex and apply to it all the lessons he had learned in the past year about filmmaking. The film would be ultra-low-budget, there would be a small cast, it would be easy to shoot on location—and Spike also promised himself that he wouldn't shoot his mouth off about the project in advance, just in case it turned into another embarrassing disaster. As with *The Messenger*, Spike drew from his own experiences to come up with an idea: "It amused me to listen to my male friends talk about how many girl-friends they had, that type of stuff—and what their reaction was if they ever found out one of their girls was straying. So I just thought, Why don't we flip the tables and do this film about a sexually active woman who is living her life like a young man, having multiple partners?"

Sensing that it would be expedient to get a better understanding of the female perspective on sex, Spike asked his Spelman classmate Tracey Willard to help design a questionnaire that he could present to some of his other female acquaintances. The questions left nothing to the imagination:

—Are there any sexual acts you perform with one man and not another?

—Do you think you are sexually adept?

—What do you think about a woman who masturbates?

—Talk about one unfulfilled fantasy.

—Do you feel all men are basically dogs?

—Does penis size matter?

—Have you ever OD'd on sex?

Some of the young women polled for the exercise might well have wondered for whose benefit these questions were being asked. But Spike argued that each needed to be answered before he felt comfort-able proceeding with his script. Research and the soliciting of opinion would be a key component for him: "You *have* to do the research. If you don't know about something, then you ask the right people who do. With *She's Gotta Have It*, I don't think I got any revelation; it was just good to hear the women whom I interviewed confirm what I thought already."

Armed with responses, Spike got down to work and established a working routine that he would come to follow like clockwork when-ever he needed to pen a project: "I wake up at the crack of dawn every day and write, two or three hours at a time. I just can't do any more. I don't type; I keep a legal pad that I write on. Once I've felt that I have enough ideas then I put them onto 3 x 5 index cards and put them in order. I use those cards to write out an outline. And, from that, I write the script, longhand, in a three-ring binder."

At this time, struggling to rub two nickels together, Spike dreamed of owning a typewriter, a fact we know courtesy of a journal he kept in which he recorded the ordeal of raising money and realizing the creative ideas for *She's Gotta Have It*. Nelson George, who had recently published the best-selling *The Michael Jackson Story*, believes that Spike had ulterior motives in composing his diary: "I remember when we first discussed the *She's Gotta Have It* book . . . and I remember thinking, He wants to do a *book*? He hasn't even got a film deal and he wants to get a book deal? I thought that he was out of his mind. There weren't even that many film books out at the time—although I think Wim Wenders had done one for *Paris, Texas* and that was one of the models for Spike's."

The account that Spike gives on how his journal became the best-selling handbook on independent filmmaking (*Spike Lee's Gotta Have It: Inside Guerrilla Filmmaking*) contradicts Nelson George's: "I never had the intention of turning the journal into a book. It was only when the movie hit that we decided to do it. I wanted the book to be a step in the demystification of film." The first entry in the journal—dated October 4, 1984—finds Spike reflecting on the newly minted title of his picture, which appears to have struck him like the proverbial bolt from the blue. In fact, he had drawn inspiration from one of the authentic cult American pictures of the 1950s: Frank Tashlin's *The Girl Can't Help It*, a showcase for the bountiful Jayne Mansfield.

Spike was further encouraged by the success of fellow NYU alumnus Ernest Dickerson. At the end of the blockbuster season John Sayles's *Brother from Another Planet*, shot by Dickerson, was released and quickly acquired a cult following, racking up over $3 million at the box office. It was Sayles's breakthrough film and earned Dickerson a feature in the November issue of *American Cinematographer*. Spike was thrilled: "I was glad that Ernest was working. All the things that he had been doing made him a better DP [director of photography]. We all wanted to be better. We all knew that his success was my success, and my success was his success, and we could both go forward together." A case in point: Dickerson, who also shot Bruce Springsteen's "Born in the USA" video under Sayles's direction, mentioned the influence of Spike Lee upon his own young career in the *American Cinematographer* article. More good news for Spike came on December 29, when he returned home to an answering-machine message informing him that he was to be named a *Village Voice* Hero of the Year for *Joe's Bed-Stuy*

Barbershop. It was a precious shot in the arm as he geared up to what he saw as potentially the most important year of his life so far. Moreover, it suggested that, whatever Spike's recent struggles, there remained a weight of expectation that the Brooklyn-based film-maker was one who could break the all-white mold of the filmmaking scene.

Over the following months of writing, Spike molded a sensual black female protagonist named Nola Darling. Jacquelyn Lee had insisted that the young Spike read Charles Dickens, and Spike takes a leaf out of Dickens's book when it comes to naming his characters: "I think that names can be a shortcut to what the character is like. We've always prided ourselves for having colorful names. I'm very particular. For me I like the name Nola Darling the best in *She's Gotta Have It*."

Still, Spike faced a huge dilemma in selecting his cast: "We just couldn't use SAG actors because of the difficulty we had with *The Messenger* when SAG had refused to give the film a low-budget waiver. We had to go non-SAG. We weren't trying to be union-busters. You have to put down a bond with a SAG film; we just didn't have the capital for that. This was really a low-budget, guerrilla-style film, and the fact that we didn't have the money wasn't going to stop us from making it."

Nevertheless, Spike was forced to go looking for as yet unheralded talent. He wrote the part of Nola with Tracy Camila Johns in mind, having first met the actress after she responded to a *Backstage* ad. Spike was immediately enamored by her charm and sexiness, attributes that would influence the character he wrote. His Nola would be a strong woman, sexually emancipated, not reliant on men and fiercely political. Of course, one of the shining cinematic examples of a provocative black female lead was Dorothy Dandridge's bomb-shell turn in Otto Preminger's *Carmen Jones*. Spike believed his own sexy black female creation would turn heads. At the same time he knew that he himself could not wholly capture a feminine perspective in his writing: "The film is still told from a male perspective, and it's about these men's perspectives on this woman who is leading her life *as* a man as far as her sexuality is concerned. We are really just show-ing the hypocrisy of men as to what they do, rather than Nola."

In this line Spike gave Nola—herself a so-called boho, or black bohemian—three archetypal black boyfriends whose very names encapsulated their characteristics. Mars Blackmon (christened thus by Spike's grandma Zimmie) was a b-boy bike messenger whose outlook and tastes were a hodgepodge of oversimplified black politics and

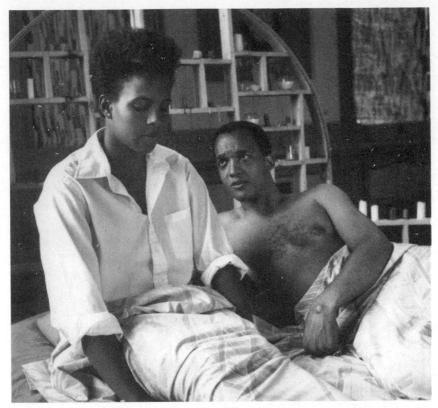

She's Gotta Have It: Nola Darling (Tracy Camila Johns) and one of her suitors, "buppie" Jamie Overstreet (Tommy Redmond Hicks). (© 1986 David Lee)

male libido, dressed up with hip-hop aesthetics. Tommy Redmond Hicks, who had starred in *Joe's Bed-Stuy Barbershop*, returned to play Jamie Overstreet, a suave "buppie" (or black yuppie) who deemed his rivals to be beneath him. The third character, Greer Childs, is a "Bap," obsessed with his own body beautiful, who enjoys an expectation of mainstream success that borders on arrogance. The role of Greer crystallized in Spike's mind once he decided that John Canada Terrell would play the part: "The character was based on John. He was just like Greer—one of those pretty boys who has straight hair, claims he's three-fifteenths Native American. That type of shit."

Spike had learned that securing his finance would be just as crucial as fine-tuning his script. But the collapse of *The Messenger* would dog him like a debt collector. The New York State Council on the Arts had awarded him a grant of $18,000 to make *The Messenger* and, happily, Spike was able to transfer these funds to his new project. A couple of months later, the American Film Institute, which had belatedly got round to processing Spike's grant application for *The Messenger*, awarded the film $20,000; Spike believed the AFI would then follow the lead of the New York State Council and transfer those funds to *She's Gotta Have It*. Their refusal to do so led him to send an angry letter to Lucinda Travis, head of the grant committee at the AFI, which Spike signed off with the classic refrain of Brooklyn Dodgers fans: "We wuz robbed." Thereafter he enlisted trusted colleagues, collaborators and friends Pamm Jackson and Monty Ross to help him in holding out begging bowls. As Melvin Van Peebles had demonstrated with *Sweet Sweetback's Baadasssss Song*, there was really no other viable alternative to this road for a black man in search of film finance. "We had to put the money together nickel by nickel," Spike confirms. "It was one of the hardest things I've ever had to do. But I'm glad that it got made the way that it did."

The initial strategy was to try to raise only the $40,000 needed to shoot for three weeks and so get the film "in the can." Spike gave the production a start date of July 1, 1985, come what may. Monty Ross was now a pivotal figure. "I was going to be second AD [assistant director] and help organize the project," says Ross. "Slowly but surely, people started falling out. They just felt like the film wasn't really going anywhere. There would be a lot of pep talks and Spike would say, 'Monty, say something! Keep us motivated!'" Spike had moved out of his uncle's house into a small studio apartment on Adelphi Street a few blocks away from the brownstone where he grew up, and he was in dire financial straits. The income from his part-time job at First Run barely covered the cost of his lodgings.

If you were a friend or associate of Spike Lee, it was your own fool luck if you bumped into him during the winter of 1984–85, as he would ask anyone and everyone he came across for a donation to his new project, whatever their own financial status. Earl Smith, still living in the Coney Island projects, was one who could not evade the beady eyeballs of his old pal: "I got an invitation to Spike's thesis film in the mail. I spoke to him after the screening and said, 'If you want to make a movie, I want to invest.' A couple of years passed and I hadn't seen him. Then I bumped into him on the train, and he asked me, 'Do you wanna invest?' I said, 'Sure,' thinking he wouldn't call me again." Smith's mother had recently passed away, and he had been hoping to use his inheritance to buy a car. Spike tried to convince his schoolmate that the cause of cinema was far more worthy: "I had $8,000 in the bank. Spike came over. I asked, 'How much do you need?' He replied, '$15,000.' I told him straight, '*What?* I ain't got $15,000.' It was a big decision, and I spoke to some people from high school, thinking maybe I could get some money for Spike. But they all said, 'I ain't donating.' To this day, I don't know why I gave Spike the money. He was a good friend. But I can't say I had the foresight to see his talent, because I didn't know anything about movies. But I gave him $8,000. A few weeks later, Spike calls and says, 'Earl, I need a favor.' I thought he was going to give me a role in the movie, but instead he says, 'I ain't got no rent money, can you lend me $500?' So I tell my girlfriend Darlene — who is now my wife — that I'm going to lend him $500. She says, 'Why? He only calls you when he wants money.' But I gave him the money, and he asked me, 'Do you want me to put this in with the money you already gave me or do you want me to pay you back?' He didn't *have* any money, so how was he going to pay me back? So I told him to take it as an investment."

Spike was also losing weight at a dangerous rate, and at one point dropped to a paltry 110 pounds. Once again he tried out for an industry job, he and Barry Brown applying for writing positions on *The Cosby Show*. The conversations began hopefully, but hope was short-lived. Spike's finances took a further hit when he quit First Run on June 28, 1985, after his request for a month's leave for filming was refused. Compounding the dire situation, Spike also split with his girlfriend of the time, dancer Cheryl Burr, and this too had a negative impact on his cash flow: whenever he felt lonely, he would call up friends for commiseration: "It wasn't long before the telephone company started threatening to cut me off." Barry Brown remembers, "It was right before they were meant to go into production, and they were in a similar situation to the one that they were in with *The Messenger*. Spike was completely disheartened, ready to throw in the towel. Monty said, 'No, give me a day, let me work it out.' And he came back and said, 'We can make this happen.'"

"As production supervisor," Ross recalls, "I felt the money that we had was right there. Spike wanted to do a three-week shoot, and I knew we couldn't do that. But I started calculating and saw that we had enough for two weeks. Spike kept saying, 'We can do the shoot in two weeks?' I just repeated, 'Yes.' Finally we ended up shooting for twelve days. At some point Spike said, 'I'll just have to worry about my actors and rehearsals and stuff like that.' So I had to make the production work. And I didn't know anything about the unions, that you needed a Teamster to drive a truck. I just made deals to get things done cheaper."

Spike had first earmarked Wayne Salazar to be production designer, but Salazar pulled out, deciding that painting his grandmother's house took priority. Spike then called upon another old contact: "When I tried to get Michael Schultz to give me a job on *Krush Groove*, one of my classmates from NYU was working in the art department of that film. I went to visit her on set and I saw this black guy at his drawing board. I introduced myself. This was Wynn Thomas. I told him then and there I wanted him to be the production designer on my films."

Another way for Spike to cut corners was to employ friends and family where possible. His sister, Joie, disappointed not to have been offered a role in *The Messenger*, was delighted when Spike now told her, "I have a part for you." He also got his father Bill to play Nola's father, and asked him to compose the score (this despite a confession in his journal that "every time I talk to my father we end up arguing"). Brother David would be the stills photographer—not that he had any choice: "Spike actually ordered me to get out of bed and dragged me out of the house to work for him. He didn't exploit; he just utilized what was available to him. He was the general. Whether it was filmmaking or the street-hockey team on the block, Spike always organized and motivated people." Indeed, Spike had more in mind for David on this assignment. During his pre-production research period he had rented Godfrey Reggio's *Koyaanisqatsi* (1983) and was struck by how the film was able to tell a story without dialogue. It gave him the idea of using David's still photos within the film: "Film is a visual medium, and in *She's Gotta Have It* there are all types of references within the frame to Malcolm X and black politics. If you look at the mural on the wall in Nola's apartment, it's a reference to Malcolm X."

Barry Brown, however, was amused to see how Spike took advantage of his family: "The first time I met Cinque was during the making of *She's Gotta Have It*. He had a Mohawk, and Spike had him do a run into the city to collect a package. He returns with the package, and as he's about to leave, Spike says, 'Where's my change?' It was maybe 65 cents, but Spike wanted it. I started smiling as Cinque left, and Spike yelled at me, 'Don't make fun of my brother's hair.' I told him it wasn't the hair I was making fun at but what a cheap son of a bitch he was. You can't even allow your brother 65 cents? I was glad *I* wasn't one of his brothers."

The only family member whom Spike could not persuade to work on *She's Gotta Have It* was Chris, who had been featured so prominently in *Last Hustle in Brooklyn*. The brothers had fallen out over Chris's use of recreational drugs. Spike reflects, "When you have kids in a family, the same parents, the same food, the same house and the same love for parents, why would one son go this way and the other son in another direction? What is the explanation?" For his own part, Chris, sick of listening to Spike's overbearing attitude and demands, could not imagine volunteering to put himself in a position where he was subservient to his older brother.

Working with his family would cause friction on later Spike Lee joints, but, as Monty Ross reports, there was no such strife on the set of *She's Gotta Have It*: "All families have their own nuances. You have to work through the squabbles. But on *She's Gotta Have It*, being around Bill Lee when it was time to work was brilliant." Spike too has fond memories of his family pulling together to get his film off the ground: "It made sense to use talented family members. You will always get the dynamics of being a big brother, and that does come into play. But I don't remember it being hard."

Perhaps the biggest decision that Spike made was to cast himself as Mars Blackmon, a move that shocked Barry Brown: "I asked him if this was wise. He's not really an actor. He said, 'I think I can do it.'" Spike had already toyed with the idea of playing an ex-boyfriend of Nola's in a flashback sequence. As he readily acknowledges, "Hitchcock is the first thing you think about when you put yourself in a film —Hitchcock and Woody Allen." In this instance, though, it was money talking: "I didn't have the money to pay anybody else." Nor did he feel that Monty Ross, who had acted in *Joe's Bed-Stuy Barbershop*, was right: "I'm not an actor; I just felt that I knew who Mars was and what he could be." Giancarlo Esposito was still smarting over Spike's decision to pull the plug on *The Messenger*, and he admits, "I was really bummed out that he decided to star in his own movie. That meant I was out. But he *was* Mars Blackmon. Mars Blackmon, to me, is a character that came right out of who Spike is." The character loves basketball, hip-hop and urban clothing; finds Nola's sexual habits most disturbing; and has an affiliation with the politics of black nationalism but neither the facilities nor the wherewithal to adequately express these views.

One crucial aspect of Spike's memorable performance came about by chance: "The whole hip-hop thing was blowing up at that time, and it was my inability as an actor to recall the lines that made me repeat stuff, just for something to do—to say things like, 'Please, baby, please, baby, baby, baby, please . . .'" Failure to learn his lines properly was one consequence of Spike overstretching himself on top of directing and producing his film. Finally gaffer Mike Hunold broke it to Spike that, when he was in front of the cameras, perhaps DP Ernest Dickerson should direct the scenes? Spike agreed, though Barry Brown notes that it would not be fair to say that Spike wholly ceded authority to Ernest. (Brown describes a telling scene on the set of Spike's and Dickerson's second feature collaboration, *School Daze*: "Let's say the camera starts on Spike, acting in the film as Half-Pint, then it goes dollying down a line of Gammites. As soon as Spike knew the camera was off him, he would come running round behind it, and he'd continue walking with it until he had to run back to his place in front of the camera and get in line)."

Undoubtedly, though, Spike relied heavily on Dickerson's advice for the look of *She's Gotta Have It*. As the DP describes it, "We were learning on the job, always trying to find new ways of visualizing a story. We weren't making documentaries and we didn't feel that we had to be realistic. If an unorthodox theatrical effect was a better way of getting a message across, we would go for that. *Raging Bull* was a big lightning rod for us, especially the speed changes and the sound design of that film. Martin Scorsese was always playing with the medium and using film expressionistically to heighten the experience the film was giving the audience. That's what we wanted to do. With Spike, it was the performance, the sound and the acting. For me it was the light and the color."

It was after Dickerson had viewed *Raging Bull* for the umpteenth time that he called Spike to say that they should think about shooting their movie in black and white. Spike, aware that Jarmusch's black-and-white *Stranger than Paradise* had found an audience, was happy to oblige: "Ernest and I were really influenced by *Stranger than Paradise* and *Breathless*, and that's what we used as reference. Though another big influence was *Rashomon*—we had people in the film addressing the camera, giving you their insight, their observations on Nola." Spike also seized the opportunity to pay homage to another of his favorite films, adding a color sequence inspired by *The Wizard of Oz* that starts with Nola clicking her heels: "You've gotta do something different, you gotta try and bring attention to yourself. You only have one shot. Ernest and I thought it would be effective—in fact, jarring—in a black-and-white film to intercut a color sequence. We were just trying stuff. But experimentation is very important, because that is where I have learned more about the craft."

The twelve-day schedule passed in a flash. As Dickerson has it, "What I remember from that shoot is the need for speed. 'Grab the camera, grab the case, grab the tripod, let's go.' Everyone, actors included, would be in the van, and as soon as we arrived at the location, we would shoot." "Spike called me one day," remembers investor Earl Smith, "and said that he was filming in Fort Greene Park. I got off from work and rode my bike there—I wanted to see what my money was paying for. I knew nothing about making movies and all I could see was Spike doing the same take over and over again. I was like, 'Who the hell have they got acting in this? They can't get one scene right. Oh, my money is fucked. . . .' I got on my bike, rode down the hill, ready to cry. My girlfriend asked, 'How was it?' I said, 'It's OK, he's making a movie.' Later he did the dog scene and he wanted me to be in that, but I wasn't going back onto the set."

The "dog scene" is so called after the peripheral barking sound made as the guys deliver their "all-killer no-thriller" pick-up lines to the camera. The "dogs" included Fab Five Freddy, Reginald Hudlin (who, one year previously, had directed a short film called *House Party* and was the younger brother of Black Filmmaker Foundation founder Warrington Hudlin), Monty Ross and Ernest Dickerson. Spike says of the scene, "It was inspired by listening to my friends and their pick-up lines, and the lengths that guys would go to get what they want. And the real pitiful thing is that some of those lines work. That is the stupefying thing. I was too shy to say *any* of that stuff."

For all such bonhomie, *She's Gotta Have It* was scraping by on donations and goodwill, and the filmmakers were in constant fear of having to shut down production even before the short shoot was done: Spike and Monty would wake each morning praying for money. At lunch Monty would leave the set and go back to Spike's apartment to wait for the mailman, hoping that he would be bearing donation checks from family and friends. "During the course of the shoot there was a time when money looked like it would run out," Monty recalls. "We shot a scene at Spike's Uncle Richard's house, and his uncle came up with champagne and beer and said, 'Hey, guys, I don't know where the film is going to go, but we love Spike and what he's doing, so let's have a moment of celebration.' Spike turned to me and said, 'We can't tell him we can't pay him at the end of the week. . . .' But sure enough, the next day some donation checks came in."

With no funds to retain an editor, Spike began cutting the film on a Steenbeck flatbed at his apartment. He soon ran into trouble when he couldn't successfully cut a fast-action sex scene inspired by Kubrick's *A Clockwork Orange*; and after Optical House, a post-production company, said it would cost $1,200 to get the effect Spike envisaged, he turned to Barry Brown for help. Brown had learned the basics of editing when cutting *The War at Home* and remembers, "Spike asked me to cut the scene where Nola and Greer are having sex, which he had trouble with. He had undercranked the camera but it wasn't nearly as speedy as he wanted it to be."

Spike also asked Brown to assist with sound, an element of film technique where Spike still had a lot to learn, though he was an eager student. Spike says, "I've always been interested in sound and how it is used. I remember seeing *Apocalypse Now* at the Cinerama in Los Angeles the first day it opened, and Walter Murch's sound design amazed me." Barry Brown is credited with sound on *She's Gotta Have It*, but he laughs at the notion today: "It's a joke. Basically, when it came to the mix, Spike had no experience at all, so I set up the tracks and got the sound-design credit."

The color sequence in the film would run for four and a half minutes precisely because such was the length of the piece of music that Spike's father had written for it. Spike knew how much music could help a movie: "I was brought up to appreciate *good* music, and music is another tool to help the filmmaker." In *She's Gotta Have It*, Nola says, "I always remember music when I was at home. I woke up to it and I fell asleep to it." Spike has no hesitation in admitting, "That's personal. You are always going to find things in my films that are personal."

Spike now desperately needed completion funds for the film. He called John Pierson, who ran the Bleecker Street Cinema and had served as a producer on Bill Sherwood's *Parting Glances*, which had enjoyed a theatrical release. Spike asked Pierson if he would invest in *She's Gotta Have It*. Pierson agreed to attend a screening of the rough cut. In his journal, Spike records how his film rocked the house at this screening. Pierson, in his book *Spike, Mike, Slackers and Dykes*, contends that Spike must have been wearing rose-tinted contact lenses: far from an unqualified success, he remembers technical problems. Looking back, Pierson reflects that the truth, as is often the case, lies somewhere in between: "I think that Spike's impression of the screening might have been true for many rank-and-file members of the audience, but it was certainly not true for the handful of industry types who were there." Despite the technical difficulties, Pierson wanted in: he invested $10,000 and became the producers' rep: "I don't want to give myself too much credit. The evidence was right in front of your eyes that this was a good film. I mean, you had to close your eyes when the color sequence came up and blink away a few things, but it was all there."

The film offers us Nola Darling (an artist, seen painting a political mural of Malcolm X on her bedroom wall), who juggles three boyfriends and fights off the affections of an African-American lesbian. Nola doesn't hide her numerous sexual partners from each other and even invites the trio to a Thanksgiving dinner in which the men

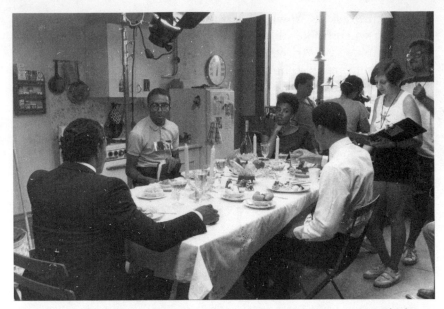

She's Gotta Have It: the shooting of the Thanksgiving dinner scene in which
Nola receives pleas for exclusivity from each of her three lovers, including Mars
(Spike, seated, wearing glasses). (© 1986 David Lee)

plead with her to choose one of them. As we discover through scenes
in which the men recount their thoughts straight to camera, Nola is an
enigma the trio cannot solve. She finally opts for the "buppie" Jamie
Overstreet, a surprising choice, given that he has just taken her by
force. The relationship quickly ends, and the film concludes with Nola
single once more but benefiting from being cut loose from her posse of
suitors.

   Although not quite the raucous sexual comedy it professes to be on
its poster, *She's Gotta Have It* is an extremely amusing début, notable
for its treatment of the black characters. Lisa Jones, who worked on
the film as a production assistant, saw a vision of the black community
that was new to celluloid: "Watching the film without the sound and
seeing shots like the slow-mo of Mars Blackmon going from the top of
the screen and kissing Nola's breast—for me, that perspective was
straight out of a loopy sixties movie. And I was watching the same
conversations about race that we were having in real life and seeing
our sense of New York and African-American culture." Black members of the audience were beside themselves that a film was finally
dealing with their lives, and in a manner that more closely resembled
their sense of their own experience than the stereotypes being offered
by Hollywood.

Nelson George was also an early enthusiast of the finished picture: "There was no precedent for a black sex comedy. I knew all the other filmmakers in New York; they were all scrambling to get something going, but nothing was really happening. Hollywood was not interested in black subject matter for the most part; certainly not in black directors. *Everything* was against this thing working. But when Spike screened the film, there was a magic that people hadn't seen before. There's nothing better—or more threatening— than that kind of art. People did say, "Shoot in color!" They had problems with his father's score, with the color sequence—people didn't like that at all. So, not everyone liked it. But there was something going on in that film that was undeniable. And I gave Spike some money—maybe $4,000."

With sales of his Michael Jackson book mounting, Nelson George had disposable income for the first time in his life and bought a house in Fort Greene, two blocks from Spike's abode. The neighborhood was still unfashionable, so George was able to use his small windfall to buy himself a good-sized pad with wooden floors and a fireplace. George began hanging out with Spike more and started to notice some bizarre behavior: "I remember being out with him a few times. He would be very silent, then he'd go, 'Nelson . . .' and he'd ask you a question about something that was way, *way* left field. I began to realize that he had these intense internal verbal monologues, even when he was in the presence of other people—but he would interject you into these monologues, and then withdraw again. He was not a guy who seemed to have a lot of psychic downtime."

Despite receiving a $10,000 grant from the Jerome Foundation[*] to add to the checks from Pierson and George, Spike was still short of funds. Even the *New York Daily News*, in a piece dated November 22, 1985, drew attention to the financial plight of the *Village Voice* hero. Barry Brown recalls, "Spike was going to sell percentage points in the film for $1,000 apiece. We didn't raise it. People at this point were saying to me, 'There's a *reason* why there aren't a lot of films about blacks: there isn't a market for it. And Hollywood's not stupid; if there was a market they would have exploited it already.' But in reality they knew the audience was there—Spike would round up statistics to show how much of the audience was black—they just didn't *want* to exploit it, even though they knew it would be a success."

[*]The Jerome Foundation, created by filmmaker and philanthropist Jerome Hill (1905-72), makes grants to support the creation and production of new artistic works by emerging artists in Minnesota and New York City.

Some would live to regret not listening to Spike. Jazz musician Branford Marsalis was another whom he approached: "Spike came to my house. He wanted me to watch his film and then invest in it. I said, 'I don't have time. I'm on the road to Europe with Sting in a couple of days.' By the time I came back, he was on the cover of *Time* magazine." This is a slight exaggeration—but it wasn't long before Spike did indeed grace the cover of America's most august newsweekly.

In January 1986 *She's Gotta Have It* was accepted into the San Francisco Film Festival. John Pierson began spreading the word that it was the hottest film of the year. Cannes caught wind of the buzz and, in March, asked to view the picture. Spike was not about to abandon his pursuit of extra finance, but he now began to dream of acceptance into the New York Film Festival in October. The big rush now was to get the money together to have the film blown up from Super-16mm to 35mm at DuArt Laboratories before the San Francisco screening. When DuArt business director Howard Funsch threatened to destroy the negative unless Spike paid up, Spike hit on Nelson George for further contributions. George was happy to help: "The thing about Spike which stood out—and I'd met a lot of artists, directors, musicians— was that I'd never met a man more confident about his destiny. Spike would always say that this is what was going to happen."

In the week before the San Francisco première, Spike sent Pamm Jackson to screen the film for Cannes director Gilles Jacob. To everyone's delight, it received an invitation to the grandest of festivals. By the time Spike got to San Francisco, distributors were starting to show interest. Jeff Lipsky was trying to snare the film for the Samuel Goldwyn Company and prepared a marketing strategy in which he wrote of Spike: "He is the first young black filmmaker to break out into the pantheon of media darlings like Jim Jarmusch, Susan Seidelman, Donna Deitch, John Sayles and Marty Scorsese." On April 2 Tommy Hicks and Spike went on a cable show called *Celebrity Showcase*, and after the appearance Spike went with Pamm Jackson and John Pierson to meet with Island Pictures. Island wanted to buy the film on condition that Spike cut three scenes: two of these—including the final scene of the film, where Nola tells her friend Opal that she will not forsake the black man—Spike was content to excise. But Island also wanted to cut Jamie's rape of Nola, and when Spike asserted that this was a deal breaker, Island withdrew the demand.

Despite a blackout that hit one hour into the world première of *She's Gotta Have It*, the trip to San Francisco was an unqualified success. Spike even got to meet a hero, Akira Kurosawa, who was receiving a lifetime achievement award. He let his hair down, met girls and

—with the promise of a deal from Island Pictures—started earmarking people for the future. Spike got on the phone to tell Monty Ross the great news: "I was sitting in a hotel room in L.A. I told Spike, 'I'm going to pack up and go back home to Atlanta.' Spike was bewildered and replied, 'What are you talking about, man? If it wasn't for you we wouldn't *be* here. You can work for me now.' I said, 'Spike, this is Hollywood. I don't know how to talk their language.' Spike said, 'I don't *want* you to talk that language.' And, like that, Spike persuaded me to go work for him."

His trips to the West Coast doubled as opportunities to meet individuals he felt might be of use to him. Spike reveled in the power that a film deal afforded him. He met with casting director Robi Reed, who recalls: "The first encounter with Spike, I will never forget. He had heard about me through a friend of mine who was in *She's Gotta Have It*, Raye Dowell. He contacted me about a party that was being given for him in the Valley, and I couldn't make it. He called me up the next day and started yelling at me. I was bemused. I said, 'We've never even met!' He asked me why I didn't come to the party, and then told me to come the next night to the closing night of *Night for Dancing*, directed by choreographer Otis Salid.* I went to pick him up in the Valley and I got lost. By the time I got to the house, he wasn't there. . . . I was writing him a note when a car pulls up the drive and Spike flies out of the passenger side. He peered at me over his glasses, under his baseball cap, and said, 'I'll be right back.' I'm thinking, This guy is really strange. . . . We head off and he finally starts to open up and crack jokes. At the theater I introduce Spike to Otis Salid and also to Ruth Carter, a schoolmate of mine. It was a very fateful evening. Later that night we ended up partying with Larry Fishburne and Giancarlo Esposito. We had no idea that a year later we would all be making a movie together."

Ruth Carter also thought Spike a tad strange but still could not help but be impressed by the unusual New Yorker: "I was working in an L.A. theater, eighty hours a week doing costumes for $100. I wasn't interested in film, so I wasn't 'up' on young filmmakers. But we all went to a nightclub and Spike was coaxing me, saying that I needed to get some experience on film. He told me to call USC or UCLA and work on a senior thesis project; it would give me some experience as to what a set was like. Now I think it's the best piece of advice that I've ever been given, and I have been giving it in turn to every young person who wants to pursue a professional career. But at that time I

---

*Salid later did the choreography for the "Straight and Nappy" number in *School Daze*.

wasn't interested. I wanted to be a theater person. I remember dancing with Spike as he was telling me this, and all I could think of at the time was how awful it was dancing with him and hoping that he didn't like me. But all he was trying to do was talk to me about film and be a friend. That night I went home and thought, I should try it. . . ."

These two attractive young women left a huge impression on Spike: "They were talented and hungry, and I wanted to start to put the team together, people whom I could work with again and again and again." Island also wanted Spike to work with them again and again, and just before he left for Cannes they produced a contract that stated he would make three pictures rather than the two that they had verbally agreed with the distributor. There was no time to argue with what Spike's team nevertheless saw as a sneaky maneuver on Island's part to get their star director tied down to them on the cheap. Still, Spike saw the deal with Island not merely as a personal success but a victory for his production company, 40 Acres and a Mule. Spike would not forget those who helped him to this plateau. Monty reveals, "Later on, after he had officially incorporated 40 Acres and a Mule, Spike said, 'OK, you're vice-president of production.' I said, 'What does a vice-president of production do?' Of course, he said, 'I don't know, I'll figure it out. You'll make $35,000 and we'll do something else after two years.' That was the most money I'd earned to date, so I moved to New York." And so, just like that, Monty swapped his matrimonial home in Atlanta for floor space at Spike's apartment while he looked for somewhere to live.

After signing the distribution deal, Spike arrived in Cannes in high spirits, flanked by a number of the cast and crew. PR guru Ginger Corbett, then just learning the ropes of the film industry, was given the job of looking after *She's Gotta Have It*: "It was mayhem. Island had given them a very small budget and they had people sleeping in the bathtubs and on the floor." When a postcard from Spike landed on Earl Smith's doormat, he faced the wrath of his girlfriend ("See what your friend is doing!? He's spending your money having fun in Europe."). The media interest in Spike was enormous, but his quiet demeanor, interspersed with bitter outcries, left many journalists aggrieved. Nelson George recollects, "A lot of reporters would call me up, because Spike would be totally quiet and give monosyllabic answers, but when you hit the right subject, he just rallied. It would go from zero to ten. And if you talked about white directors directing 'black films,' such as Steven Spielberg's *The Color Purple*, he exploded."

"It's not Spielberg per se," Spike reflects. "I've always acknowledged that he is one of the greatest directors ever. I wasn't talking about *Jaws* or *Close Encounters*. I was talking about *The Color Purple*." Spike had watched this film with Nelson George, and it aroused his ire. "At that time," says Spike, "there were a lot of these books—not just Alice Walker's—that were coming down hard on the black male. It seemed to me then that if you had a manuscript with that kind of slant, you were given a book deal." In any event Spielberg was onto a loser with *The Color Purple* as critics such as Nelson George were already disgusted that the figure of Mister had, since the publication of Walker's novel in 1981, become the best-known of all African-American male literary characters. Spielberg's film ended up being remembered mostly for the feat of alerting America to the acting talents of Oprah Winfrey.

As Cannes wound down, Spike was awarded the Prix de Jeunesse but left the festival downhearted, once more claiming, "We wuz robbed" when he didn't also carry off the Camera d'Or for Outstanding First Feature. Some reporters, unhappy with Spike's attitude in interviews, saw this as another sign that the Brooklyn native had a chip on his shoulder. Nevertheless, a momentum had been established, as Nelson George remembers: "The Cannes ticket took the whole thing to the next level, and when he came back it was a different world. One of the greatest moments and the greatest parties I have ever been to was after the première of *She's Gotta Have It*, hosted by the Black Filmmaker Foundation in the Puck Building in New York. Coincidentally, the other film showing at the Cinema Studio in Manhattan was *Mona Lisa*, another Island film, starring Cathy Tyson. It was like a generational coming of age. I cannot emphasize it enough. It was like young, black, hip New York had a film to call their own, a film that on some level represented their reality: the buppie, the b-boy, the boho girl, all that stuff. I was so struck by it. He had awakened me, and I'm sure a lot of people, particularly African-Americans, had that realization about themselves."

In August 1985 Island had successfully released Hector Babenco's *Kiss of the Spider Woman*: against all expectation, the film was a box-office hit and so became a template for "counterprogramming." Island followed the same strategy with *She's Gotta Have It* and it was released on August 15, 1986, at the Cinema Studio theater on 66th and Broadway (since torn down, there's now a Barnes and Noble on the site). The *New York Times* review by D. J. R. Bruckner criticized the film's visual presentation and technical proficiency, but for the story Bruckner reserved the highest praise: "Stripped of some of the distractions of this presentation, their story has a touch of the classic." Several critics were sympathetic to the plight of the young filmmaker and would gloss over what they saw as the film's faults. An example of this attitude is the view of social critic Stanley Crouch, who saw a negative as a positive: "The thing I found most interesting was that the woman was so boring. I said that to Spike once: 'There is nothing interesting about Nola. She looked nice but she was totally soulless, really shallow.' I thought that was profound. It creates a double-level pathos, because you feel sad for her. She's nowhere near what the guys make of her, and you feel sorry for the guys because they can't see that she has nothing to do with the fantasy that they have."

This would not be the last time that Spike faced criticism that women in his films were one-dimensional. Of Nola Darling, Spike says, "I think the mistake that people make is that they don't put the film in context. It came out in 1986. There might have been one other picture in the whole of the United States where there was a leading part for an African-American woman. When you have those types of numbers, you have unrealistic expectations about those characters: that they need to represent all African-American women. There was no way that Nola Darling was meant to represent every black woman in America. This is just one particular woman."

There was one major hurdle that Spike had not yet overcome at the time of release: the film had still to get an R rating from the Motion Picture Association of America (MPAA). "The MPAA is made up of white middle-class people out of L.A., and L.A. is the most segregated place I have ever been," says Barry Brown. "Segregated beyond race: segregated in terms of class, money, position and what your profession is. I think they had a hard time with black people just being people—and especially a sexually active young black woman. It flipped them out. They could not come back to us and say, 'We are going to give you the harshest rating we can because the people in the film are black.' The only thing they could focus on was this fast-action sex scene. They said, 'No doggy style.' They also said, 'There is one spot where you can see a penis.' We said, 'OK, tell us where, we'll cut it.' We recut it three times, and on the third time they rejected it we then asked them to give us specific frames that they had a problem with." Without MPAA approval, the film would be classified X, a big blow for any film since major theater chains refused to book X-rated films. Barry Brown insists that no penis was ever visible; John Pierson argues the contrary. In any event, as Brown remembers, "It was a month before the film came out, and Spike was confident that they would give the film an R. The MPAA took their time over seeing it again, and by the day of release they still hadn't seen it. The film came out and it had still not been officially given an R rating." The poster for the film stated that the film had an R rating, which would allow teenagers to see the film if accompanied by adults; the MPAA took full advantage of this misuse of their trademarked rating system by threatening Island Pictures with breach of copyright for using the R symbol on the poster unless they cut half of the offending sex scene.

As Spike tells it: "I've always had a checkered relationship with the MPAA. What has been really difficult for me to understand is how they distinguish between whether sex or violence is more detrimental to young minds. I think that they've been too lenient on violence and that they're too controlling on sex. What you have to realize about the sex thing is that there are no guidelines. They tell you something is an R on one film, and the next year you do the same thing and they give you an X rating. They're too flimsy, their guidelines."

Spike was forced into making an emergency call to Barry Brown: "My son had just been born, and Spike calls me up and says, 'Good, you're back. You've got to go to the theater and cut half the scene.' We called up the projectionist. I think that the film had been shown two or three times. And I cut the scene in the projection room. Then I was worried about the soundtrack, so I had to wait around for the next screening to make sure it matched." Brown did notice one thing that he hadn't anticipated: "I watched people as they came out of the film. They were *aglow*—especially the young women."

Word-of-mouth was spreading. Actor Delroy Lindo recounts a common experience: "One Saturday I tried to go and see *She's Gotta Have It* with my lady. It was playing in three theaters—the first theater was sold out, so we take a bus uptown, and at the next theater, on Broadway near Lincoln Center, there's a huge line of people waiting. There's a guy standing outside, selling merchandise. Someone on the bus says, 'That's the director.' And this is pertinent—because that is one of Spike's most brilliant characteristics, his eye for marketing." Lisa Jones says of Spike's merchandising activity: "He knew that all this stuff was driving his movies. He definitely never had an interest in being a poor artist." The *Village Voice*, continuing its love affair with their Hero of the Year, put Spike on its cover under the headline *Birth of a Salesman*.

Of his decision to hit the streets, Spike says: "We had to be entrepreneurs, we had to be innovative. Millions of dollars weren't being spent on print or TV ads. I'd always made and sold T-shirts when I was growing up—I had a ton of them. We made up some shirts for the crew, and we started selling them." Earl Smith was also on the streets, helping out: "We were selling so many shirts that I started to think, Maybe I'll make my money back. Eddie Murphy came to one show; he bought out the whole theater. We also went to the Labor Day West Indian Parade and set up a booth. We had a big advantage over other vendors, because if you came to our booth you could meet Spike Lee. We made $15,000 that day. We set up street teams at all the cinemas, and if shirts weren't selling, we would tell the vendors to say, 'Spike Lee is going to be here after the show! Get your T-shirts now and he'll sign them after.' We'd promise to give their money back if he didn't show. He was probably getting writer's cramp from signing his name so many times. We then started selling postcards to people who didn't have $10 for a shirt."

He may not have been about to buy a house in the Hamptons, but Earl Smith was not to be too disappointed by the yield from his investment: "Three weeks before Christmas and I'm almost broke. Spike calls me up and says, 'Earl, you have to meet me at the lawyers' office.' I'm like, 'What's going on *now*?' I was going to this meeting with Spike's words ringing though my mind—'Earl, this is an investment, you can lose your money. . . .' I get to the office and this guy is talking about how much it cost to advertise the film, and I'm thinking, Damn, I'm not going to make any money now. An hour passes and he's still talking, and I just want him to hurry up so I can go home. Then he says, 'Earl Smith,' and gives me an envelope. I don't even open it. I say thank you. I'm tapping my fingers and I'm on the train, then a big smile . . . $8,500. I go home, show my wife and say, 'Here, you see, OK?' A month or so later, I get called back to the lawyers' office and I think, I ain't even going to work today. I get there and they give me a check for $15,000. I get another check later, and I'm thinking, This is *great*. . . ."

She's Gotta Have It was on its way to making $8 million domestically. And for all the film's attractions, most of the attention appeared to have settled upon Spike's character, Mars Blackmon, the bumbling basketball fan infatuated with pop culture, the b-boy who made love with his Nike Jordans on. Mars had audiences in stitches. Ernest Dickerson states: "I remember when people saw *She's Gotta Have It*, they were wondering, 'Who is this guy playing Mars Blackmon?' and when in the credits they found out he was the director, there was a huge gasp from the audience. I think Spike's acting had various degrees of success. He started out definitely wanting to be a director, but I think acting was a trap he got into after *She's Gotta Have It*."

Spike claims to have been unsurprised by the reaction to the movie: "I really believed there was an audience for the type of films that I wanted to make, dealing specifically with the African-American experience in America. After *She's Gotta Have It*, some critics called me the 'black Woody Allen.' There's nothing wrong with looking for a point of reference, but I think that a lot of times critics are lazy, and laziness just boxes people in, without any effort to try and dig deeper below the surface. I had only done one film: how could they tell what was going to be my direction? So I laughed when I heard that. Woody Allen probably laughed too, in the same way that Steven Spielberg laughed when *Newsweek* put M. Night Shyamalan on its cover and declared he was the new Spielberg."

Midway through the eighties, hip-hop and black American film were each, in their own way, generating huge cultural voltage and reaching substantial black audiences. Spike Lee's success partly came from being at the apex of both these movements, or so believes Nelson George: "Spike was able to tap into energy at all levels. Hip-hop was ascendant and coming at the same time that Spike was making black film ascendant—two energies feeding off each other. Mars Blackmon is probably one of the first hip-hop figures on film. Now it's institutionalized; *then* it was an idea. I think this period was unique, in that you had two sorts of African-American art forms coming into public view at the same time. Spike made it cool for nerdy black guys, for the first time ever, perhaps." It was indeed "a moment." Run-DMC released the seminal *Raising Hell* album and enjoyed a crossover *Billboard* hit by releasing their version of Aerosmith's "Walk This Way," recorded with Joe Perry and Steve Tyler. They then headlined a huge tour alongside Whodini, LL Cool J and the Beastie Boys. DJ Jazzy Jeff and the Fresh Prince (a.k.a. Will Smith) released "Parents Just Don't Understand" and had a surprise smash. The New York theater scene jumped in on the self-examining act when George Wolfe's critique of black intelligentsia, *The Colored Museum*, opened at the Public Theater.

In an interview with Nelson George that prefaces his journal entries in *Spike Lee's Gotta Have It*, Spike rails against a criticism made in the *New York Times* that his film was technically flawed. But, over time, as his body of work has developed, he has turned his critical eye upon the picture. "He says that he can't watch the film," states Monty Ross, "but he's being really hard on himself. He should like it for sentimental value. I don't want to sound like an old uncle, but that is the first one, the one that you don't know if it will be a success. The film stands the test of time." Ironically, Spike's main gripe is with the scene that was potentially the deal breaker with Island. He laments: "The rape scene, that is the one scene in all my films that I would redo. I think the

rape and especially its aftermath were too flippant. I didn't really show
the violation that it is. It was ill thought out and ill conceived—all the
ills that you can get. It just made light of rape, and it really comes
down to immaturity on my part."

Another aspect of the film with which Spike was dissatisfied was the
acting, which goes some way to explaining why he wouldn't use those
particular actors in prominent roles again. By the end of the film, he
had fallen out with Tommy Hicks. But then nor did he like his own
performance as Mars, and he made noises— at least to Nelson George
for the *Spike Lee's Gotta Have It* book—that he wouldn't act again.
Nevertheless, he lapped up the pleasure of having a $13,000 billboard
bearing his picture on Sunset Boulevard and even persuaded Island to
launch an Oscar campaign in pursuit of a nomination for Best Screenplay and a Best Musical Score nomination for his father. All of a sudden, women who wouldn't have looked twice at him previously were
taking note, as he became an arbiter of what was perceived as hip in
America. "Spike had become a famous person," remembers his once
unwilling dance partner Ruth Carter, "and I regretted not writing him
back when he had sent me a postcard from Cannes. Finally one morning I get a call: 'Ruth . . . hello . . . Ruth . . . hello.' It's a thing that
Spike does; he uses silence on you as sort of an intimidation tactic—it
took me about five years to stop being intimidated by him. Anyhow,
what he said to me was, 'This is the man of your dreams.' Then he
said, 'I want you to be the costume designer on my next movie.' He
sent me the script and the next day I quit my job."

In contrast, Barry Brown, who had already sampled the success of
an Academy Award nomination, was amazed at how low-key Spike
remained: "There is a moment where everything changes. I had that
too, and I went nuts, beating myself up, going off the rails. And it's
easy to do; you have to fight it. Spike had the moment with *She's
Gotta Have It*. Eddie Murphy called up and said, 'Spike, we have to
make a movie together,' and Spike says, 'Eddie, what movie are you
and I going to make together?' If that had been me at that point, I
would have made the film with Eddie Murphy. . . . Also Spike got a
call from L.A. from an executive at a studio. Spike didn't know who
he was, but he wanted Spike to get on a plane and meet him in L.A.
Spike was furious. He said, 'I didn't call you, you called me. I don't
know who you are. If you want to see me, you get on a plane and
come here and I will meet with you in Brooklyn—and don't even talk
to me about Manhattan, I mean *Brooklyn*.' Holy Moses, I didn't
know how he could talk to people like that. But he was fighting not to
let it go to his head, not to lose it."

In the time it took Mike Tyson to go from amateur Olympic flop to heavyweight champion of the world, Spike had gone from a forlorn figure on the New York subway, yearning for Hollywood, to the rising star of the New York independent film scene. Not only had his status taken a 180-degree turn: so had his game plan. It was the breakthrough year for African-American entertainers and art forms; and now Spike expected Hollywood to come to him.

4 *School Daze*

In the wake of the spectacular success of *She's Gotta Have It*, Spike Lee had two things on his mind: Miles Davis and finding a home for 40 Acres and a Mule. Spike didn't think twice when Warner Bros. asked him to direct a promo video of a cut from Davis's *Tutu* album. Spike knew why he had got the call from the "Picasso of Jazz," widely regarded within the music industry as an egomaniacal control freak: "The fact that Miles knew my father meant that I got a pass. He was known to be really rough on people. The first time that you would meet him, he would grill you, then kick your ass."

The family connection may have won Spike the job, but it would not save him or his crew from the wrath of Miles. The video was the first gig with Spike for property master Kevin Ladson: "My job was to re-create Miles's artwork. I remember passing Spike on the stairwell the first time, thinking, Yeah, we're going to meet today. . . . I wasn't even thinking, Wow, I'm working on a Miles Davis video. It was all about Spike for me. But in the middle of shooting I brought the artwork up to the Puck Building, where we were shooting, and Miles saw me and said, 'That's great, wonderful.' Then he came up closer and yelled, 'Man, you fucked up my artwork!' He cursed me out five different ways. Spike says, 'Hey, what's your name?' I reply, 'Kevin.' He says, 'Kenny, can you go back and redo it?' I said, 'My name is Kevin.' 'Kenny, can you just go and do it?' I was sure Spike would never hire me again." In time Ladson would learn that the ultimate sign of approval from Spike Lee was when he remembered your name.

Shooting the Davis video was an unexpected bonus, but Spike was impatient to build on his début feature hit. He dusted off the *It's Homecoming* script he had begun at Morehouse and began reworking the story. He also found the perfect location for the 40 Acres head office: an old renovated firehouse at 124 DeKalb Avenue, Brooklyn, one of the properties that he had openly coveted (much to Barry Brown's derision) when he was merely a struggling filmmaker. The spectacular building—a stone's throw away from the Fort Greene Park setting for *The Wizard of Oz* sequence in *She's Gotta Have It*— was not simply a way of affirming that there's no place like home: like the name of his company, it was a statement of intent—namely, that Spike didn't intend to abandon his roots.

Spike's first feature had introduced the world to Fort Greene, and he soon had upwardly mobile black New Yorkers realizing there was somewhere other than the Village to live. "I was a Manhattan girl and spent all my time in the East Village," states Lisa Jones. "Getting off the train in Fort Greene, I didn't even know this world existed—these stately brownstones, black families walking around, a kooky kind of middle class." Jones, though, was more impressed with what the converted firehouse of 40 Acres represented: "I think the most important thing that Spike did was in deciding that he wanted to create an institution," she enthuses. "He wanted there to be a legacy. He didn't just get jobs for himself. He allowed a whole generation of young people access to the industry. From early conversations he was telling me about Micheaux and how the history had been lost, and *he* wasn't going to be lost like that. And there was some political importance there, certainly for me, coming out of a black nationalistic background." Spike was fast being seen, even after only one movie, as the emblem of a new generation of black New Yorkers. But the young director was wary of too much responsibility being heaped upon him. At the time he wrote, "I'm determined to not let Spike Lee and 40 Acres and a Mule be seen as the saviors of black people like Richard Pryor's Indigo films. I'm not trying to right everything that's been wrong with black film and black people over the last hundred years."

Some of the pressure would dissipate after the release of Robert Townsend's *Hollywood Shuffle*, to which Samuel Goldwyn and Jeff Lipsky had turned their attention after losing out to Island in the fight for distribution rights to *She's Gotta Have It*. Townsend, an actor who had appeared in *A Soldier's Story* (1984) and worked with the ill-fated Indigo, had his own painful tale about having to use credit cards to finance his movie. *The Hollywood Shuffle*, penned by Townsend and Keenan Ivory Wayans, was a semi-autobiographical account of a black actor struggling to get a role that is not that of a gangster, slave or Eddie Murphy–type clown. Released on Spike Lee's thirtieth birthday, March 20, 1987, the film constituted another attempt to show that there were numerous stories that black people wanted to tell on film. Its box-office success proved that the black audience who attended *She's Gotta Have It* was still out there in substantial numbers and that Spike Lee was not the only African-American director in town. The summer of 1987 also signaled a slight stall in Eddie Murphy's meteoric rise: the final gross of *Beverly Hills Cop* 2 fell $80 million short of the original's $230 million. The end of 1987 also saw the ascent of Denzel Washington, whose turn as Steve Biko in *Cry Freedom* would earn him an Oscar nomination as Best Supporting Actor. Spike admired Washington's performance and, in total contrast to his experience with Eddie Murphy, envisaged one day working with him; but he disliked Richard Attenborough's film, which told Biko's story through the investigation into his death by white South African journalist Donald Woods, played by Kevin Kline. Spike saw *Cry Freedom* as one more film to add to a growing genre that might be labeled White Directors Messing Up Black Stories.

Spike knew that the public could be fickle when it came to one-hit wonders who failed to consolidate their first successes: he had seen too many sports stars fade into oblivion after one great season. At the same time, he was also conscious of the need to protect his personal image. A business proposal from California Wine Cooler, enamored by Mars Blackmon's urban outreach, was politely declined; so was Janet Jackson's idea for a rap record based on "Please, baby, please, baby, baby, baby, please." As a director Spike resisted making TV shows or commercials because it would entail giving away final cut and becoming one more black artist subservient to the whims of the white "gatekeepers" in charge of the networks and agencies. However, he was more than happy to appear on *Saturday Night Live* both as himself and as "Mars." Spike wrote and directed a few skits for the show, hosted by *The Cosby Show*'s Malcolm Jamal-Warner. One of these used Run-DMC to lampoon the media stereotype of black men as criminals and send up Spike's own fast-growing reputation as an overzealous commentator on racial politics.

Then Nike called, asking Spike to work on commercials to star a promising young basketball talent named Michael Jordan. Spike agreed to appear in the ads with Jordan, as Mars Blackmon: "*That's* when it really blew up, that's what really got my face known—not *She's Gotta Have It*," says Spike. "To me, it was natural for Mars to wear those sneakers—that was the trend at the time. Bill Davenport and Jim Riswold at the advertising agency Weiden Kennedy saw the film and they saw Mars's infatuation with Nike, and they got the idea to pair Mars and Jordan together. Some people think that I meant it all along, but I never intended that to be the case when I wrote the script." One dissenter is John Pierson, who goes so far, in *Spike, Mike, Slackers and Dykes*, as to record that when they drove together to the world première of *She's Gotta Have It*, Spike expressed two wishes: first, to have Stevie Wonder compose a soundtrack for him; and, second, to appear in a Nike commercial as Mars, alongside Michael Jordan. . . .

"It must be the shoes": Mars Blackmon (Spike) and Michael Jordan, on behalf of Nike. (© 1988 David Lee)

Nike was then an upstart company, looking to overtake Adidas in the sneaker market. Adidas was the brand eulogized by Run-DMC ("On stage, front-page, every show I go/It's Adidas on my feet, high-top or lows"), and Nike needed a figurehead to capture the imagination of the urban black market, that same hip-hop generation to whom films like *Krush Groove* and *Wild Style* were trying to appeal. Nike founder and CEO Phil Knight recollects, "We were first introduced to Spike Lee by Michael Jordan. He'd just seen *She's Gotta Have It* and he kept going around saying, 'Please, baby, please, baby, baby, baby, please.' I said, 'What the hell is that from?' And he talked about this movie and told the Weiden Kennedy people about Spike. To this day, I still haven't seen this movie."

Spike was left alone to work his magic on the Nike commercials, but when he shot Branford Marsalis's "Royal Garden Blues" music video, the behind-the-scenes shenanigans confirmed his fears that relinquishing creative control was a dangerous business. He made a simple video that met with the ire of both Marsalis's manager and Columbia Records. They were dismayed that Spike didn't deliver a formulaic MTV-oriented approach, as was the vogue of the time. Both sides refused to back down, and finally Spike walked, Columbia then bringing in their own editor. Fortunately his friendship with Branford was not affected: the sax player was happy to let others decide the fate of the video. Today he remarks, "I wouldn't expect Spike to tell me how to play saxophone, so I don't tell Spike how to do his job." Marsalis also agreed to star in a short film, *Horn of Plenty*, that Spike wrote and directed for *Saturday Night Live*. The piece drew inspiration from his father's struggles and his desire to play only the type of music that he loved, no matter what the financial or emotional consequences. Marsalis plays a down-and-out jazz musician who can't get a gig and is reduced to playing on the street to raise money for his family. On a street corner young urban kids make fun of the old-style music he plays, and, like a cartoon, a rain cloud follows Marsalis wherever he goes.

In the course of working together, Spike and Marsalis struck up a friendship that wasn't restricted to work. "We used to get shitty Knicks seats," Marsalis recalls, "and the Knicks were horrible at the time—Hubie Brown was the coach, and there were a lot of empty seats. We would sneak up to the bench and scream, 'You fucking suck! We need a real coach!'" Over the next decade, Spike would have cause to lament numerous other Knicks coaches as Mars's hero Michael Jordan and his Chicago Bulls achieved a formidable domination of the sport. But coaching was a discipline close to his heart, not least because he saw the filmmaker's craft as somehow analogous: "In sports you have to have the right pieces to stick together, and it's like that when you direct a film."

In this line Giancarlo Esposito then became a recipient of what soon came to be known in 40 Acres circles as "the Spike Lee phone call": "It was the early-bird special with Spike. You get that phone call, 'Come straight to Atlanta.' I knew that meant he was going to shoot something for *It's Homecoming*. I asked him who else was coming? He said, 'Vanessa Williams, Fish, Ernest Dickerson . . .'" Spike fondly remembers that the Atlanta weekend left Vanessa Williams frequently open-mouthed at all the beautiful black flesh on show in the vicinity. (It was a youthful display of her own beautiful flesh before a camera lens, eventually published in *Penthouse*, that had caused Williams to be stripped of her Miss America title in 1984.) Spike and Ernest took the opportunity to shoot footage of Morehouse's football game against the visiting Howard University squad, in the hope that they could incorporate some of it in the forthcoming movie. Spike even got his old Morehouse teacher Dr. Eichelberger to don a referee's outfit as part of the sequence. All Eichelberger recalls about the experience was the ill-fitting outfit: "Those damn tight shoes he made me put on! I have a size-thirteen foot and I had to wear a pair of size nines for three or four hours." In the end, adding insult to injury, Dr Eichelberger's pains would be in vain.

Also on this Homecoming weekend trip were John Pierson, Laurie Parker (a production executive from Island) and Loretha Jones (Spike's lawyer). Pierson recalls, "Between Loretha, Laurie and me being around, there was some confusion over who was going to be the producer for Spike Lee. I had my hands in a few other first-time projects, so it certainly made sense for me not to worry about that. But Loretha at the time was super-aggressive." Despite the tension, Esposito says, "We had a wonderful weekend. We shot some stuff that he called second unit, but it was another three to six months before we shot the movie."

During those six months, Spike's deal with Island came apart and the film, now retitled *School Daze*, found a new home. In January 1987, a week before pre-production was due to commence, Laurie Parker called to tell Spike that Island couldn't meet the budget. Spike says, "When Island acquired the rights I didn't know that they had a ceiling on how much they wanted to put into my pictures. *School Daze* they said that they couldn't do. I said, 'Good, I'll take it somewhere else.'" Hindsight may have salved Spike's memory, as Monty Ross remembers Island's late withdrawal provoking extreme stress: "We had set up the production office in Atlanta, and we had to shut it down for a brief moment before we heard Spike got funded."

Loretha Jones's endeavors at the Homecoming weekend paid off: the producer credit was hers when she helped take the script to Columbia Pictures. After their failure with Indigo, Columbia, now headed by David Puttnam, had since seen Island and Samuel Goldwyn jump ahead of them in capturing a black audience: now they wanted a piece of the pie. They were even willing to concede final cut to Spike, a demand he insists on putting into every contract: "The precedent was set with *She's Gotta Have It*. And I have always been able to keep final cut because my films haven't really cost that much." *School Daze* was greenlighted at $6 million, dwarfing the $175,000 spent on his début.

Esposito was enamored by the changes Spike had made to the script: "*Animal House* was a silly film about a white fraternity, whereas I thought that Spike dealt with some more difficult issues here. The original *It's Homecoming* script wasn't a musical; it was a film with music in it. Spike kept working on the piece over six or seven months, streamlining it from the original 175-page script to be an interesting look at black fraternities, the relationship between African-American males and females, and friendships and moral values that are hazy in the African-American community."

The plot had also changed—from being about a small black college named Mission, struggling against being absorbed into the large majority-white state university, to looking at how students at Mission were politically divided along interracial lines over the school's investments in apartheid South Africa. The lack of brotherhood among blacks was to be shown on a micro-level by the tension between light-skinned and dark-skinned students. (This interracial division dated back to slavery, when lighter-skinned blacks would be given jobs as servants in the big house, while their darker-skinned counterparts worked the fields.) Heading the campaign against the school's investments is the dark-skinned Dap, and his political rival is his onetime best friend, light-skinned Julian, also known as Big Brother Almighty in his role as head of the Gamma Phi Gamma fraternity. Dap's loathing of fraternities is challenged when his cousin Half-Pint announces he is going to pledge Gamma Phi Gamma, and soon after his dark-skinned girlfriend (who, because of her complexion, is known as a Jigaboo) announces she wants to join a sorority. Dap sees sororities as home to Wannabes: black girls, nearly all light-skinned, whom he mockingly refers to as Oreos (black on the outside, white on the inside).

Spike says of the script, "It was my own personal experience of four years at Morehouse that was the template for the film. I'd never heard of fraternities until I went down south, to be honest. I would just find it amazing that people had so little self-esteem that they put themselves through these really bad experiences just to belong to a group. But everybody had their own different reasons. Some people joined on a legacy because their parents were in fraternities or sororities. But I knew who I was and I didn't need to be validated by being in a fraternity. I didn't want my ass beat either. I would ask my friends, 'Why are you pledging? Why do you have a need to be hit by a paddle so that you can belong to a group?'"

Bill Nunn was not surprised that Spike wanted to revisit his college experiences: "When you're a writer, you write what you know, and at that time in his life it was all he knew. He didn't have that much life experience, so going to school in the south was probably a profound experience for him." Ernest Dickerson suggests that Spike also wanted to show another side of the African-American experience: "Spike and I both went to black colleges, and that experience had rarely been done on film, so we wanted to capture it."

But Spike also saw his script as a bigger canvas for a study of the African-American experience: "People sometimes think that my source of inspiration is just filmmakers, but it is athletes, musicians, so many people—Malcolm X, Dr. Martin Luther King, Willie Mays, Muhammad Ali, Walt Frazier, John Coltrane, Miles Davis, Joe Louis, Jackie Robinson. . . . These guys are legends, very strong African-American men who took no shit from anyone, who were also top of their field, geniuses, visionaries, at a time when you could get smacked down for taking a stance. But their convictions were never in doubt. They knew they were right and they weren't going to compromise. You'd have to look long and hard today to find an athlete who would make the sacrifice that Ali did when he refused to fight in the Vietnam War. So the opening credit sequence of *School Daze* was trying to show—in a very short time, visually, through still photographs—a very condensed version of African-American history. Slavery was the reason why there are schools for blacks. Historically, blacks were unable to enrol in white institutions – that is their heritage. What we did was use a historically black college as a microcosm of black America, hoping to highlight the so-called differences that I feel are petty, that keep blacks from being a unified people—class, skin color, hair type, that type of stuff."

Spike was keenly preoccupied by the images people sought to present of themselves and was publicly critical of actress/comedienne Whoopi Goldberg for this reason: "I complained that Whoopi Goldberg was wearing blue contact lenses. Number one: I had read Toni Morrison's great novel *The Bluest Eye* about this young girl wanting to have blue eyes. I know it's passé now, but when it first came out, I just couldn't believe it. Number two: it looked unnatural, fake—dark-skinned black people with blue eyes, they looked like zombies. I had a hard time getting past that. 'What is wrong with your God-given eyes?'"

The production of *School Daze* was dealt a blow when the administrators at Morehouse, evidently irked by Spike's refusal of a request to see the script, denied their alumnus permission to shoot on campus, only days before shooting was to commence. This restriction also applied to the footage Spike had shot at Homecoming the previous fall. "Morehouse can be quite conservative," says Ernest Dickerson. "They rely upon grants given to them, so they don't want to be too radical and rock the boat. They were upset, in a sense, with the sex in *She's Gotta Have It* and they wanted assurances that *School Daze* wasn't going to have more of the same. So they wanted script approval, and there was no way that Spike was going to give them it. Parts of the script were very political—black schools being funded by corporations that do business in South Africa. We were talking about some things that were taboo in the black community, even amongst people of color. There is a hierarchy of color, and the lighter you are, the better: *School Daze* dared to air that dirty secret. And they took away all the locations, so we kind of had to make up the look of the film as we went. There were many occasions where there was only one location that Wynn Thomas could make right."

When the college did get wind of the script, Spike recalls, "They criticized me for airing dirty laundry or said that I made up a lot of the stuff that I depict. I don't think that an intelligent person would think that white people didn't know about that stuff already. I'm sad to say that intra-race racism is something that is with us. The president of Morehouse, Hugh Gloster, said that the actor I cast, Joe Seneca, looked too much like a Sambo to be a college president. In actual fact, Morehouse enrollment went up after *School Daze* came out, and they saw that the final product wasn't the bad thing they thought it would be."

Behind the scenes at Morehouse, Herb Eichelberger claims that ignorance contributed to the administrators' decision not to let Spike shoot. Eichelberger says, "The people there were so conservative in their thinking that they didn't give this young guy a fighting chance, because they didn't understand what he was trying to say. Being religious-based colleges so to speak, United Methodist colleges, the sex scenes were probably a salient issue. But they didn't understand the parameters of filmmaking. I think that if the schools had made it easier for him, then I'm not saying that the outcome would not have been any different, but it would have made for less stress on his part."

The students at Atlanta, whom the producers hoped would work for free as extras, had a totally different view of the filmmaker. "When he went back there, it was like, 'Spike Lee is back!'" says Giancarlo Esposito. "He was a star. He had come back with a camera, and somebody had given this nigger money to do something. Remember, Spike was like a good student with glasses, a nerdy character—*no one* thought that this motherfucker was going to make it. He showed everybody."

"*School Daze* was the next step," claims Monty Ross. "We had made an independent movie and now it was time for a studio movie, with unions, the scheduling, the big budget, the banking issues. Spike wanted a certain response. It was the opportunity for African-Americans to expand. Spike was writing the script, directing and writing books about the whole experience—all of this when he *could* have been focused on having an entourage of fifty people. But he was totally focused on the bigger picture."

Spike was critical of the fact that Eddie Murphy was not using his exalted position within Hollywood to give African-Americans a break into the film industry—he failed to see how Paramount could possibly refuse any Murphy demand, given the cash he was raking in for them—and so he was determined to lead by example in promoting African-American talent. Whenever he found a talented African-American whom he felt was the best person for the job, he would appoint them, whether or not they had the right union credentials. Spike refused to buckle under pressure from both the union and the studio to follow the established rules: from *She's Gotta Have It*, Ernest Dickerson, Wynn Thomas, Monty Ross and his own family members remained on board at 40 Acres. Tracey Willard, who had helped with the "sex questionnaire," was given a job as an administrative production assistant, and Spike gave the two girls he had met while partying in the Valley, Robi Reed and Ruth Carter, a chance to break into the industry.

Robi Reed says, "I don't believe any studio would have given me a movie where I had to cast eighty people. Even after *School Daze*, when I had also cast *A Different World*, Eddie Murphy wanted me to cast *Harlem Nights* and he had to fight for me from the inside." Spike had clear instructions for Reed about the type of actor he was looking for: "We wanted multitalented people who could sing, act and dance, and look of college age. We didn't require anybody to have years of experience in theater or TV. Tracy Camila Johns lost out because she wasn't so strong dancing and singing. The auditions were huge events

—everybody auditioned, including Ving Rhames,* Eriq LaSalle† and Tommy Davidson.‡ Reed would take many of the actors from these auditions on *School Daze* to work on *The Cosby Show* spin-off *A Different World*, set on the campus of Hillman, another historically black college. Television, spurred on by the success of *The Cosby Show*, had stepped up its attempts to increase the number of African-Americans on screen. PBS had commissioned a six-part historical series on the civil-rights movement, *Eyes on the Prize*, and Oprah Winfrey's eponymous talk show was on air. Spike, turning on the tube, once again felt sure he was in touch with the zeitgeist.

Even before auditions began, Spike had in mind whom he wanted for his leads. He took the opportunity to get the actors whom he had let down on *The Messenger* back on board. Larry Fishburne—"Fish" to his friends—had invested in *She's Gotta Have It* and knew that it was not uncommon for film financing to collapse; he took the role of Dap without qualms. Giancarlo Esposito was called on to play Dap's adversary Big Brother Almighty. Vanessa Williams, earmarked to play Esposito's girlfriend, eventually passed on *School Daze* and the lead female role went to seventeen-year-old Tisha Campbell who, according to Robi Reed, "had blown us away" at the auditions. Spike also wanted 40 Acres to give opportunities to talented actors who had impressed him over the years, especially those he had seen in repertory theater, such as Samuel L. Jackson and Bill Nunn. Nunn remembers the unorthodox casting process: "I took over delivering the *New York Times* from Monty after he left Atlanta. They had a screening of *She's Gotta Have It* in Atlanta and I ran into Spike, who told me, 'I'm doing a musical, bring your headshot to my grandmother's house tomorrow.' The next morning, after I finished delivering the newspapers, I stopped by there, and he said that he wanted me to be in *School Daze*. It happened right there on his grandmother's porch."

The advent of Spike Lee presented a rare opportunity for the types of black actors depicted in *The Hollywood Shuffle*. Unsurprisingly, Roger Guenveur Smith canceled a holiday to Barbados to go to the audition in L.A. His opening gambit was to tell a sick joke that duly earned him the role of one of the pledgees, and he was proud to join the ensemble bound for Atlanta: "I'll never forget the first time that we

---

*Rhames had appeared in *Native Son*, later becoming known for *Pulp Fiction* and *Out of Sight*.
†The *ER* star had then appeared in *Rappin'* but his SAG status excluded him from *She's Gotta Have It*.
‡Unknown at the time, he became a household favorite for his performances in *In Living Color*.

all met for *School Daze*. We were all at a big table. There was East Coast talent and West Coast talent; it was a tremendous coming together. There was this tremendous energy, because we knew, almost conspiratorially, that somehow we were part of something new and important." Kadeem Hardison, Jasmine Guy, Tyra Ferrell, Leonard Thomas and Kasi Lemmons also joined the roster in Atlanta. But Spike's process was not entirely devoted to discovering new stars. He had grown up admiring Ossie Davis, whose *Ossie and Ruby* TV show had iconic status as one of the few that starred African-Americans. Davis remembers, "Ruby and I had done a book and we invited Spike to the book party. He told us about *School Daze*. I was working on a play, *I'm Not Rappaport*, at the Booth Theater at that time. The part of Coach Odom was like a guy I knew, but I was working in New York and he was shooting in Atlanta. He said, 'It's a day's work and if you come to Atlanta on a dark day we can pull it off.'" Davis, excited by this new black talent, also took a pay cut to appear.

Now the crew had to be assembled, and Spike gave Barry Brown a new starting position. He had been impressed with Brown's speedy cutting abilities on *She's Gotta Have It*, and so wanted him to edit *School Daze*. Brown was somewhat circumspect: "I wasn't a film editor. At that time I'd only cut on 16mm, and on *The War at Home* we figured out things on the go. 35mm is different. I had to ask someone to get me into a feature editing room so I could understand it." Brown, also embarrassed by his dubious sound credit on *She's Gotta Have It*, suggested Tom Fleischman do the mix on *School Daze*. Brown had worked with Fleischman, the son of famed editor Dede Allen, on *The War at Home*. Fleischman was immediately struck by Spike's work-obsessed manner: "Spike seemed very personable, quiet, serious, knowledgeable, no-nonsense; he seemed to know exactly what he wanted." Spike also used a music supervisor for the first time, and this was one of several positions where the studio demanded that he use established union members. Alex Steyermark's name was put forward. "Spike was trying to do something that was far more complicated than *She's Gotta Have It*. He's fascinated by state-of-the-art technology, and he was eager to have his father compose music. But it was difficult, because Bill is a purist who wouldn't allow us to use reverb. And he would write the music cue first and figure out what the tempo should be based on how long the scene was, rather than write for the scene specifically."

Lisa Jones was asked to double up on her role within the growing Spike Lee cottage industry, undertaking second assistant director chores while also writing a book on the making of *School Daze*: "I took notes on set and then interviewed people later on. I had my little perch in the firehouse, where I could look down and hear all of the events. I was the invisible voyeur. And Spike made suggestions, but he didn't ever try to dictate the questions that I asked the crew." Monty Ross remembers Spike's excitement at putting together the 40 Acres team: "We had Ruth Carter, Robi Reed, Ernest Dickerson, Barry Brown, Bill Lee and Wynn Thomas—Wynn introduced us to the need to create the right environment for the actors and actresses. That was the team, and Spike said, 'Hey, this is the band that can make hits!'"

Meanwhile, life also began imitating art. One of Mars Blackmon's most amusing statements in *She's Gotta Have It* was that he had given Jesse Jackson the idea to run for President. Reverend Jackson, running once again in 1988, was invited by Spike to the set of *School Daze* the day before shooting was to commence to say a prayer for the production. Monty Ross says of the visit, "It was great—Jesse brought his spirit. People weren't used to that kind of thing, especially the folks on the crew who had been used to the Hollywood environment. Now here we were praying with Jesse Jackson." Jackson also asked Spike if he would shoot a commercial for him when he had finished shooting *School Daze*. Spike agreed to do so.

The first day of shooting was to take place on location at the local Kentucky Fried Chicken, in which a group of students and townies almost come to blows. "That scene at the KFC is all about class," says Spike. "The people who lived around the schools resented us, and a lot

Reverend Jesse Jackson giving his blessing to the production of *School Daze*. (© 1988 by David Lee)

School Daze: tension at Kentucky Fried Chicken between Laurence Fishburne and Samuel L. Jackson. (© 1988 David Lee)

of people at the school looked down at the townies, thought that they were stupid. So there was actual antagonism." Filming the scene, Sam Jackson, playing a townie, was surprised at the laissez-faire attitude Spike had when giving instructions to the actors: "Me, Giancarlo Esposito, Bill Nunn and Fish, we were essentially theater actors with an understanding of characters and how to embody them and what we wanted to do. So we started to flesh the characters out, and Spike just kind of sat back and watched us do it and accepted it. Spike is a shooter: he sets up shot and kind of walks away from you—he doesn't stand around and give you a lot of thematic talk about intentions or the mood of the scene. He just says, 'Are you ready? *You* ready? *You* ready? OK, let's go.' Apparently he either trusted us or he was more concerned with the setup of the shot or something else, and he left the rest to us. And it was fine." This was not to say that Spike let the

actors call the shots. As an actor of no little experience, Fishburne was
taken by surprise on that first day when Spike refused his request for
another take. The director's explanation took the form of a sporting
analogy: "You can't hit a home run every time." Once his initial anger
at the implicit rebuke subsided, Fishburne took his own form of
revenge by calling Spike "Coach" for the rest of the shoot; but unbe-
knownst to Fish, Spike the sports fan took this as a compliment.

Giancarlo Esposito says the script was loosely written to allow for
improvisation, and yet Spike was not as hands-off as Jackson suggests:
"Spike's response to any comments is that he listens, and if he thinks
that they're valid he will give you respect. But it would be a hard thing
to get him to change his mind. Spike is his own man. We had a scene
where Larry and I are on the quad. I hated my lines so I reworked them,
and I told Larry, 'I'll say it on camera and you respond.' We did an electric scene. And Spike was on a ladder with a bullhorn. We finished, and
everybody knew that we'd changed the lines because there was complete silence. He screamed, 'What did you say?' Larry and I didn't
answer. Spike said, 'Whatever you said, and whatever Larry said, do it
again, just like that!' And that was his stamp of approval."

Spike's natural approach was not to pamper his staff, and this
caused some resentment. Costume designer Ruth Carter for one felt a
tad undervalued: "I don't think anybody knew what I had to do, the
amount of work involved, so no one empathized with me. I remember
going to Monty Ross and saying, 'I have a problem.' Monty was the
guy who was at Spike's side, who was approachable. But there were
days when you wondered, Does Spike approve of me? He had some
fucked-up ways. He would show favoritism constantly, like somebody
would walk in with a great T-shirt and you would find out that Spike
had given it to them. So you would think, Why didn't Spike give *me*
that shirt . . . ? And you'd be deflated and daydream about being in his
good books. But Monty would say, 'Ruth, Spike thinks you are wonderful,' and I would feel better. I don't know why we needed that
approval, but maybe he thought that if he showed too much, you
might get lax. But I desperately needed it. And he wouldn't give it. It
wouldn't happen until the movie was over, then all of a sudden you
would get gifts." Randy Fletcher was first AD and, despite his
formidable size, he too found Spike's demeanor was geared to intimi-
date: "Because he doesn't talk, he can scare you in the beginning,
because you don't know if you are doing things right or not. But he
has an eye communication that says everything without the need for
words. He would just look at me and I would know. And he gave me
a lot of confidence, because we were all young, filmwise."

When he thought it necessary, Spike could be very demonstrative of his anger, and would explode when he was extremely disappointed. His youngest brother, Cinque, found himself in the firing line for his poor acting on *School Daze*: "I was apprentice editor. I was also an actor but I got cut because I was terrible. The one thing Spike hates is people who don't know their lines; it's like sabotage to him. I kept on saying 'Pee' instead of 'Phi.' Spike made me stand in the corner and face a wall in front of everyone for a couple of minutes. That was my first brutal experience with Spike on a film set." Spike was bemused when Jim Jarmusch later asked Cinque to appear in *Mystery Train* and *Coffee and Cigarettes*.

While still a mass communications major at Morehouse, Spike shot a four-minute dance piece on Super-8 featuring Melody Ruffin dancing to "At the End of the Rainbow," sung by Patti Austin. Ruffin had performed at the coronation Spike directed, and from that moment on he knew that he wanted to make a movie with MGM-style musical numbers. In *School Daze* he got to fulfill this ambition, and "Straight and Nappy" was the grandest sequence in the film, the song designating the main battleground between the Wannabes and Jigaboos,

School Daze: showdown at Madame Re Re's between the Wannabes and Jigaboos. (© 1988 David Lee)

warring factions loosely modeled on the gangs in *West Side Story*. Since his days at Morehouse when Spike had affected a big afro, he considered hair a political issue, and this conviction was lavishly reflected in the drama of *School Daze*: "There *is* a cultural signpost with black hair. In the Kentucky Fried Chicken joint, the townies have jheri curls, and I still hate them to this day. The person who invented jheri curls should have their pubic hair put in jheri curls. . . . But that was the inspiration for 'Straight and Nappy,' which my father wrote the music and lyrics for." Such was the depth of Spike's feeling on the issue of personal style that Giancarlo Esposito saw a chance to tease his director: "Spike was on at me about my haircut. 'What's your hair going to be like?' I remember I was feeling a whole Bauhaus thing. I wanted my hair to be parted in the middle, really severe, and then cut back in and tight on the side. And it was a chance to dog Spike, mess with him."

The manner in which Spike wielded his power even caused a real fight to happen when the crew were filming the Greek Show, a center-piece moment of the Homecoming weekend. Spike says, "Branford Marsalis said something, and people started swinging. I never really found out what happened, but I kept the cameras rolling. *That's* when you get the special stuff, when there's something that you're not expecting." Cinque remembers Spike being delirious as his cast really started to split down color and class lines, and he recounts how Spike encouraged the antagonism between the lighter and darker members of his cast: "Larry Fishburne was taunting the other guys in the scene. It broke out into a real fight, and Spike jumped on stage throwing fake punches—he loved that. He set up the actors so it was light-skinned people in one hotel and dark-skinned people in another. That created friction. I think he liked that. It was a shitty hotel. I had mice in my room." By contrast, the light-skinned members of the cast enjoyed plush accommodation. In short, Spike was encouraging the same prac-tice that his film was lambasting. He argues that this was the only way he could get a realistic performance from his actors: "For a lot of peo-ple it was their first time on a movie, let alone their first movie on loca-tion. On location you spend a lot of time together, because there's nothing else to do—everybody goes back to the hotel. And these were inexperienced actors. I didn't want anybody to get too chummy. I thought that if there was a real-life friendship it would spill over onto the screen." This attitude affronted some of the more experienced actors, and Esposito and Fish refused to toe the line. "Spike hated the fact that Larry and I got an apartment together," Esposito remembers, "but we had done films before. When people weren't allowed to see their acting friends, I was like, 'How juvenile of the cat to do this.' But I feel differently now. I feel that he was bright, because he made people turn on each other. He made people understand that they *were* different."

Lisa Jones, who was staying in the nicer hotel, also considered it a shrewd move on Spike's part: "Behind the scenes the dark skin/light skin divide was operating. It created a lot of tension and drama. But there was still a sense of camaraderie. I remember at the 'Straight and Nappy' performance, it was a long shoot, people clapped at the end and the set was auctioned off—people were desperate just to have a little piece. And they didn't really want to leave. To be part of the film was amazing. If you walked down the street with a crew jacket in Atlanta, people would give you deep respect."

Giancarlo Esposito, an actor who attains authenticity by staying in character on and off screen, took full advantage of that respect: "Atlanta is an amazing city with amazing women. I went buck-wild, crazy. I was acting out my part of Big Brother Almighty, I could do anything I wanted—the city was in the palm of my hand." Such machismo did not sit so well with many of the women on the shoot. Lisa Jones says, "For me, coming into that world after working in journalism, theater and performance art, I found it so insular, so anti-intellectual and so sexual. It's always been a struggle for me—although I love movies, I'm not so enamored by the movie world and how full of itself it is. Spike wanted to tell the story that he was interested in. Working on the set, if we grumbled at the time about the sexual politics, he would say, 'That's your movie. If you want to go see that movie, write it and direct it.'" Political correctness was never going to be Spike Lee's forte: as he wrote in the *She's Gotta Have It* book, "They are waiting for a black lesbian film—I'm not doing it."*

For Spike, trying to put all the elements together was like making his début film all over again: "*School Daze* was a big jump. Basically the crew of *She's Gotta Have It* was like an NYU-student-size film. *School Daze* was a lot more people than I ever worked with before, so it was a transition. There was no primer or guide to what I was doing. So I was learning on the job. I read a statement by Kurosawa, who at the age of eighty-five said that there was a universe of cinema that he still had yet to learn. When a great master says that, it's a very humbling experience. And it really makes you examine your own shit and say, 'Yo, I got to get in the woodshed and become tighter, and always be on the quest for knowledge and growth.'"

*See Chapter 17.

Barry Brown recalls a masquerade of professionalism on set: "I remember that I didn't want to get into a conversation with the Columbia executive because I didn't want her to realize that I was so inexperienced. Both Spike and I were learning so much at the time neither of us felt comfortable about me cutting while he was shooting. After the shoot Spike was in the editing room every day." But Columbia understood the difficulties faced by individuals working on a production of this scale for the first time. Stills photographer David Lee, now endowed with a salary, benefited from some useful friendly advice: "On *School Daze* I still didn't have the right equipment for the job. There's a blimp that you put on a camera to silence it. I didn't know what that was. I'm trying to process the film in the dark in the hotel bathroom—I didn't even know there were labs for that. I was completely naïve. Then some kind people at Columbia were on set and they kind of explained things for me. They even bought my first blimp for me. I was ecstatic that now I could actually get some sleep."

Not everybody was so understanding of the delays and difficulties in making the film. Production manager Matia Karrell, who had worked on a number of film sets and was assigned to *School Daze* by Columbia, was tearing her hair out because Spike promoted so many inexperienced individuals. In particular, she lamented the fact that in her eyes the two production assistants in the costume and production-design departments were better equipped than their immediate superiors, in terms of experience. Her criticisms were not popular, especially as they implicitly espoused the virtues of white staff over the black individuals that Spike was keen to promote. Karrell was frustrated at a hiring policy she saw as making her already tough job tougher; she was not open to the argument that Spike was offering opportunities to people of color who had historically been discriminated against. In *Uplift the Race: The Construction of School Daze*, the companion book penned by Lisa Jones, Karrell recalls: "Monty and Tyrone [Harris, locations manager] were in my office at the end of the production and were discussing how to make a location work. I don't remember what the issue of concern was, but I said something to the tune of 'Is this Filmmaking 101?' Monty got very upset about that and I had to apologize later. I had to make him understand that my frustration was a bigger frustration. It wasn't directed at them personally, but at having to take up the slack on so many areas. Sometimes Tyrone would say things like, 'Is this so bad? I didn't do so bad, did I, for a black man.' . . . I think that if he had been a more experienced locations manager I wouldn't have had to expend that energy. But it's OK, because it made me remember why I wanted to do this film. Spike, he's in it for all the right reasons. And it made me think about life in bigger terms. Sometimes you have to remember that life is not a business, filmmaking is not just a business. It is a business about people."

Ossie Davis, who appeared on the set for one day, says that from the perspective of the outsider looking in, there was nothing different about this set than any other he had been on. In fact, "I was impressed when I got to Atlanta, because I was met by Grace Black, a production executive whom I had worked with before, and she said Spike was ahead of schedule and under budget. And I sort of like that: the way he works, organizes things."

Spike wanted to assert his creative control beyond the production of the movie itself. He had been disappointed that Island went with what was his third choice for the poster on She's Gotta Have It and now took steps to ensure that his own concept for the marketing of School Daze would not be so easily ignored. Spike turned to Art Sims. "At that time African-Americans had no jobs in Hollywood," says Sims. "Spike was saying, 'I want to use Art Sims's 11/24 advertising agency. They're doing my work and that's it.' The studio didn't like it at all. Spike fought a lot of battles that opened doors—that are still opening doors. Hollywood is still a good-ole-boys network in many ways. All the other directors just wanted to make their movie and get paid, but Spike refused to give in. It wore on Spike too. Sometimes he got mad at me, because the pressure was so much. There was one executive on School Daze who still tried to get the studio's view implemented. She said, 'I want you to do Spike's face with his eyes bugging out, with a slaphappy expression on his face.' I told her that Spike wouldn't like it. But the executive insisted, 'This is going to be the one-sheet and he's going to like it.' When Spike saw that image, all hell broke loose. I saw that lady packing her bags the next day."

With marketing in mind, Spike also broadened the film's musical palette by conceiving the idea of a go-go track entitled "Da Butt," and then asking Marcus Miller (co-producer of Miles Davis's Tutu) to write lyrics for the band EU. "I knew 'Da Butt' was going to be a hit the first time I heard it," Spike recalls. He also made a deal with Manhattan Records to release the soundtrack for School Daze, having been disappointed by Island's paltry effort to exploit the secondary music market. Spike had seen the benefit of merchandising on his début film, and how soundtracks could help sell films such as Grease and Saturday Night Fever. He even had misplaced hopes for the girl band he created, the Gamma Rays: "I made a mistake with the Gamma Rays. I should have had three of them like the Supremes." The other mistake he made was to give the four actresses the same deal, despite Tisha Campbell being the obvious lead. Tisha's mother was also her manager and encouraged her daughter to sue Spike. Campbell walked away with an extra $25,000 from an out-of-court settlement.

Spike knew he was in for a rough ride as soon as Columbia started to show *School Daze* to test audiences on August 18, 1987. Barry Brown accompanied Spike to the first screening in Philadelphia: "It was the first time either of us had previewed a movie, and he was in the middle of the row and I was at the end, but there was a point where the Gamma Rays start singing this song, 'Don't Let Nobody Turn You Around,' a song from the civil-rights movement, and this audience just *moaned*. It was one big groan. I mean, *everybody*, four or five hundred people moaning, which was a horrible thing to experience—my stomach just dropped. I look down the row, Spike Lee does the same. We both look at each other and it's a look that says, 'God, isn't this horrible?' So from that point on we always sat together at screenings." But the offending scene was cut.

Columbia were getting cold feet over the movie as the test-audience results were not looking positive. By the time the film was ready, David Puttnam had resigned from Columbia, suffering from chronic fatigue syndrome and somewhat beaten down by the range of diplomatic difficulties that had come with the job. He was replaced by Dawn Steel. Spike was convinced that she wanted to kill the film because it was a Puttnam project, and took to calling her "Steely Dawn." Steel was on the receiving end of Spike's ire when she suggested that *School Daze* shift its release date so as not to clash with *Action Jackson*, a beat-'em-up starring Carl Weathers and Vanity. Spike was furious at the implication that the black audience would be split between two such wildly disparate offerings. Steel could not expect that the Nike ads that were starting to air in late 1987 would have such an impact on the popularity of the director.

The Spike 'n' Mike "It's gotta be the shoes" ads not only exposed Spike Lee to an audience that wouldn't have dreamed of lining up to see *She's Gotta Have It*; they also persuaded a whole generation that Nike Air Jordan sneakers were an accessory they couldn't live without. Nike quickly became the biggest sporting brand in the world, and Phil Knight would never forget the contribution made by Spike Lee: "I think that the commercials had his fingerprints all over them. Everyone remembers what a great success the Jordan line has been— perhaps the biggest success in the history of the sporting-goods business. It continues to sell at a very high level. But in that year before the

Spike and Mike adverts, the sales of Air Jordans actually went down. It was those advertisements that really revived the brand."

"Yo, Mars Blackmon here, with my man, Michael Jordan." Thus the opening line to an advertising campaign that is often cited in lists of the best TV spots in history. Nike hoped that Spike would put them in touch with urban culture but had no idea of how well he would do so. The ad upped the ante of sports merchandising. "This was one of the great American moments in Madison Avenue advertising," says Robert Thompson, founding director of the Center for the Study of Popular Television at Syracuse University. "The idea that people don't get good at something because of practice and the right genes, but rather with the right attitude and the right shoes—it was brilliant."* Everybody wanted a piece of Mars Blackmon: he was seen as the epitome of street cred and Spike became a bona fide celebrity. "I think it was very glamorous for him, meeting celebrities, the sports figures he admired," says Lisa Jones. "He did things and made choices that I bet he wouldn't make today—talking about certain political issues on *Nightline*, becoming something of a spokesman."

Eventually *School Daze* opened, as Spike wanted, on February 14, 1988, and the timing was crucial, coinciding with the 1988 All-Star basketball game, in which the best talents of the Eastern Conference faced off against the Western stars. Jordan played like a legend and was named Most Valuable Player. The news was greeted with countless reruns of the Spike 'n' Mike ad. *School Daze* needed the boost, as many critics agreed with Bill Nunn's assessment of the movie on his first viewing: "I was disappointed. I thought that it was going to be all-round better. But like other Spike films—you can say, 'Man, this sucks,' and then watch it again and flip over. That's the way that movie has been for me." Others were not willing to give the film so much time of day. Rita Kempley of the *Washington Post* wrote, 'Tell an inexperienced director he's a genius and you create Dr. Frankenstein. *School Daze* with its pompous patchwork plot is an arrogant, humorless, sexist mess." Spike would now understand why many directors avoid reviews: he was particularly taken aback by the critical suggestion that one of his heroes, Vincente Minnelli, would be turning in his grave at the poor musical numbers in *School Daze*.

Despite the critical mauling and the fears of the studio, *School Daze* did unexpectedly good business. Its gross of $14.5 million would make it Columbia's most profitable film of the year. (The infinitely more expensive *Action Jackson* grossed $20 million, a disappointing

*Quoted from "Air Jordans" by Damien Cave, on Salon.com.

return given its higher budget and marketing push.) Spike had no doubt that the box-office return of *School Daze* vindicated his position. The film's gross had benefited from the personal popularity of Spike Lee, much of which was attributable to the Nike ads. At this stage in his career Spike was being admired more for his acting and his cult of personality than his filmmaking. But he had already begun working on a project that would leave no doubt about his credentials as a director.

5 *Do the Right Thing*

Gotta give us what we want
Gotta give us what we need
Our freedom of speech is freedom or death
We got to fight the powers that be.
    Public Enemy, "Fight the Power" (Shocklee/Sadler/Ridenhour)

By 1988 rap acts were selling out stadiums across America and starting to dominate the *Billboard* black music chart. And, as we have seen, Spike Lee—at least in his Mars Blackmon b-boy makeup—had become the cinematic embodiment of a rap scene that was carrying black political perspectives into pop culture. Thus Def Jam mogul Russell Simmons approached Spike to direct *Tougher than Leather*, a follow-up of sorts to *Krush Groove*, aimed, like its predecessor, at showcasing the rap stars on his label. Spike's relationship with music labels had improved since he had butted heads with the management of Columbia Records over Branford Marsalis's "Royal Garden Blues" promo. While filming *School Daze* he also shot music videos for three of the acts who had appeared in the movie: Phyllis Hyman ("Be One"), the Rays ("Be Alone Tonight") and EU's go-go smash "Da Butt." None of these clips matched the skill and craft that he displayed in his video for Anita Baker's "No One in the World" in 1987. But despite his growing facility in directing musicians and artists, Spike turned down the *Tougher than Leather* offer: as he remembers it, "the script was a reworking of the blaxploitation genre—Run, D and Jam Master Jay spend the entire film running around shooting people—and I never went to see those films. I didn't like them."

The growth in rap's popularity since the release of "Rapper's Delight" in 1979 was emblematic of a shift in the cultural tastes of African-Americans. Rap music—unlike gospel, rhythm and blues, or the pop crossover sounds of Michael Jackson—was revisiting African roots through its syncopated polyrhythm and raw street-talk expressiveness, distantly derived from the songs that were developed as a mode of communication by African slaves. Rap's crucial break from the preceding black musical traditions of the twentieth century was that the street-talk style, similar to that used by Jamaicans in "toasting," served as a celebration of the black working class; one that also criticized the sociopolitical system that blocked the progress of African-Americans.

Spike had hoped the script to *Tougher than Leather* would embody just such a vision of rap music's potential, which meantime reached an apex with the July 1988 release of Public Enemy's stunning second album *It Takes a Nation of Millions to Hold Us Back*. The "PE," who had signed to Def Jam in 1986, were the self-proclaimed "Black Panthers" of rap, and in their music they went further than any of their peers in addressing the problems of the African-American working class. A best-selling single from *It Takes a Nation* proclaimed "Don't Believe the Hype," but the sounds emanating from MC and group founder Chuck D and his crew of Flavor Flav and DJ Terminator X surpassed even the most exalted expectations of what rap could achieve. The band were backed up on stage by the S1Ws ("Security of the First World"), so called to demonstrate that the black man would not be relegated to Third World status. The influence of the Panthers was prevalent both in the political nature of PE's lyrics (often supplemented by the sampling of Malcolm X speeches) and in their on-stage presentation, S1Ws toting fake Uzi machine guns in a posture of militant action. Spike recognized a kindred spirit in Chuck D, and extols him still as "one of the most politically and socially conscious artists of any generation. It was in pre-production for *Do the Right Thing* that I got an idea for a song, and I knew the person that I needed to go to was Chuck D. The first demo they did, I sent back—I didn't feel it was right. Then Chuck came back with 'Fight the Power.'" The song was eventually completed after the shooting of the film. Not only would it be the perfect accompaniment to Spike's cinematic essay on black urban life in New York; it would become an anthem and carry rap music further into mainstream America.

As Spike Lee sat down to research and write his third picture at the start of 1988, fifteen-year-old Tawana Brawley's claims that she had been abducted and raped by a group of men—some carrying police badges—were making headlines on a daily basis in New York and nationwide. Brawley later retracted her claims but told others that, although penetration did not occur, other types of abuse, some sexual in nature, certainly had. Forensic tests found no evidence of sexual assault: this was only one of many discrepancies in Brawley's story. The politically ambitious Pentecostal preacher Al Sharpton and two attorneys, Alton H. Maddox and C. Vernon Mason, used the Brawley case to highlight their conviction that the police and the judicial system were racist and corrupt; but they refused to recant even as evidence mounted that Brawley had lied. Spike Lee also ignored the growing evidence against Brawley and decided that his forthcoming film wall would feature graffiti proclaiming "Tawana told the truth." Several court cases would prove the opposite. In the course of his commentary for the 2001 Criterion Classic edition of *Do the Right Thing*, Spike claims that the slogan was not a show of support, rather just the kind of statement he thought would be spray-painted on a wall in Brooklyn in 1989. Nevertheless, the Tawana graffito remains for Spike "one of my favorite uses of background in my films"; and, like Sharpton, Spike steadfastly refuses to say that there was no element of truth in Brawley's claims.

The recent history of relations between the New York Police Department and the city's black populace suggested at least that Spike had good reason to believe Brawley's claims when first asserted. Despite the cosmopolitan makeup of New York's citizenry, many, including Spike, felt that under Mayor Ed Koch the city had become an uncomfortably simmering melting pot of racial tension. On December 20, 1986, a few months after *She's Gotta Have It* established Spike as a local celebrity, a twenty-three-year-old African-American construction worker named Michael Griffith was killed after being chased by an Italian-American mob in Howard Beach, Queens. Griffith was with two black friends, Cedric Saniford and Timothy Grimes, when their car broke down in front of a pizza parlour. They wandered inside, hoping to call for help, and when they were refused the use of the phone they sat down to eat. Soon after, two police officers answering a call citing "three suspicious black males" walked in, but left as soon as they realized the calls were unwarranted. Thereafter, a group of white men—among them John Lester, Scott Kern and Jason Landone—chased the black youths out of the pizzeria toward a gang of accomplices waiting with baseball bats. Grimes escaped after he pulled a knife; Saniford was knocked unconscious and, as a severely beaten Griffith tried to stagger away from his pursuers, he wandered onto the busy Belt Parkway, where he was hit and killed by a passing automobile. New York erupted, witnessing its largest black protest rallies since the civil-rights movement.

The protection of New York's finest appeared to offer little comfort to the city's black citizenry. Yvonne Smallwood was sitting in a car when her companion was issued a traffic violation ticket; she complained to a police officer that the police would be of more help if they concentrated on pursuing drug-dealers. The police officer writing the ticket took offense and beat Smallwood to death. A similar fate befell Eleanor Bumpers in 1984, when the police were called in to evict this sixty-seven-year-old arthritic woman with psychiatric problems from her Bronx home. Bumpers answered the door holding a kitchen knife for protection against her "enemies," as was her wont: the policeman on the scene blew her hands off and then, as if to make sure, shot her dead. Disturbingly similar outrages were not uncommon. Edmund Perry, a seventeen-year-old black student, was murdered ten days after high-school graduation by a policeman who claimed to have been in a fight with him; graffiti artist Michael Stewart was apprehended by eleven policemen in a white transit van and choked to death—the evidence of Stewart being strangled by the police was "lost."

Spike had previously conceived of a film called *Heatwave* to be set on the hottest day of the year. "In New York you have eight million people on top of each other," he points out, "and people get crazy when it's hot. Things start to get frayed. If you bump into someone, you might get shot." Piecing together his story, Spike wondered what might happen if a black person was murdered by police on a hot, humid New York summer's day. He then borrowed details from the true-life accounts: from Howard Beach, the baseball bat, the pizzeria, conflict between blacks and Italian-Americans, and a call issued by blacks to boycott pizzerias for one day in protest of the Griffith death. From the case of Michael Stewart, he took the lethal choke hold. But as he acknowledges, "there were many different things that influenced *Do the Right Thing*. I remember seeing an old *Twilight Zone* where a scientist had conducted a study showing that the murder rate goes up after the temperature hits 95 degrees. I wanted the film to take place in one twenty-four-hour period and wanted it to take place on the hottest day of the summer. There was also a big incident in Brooklyn College, where black students and white students were fighting over what music was being played on the jukebox. In terms of the racial climate in the city at that time, Mayor Koch had really polarized a lot of New Yorkers."

Spike was determined to contribute to the downfall of Koch, who had been mayor of New York since 1978: "We knew that when the film came out it would be right before the Democratic primary for mayor. We felt that we could have a little bit of influence . . . and every time we could nail Koch, we would. Though, interestingly enough, people like Joe Klein and David Dedley wrote that the film would hurt David Dinkins's chance of becoming mayor." In fact, Dinkins went on to be elected New York's first black mayor, and from this experience Spike developed a unique and contentious reputation as the one American director who consistently made pertinent and up-to-date political comments in his films, which he hoped would influence the political climate at the time of a movie's release.

Spike had noticed a common thread in many of the notorious instances of racism in New York, something he had first witnessed growing up in the Italian-American neighborhood of Cobble Hill. "Historically," he suggests, "there has always been a dynamic between Italian-Americans and African-Americans that sometimes turns into violence." This proposal struck a chord with Giancarlo Esposito, who felt that in *Do the Right Thing* Spike was displaying a surprisingly strong grasp of the subject matter at hand: "My father was Italian, from Naples, and my mother was black. I felt that Spike really understood the consciousness of Italian people, probably even more so than he understood black people,* which to me was surprising. Bottom line, the reason I think that Spike understands Italians is because they are good people, people who really care about the community. They're very different from what Spike would probably coin 'white people,' and I think that's why he relates to them. You can see this in *Jungle Fever* too. I think the stuff in the coffee shop in that movie is some of the best stuff I've seen in a Spike Lee movie—he really got the nuance of those relationships."

As soon as Spike decided he would set his film on the hottest day of the year, he sought out the visual input of Ernest Dickerson, who had —in the wake of a divorce, and like many a Bap and buppie—moved to Fort Greene: "I remember Spike had a yellow legal pad and the title on it was *Heatwave*. He said to me, 'I want you to really think about how you can give the feeling of the hottest day of the summer. What can you do visually to make the audience sweat?' Even before he showed me the script, he threw that at me. I've always been influenced by the psychology of color. I think it's been proven that when you look at the color red your heart beats faster, and when you look at blue and green your tendency is to calm down. So I thought, What if the color scheme was all reds, yellows and earth tones, and nothing blue? On the East Coast, the weather changes a lot. Spike made sure that I had enough time to work that out, because the decision that I made ultimately determined where we were going to shoot. I knew that we needed to shoot on a street that traveled from north to south, because where the sun traveled east to west, one side of the street was always going to be in the shade. So if it was raining I could shoot cloudy conditions and make it look like the shaded side of the street."

Spike wrote *Do the Right Thing* at a furious pace, taking only

*Spike vehemently disagrees with this suggestion.

twelve days to complete the first draft. The film would take its lead from Richard Wright's *Native Son*, the great black literary work of protest. *Native Son* shocked many on its publication in 1940, as it broke from a stance popular among black authors of the time, who were advancing the idea of the sophisticated and cultivated "new Negro"—so called because this creature could assimilate into mainstream American society without difficulty. Instead Wright (as would Ralph Ellison a few years later in *The Invisible Man*) sided with the more aggressive and disillusioned black masses, turning the psychic and physical violence of black life outward onto white America. Likewise, Spike abandoned the confines of the black community that housed *She's Gotta Have It* and *School Daze* and turned his attention to modern America from a black urban working-class perspective.

The opening line of the script was the very same cry of "Wake up!" that had served as the ambiguous end to *School Daze*. "That is a call to everybody, not just African-Americans, to look at what is going on around them," Spike contends. Set on a single block in Bedford-Stuyvesant, *Do the Right Thing* centers on the relationship between Sal and Mookie, employer and employee. They work at Sal's Famous Pizzeria alongside Sal's two sons, Vito and the racist Pino. Sal is proud of his Italian roots: the wall of his pizzeria is adorned by pictures of Italian-American idols, and he doesn't consider himself racist—indeed he employs Mookie, operates in a black neighborhood and shows rather more affection for Mookie's sister Jade than Mookie is comfortable with. Mookie, much like Mars Blackmon in *She's Gotta Have It*, is a father less interested in looking after his family than in lining his wallet: like Mars, he doesn't live with his girlfriend and their child. Spike says, "This is just a comment on young African-American males who are bringing babies into the world and aren't being responsible adults." Over the course of the day, as Mookie delivers pizzas around the neighborhood, we meet the prominent residents of the block and observe racial tensions simmering under the summer sun, until finally a riot breaks out at the pizza parlor after Sal smashes the PE-pumping ghetto blaster that is the proud possession of Radio Raheem. Police are called to the scene, and Raheem winds up in a choke hold that proves fatal. Mookie retaliates by throwing a garbage can through his employer's window. The film ends with Mookie returning to the scene of the devastation the next morning, so that he can collect his outstanding wages from a distraught Sal.

With the production shooting in New York, Spike made the decision that he needed producers, not to say a production manager, who knew the Big Apple to its core. As First AD Randy Fletcher recalls, the *School Daze* producers had in any case fallen permanently from favor when they tried to put a crimp in Spike's leisure pursuits: "We were in Atlanta and Spike wanted to go see a boxing match. He said, 'I'm wrapping early, I'm going to the fight.' He knew what he was doing— if we lost four or five hours, he'd make it up. But all the producers were saying Spike couldn't go. I said, 'Are you all *crazy*? You're going to tell him he can't go to the fight?' And Spike remembers stuff like that. By the time of *Do the Right Thing*, they were all gone." Instead Jon Kilik, first introduced to Spike by David Puttnam, was brought in to be line producer. Kilik would become a pivotal figure at 40 Acres, and he says of his encounter with Spike: "We met up while he was still working on the *Do the Right Thing* script, and this is the process that has been repeated over fifteen years on eleven films: he will tell me about the idea, he'll start to paint the outline, then describe how he wants to shoot it, *where* he wants to shoot it and *when* he wants to shoot it."

Spike had been all set to make *Do the Right Thing* with Paramount when they abruptly got cold feet and asked him to change the ending. He refused and shopped the film around to Touchstone, before Sam Kitt picked it up for Universal. Spike hoped to make the picture for $10 million, but Universal would not go over $6.5 million. They suggested that Spike shoot in Baltimore or Philadelphia with a non-union crew to save money, but Spike was determined to shoot in Brooklyn and gave Kilik the task of negotiating with the unions: "It was going to be a combination of working with non-union people that Spike wanted, yet somehow doing it under a union contract and a formal union structure. Spike had quickly established a profile, and the budget of $6.5 million was high enough so that the unions weren't going to ignore the production. So there were two unions here, NABET [National Association of Broadcast Entertainers] and IATSE [International Alliance of Theatrical Stage Employees] and we sat down with both of them and tried to tell them, 'We are going to be working on the streets of Brooklyn and we are going to be using these people. We'd like to work with you, and we would like to supplement our crew with your membership.'" Spike had originally planned to sign a contract with IATSE, but they proved too expensive. So they went into negotiations with NABET for a month, and the outcome was gratifying for Spike: "NABET was the younger of the two unions and they were willing to work with us. They brought in probably fifteen people, and maybe a third of the crew weren't members of the union prior to the shoot. It helped us establish a traineeship intern program, which led to membership for probably another five or ten people each film. It was really a great situation for us *and* in the end for the union, because we did it under their banner, so we helped put them on the map also."

In positions where NABET had no black members—such as the hairstylist, stills photographer and second assistant director—Spike was granted permission to use non-union crew. As David Lee puts it, "It was a great play on Spike's part. The unions couldn't say no; they would have no justification in not allowing the people who had the hours into the union. Spike showed that there was no black props man in the union, or indeed black people in other positions. I'm eternally indebted because I got into the union on *Do the Right Thing*. And it was really with that film that Spike was first able to exhibit some clout and challenge people—through the movie itself, but also challenging people in the industry over the incredible inequalities or absence of people of color on their roster."

Lisa Jones, back again to write the book of the film, elucidates: "Other people were pulling Spike and getting his attention; he was doing the commercials and stuff. His mega-operation had begun, but he still had a very clear sense of the brotherhood. One thing that he always mentioned to me was that a great influence on him was that his great-grandfather founded Snow Hill Institute in Alabama. It was through this autonomous black institution that there was this idea to uplift the race. It always stuck in his mind, and training people and furthering their opportunities really connected him to his great-grandfather." As Randy Fletcher explains, this connection bore fruit on *Do the Right Thing*: "Spike started the intern program and he let me oversee it, so I would interview all the people who wanted to become interns. Already we had two hundred people coming for thirty spots."

The crew was gathered: Ernest Dickerson, Monty Ross, Ruth Carter, Robi Reed, Wynn Thomas, Barry Brown, Randy Fletcher, Alex Steyermark and Tom Fleischman. Casting the film would not be so straightforward. Spike had wanted Fish to play Radio Raheem, Robert De Niro to play Sal, and Matt Dillon for Pino, but he was turned down by all three: "Larry Fishburne didn't like the script and thought the part was too small for him. De Niro said the part was too similar to others he had played. And Matt Dillon's agent didn't want him to do it." For Sal, Spike then looked at Danny Aiello, who had recently done *Moonstruck* with Cher. Spike knew he had his man when Aiello informed him, "My politics are on the right of the most right-wing person you know." Spike then cast *School Daze* alumnus Bill Nunn as Radio Raheem, alongside Sam Jackson as DJ Mister Señor

Love Daddy and Giancarlo Esposito as the confrontational neighborhood radical Buggin Out.

As the start date approached, Spike agreed to act with Danny Aiello in a radio play by dramatist John Patrick Shanley, who had recently scripted the feature film *Five Corners*. Shanley was a writer Spike admired, but *Five Corners*'s greatest impact upon him was in the performance of little-known Brooklyn-based actor John Turturro as a violent sociopath. Spike approached Turturro with his new script. Turturro recalls, "There was something about that script that made me think this could be really interesting. Spike asked me which role I wanted to play. I wanted to play Pino, the racist, because he's the more interesting out of the two brothers. And during the course of the film we became friends." Indeed, *Do the Right Thing* would prove to be only the first in a long and fruitful sequence of Lee–Turturro collaborations. "I've seen him go through a lot of things," the actor reflects. "We're both the same age, we grew up in similar kinds of family situations—my friends were black growing up, his friends were white growing up—we definitely have things in common. I think we were even born a few weeks apart. And I had a very specific position within his movies—I'm like his Caucasian thread."

Spike cast himself in the role of Mookie and enlisted Joie to play his sister; but it was in the unusual surrounds of an L.A. nightclub called Funky Reggae that he found the beautiful dancer who would play

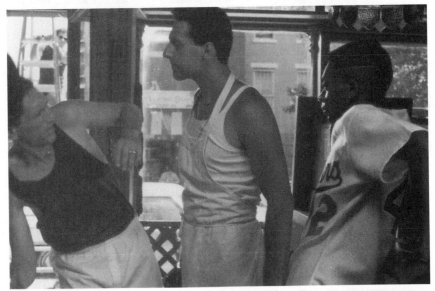

Do the Right Thing: Vito (Richard Edson), Pino (John Turturro) and Mookie (Spike Lee). (© 1988 David Lee)

Do the Right Thing: Joie Lee and Giancarlo Esposito rehearse under Spike's watchful eye. (© 1988 David Lee)

Mookie's girlfriend, as he relates: "They were having a birthday party for me, and the go-go band EU had flown in from DC. It was a *great* party. And this girl was dancing on top of a speaker, so I told her to get down because I didn't want her to fall and break her neck, then find out that I'm the one being sued. And when I told her to get down, she cursed me out. Now, you know how Rosie speaks—I had never heard a voice like *that* before. And I started speaking to her, and it turns out that she was from the same neighborhood in Brooklyn as I was from. That's where I started to get the idea of making Mookie's sometime girlfriend Puerto Rican."

Rosie Perez was not so struck by this short black man, who looked smaller still from atop a large speaker: "At first I said no. I wasn't an actress. I was at college. I had no interest in being an actress—the mere thought of it never entered my consciousness, or *sub*consciousness. But Spike saw something that I clearly didn't that first night we met.

He kept laughing at me, shaking my hand, repeating, 'This is fate, this is fate. . . .' He assured me it would be all right. When I read his script, a lot of the vernacular of the character stuck me strongly. I was like, 'Whoa, this line is used in the exact same way as I use it. . . .' So I read it and I loved it, and when I went back to tell him, he told me, 'Now you have to audition.' I said, 'Wait a minute, you just gave me the role.' He said, 'Asking if you're interested is not an offer.' "

Meanwhile, *School Daze* veteran Roger Guenveur Smith was begging Spike to be included in the new project: "I felt that I could contribute in some way to the Brooklyn piece. Spike was in L.A., I was there, we had a very brief meeting and he gave me a draft, which was prefaced with a quote from Malcolm X—not the one that was eventually used in the film. So I thought about a character who was maybe trying to sell personally colorized portraits of Malcolm and Martin Luther King, and I remember having seen that photograph of the two of them and being rather startled by it, because of the popular propaganda that these were two men who were diametrically opposed. But you could tell in that photograph that they had a genuine love, admiration and respect for each other. We had another meeting after I had read the draft, and I pitched Spike the idea of Smiley, a guy who tries to sell this photograph, and he thought it was a great idea. We just expanded it from there and the character of Smiley continued to grow.* Smiley became more aggressive and eventually became the moral spine of the piece, the one who actually burns the pizza parlor."

Having decided upon his cast, Spike needed to find the right location: "It was a challenge to shoot the whole film on one block. I wanted brownstones, so Wynn Thomas had to find a block that had them, as well as empty lots in the corner, so that we could build a Korean fruit-and-vegetable stand and a pizzeria directly across from it. Plus you want to have a block that you can control, one that didn't have a bus going through it, because the city wouldn't reroute a bus for me. Also we had to shoot it in Bed-Stuy because at that time it was the most well-known black neighborhood in Brooklyn." The location also allowed Spike to pay homage to local hero Mike Tyson, and he ordered that a huge mural of the boxer be painted on a wall that looked onto the location of Sal's Famous Pizzeria. Tyson was a symbol of the strength of Brooklyn's African-American community. As well as being the youngest heavyweight champion in history, he had in 1987 become the first undisputed champion of the world since Larry

*Spike now jokes that, had it been up to Roger, Smiley would have been in every scene.

Do the Right Thing: Spike and Ernest Dickerson on location. (© 1988 David Lee)

Holmes. On the night of the 1988 All-Star Game, Tyson had married actress Robin Givens. On June 20, 1988 he defeated Michael Spinks in ninety-one seconds—one of the most awesome displays ever witnessed in the sport. But during the shooting of *Do the Right Thing* Tyson broke his right hand in a street brawl with Mitch "Blood" Green, and the start of his demise was evidenced a few months later when Givens, sitting next to her husband for an interview on Barbara Walters's *20/20* TV show, informed the world that living with Tyson was "frightening" and described the boxer as "incredibly abusive." (She filed for divorce shortly thereafter.)

Hollywood studios tend to discourage location shoots due to the difficulties of controlling such external factors as traffic, noise and the public. *Do the Right Thing*, however, would take over a block in Brooklyn for some eight and a half weeks. "People on the block were fantastic," claims Spike. "You have to realize that every time you shoot on someone's block or in someone's house you are being an inconvenience to them. So, knowing that, we tried to make it as pain-less as possible. Of course, there's always going to be some anger—they're mad because they can't park their car in front of their house or they've been told they can't play their music loud or that they can't walk down the block in the middle of shots." The *Making of Do the Right Thing* documentary, shot as part of the electronic press kit (EPK) for the film and directed by leading black documentary film-maker Sinclair St. Bourne, picked up on some of this local animosity toward the filmmakers. To help appease the locals, Spike brought in Preston Holmes, the production manager who had turned Spike down for a job on *Krush Groove*: "At the time, one of the things that I sort of prided myself on as a production manager/line producer was going into the community and building a positive relationship between them and the production. We were able to provide some jobs. People had certain skills. I remember there was an unemployed construction worker who was put to work in the construction department, and he eventually got into the union as a carpenter. There was another kid who just hung around who became the driver for Spike."

Monty Ross and Preston Holmes decided that the production would take the unusual step of rejecting police protection from the New York Mayor's Office of Motion Pictures in favor of the Fruit of Islam (FOI), the security wing of Louis Farrakhan's black national-ist/separatist Nation of Islam. The decision evinced the low esteem in which the NYPD was held by the management of 40 Acres, but Spike's association with Farrakhan would be attacked in the media for years to come: they charged him with hypocrisy in attacking racism whilst at the same time supporting an organization headed by an anti-Semite who openly called for exclusive black communities in America.* Pres-ton Holmes believes that the local reaction to the Fruit of Islam in Bed-Stuy validated the decision to employ them: "It's an amazing kind of respect that they get in black communities all over the country, and one of the problems in the community where we chose to film was drug dealing. Because of the influence of the Nation of Islam, that disappeared for the entire time we were there." Of course, the dealers simply upped and set up shop around the corner, a further sign that crack, the affordable and highly addictive cocaine derivative, was transforming the drug trade in America's inner cities.

But for everyone involved in Spike's third feature it felt like a charged moment, a time to survey the positive changes in African-American life. Giancarlo Esposito describes the mood: "The whole

---

*See Chapters 8 and 12.

idea of 'fighting the power' was indicative of what everybody in the African-American community had felt for so long. And *Do the Right Thing* changed the way we thought, as actors making movies, because literally all of us who hadn't made a movie in Hollywood at that time, we were now making a Hollywood movie in Brooklyn. I'll never forget the opening of the picture, the dance and the soundtrack—which, to me, was the best of Public Enemy. And Rosie Perez in boxing gloves —just the whole visual idea, the look of her, the big gloves and the huge breasts, a spicy, sassy Puerto Rican woman. It was amazing."

Perez may have cut a fine figure in the film's title sequence, but during the shoot itself she remembers feeling far from invincible, if not something of a victim: "Spike wasn't getting what he wanted from me. He kept on asking me to do the number over and over. I was completely exhausted. I developed tennis elbow because of the sparring I

Do the Right Thing: Rosie Perez in costume for the shooting of the celebrated title sequence. (© 1988 David Lee)

was doing. I was on crutches by the end. It was really, really hard. I was hating Spike, and I was so furious and so exhausted, yet I was exhilarated at the same time. It was like, 'I'm gonna get this, I'm gonna show you I can do it.' And that's exactly what he wanted from me, from the beginning. All over the world, people still come up to me and ask me about the passion of that scene. It made me realize, 'Spike is fuckin' dope. He is *good*. . . .'"

Giancarlo Esposito also notes that on this project Spike was far more confident of his writing and storytelling abilities: when they differed over the dialogue for the scene in which Buggin Out clashes with a white neighbor, Spike heard out Esposito's suggested improvements and mulled them over: "And when we finished he said, 'No, it's too expository, go back to the way I wrote it.' When he goes with it and he feels it's right, he knows it in his gut." Still, this conviction led Spike to several run-ins with Danny Aiello, and their mutual antagonism came to a head on the night Spike filmed the climactic riot at Sal's pizzeria. John Turturro says of the night shoot, which overran into the wee hours: "A lot of people got hurt. It wasn't really choreographed well. Martin Lawrence and Steve White were punching me for real. On another take, Martin fell and I tried to catch him, and I stuck a finger in his eye trying to help him. So it was almost like the filming was mirroring the story by this point. And Danny didn't want to do something that Spike wanted him to do." Bill Nunn elucidates: "Danny didn't want to use the word 'nigger.' He went into a big thing about his background, how he wasn't racist. To me, it was comical. I'm sure everyone has *some* racism in them. How are you going to say that you're 100 percent not racist?"

Randy Fletcher watched Spike argue with Aiello over the action in which Sal smashes Raheem's radio, so kick-starting the riot. Aiello disagreed with everything Spike wanted to do and point-blank refused to be slung across the pizza counter in a moment akin to western saloon humor. The two were going at each other to such an extent, Fletcher remembers, that "I saw the tone in people's voices start to get a little edge there. I just asked everybody to leave the set, so it was just Spike and Danny left. Then they were in there another ten or fifteen minutes, shouting at each other, and Spike didn't even realize that the set had been cleared—that's how focused he was on the situation." Looking back, Spike is nonchalant: "Danny has his own ideals and that's just the way it is—he had a viewpoint and I had a viewpoint. He wanted Sal to be the most lovable pizza owner in the world, but that's not the character I wrote." In a subsequent interview with Gavin Smith for *Film Comment*, Aiello would claim that he more or less wrote the part of Sal. Spike says, "That's Danny. He gave a great performance. He was nominated for an Oscar. So I just let him take all the credit that he wants." Barry Brown jumps to Spike's defense: "I remember saying to someone, 'So you think Spike just set up the camera and Danny made up the lines in those scenes? Who do you think created those scenes? There's only one guy credited as screenwriter.'"

As with *School Daze* Spike seemed to be provoking his actors to assume the attitudes of their characters away from the set, but then, according to John Turturro, the director didn't even have to try all that hard: "Being around all these black people on the crew—which you'd never seen on a movie before—it was just a different energy. Even watching the dailies was like going to see a movie on 42nd Street: everybody would yell and talk back to the screen. I was shy at first, because I played the racist guy—at rehearsals I would talk really low. Then once I got to know everyone we added a lot more things to it. I improvised a lot. But there was a craft service girl who wouldn't talk to me: she saw me saying, 'Nigger nigger nigger' so many times that she started to think that maybe I just *was* that person. She wouldn't even give me water."

Midway through the shoot the foremost black figures in American film enjoyed a celebratory summit as Spike took his entire cast and crew to the Eddie Murphy residence in New Jersey for a party and barbecue. As Rosie Perez remembers it, "We took over his house. It was pure decadence—we celebrated by drinking so much champagne. We had so much fun. For me it was even better than being discovered by Spike. In all the time I have worked in Hollywood, and all the parties, I have never had such pure unadulterated fun working on a movie." Production assistant Mike Ellis recalls that Spike finally got to know his name: "I went in a van with Sam Jackson, Steve White, Giancarlo Esposito, a bunch of folks; we got there at 11:30 in the morning. By the time Spike got there, I was opening the door telling people where to change their clothes, where the pool was. There were guys in tuxedos serving champagne, and I did a great deal of flirting, which helped change the 'my man' status I had in Spike's eyes. Eddie Murphy was hilarious; he was trying to talk to two girls from the crew, and he changed his clothes about four times."

Nevertheless, by the end of the shoot Rosie Perez was not so enamored of her director. It was the film's sex scene that raised her hackles, one wherein Spike himself as Mookie lavishes his attentions on Perez's Tina by taking an ice cube to various overheated zones of her body. As

Ernest Dickerson remembers, "It was a pretty heavy scene for anybody to do, especially someone who's doing her first film. And Rosie was nervous, so we spent a lot of time talking about it before. I said, 'Look, I want you to feel that you can trust us. We will do anything we can to make you feel as comfortable as possible so you can do this scene.'" "The ice-cube sequence was very disturbing to me—very disturbing," Perez recalls. "I mean, I had just lost my virginity in college. And it wasn't what I had expected. I found it much more exploitative than what I had read—on the page it seemed like an intimate moment between boyfriend and girlfriend. What it came out as was some guy getting some ass via his baby-mother, and that's not how I had interpreted it."

Dickerson recalls, "Darnell Martin[*] was my camera intern, and I bumped her up to first camera assistant so that it would just be Spike and myself and another lady in the room when we shot the scene. And then Spike was acting and directing, and I remember that Rosie did get very upset." "Eventually I burst into tears," says Perez, "and I said, 'Don't keep filming.' It was just like a volcano silently erupting, and when it did, I just cried. That was the only way that I could handle it. And I remember Ernest said, 'I can't keep filming,' and he shut off the camera. Darnell Martin gave me a hug—I remember we became friends after that." "I did say 'Cut,'" Dickerson says, "because at that point I'm pretty sure we already had it, and Rosie was getting upset, and I wanted to make sure she didn't feel exploited and, as a result, clam up on Spike for the rest of the film."

"I don't know how Spike felt about that situation," says Perez. "And I felt bad, like, 'Oh, I disappointed him, oh God, I don't understand what's going on. . . .' It's the one thing that has always bothered me. I've got over it, but I need to express this, because I feel it's important that a girl who is nineteen or twenty years old who goes into this new world be forewarned and be taken care of. I was too young, and Spike picked the fruit from the tree too soon. Although my age says that I was an adult, my life experiences and my personality and my emotional sensibility weren't there yet. I just think that he was irresponsible to put me in that position. He was the older person, the captain of the ship, and I really truly feel that as soon as he saw that I wasn't comfortable—completely shaken—he should have done something to help me." Spike insists he has been careful to ensure that he gets sex scenes "right" without straying into exploitation: "You just have to be on good terms with the actors and talk stuff out before-

[*]Later the director of *I Like It Like That* (1994).

hand. A perfect example is *She Hate Me**—I had many different discussions with many different women and also with Anthony Mackie, so they knew. And this was before they even agreed to do the film. But actors want to know. 'Here it says, "They make love." What type of acts are we talking about? What's going to be seen?' I have no problem with that. At the same time, I still want to allow myself some flexibility. But shooting a sex scene, that is something that is very mechanical—'Will you move this way? That way? Raise your leg?' And for the most part the crew isn't allowed to be there—I close the set, make it as comfortable as possible."

Rosie Perez's final word on the *Do the Right Thing* experience is conciliatory: "But who am I to tell a director what they should be doing? I think that Spike's message is much bigger than that one issue, and I think that sometimes we can get very choosy about what he's trying to say. Outside of whether you feel the portrayal of women is positive or negative, there's so much more that he's saying outside of that that it's *unbelievable*." Lisa Jones, though, perceived the makings of a major problem in the treatment of women in and around 40 Acres productions: "Political hip-hop had come on the scene. But at the time I was really questioning hip-hop politics and removing myself from the 40 Acres scene. Spike was down with Public Enemy, and I wasn't necessarily feeling all that enamored by it. There were a bunch of us who didn't like it, because sexism was coexisting with all the right-on politics. And what was the message of all that politics anyway? That you should walk around wearing an X on your shirt? What was beyond that? It ain't even defined *now*. 'Fight the Power'? It was more 'Create your own power.' And after growing up in the black nationalist world, with its own contradictions and sexism, for me it was like, 'I'm not buying *another* sexist ideology.'"

A problem faced by black nationalism, by political hip-hop and ultimately by *Do the Right Thing* was the degree to which African-Americans were forced to see themselves as mere reflections of how they were perceived by the dominant white culture, wherein all too often dark skin was decreed as ugly (a topic Spike touched on in *School Daze*) and males dominant over females. The problem for Lisa Jones was that Spike, in common with various rappers and black nationalists who could identify prejudice and oppression when it came in the guise of race or class, either did not want to deal with—or completely overlooked—the tendency of the mainstream culture to encourage males of *whatever* color to believe that they enjoyed a rightful position

*See Chapter 17.

of dominance over the female of the species. This unreconstructed male chauvinism would pepper characters in Spike's movies: eventually the director would hold his hand up and admit, "I need to work on the depiction of females in my pictures."

In the course of post-production, the final scene of Do the Right Thing, which had once led to Spike's deal with Paramount collapsing, would again cause problems. Barry Brown remembers, "Jim Jacks and Sean Daniels, the executives at Universal, were very concerned about the ending of the film. They really didn't want Mookie to walk away

Do the Right Thing: Sal (Danny Aiello) and Mookie (Spike) square off over Mookie's salary. (© 1988 David Lee)

with Sal's money. I was adamant in myself—Spike has been there, I have been there, broke, and you've got nothing coming in down the line, you can't see where the next money is coming from—you don't walk away from $250 lying on the ground. You have to pick up the money. Otherwise it's bullshit." Spike concurs: "Money is all Mookie cares about. That is his god. When Sal throws the money at him, if he had any self-respect he wouldn't take it. But he's about the money, so he took it. Sam Kitt, another executive at Universal who was assigned to the film, he felt the same old shit where the studio wants their main characters to be the most lovable people, otherwise people won't like the movie. I don't agree."

Village Voice critic Stanley Crouch, who didn't care for *Do the Right Thing* in general, was specifically unimpressed by its final scene and sided with Sam Kitt: "It's too cartoonish and too irrational. You can't have a guy working for you and he picks up a trash can and starts the riot that causes your business to be burned down, then he comes up the next day and demands the $250 that you owe him. I don't know anybody except that character of Sal who would pay Mookie the $250, even throwing it back at him. I just don't think so. . . ."

But Spike had demonstrated on *School Daze*—when he cut a song after witnessing the derision of test audiences—that having the power of final cut did not mean that his first cut was the be-all and end-all of the movie. "Spike is a guy who's going to listen," says Barry Brown. "Spike comes across as being this hard-ass, and once he's formed an opinion, he is. But he usually comes to an opinion from an educated perspective. And finally he said, 'No, Mookie has to pick the money up.' The studio wanted us to come up with something else. And so, before the screening, Jim Jacks said, 'What did you guys do at the end of the movie?' I said, 'Well, you know Smiley's photo of Malcolm X and Martin Luther King? We're going to have that photo up, and there's going to be a quote from Martin Luther King and one from Malcolm X.' Jim Jacks said, '*What!?* We're not joking around here—we're not like some kids in a playground. It costs a lot of money to do this screening, and you guys come up with *quotes*!?' He was yelling at me in this theater. Finally Sean Daniels comes along and pulls him off. That's one thing that Spike would never do—be around before a screening, so that the executives could get to him. And he was never around afterward either. So I would go down and have a drink, and they would grab onto me. So what happened when they saw the quotes at the end? They came around and said, 'We apologize, we're sorry, it really works. . . .'" Roger Smith was ecstatic to see that his last-minute introduction to the picture had enjoyed a life through to post-production and beyond: "It's pretty amazing that we brought to *Do the Right Thing* this obscure image of Malcolm standing with Martin Luther King, and now it's a standard image that you see everywhere."

Not only Spike but the whole of the 40 Acres crew were growing in confidence and filmmaking ability. In the making of the film, a great realization came over Barry Brown: "It hit me that every scene had a center to it. Once you've found the center, you work from that point. But it can come at the beginning, the middle or the end of a scene. Take a scene like the one in the middle of the film where Mookie comes to ask Sal for money, and the camera just pans between them. Sal says, 'If I give you the money now, I'm not going to see you tonight.' Mookie says, 'I'm gonna remember that. . . .' That's Mookie's scene—one thing you get out of it is the frustration of the kid. It's not Sal's scene, because Sal's not affected; he won't remember the conversation. But for Mookie it's one of the things that leads to him throwing a trash can through the window. Mookie is the center of that scene. It's got to have this effect on him, and you've got to make sure that you convey it. So I cut the scene around him."

Many who saw an early cut of the film quickly formed the view that the 40 Acres production team had improved beyond recognition. Jonathan Demme was invited to a screening at the mix stage and eagerly told the filmmakers, "You're in the big leagues now." John Pierson says, "I know that Spike doesn't like people saying this, but what shocked me and a lot of other people was how quickly he went from *She's Gotta Have It* to making a film like *Do the Right Thing*." Nelson George offers his own interpretation of why Spike was able to make the step up: "Watch *School Daze* and *Do the Right Thing*, and you see an amazing thing: a guy who makes a film, learns from his mistakes and makes the next film better. Sometimes you have to fail to succeed. It's almost like he looked at the blueprint for *School Daze* and adjusted. In terms of how he did the production, he made sure that the film took place on one block that he could control rather than be at the mercy of all those people down in Atlanta. Spike tried to do a three-day structure in *School Daze*, and you totally lose track of time in that film, you don't know what day of the weekend it is. So his next film took place on one day and was very tightly controlled structurally. Things that are all wrong with *School Daze* are all right with *Do the Right Thing*."

On April 19, 1989, a twenty-eight-year-old white woman employed as an investment banker by Salomon Brothers of Wall Street (and whose name would remain undisclosed until 2003) was attacked and raped, allegedly by a gang of black youths, while jogging in Central Park. Business tycoon Donald Trump took umbrage and posted a full-page advertisement in the *New York Times* calling for the state's reinstatement of the death penalty. Caught up in the outrage sweeping the city, a *New York Daily News* columnist wrote, "The phone lines to this newspaper are busy with people screaming, 'Call the case for what it is: black savages rape white girl.'" The *Amsterdam News*, favored by a black readership, likened this outcry from what it saw as "white New York" to the false conviction and near-execution in the thirties of nine black men, the Scottsboro Boys, for allegedly raping two white girls. The jogger herself could not remember anything of the incident, and Spike Lee told Nelson George on the Thursday after the attack, "I know in my heart if these kids had raped a black woman it would have been on page fifteen. Editors would have thought it's another example of niggers killing niggers."

It was against this backdrop that Spike, one week later, shot the promo video for Public Enemy's "Fight the Power." The song harangued American society, the media, capitalism and the failure of integration for reinforcing racism. The concept of the video was to re-enact the 1963 March on Washington, at which Martin Luther King made his "I have a dream" speech—only with Public Enemy at the head. The song, the timing of the shoot, the celebrities involved and the symbolism evoked by the video captured the imagination of New York's African-American population and they congregated in large numbers to be a part of the shoot. Spike was relieved that the risk he had taken in not paying extras to turn up had paid off.

Five black male teenagers were convicted of the attack on the "Central Park jogger": according to the NYPD, the kids had been on a vicious "wilding" spree (this a supposed piece of street jargon, describing heedless behavior and derived from Tone-Loc's hit record "Wild Thing"). "Wilding" entered the vocabulary of New Yorkers. But in December 2002 the New York Supreme Court quashed the rape convictions of the five teenagers after Matias Reyes, a convicted serial rapist, claimed that he and not they was responsible for the attack. New methods of analyzing DNA corroborated Reyes's story, and the Prosecutors Office would later release a statement that "there is sub-stantial reason" to believe Reyes acted alone, though the Police Department argued that he may have been a sixth attacker. Anne Murray, NYPD bureau chief at the time and now a private investigator, was reported as saying, "I knew the coverage would be very different if the victim weren't white." The videotaped "confessions" of the five

Flavor Flav, Spike and Chuck D on location for the music video of "Fight the Power." (© 1988 David Lee)

teenagers are now seen as examples of police malpractice, due to misconduct that took place before they were made.

Do the Right Thing was unveiled to the world in a competition berth at the Cannes Film Festival in May 1989 and was considered a favorite for the coveted Palme d'Or. Monty Ross, who on this Cannes visit did not have to sleep in the bath tub of a hotel room, remembers, "Miramax were distributing *sex, lies, and videotape*, and Steven Soderbergh saw *Do the Right Thing*, and whenever he would pass us in Cannes he would show great respect to Spike. Then at the final awards ceremony, when *sex, lies, and videotape* won the Palme d'Or, I remember that Steven looked right at Spike, and they looked at each other, and Steven had this shocked expression that said, 'I won!' But he knew *Do the Right Thing* was the better film at Cannes that year." Spike was furious, not least when he heard that he had lost out essentially because of the ending of his film: "Wim Wenders, president of the jury, was said not to like the fact that it's my character, Mookie, who throws the garbage can through the window of Sal's Famous Pizzeria. Apparently Wenders considered it an unheroic act. Are you telling me that James Spader in *sex, lies, and videotape*, who tapes women and watches them so he can masturbate, is heroic?" In any event, Spike left Cannes empty-handed, remarking, "I have a

Louisville Slugger baseball bat with Wim Wenders's name on." His comments were perceived as those of a sore loser.

He returned to New York to discover that the screening at Cannes had several leading American film critics up in arms about the incendiary nature of his film. David Denby in *New York* magazine, Richard Corliss in *Time* and Jeanne Williams of *USA Today* all argued that *Do the Right Thing* was of no value except as agitprop to incite the black community to riot. This criticism met with fury within 40 Acres. Monty Ross says, "That is folks not doing their homework. Black people do not riot because they go see a movie. It's not that intense. It's not like it used to be in the sixties where it was *expedient* to start a riot. When black folks go to the movies, they've given up their money and, just like everybody else, they're thinking first of all it better be a damn good movie." Stanley Crouch was critical both of the film and of the concern among his journalistic colleagues that its scenes of racist violence might spur imitative behavior: "Most serious black gang crime is black-on-black. Movies do not pose a threat to society in this way. The only kind of threat you could pose today would be if you could convince all these black men to avoid spending $100 on tennis shoes—*that* would be a threat. But if somebody puts out a film where the message is maybe a little too heavy for the mainstream? First, the powers-that-be know that people will not go to see it. And secondly, they know how to smother it, just in case. All they do is put out a movie against the one they're scared of, one that opens with all these athletic bodies in the showers with their breasts out. . . . The political movie will soon be forgotten. Having a Negro as a threat, that is just over. It wasn't so much that white people were threatened by Spike; they just liked to *think* that they were. So the Negro kind of functions like an offshoot of the old horror-film characters: it's like what Dracula and the werewolf are all about. People get frightened, then they leave the theater and they know that it's only a film, there's no Dracula. And they know there's no black revolution out there either."

Expensive sneakers, however, were a big issue; and they formed a key part of a scene in *Do the Right Thing* wherein Spike attempted to comment on the gentrification of Fort Greene, as poor blacks moved out to be supplanted by an influx of the white middle class attracted by the burgeoning artistic reputation of the area. The character who embodies this trend is Clifton, played by John Savage, and Spike shows his dislike for Clifton by dressing him in a Larry Bird T-shirt. (The famous Boston Celtics player was lampooned in *She's Gotta Have It* as the "ugliest motherfucker in the NBA.") The dramatic spur of the brief scene sees Clifton accidentally wheel his mountain bike over Buggin' Out's pristine new pair of Nike Air Jordans, which he had earlier been seen cleaning with a toothbrush. Esposito's comic tirade at Clifton builds to a larger charge—"Who told you to buy a brownstone on my block, in my neighborhood, on my side of the street? Yo, what you wanna live in a black neighborhood for anyway, man? Motherfuck gentrification!"

Still, the aura of commodity fetishism around the Nike shoes prompted an accusation that Spike, one of the public faces of the Nike brand, was indirectly responsible for a contemporany crime wave that saw people being mugged or even killed for their Air Jordans. Phil Knight, CEO of Nike, thought it ludicrous that this association be made: "We work to get product placement in a lot of different movies, and when I think of all the things that Spike Lee has helped us with and been beneficial to Nike for, product placement is not near the top of the list. I'm proud that he has them there, but I don't think that those scenes really have had that great an impact. The muggings are distressing, and sometimes guys are getting killed. It's crazy; you hate for that to happen and you hate for Spike and anyone else to be burdened with the questions related to that. But he handles the stuff on his feet so well." Spike argued, "People saying that Nike was responsible for the crimes being committed—that didn't make sense. People get robbed for a lot of things—money, bomber jackets, cars. Is somebody going to boycott Mercedes-Benz because cars are being stolen?"

But controversy was dogging Spike like a stalker. Professor Griff, so-called Minister of Information in Public Enemy's S1W crew, gave an interview to David Mills of the *Washington Times* in which he spouted an erroneous anti-Semitic and homophobic diatribe, alleging that Jews were "responsible for the majority of the wickedness that goes on in the world . . . the Jews finance these experiments on AIDS with black people in Africa."[*] In the inevitable and rightful furor that ensued, Universal started to get cold feet. Public Enemy had provided more than just a title song to *Do the Right Thing*: the numerous airings of "Fight the Power" from Radio Raheem's ghetto blaster served as the film's backbone. Spike was forced to make several calls to Chuck D to find out what was going on within the group, and this became a factor in Chuck D's decision to suspend Professor Griff from the band.[†]

---

[*]In his support Professor Griff cited Henry Ford's anti-Semitic text *The International Jew*, plus a book circulated by the Nation of Islam called *The Secret Relationship Between Blacks and Jews*.

[†]Professor Griff would later claim that his words were taken out of context and he does not believe the statements as they were presented by David Mills.

Spike was also criticized in some quarters for making a film about the urban black population and not addressing the issue of drugs. In his defense he asserted, "This is a film about racism. Drugs are too big an issue to have to share space with a film on racism." Roger Smith believes that Spike's open discussion of racism was bound to provoke criticism in the mainstream media: "It's not simply true of Spike Lee, it is true of *any* man who chooses to be articulate about the great dilemma of America, which is race. We suffer from a tremendous historical amnesia, and that is played out every day in this country. Americans don't want to be reminded of this great tragedy. It's something that we would much rather ignore. I think that what is particularly disturbing about Spike is that he achieved an obvious economic stronghold—he's not a pauper, he lives well and unapologetically so— but he is still engaged in popular American culture, and in this American forum that kind of economic achievement is then supposed to translate into silence on matters of race and class."

As Monty Ross notes, one benefit of the intense media interest in *Do the Right Thing* was that it ensured the film would be one of the most keenly anticipated releases in a summer otherwise dominated by Tim Burton's *Batman*: "When the *New York Times* dedicates, like, six *weeks* in its editorial section to talking about the neighborhood and crime and the mayoral election, all in connection to this film, you scratch your head a little bit and say, 'Wow.' That made a tremendous impact. I think that what Spike wanted to get across is that you can make a film that gets people thinking about issues and can also be entertaining." Bill Nunn recalls, "There was a sudden shift in expectation. This was a Spike Lee joint that raised the bar to the next level and entered mainstream American consciousness. I was in Atlanta doing my thing and I guess a month or two before the movie was released I started getting phone calls, people calling me up and flipping out. I'd never been interviewed by so many people before. I think it's a historical moment in film—and one of those films that students are going to be watching in the future."

Spike came away feeling that the views of some of his characters had been unfairly attributed to him: "They don't do that shit to Woody Allen. I remember having an argument with some critic from the gay magazine *The Advocate*, who accused me of being homophobic because I had one of my characters call another a faggot. I was accused of being homophobic for just depicting homophobia—I don't understand that thinking." John Turturro also felt that Spike was not being given a fair crack of the whip: "I think that a lot of critics didn't review him in a social context; they held him to other kinds of criteria.

They didn't really understand that he was one of these guys getting a chance to do something, and they critiqued him as if there were twenty other black filmmakers at the time. They held him up to a different kind of critique that maybe they would not do with a white director."

Edward Norton was a student at Yale at the time of *Do the Right Thing*'s release and he remembers his surprise at watching the film: "I think that, for me, the disconnect between seeing what was written about the film and the feeling that it had provoked in me was the beginning of an ongoing observation I've had over the years about the incredible misrepresentation of Spike Lee's work. The failure of the mainstream critical community to understand the true message of that film, the underlying humanity and compassion of it, was astonishing to me. When a certain kind of blind acceptance of what people have to say informs your view of life to a certain degree, and you then have that first experience of feeling like you are a generation and the things you believe, the values that you have are being attacked and misrepresented—in a way, that's your first experience with culture clash, and it's an intense one. I felt people were responding in exactly the opposite way to the people who were writing about the film and saying, 'This is a dangerous film, it's going to cause violence.' I sat there thinking the exact opposite. What I realized, way down the road, is what made people uncomfortable with it was that it didn't offer any easy answers."

Do the Right Thing finally freed Spike Lee from the shackles of the Mars Blackmon persona. The film took in $28.5 million domestically at the box office, but although it was Spike's best grossing picture to date, he was disappointed with the figure: "The box office was damaged by all the negative publicity. It scared white audiences away from the film." In a *Sight and Sound* poll of the best films in the last twenty-five years *Do the Right Thing* would rank sixth. For Nelson George, the 40 Acres head was at the center of the foment going on in black culture: "Spike is the exemplar of that middle generation between the civil-rights movement and the hip-hop generation. In 1989 a picture was taken by Anthony Barbosa in the 40 Acres firehouse—it had myself, Spike, Chris Rock, Run-DMC, Russell Simmons, Lisa Jones, her sister Kellie, who was an art curator, George Wolfe, Vernon Reid, Reggie and Warrington Hudlin, Alva Rogers, who was in *School Daze* and *Daughters of the Dust*, Fab Five Freddy and Lorna Simpson. . . . It was an interesting group of people who were all coming up at the same time; and Spike's the reason we took the picture at the firehouse. Spike already had the building—he was already being institutionalized."

6 *Mo' Better Blues*

Giant steps had been made by the enterprise that was 40 Acres and a Mule. Monty Ross recalls, "The phone was ringing off the hook, and that made it difficult to work. A lot of people were phoning trying to get *jobs* and be a part of 40 Acres. You're starting to be at your height in terms of celebrity and you have people ringing the doorbell. And you want to do *everything*. Jesse Jackson is dropping by, other

Spike, photographed before a poster for "the greatest album ever recorded."
(© 1989 David Lee)

celebrities,* all in that space." But Spike now wanted 40 Acres and a Mule to expand, break out of the mold—be more than just a production company.

Earl Smith, Spike's school chum, was working as a basketball director on Coney Island when Spike called to offer him more money to work at 40 Acres. There wasn't a particular job Spike had in mind; he just needed more bodies and someone he could trust on the inside to do whatever was necessary. Earl was put to work on a new venture: "Spike started a T-shirt business from the garage at the bottom of the firehouse. People were ringing the bell for a 40 Acres baseball cap, and it got to the point where we couldn't do everyday 40 Acres business. We had people from Japan coming over, wanting to buy ten, fifteen thousand dollars' worth of merchandise. That's why Spike bought a building on the corner of South Eliot and DeKalb Avenue, and planned to open up a store."

The success of the "Fight the Power" single, following EU's number-one hit "Da Butt" from the *School Daze* soundtrack, made Spike feel like he had the Midas touch with music as well as film. Plans were put in motion to create a new subdivision in the company, 40 Acres and a Mule Musicworks, which would "enlarge the legacy of African-American music"; this just as the emergence of a West Coast rap scene, centered around the ganglands of Los Angeles, was bringing a glamorized image of ghetto violence into the mainstream. Ice-T's title song to Dennis Hopper's *Colors* and NWA's *Straight Outta Compton* would shortly divert attention away from the Afrocentric aesthetic that had been prevalent in the New York rap scene. Then again, a further dimension to the genre was being explored by De La Soul's début album *3 Feet High and Rising*, with its happy middle-class self-consciousness and smart lyrics, as showcased by the hit single "Me, Myself and I." The album was a perfect riposte to the misguided "rap breeds violence" critique—long espoused by those threatened by the political musical expression of young black rappers—that first gained credence after a 1986 Run-DMC concert in Long Beach led to riots among gangs of blacks and Hispanics. The issue would be famously reinforced by Ice-T's single "Cop Killer," which was inspired by the Rodney King incident.†

The type of musical lineage that Spike wanted his label to acknowledge was exemplified by Ernest Dickerson's directorial début, a film that Spike hosted, entitled *Spike and Company—Do It A-Cappella*, a

---

*In the *Do the Right Thing* book, Spike talks about the range of celebrities, from Sean Penn to Melvin Van Peebles, who would come to his parties.
†See Chapter 8.

Public Broadcasting Service production exploring the a cappella vocal tradition. Spike had discerned a growing problem with the laissez-faire attitudes of black Americans toward their history: "Jazz is an art form that we created. And, very sadly, it's musicians like Wynton and Branford Marsalis, and Terence Blanchard and the older cats who are trying to save this tradition, which a lot of young black kids—not all of them—aren't hearing; so the black community loses part of its tradition, in the same way that we lost blues. If it wasn't for young white kids, blues would be a historical relic. The first time I heard Bob Marley's "I Shot the Sheriff" I thought it was a rip-off: I thought Eric Clapton's version was the first, because I didn't know anything about reggae. White college kids were into reggae way before most black kids, mostly because they were smoking herb. . . . But I remember the general African-American attitude toward Bob Marley and Rastafarians—we looked at them like they were crazy, all that matted hair. . . ."

The 40 Acres ethos was about more than just making money: Spike wanted to set up programs that would give African-American and underprivileged kids opportunities to get professional instruction. Plans were mooted for a summer basketball camp, and Spike inaugurated the 40 Acres Institute, a film program to be taught at the Long Island University campus in Fort Greene: "We gave a class every Saturday morning, and each class would have a different guest. I remember Robert De Niro came, Martin Scorsese, the Hughes brothers. They were all good guests." The 40 Acres Institute was, like the books that had accompanied each of his films, an attempt to challenge the conventional wisdom that filmmaking was a secret and magical society. Spike wanted to ensure that the students knew this above all: "You don't need to go to film school to be a director. It's enough to get a camera, or work on a set, and learn the craft. But you need to live, and make comments on that life."

In the Institute seminars, which Spike had committed to videotape, he would rail against the depiction of African-Americans in mainstream movies: he decried Alan Parker's civil-rights picture *Mississippi Burning*, which, like *Cry Freedom* before it, overstated the contribution of sympathetic whites in changing social attitudes toward blacks. He also lamented Dennis Hopper's *Colors* (indeed, Nelson George argued that the film unintentionally spread L.A. gang culture across America), Keenan Wayans's low-brow blaxploitation comedy *I'm Gonna Git You Sucka* and the awful *Tougher than Leather*. Compared to most Hollywood output, Spike was still plowing a solitary furrow in terms of the characters and stories he chose to portray. Danny Glover in *Lethal Weapon* and Morgan Freeman in *Driving Miss Daisy* were winning plaudits, but for playing trusted sidekicks to white counterparts. Eddie Murphy's directorial career began and ended with the dismal *Harlem Nights*. At this juncture, a long-standing aversion to Hollywood's stock depiction of the black jazz musician inspired Spike to make his fourth feature in five years.

Spike is emphatic in his belief that John Coltrane's *A Love Supreme* is the greatest album ever recorded. Come the autumn of 1988 he was looking forward to seeing Clint Eastwood's Charlie Parker biopic *Bird*, his excitement mixed with a certain trepidation, since the portrayal of black jazz musicians in American film had an uneasy history. From the very first "talkie," 1927's *The Jazz Singer*—in which Al Jolson covered his face in burnt cork and sang "Mammy"—until Nat King Cole played W. C. Handy in *St. Louis Blues* in 1958, and despite the African-American roots of the art form, the black jazz artist was simply a sideshow in so-called jazz films. Many of these featured such legendary artists as Duke Ellington, Bessie Smith, Louis Armstrong, Billie Holiday and Jimmie Lunceford, but used essentially as novelty acts. The culture and tradition of jazz were ignored, as Hollywood concentrated on the only acceptable jazz hero—a white one.

The aural landscape of jazz had in the meantime been revolutionized by Charlie Parker, Thelonious Monk and Miles Davis—but this was not an understanding one could glean from watching American movies. Hollywood continued to ignore the political and sociological circumstances that provided inspiration for the introspection and musical expression of jazz artists. The eventual acceptance of the existence of a black jazz scene in *St Louis Blues* was followed slowly but steadily by more pictures focusing upon black jazz artists—*Paris Blues* (1961), *A Man Called Adam* (1966) and *Lady Sings the Blues* (1972)—and drawing them as individuals beset by personal problems and social tensions, far from the happy-go-lucky figures of earlier jazz movies. But the 1986 release of Bertrand Tavernier's *'Round Midnight* confirmed that the passage of time had changed little. And as Spike sat through Eastwood's *Bird*, he felt a compulsion to tell a different kind of jazz story: 'In a lot of ways, *Mo' Better Blues*—apart from me being the son of a jazz bassist and growing up amongst the music—was a reaction to two films: *Bird* and *'Round Midnight*. Clint Eastwood is a great filmmaker, but I don't like *Bird*. And I don't like *'Round Midnight*. That's not said to negate the filmmakers—they could both say they love jazz just as much as I do. They probably know more. But at the same time, if you look at both of those films together, there's really no joy, no warmth. In every scene it's raining . . . *Bird* is one of the darkest films that ever had a theatrical release. You can hardly see an image on the celluloid. It's like, 'Oh, these jazz musicians are so tormented, they never laughed, they never had joy in their life, they're all tragic and torn and twisted.' Of course, that might have been a small part of it. But at the same time, I was thinking about the musicians I grew up with, of my generation—Branford and Wynton Marsalis, Terence Blanchard, Donald Harrison. These guys weren't rich, but they were making good money. And they played basketball, football, they loved sports, they had family, they had girlfriends, had a good time going out, living— they're not simply moping around lamenting the misery of their lives."

The difficulty in translating the essence of jazz to film is highlighted by Spike's own selection of preferred jazz films: "My favorites are the documentaries *Jazz on a Sunday Afternoon*, about the Newport Jazz Festival, and *Straight No Chaser*, on Thelonious Monk. The guys that we knew, the ones of my generation, *Mo' Better Blues* was just a little bit of the world at that time. But I don't think that we made the definitive film on jazz. I didn't want to make a Coltrane biopic, because who would play Coltrane? I think I knew in my mind that the first biography I would do was Malcolm X. I didn't *tell* anybody that, but I always believed it." News was filtering through that Warner Bros. wanted Denzel Washington, fresh from an Oscar nomination, to star in a Malcolm biopic under the direction of Norman Jewison. Spike was furious that the studio was about to repeat the same error that blighted *Cry Freedom* and *Mississippi Burning* and allow a white director to ruin a black story—but that was a fight that would have to wait until after he had completed his own jazz opus.

Spike originally wanted to pay homage to Coltrane by naming the film *A Love Supreme*. But in order to do so he needed to obtain Alice Coltrane's approval to use both the song and the title: "Alice, because of the profanity in the film, didn't want us to use the title. I understood that. I was just happy that she didn't stop us from using the song, so we still had to get permission to use 'A Love Supreme' at the end. If she had refused that, I would have been heartbroken." After toying with the title *Beneath the Underdog*,[*] after Charlie Mingus's biography, and *Variations on the Mo' Better Blues* because it sounded like a jazz composition, Spike settled on a shortened form of the latter: "I got the term 'Mo' Better' from a former Spelman girlfriend, Patti Hailes. The title of a film is an all-important marketing tool. It's the first thing people hear and see. A good title is a plus. But it's no substitute for a good film."

*

---

[*]In the movie this eventually became the name of the club at which the band plays.

"Music" is definitely one of the key words that spur Spike Lee into conversation, ever present in the internal dialogues that Nelson George believes him to be plagued by. Although Spike, in a show of teenage rebelliousness against his father, never considered becoming a musician, he says, "growing up in that world and hearing the stories definitely influenced me. It still bothers me today when you go to a function, and you have a trio there, or a pianist, and they're playing really good music—and people are talking, laughing and clinking glasses. Sometimes I think, Shut the fuck up, listen to the music! I've always had admiration and utmost respect for musicians, because for me—and I know I'll get in trouble for saying this—for *me*, I think musicians are the greatest artists in the world. I put them over painters, poets, over writers. You get me the greatest musician, I'll put them up against the greatest painter, the greatest sculptor, the greatest actor, and the musician will come out on top. Music is the greatest way to express the artist, their heart and soul, their essence and their spirit—to express God."

Even before Spike wrote the *Mo' Better* script he had in mind the musicians and composers he wanted to be involved in the project. Alex Steyermark returned as music editor and, in his third collaboration with the director, was starting to recognize his working method: 'He has that quality that all prolific filmmakers have, in that no film is perfect—it is what it is. Fassbinder was like that to me—each film has a new set of problems that he is confronting as a filmmaker, like a new challenge from a film-making standpoint. Then he solves that problem, and then he produces a new challenge with each film. And so with music in his films, he's been doing the same thing. It is just getting more complicated. The biggest challenge on *Mo' Better Blues* was that it was the beginning of digital and we were basically mixing the music to pictures from the master tracks for the first time. Also the film had the added component of the musicians performing live on camera."

A musical ear was an important ingredient in the casting of the film. Spike finds it particularly grating when he is watching a film about musicians that features actors who are clearly miming and, more often than not, playing notes different from the ones that are heard: "What I think Tavernier did great in *'Round Midnight* was getting Dexter Gordon. That was the move—to get the real McCoy." Thus it came naturally for Spike to approach first Gregory Hines and then Branford Marsalis to take the role of saxophonist Shadow Henderson in *Mo' Better Blues*. Marsalis says, "I turned it down. I thought all along that when you have a role that has that much meat and is that important, then you need somebody who knows what the fuck they're doing—

because, you know, Spike is a very dear friend of mine and sometimes I got the feeling that Spike was giving me a role out of friendship. I think that Denzel played the role much better when he was next to an actor like Wesley Snipes, who was equal to the task, than if he had been around some novice, carrying my sorry ass all the time."

Spike had wanted to work with Denzel Washington for some time: "I had seen him on Broadway in *A Soldier's Play* and in some other stuff on television. But he was just someone who—and I don't think I was the only one who thought this—you could tell was going to be huge." Washington had just appeared in the play *Checkmates* on Broadway, and Spike knew it would do no harm to his ambition to direct *Malcolm X* if he was on good terms with the actor considered a shoo-in for the title role. Casting director Robi Reed says, "It wasn't difficult to get Denzel into *Mo' Better Blues*. He wasn't yet getting leading-man roles, if you think about it. In *Glory* he was a co-star, he was supporting.* He *wanted* to be a sex symbol. He hadn't got to that point yet. So really *Mo' Better* was his first starring role." Washington was cast as Bleek Gilliam, trumpeter and front man of his own quintet.

Wesley Snipes, who had turned down a role as one of the young street kids in *Do the Right Thing* to appear in the baseball comedy *Major League*, was cast as Shadow. Monty Ross recalls, "Wesley kept on going around telling everybody that he was working with Spike so that he could become a big action star like Schwarzenegger or Stallone." Appearing in their third Spike Lee film—in common with Sam Jackson—Bill Nunn and Giancarlo Esposito played band members. Struggling to find an actor who could play drums, Spike employed drummer Jeff Watts to complete the Bleek Gilliam band. Spike cast himself as the band's manager (ironically named Giant) and sister Joie as one of Denzel's girlfriends. Keeping to the family theme, the owners of Beneath the Underdog were played by real-life brothers John and Nick Turturro. Spike cast the unknown Cynda Williams to play a wannabe singer and Gilliam's girlfriend; but his plan to promote the actress as a singer subsequent to the film's release met with Branford Marsalis's derision: "There is a little bit of Cecil B. De Mille in Spike. He liked discovering new talent. One of the things that I begged him not to do was let Cynda Williams sing. Raymond Jones did an excellent arrangement of 'Harlem Blues': that song could have been a bigger hit with a singer singing it —not with her singing it." Sam Jackson was cast as a henchman with a limp—the actor had been involved in an

---

*Edward Zwick's *Glory*, in which Washington played a private in the first all-black Union company to fight in the Civil War, was due for release just after Spike's film wrapped on December 1, 1989.

Mo' Better Blues: the Bleek Gilliam Band—Bill Nunn, Denzel Washington, Jeff Watts, Wesley Snipes, Giancarlo Esposito and manager Spike. (© 1989 David Lee)

accident with a subway train that miraculously only left him wearing a leg brace. Jackson admits that drugs were becoming part of the scene: "Everybody knew—I don't know about Spike—but a lot of us were drug users. We smoked reefer and drank and did a lot of stuff while we were working, most of us. It wasn't a big secret, but I guess my being a drug addict might have been a secret to a lot of people."

Spike needed to find a new editor because Barry Brown was busy trying to resurrect his directorial career with *Lonely in America* (memorable mainly for an opening sequence that features Spike Lee buying a copy of *Time* magazine with his picture on the cover). Spike called Sam Pollard, who recalls, "My son, who was nine or ten at the time, said, 'Dad, Spike Lee is on the phone.' I said, 'Come on!' So I got on the phone and he said, 'Hey, man, it's Spike, I'm doing this film called *Love Supreme*. I got your name from Preston [Holmes] and I want you to edit it.' I was in the middle of working on *Eyes on the Prize*, so when Spike told me his production schedule, I said, 'Thanks for the call, I'll talk to you next time.' I didn't think that I would hear from him again." But Spike wasn't to be deterred: "About a month later, Spike called again, asked me again if I was free. It was getting close to Labor Day weekend and he was going to Martha's Vineyard for the holiday. This shows how life is, because, coincidentally, I was going to the Vineyard too. We met at a coffee shop and we spent forty minutes together. I did most of the talking. Basically I talked myself into taking the job."

Mo' Better Blues opens with a mother forcing her son to play a musical instrument, though her musician husband is far more willing to let the boy go out and play with his friends. This broadly reflects Spike's experience of his own mother's encouragements, but then Spike sees the phenomenon as fairly universal: "You can't underestimate the influence of parents or parental figures—whether it's the parent, the grandparent, coach, teacher. . . . With successful people, there is always a mentor who took an interest in that child and saw some talent, some potential. Again, in sports, a lot of times if the father for whatever reason thought that he was going to be a pro but didn't make it, his dreams don't die. He transfers them to his child. It's universal. It doesn't have to be sport. It could be anything you like—the thing you couldn't do. The smart parents are the ones who pull back when they see that their kids don't want to do it. The worst thing to do is to force your child to do something that they don't want to do, because they are going to end up hating it. *Hating* it."

A dilemma plaguing Spike at this early juncture in his still ascending career was the strain caused by the combined needs to make money, make art and please an audience without selling out. This is reflected by the battle in *Mo' Better Blues* between Shadow and Bleek, as they feud over the type of music they believe the band should be playing. Shadow feels they should play for the crowd; Bleek is only concerned with creating dynamic, original music. Spike says of this tussle, "I'm talking about art in general. And I think that the big argument that happens between them is over art versus commerce, and that's been going on for a long time. I always felt that if you're a filmmaker and you tell a good story, you might not make a hundred million dollars but you're not going to go broke. You can always make films. I've always tried to make thought-provoking entertainment and that's always been my goal—and there are some that are more successful than others. I've never wanted to make a pure popcorn movie. There's nothing wrong with that—some of those I go see in the summertime, but it's not something that I want at this point—though I try to stay away from saying 'Never.'"

Spike also returned to the debate aired in all of his feature films to date: the failure of black support for black endeavor. This time, it was conducted in the sphere of black musical artistry: "A lot of the arguments about black people not supporting certain acts I got from

Branford and Wynton. They both said that they would love to see more black faces in the jazz clubs they play in; they had seen a lot of black people who nearly starved to death because they sacrificed everything to play music—some of those lines are repeated verbatim in *Mo' Better Blues*. I actually put more black faces in the audience than you would have thought realistic—not because I wanted to get more black extras working, but because we just wished that it could be more like this."

Spike went into pre-production armed with his biggest budget to date: $10 million, courtesy of Universal. The commercial failures of *Bird* and *'Round Midnight* were cited by studio head Tom Pollack as reason not to give Spike the $11.5 million that he wanted. Spike immediately assigned a musical coach to each of his four actors in the band: "Even if you didn't do it for them, the great actors would do it themselves. If they're doing a cop movie, they go out in a cop car on shifts and stuff—that is something the actor does; you want to try to absorb the world that you supposedly live in, then it becomes second nature. And I wanted to get these guys thinking like jazz musicians, so that it would be believable on film." Branford Marsalis recalls teaching the actors how to pull off the task that Spike had set: "I just tried to demystify the playing of the music. I told Wesley, and I even told Denzel, a lot of it has to do with the physicality of it. The reason an actor looks bad playing an instrument is that they don't think choreography—it's like, if you're hitting high notes, your body language should reflect high notes, you should bend. If you're hitting low notes, you should squat your knee down and haunch to physically manifest the sound. And the most important thing is that you learn the solos so well that your fingers are moving when the sound is moving. Nobody can sit there and tell whether you're hitting the right buttons or not."

It was a task that proved most difficult for Giancarlo Esposito—surprisingly, in that he was the only one of the actors with a degree of proficiency in playing an instrument, having had several years of piano lessons. He remembers, "I was under pressure to learn to play a specific piece of music. If you said, 'Learn this music because you have to play a concert tomorrow,' that's one thing; but if you're telling me to learn it in a certain way because you just need me to be in the right place when the camera comes at me, it's harder. For me, the music was much more difficult than I had the ability to play. You're not asking me to play 'Mary Had a Little Lamb,' so I found it to be an incredible challenge—one I don't think I met as completely as I would have liked to. . . . There was one day when we were at Long Island University watching the dailies, and Spike burst out laughing from the back row because my hands were doing one thing and the piano was playing another. Thankfully he didn't use that."

The actors at least had no trouble stepping into the lifestyle of musicians, as they discovered that the kudos of being actors were poor by comparison. Bill Nunn smiles at the memories: "I'm telling you, we had the best time on that movie. You got a bunch of guys at a nightclub dressed to the nines, with beautiful girls in the audience, and pretending we're playing the instruments and being treated as if we really *were* playing the instruments. So you can do the math from there." Spike remembers, "They loved it. I mean, I wasn't hanging out with them—but I know they would go out to clubs together and ask women, 'Do you want to hear me play.?'" First AD Randy Fletcher had his work cut out keeping up with all the comings and goings: "We were young and it was a fun movie to work on. It was like having all the people that you grew up with getting paid to laugh and have a good time together. You put those guys who were in the band in the same room and that shit was hilarious. A bunch of times I went out with them in New York and they were acting and being treated like rock stars. People would tell us that we'd have to leave because we were making so much noise, and it was not easy to get these actors to be quiet at times. On set, I was probably the only one that had to yell and scream. Trying to keep track of the guys, that was the other job that I had to do, which was rough. But I had a special relationship with those guys. They trusted me, and I kept my mouth closed."

Despite the general feel good factor on set, Spike ran into problems with his family. A jazz purist such as Bill Lee was always going to demur when technology made certain demands on the soundtrack, demands that were taxing even to the most tech-savvy music specialist. Alex Steyermark says, "There were also disputes between the other musicians and Bill over how the music should be played." Branford Marsalis, never shy of expressing an opinion, says, "On one song Bill said that he wanted the song to be a swing tune. I said, 'This is not a swing tune, it's a funky tune,' and I told Spike, 'The song had the potential to be the most popular song on the CD; you don't want to mess this up.' Spike said, 'Yeah, you're right.'" These arguments were played out in public, recalls Randy Fletcher: "I remember a couple of times where we were doing musical things, and Spike's father was there. Spike would say to me, 'OK, give it a couple of minutes and be polite, clear my father off the set or tell him, "That's enough."'" He would look at me and then look at his father, and I would know that it was time for his father to leave. There were certain things that his father would do that would *ensure* that he got removed from set."

Spike and his father, Bill Lee, at work together on *Mo' Better Blues*. (© 1989 David Lee)

Monty Ross felt that the disputes and arguments on set were essentially of a musical nature: "Bill's a purist—there are certain elements in music and those elements are the *only* ones. It was always about the music. But Spike said, 'We need something that is more representative of where the young musicians in the audience are too.'"

The hurt that Spike felt over his mother's death still raged within him, and although this did not spill out into on-set arguments with his father, the topic was very much off limits. Randy recalls an ad-libbed sequence in the film that takes place in a dressing room, between the band members and their manager, in which "somebody said something about Spike's mother. Spike's mother had been dead a few years and that was in his heart. If you look at Spike's face—and everybody is still trying to be in character—it was a little awkward situation. And Spike said, 'Why have you got to bring my mother into this?'" Lisa Jones interprets the father-son situation like so: "In some sense, that film was, if not a tribute to his father, some sort of musing on his father's life, being about his own dilemmas as a man and his relationships. I think that it's hard to work with your father, *period*. I think that Spike was coming to that realization, and so maybe he was paying homage before he made the break. In the companion book there's a section that was his way of just documenting his own father's life."

Indeed, in the chapter titled "Eight Bars In," Bill Lee writes that his grandfather, who wrote a book *Twenty-Five Years in the Black Belt* about founding the Snow Hill Institute (a normal and industrial school for "colored boys and girls"), was the most important person in his life. Bill's father played the cornet and ensured that all his seven children would play an instrument and be part of the Lee Family Band. Bill was taught drums, but when he heard the North Carolina A&T band, who added jazz beats to simple military songs, he would —against his father's wishes—try out jazz beats. Bill was a basketball star when he graduated from Snow Hill Institute and wanted to be a coach rather than a musician, but at the last moment, after hearing Charlie Parker, he decided to learn the bass violin rather than study physical education at Morehouse. At Morehouse he met Jacquelyn Shelton, and after graduating, against his father's wishes, he moved to Chicago to play bass. In 1952 he and Jacquelyn married.

In Chicago they would meet many of the jazz greats, including Duke Ellington. The headline acts could not afford to pay musicians to tour with them, so Bill worked as a local musician, taking gigs backing acts as they came into town. A desire to improve his own position led to him moving his young family to New York in 1959. Bill was traveling around looking for somewhere to play and have his art appreciated. In New York, he lugged his bass around, jamming, trying to make a name for himself and get a few gigs. By 1966 he was working frequently as a studio musician, but this dried up when he insisted on playing with a friend when he was called in to work. The work ended when Bill responded in the negative when the studio asked if he had plans to play Fender bass. As work was scarce, he went on to manage a band and perform for his own groups rather than for someone else. He talks about compositions he has written that have never been performed, novels he has written that have not been published: he comes across as a man who has dedicated himself to art above all else.

If Spike had any doubts about replacing his father as composer, they were eradicated when he passed Terence Blanchard sitting at the piano. Blanchard reminisces: "I'd been working on a tune for a solo album I was getting ready to do for Columbia Records. Spike comes over and says, 'What's that? I like that.' I said, 'Well, it's a tune called "Sing Soweto." I wrote it for some kids in South Africa.' He goes, 'Can I use it?' When he went to edit the film, I guess he felt like he needed some more music. He called me and said, 'Hey, man, can you write an arrangement?' I said, 'Sure,' never having done one before. I remember that I just sat at the piano, because I was taught that all the orchestration can really just be derived from playing the piano. Spike dug it when he heard it. For me, I was just happy to stand in front of the orchestra, because he gave me a chance to conduct it for the session. I was tickled pink because it was the first time that I had a chance to stand in front of sixty people, wave my arms and have them play something that I'd written.[*] Spike walks up to me and says, 'Man, that's cool, you got a future in this business.' I left feeling on top of the world, and as I walked through the building, there was a guy doing an analog-to-digital CD re-recording of Stravinsky's *Rite of Spring*. I remember that brought me right back down to reality. I immediately knew what the defects were in my arrangement for Mo' Better Blues. I had treated all of the various sections of the orchestra as separate entities. I didn't mix and combine those elements to create interesting colors and textures." Branford Marsalis for one felt that Spike was making a good decision in replacing his father: "Terence is more of a writer than Bill is, and Terence has a lot of training that Bill didn't have: he learned how to write for strings and he played classical music and he *listened* to classical music."

Compounding the sense of family strife around Mo' Better Blues, Spike was having as much—if not more—trouble with his sister, Joie, than with his father. She was cast as Indigo Downes, a young accountant with whom Bleek Gilliam dallies when he is not with Clarke (Cynda Williams). It was Joie's biggest role to date, but as she recalls, "Every experience working with Spike was hard—Mo' Better Blues was definitely the hardest. I know Spike wants me to do well. I'm his sister. He wants me to be in the same company as all these actors whom you wouldn't think twice about casting, and he doesn't want people to say, 'She's in the film because she's his sister.' But it's very hard to distance the family relationship when we're on set—I don't know if it's *possible*. But that is part of the experience, actually—he is my brother, and I'm working with him, and he's a world-renowned director." Freud would perhaps somersault in his grave, but it is a fact that, for *Do the Right Thing*, Spike, as an actor, played with his sister's lips and, as a director, filmed her in the shower; and for *Mo' Better Blues* he filmed her in a sex scene with Denzel Washington—"an experience that I would not repeat," he recalls. Joie is of like mind: "Oh God, it was a horrible experience for me. I don't think that I ever got there, that I was ever private or intimate with Denzel—and I think that it shows. It didn't create tension between us, I don't think that, but I wasn't able to make the separation between being the character and being Spike's sister. We never talked about it. What is there to say? I don't discuss that aspect of my life with my brothers. I just don't even expose that. I didn't

---

[*]Spike claims that it was his father who gave Terence the chance: Bill was at the conductor's stand and told Terence, "Since you wrote it, you should conduct."

really know what I was doing. I didn't know how to ask for help. I didn't have enough experience under my belt or training to be able to make the separation, so it was horrible. And it still makes me feel uncomfortable—I can't watch it. That is just humiliating, humiliating. I seem to experience that a lot with my brother. . . ." Someone who was physically rather than emotionally discomfited by the shooting of this scene was property master Kevin Ladson: "I used to have this habit of sneaking into closed sets to watch the sex scenes—peeking out for a glimpse of flesh. On *Mo' Better Blues* I snuck under a table looking at the bed where Denzel and Joie were doing it. I'm like a little child, and it's totally juvenile—but I was having absolute fun."

The sex scene between Denzel and Joie is intercut with scenes of Denzel sleeping with Clarke, and this sequence handsomely displayed the skills of Sam Pollard. The editor, however, passes the credit on to his director: "Spike remembers so much about what he has shot, he knows the kind of direction that he wants the scene to go into. People approach me and say, 'The sex scene jumping between the two girls and Denzel, your work is so brilliant there.' I always say, 'Hey, listen, that wasn't me.' Spike had thought that out, storyboarded that whole scene. He knew exactly how he wanted that scene to be. I maybe finessed it in a couple of places, but the whole concept was his. This guy is a very strong director." This was another instance where Spike took a real-life experience and put it on film. While he states the undeniable ("These were good-looking young musicians, and I don't think that it was a revelation to see jazz musicians with multiple sexual partners"), he also adds intriguingly, "I don't know where I got the specific idea for the double love scene. It definitely wasn't making love. I might have called a woman another name and I was in a jam."

But Spike's strong directorial vision of the finished film would ruin Pollard's initial experience of working at 40 Acres and a Mule: "It was an eleven-week shoot. By this time I had been editing for fifteen years. We started screening dailies, and by the second week I'm expecting Spike to say, 'Start cutting.' But he tells me, 'I don't want you to cut anything yet.' OK—four weeks go by, and I ask Spike again, and he says, 'I don't want you to cut anything yet.' Now I'm starting to get really angry, because even though I'm being paid a full salary, all I do is come in every day, look at some dailies before the assistants sync them up, and go to dailies at six o'clock. So seven weeks go by, Spike doesn't want me to cut. Eleven weeks, the whole shoot is over—I haven't cut a frame. I'm thinking this is going to be a terrible job. I'm thinking this director is going to be sitting behind me while I make every cut—he's gonna ruin my life. But the shoot is over, so I figure that come Monday we're gonna start editing. Spike says, 'No, I'm going on vacation, I'll be back in a week.' 'Do you want me to cut anything . . . ?' 'No.' Twelve weeks, full salary, and I haven't cut a frame of *Mo' Better Blues*. Thirteen weeks, Spike comes in, he starts screening all the dailies of Scene One that he already screened seven weeks ago, from beginning to end. Then he tells me to cut the scene. Then he goes away and he screens all the dailies for Scene Two and wants me to start cutting again. That's his strategy. That's what we do for the whole film. I figure, there's no *way* I'm working for this guy again. So we get to the end of *Mo' Better Blues*, I figure it's been a nice relationship and this will be it. Then he asks me to cut *Jungle Fever*. I say yes but I feel a little trepidation. By the time we get to two weeks of dailies on *Jungle Fever*, Spike asks me to start cutting. Obviously, he just didn't really trust me on *Mo' Better Blues*."

The first signs that African-Americans were truly becoming a force behind movie cameras were seen at the 1990 Sundance Film Festival: Steven Soderbergh donned a *Do the Right Thing* T-shirt as he went about his business as a jury member, looking for the best dramatic film in a competition that included the Hudlin brothers' *House Party*, Charles Burnett's *To Sleep with Anger* and Wendell B. Harris's exuberant *Chameleon Street*, which walked off with the top prize. On February 11, 1990, Nelson Mandela was released after twenty-seven years in a South African jail. A couple of weeks later the nominations for the Academy Awards were announced: *Do the Right Thing* was nominated for two, Danny Aiello for Best Supporting Actor (pitted against Denzel Washington in *Glory*) and Spike in the category of Best Original Screenplay (alongside Cannes nemesis Steven Soderbergh). Spike was downcast that *Do the Right Thing* had not been nominated for Best Picture, yet his disappointment was put into perspective by an unexpected sadness the week before the Oscar ceremony.

On March 18, as Spike was gearing up for the second test screening of *Mo' Better Blues* in Philadelphia, he received news by phone that Robin Harris, who had appeared in both *Do the Right Thing* and *Mo' Better Blues,* had died of a heart attack. It was the first death in the 40 Acres family. At thirty-six, Robin had looked as though he was about to break into the big time; sandwiched in between the Spike films was a starring role in Reggie Hudlin's amusing musical comedy *House Party*, which took in a staggering $26 million at the box office. Its successful formula, avoiding big social issues to depict a teenager who just wants to have fun, was a precursor to the phenomenal success of *The Fresh Prince of Bel Air,* a sitcom starring rapper Will Smith that would début later in the year. Spike remembers, "We were all devastated by Robin's death. In fact, all of us who knew Robin think about him all the time. He used to play at this comedy club in L.A. and he would MC the show. To go to the bathroom you had to climb some steps—and people would urinate in their pants rather than go up there, because there would be a chance that Robin would see you and snap his fingers, the spotlight would pick you out and he would tear you up. I saw him rip Mike Tyson, make an ass of him—he had everyone crying, because at the time Mike was heavyweight champion of the world, and he was helpless, like a two-year-old, because Robin Harris was killing him. That's how I got the notion to put him in *Do the Right Thing*. When it came to *Mo' Better*, I can't write that stuff, so I just said to Robin, 'Go out there and do your stuff.' And it's so funny—a lot of people who were supposed to have a day off from filming *Mo' Better* would call in to see if Robin was working, and if he was then they would come to the set anyway. Everybody wanted to be there, he was so funny. It was a great tragedy that he died. If he had lived, he would have been huge."

At the Oscar ceremony on March 26, Kim Basinger, introducing a clip from Best Picture contender *Dead Poets Society*, departed briefly from her script to lament that *Do the Right Thing* had not even been nominated. ("The best film of the year, *Do the Right Thing*, is not on this list," she said.) David Lee says, "I will always remember Kim Basinger. She was shaking up there. The idea that Spike wasn't nominated seemed so terrible to her. I remember that moment as being great." But Spike's week ended as it had begun, on a low note. *Driving Miss Daisy*, in which the Oscar-nominated Morgan Freeman played a black chauffeur who befriends an elderly Jewish racist (Jessica Tandy), walked away with the Oscar, which seemed to be another kick in the teeth to the race politics of *Do the Right Thing*. Spike was beaten out to the Best Original Screenplay award by Tom Schulman for *Dead Poets Society*; Danny Aiello lost too, albeit —a silver lining, perhaps—to Denzel Washington.

On Sunday, July 22, rain in New York did not deter a line of people from attending the opening of Spike's Joint. The enterprise had a nationalist underpinning. Like the construction firm used to build the shop, the enterprise was owned by a black man, it was situated in a black neighborhood, the employees were made up of local and predominantly African-American kids, and Spike was making the best use of his business contacts. Nike goods were found in the store, as were Gap and Levi-Strauss, who had enlisted Spike to make commercials. Nelson George wrote in the *Village Voice* at the time that anybody who saw a contradiction between Spike's nationalism and his capitalism had their "head stuck in the sixties. In the face of modern corporate infotainment monoliths, the most realpolitik counterstrategy is to be in business with as many as possible. Diversifying protects you against cooptation by any single corporate entity or industry. With revenue flowing in from commercials, books, music videos and merchandising, Spike has some major cushion should Hollywood get tired of his methods or his mouth."

On August 3 *Mo' Better Blues* opened to mixed reviews. But there was not much debate on the film's merits as a study of jazz. The press were more concerned with arguing over whether the portrayal of the two Jewish managers of Beneath the Underdog was anti-Semitic. The miserly Flatbush brothers were branded as unflattering Jewish stereotypes by the Anti-Defamation League of B'nai B'rith (ADL). The *Hollywood Reporter* (August 7, 1990) reported that ADL director Abraham Foxman complained, "Moe and Josh Flatbush as greedy and unscrupulous club-owners dredge up an age-old and highly dangerous form of anti-Semitic stereotyping. The ADL was disappointed that Spike Lee—whose success is largely due to his efforts to break down racial stereotypes and prejudice—has employed the same kind of tactics that he supposedly deplores." John Turturro was surprised by the ADL complaints when they broke: "We had never even discussed the characters' backgrounds. To my mind they were half-Italian, half-

Mo' Better Blues: Nick and John Turturro as the controversial Flatbush brothers. (© 1989 David Lee)

Jewish. Sometimes in Spike's movies you lose a lot of scenes because he lets a lot of people improvise, and I think if we had seen a little bit more of the brothers throughout the whole film people would have got the comedic vaudeville turn that we were doing. I was shocked by the reaction. My wife is Jewish. There have always been Jewish managers of clubs, and that is a natural antagonistic relationship, between an artist and a financier/owner. We never made an issue of it. It was the media that called the Flatbush brothers 'cheap bastards.'"

Spike had no choice but to respond to the accusation. He remembers, "I thought it was bullshit, but at the same time, they were some very serious charges, because my lawyer at the time, Arthur Klein, a Jewish lawyer, said, 'Spike, this could be very detrimental to your career.' And he urged me to write a letter for the op-ed section of the *New York Times* saying 'Why I am not anti-Semitic.' I just found it foolish—and funny—the idea that somehow, in the history of America and of popular music, no Jewish people ever exploited black musicians." John Turturro saw the reaction as part of an endemic institutional problem with the American media: "I think a lot of stuff written about Spike's movies in those days was from all these white writers, writing about a culture that they didn't grow up in. I'm not saying that I'm an authority—I grew up in an area where I was a minority, then I moved to an area which was mostly Italian-American and I'm like the darkest kid and they thought that I was Arabic or maybe a mulatto. I had a lot of fights. Then I got bussed out to high school, which was all black. When I was growing up, my friends were black. I'm actually not that comfortable if I'm in a completely white situation – I feel a little bit ill at ease. But I think a lot of journalists are white and they want to put an angle on the story. And it gave them a story to write about. It was supposed to be funny to see the owners of the club. And if you look, some of those scenes, they *are* funny. Along with Robin Harris, we were the comic relief. The accusations were really out of context, and it was bad. First I had to defend Spike that he's not a racist, then I have to defend him that he's not an anti-Semite. The tone was set after *Do the Right Thing*. And he gave them plenty of fodder. . . . I think if he looks at it now, he'd say, 'You know what? I'll say what I have to say at the right time. Let them hang themselves and see what happens.'"

But Spike is rarely content to sit out these arguments on the sidelines: "Well, automatically those groups, the Jewish Defense League and the Anti-Defamation League, think that all Muslims are in the Nation of Islam and everybody under Farrakhan is anti-Semitic; and therefore, since I employed the Fruit of Islam, it means I'm anti-Semitic. It's really crazy. Take John Walker Lindh, the so-called 'American Taliban': they asked him why he converted to Islam; he said he saw *Malcolm X*, so they are blaming *me* for his conversion. And if he hadn't converted to Islam then he would never have been in the Taliban, so they connect the dots and I'm to blame. Luckily, people didn't go for that. But it's very tricky: if you say, 'Spike, 85 percent of the players in the National Basketball Association are African-American,' it's OK. However, if you say, 'A large part of the entertainment industry is populated by people of Jewish persuasion,' you're called 'anti-Semitic.' To me, there seems to be a great big disparity to that—I'm not complaining, it's a fact. I've been making films for almost twenty years, and when I have to do a studio film I have to say that the majority of people that I have dealt with and have worked with have been Jewish. My former lawyer, Arthur Klein, my agent at William Morris, Dave Wirtschafter, Jon Kilik, the producer of my films over the years, are all Jewish."

The rise of anti-Semitism among black Americans (at a time when it could be claimed that anti-Semitism in general was on the wane) increasingly occupied the minds of some leading scholars. Black academic and leading social commentator Cornel West met with Jewish counterpart Rabbi Michael Lerner for a discussion of what they saw as the worsening relationship between blacks and Jews in America. They began writing a book together that was eventually published in 1995, entitled *Jews and Blacks: Let the Healing Begin*. It points out that Jews and African-Americans famously campaigned together during the civil-rights movement, and yet a tense relationship between the groups developed as supporters of the expansion of Israel utilized the emancipation rhetoric of the civil-rights movement and the need for identity in supporting the 1967 and 1973 wars that saw Israel, contrary to U.N. resolutions, take land from Palestinians. It catalogs how the situation worsened in 1984 with the presidential campaign of Jesse Jackson, who called New York "Hymietown,"* and the rise of Minister Louis Farrakhan. The antagonism was played out on the airwaves with Leonard Jeffries[†] on one side and Howard Stern[‡] on the other. Cornel West would argue: "Jewish racism and black anti-

---

*Jesse Jackson quite rightly apologized for the remark and he ran his 1988 campaign with his pro-Palestine arguments safely backed up by Edward Said.

[†]Former head of the Black Studies Department at the City College of CUNY, removed in 1992 for his anti-Semitic beliefs. He famously challenged the decision in the courts and his initial successful claim for damages was eventually overturned.

[‡]American radio personality who made a name for himself for his outlandish and shocking behavior aimed in particular at certain religions and ethnic minorities that had him being coined as a "shock jock." He was suspended by Clear Channel in February 2004 for his overuse of the term "nigger" on his show.

Semitism are not only as American as cherry pie; they also are human responses to insecurities and anxieties."

As leading academic Dr. Henry Louis Gates Jr. pointed out in a *New York Times* op-ed of July 20, 1992, these "insecurities and anxieties" are not simply those from a battle between Jews and African-Americans but stem from the efforts of one black élite to supplant another in a fight over who is the official voice of black America. Fomenting anti-Semitic views benefits groups such as the Nation of Islam, who "preach a barricaded withdrawal into racial authenticity. The strategy of these apostles of hate, I believe, is best understood as ethnic isolationism—they know that the more isolated black America becomes, the greater their power. And what's the most efficient way to begin to sever black America from its allies? Bash the Jews, these demagogues apparently calculate, and you're halfway there. . . . The brutal truth has escaped many [puzzled Jews] that the new anti-Semitism arises not in spite of the black-Jewish alliance but because of it." Similarly some Jewish groups also benefit from being the victims of anti-Semitism. So when sympathetic black intellectuals such as Cornel West suffer from vicious attacks on their work from those claiming to speak for the Jewish world, the groups that benefit most are those extremists who thrive on such soured relations.

Spike willingly states that he cannot duck questions of politics simply because he is a celebrity and not a politician: "A lot of my films have political content, so I can't complain about being drawn into that stuff. But still, how this fuss started with people saying that I was anti-Semitic because of the Flatbush brothers . . . that was really stretching it." In terms of the issue of on-screen representation, the director believes there is a cultural oversensitivity at work: "They talk about stereotypes, but the least seen stereotype in Hollywood is that of Jewish people. Do you know how many commercials there are on television depicting Italian-Americans as the Mafia?"

Spike argues that his own position on the "feud" between Jews and African-Americans is that "the argument between us is overplayed. What really blew the whole thing up was Jesse Jackson's 'Hymietown' comment. Before that, I would say that there was a history of black people and Jews coming together for the civil-rights movement. For a long time the NAACP was partly funded by Jewish people. That is probably why there was such a shock on the part of Jewish people when any criticism of them appeared from African-Americans— because there was seen to be this solidarity. Now it's felt that there is this great anti-Semitism on the part of African-Americans. But for the most part I don't think a lot of African-Americans, especially in New

York, make this distinction between white people and Jewish people. I don't even know if the relationship between African-Americans and Jews is in such a terrible state. The thing that gets me is that there is this unwritten law that you cannot be critical of Jewish people—that if you speak against a Jewish person or an institution that means you are anti-Semitic." This applies not simply to the representation of characters in movies but to the actions of states and governments on the world stage, and as Spike adds, the Palestinians are really being treated how black people were being treated as a whole a long time ago.

Mo' Better Blues, made for $10 million, went on to gross $25 million and cemented Denzel Washington's reputation as the leading black actor of his generation. His impact was something Lisa Jones would not forget: "I interviewed Denzel for the *Mo' Better* book, and he was fascinating. He told this one story that stuck in my mind, about somebody, a preacher, I think, writing the word 'destiny' on a piece of paper for him, telling him that he was really going to change the world, and that he needed to keep that in mind as he proceeded in life. Denzel had that paper in his wallet. I was touched by that. Maybe it was the way he told it—he was such an interesting storyteller—but I think that it taught me a lot about how all you have at the end of the day are the choices that you make and your integrity—and that can go pretty quickly if you don't safeguard it. Making those wise choices will serve you well. As Spike liked to say, 'Don't take the short money.'* That was a line from *On the Waterfront* and it was one of Spike's favorite phrases. I used to throw it back at him all the time—if I thought that he was making a decision that, you know, was not the right one.'"

---

*Budd Schulberg says of the origin of the catchphrase: "When I wrote that, and the whole stuff about the contender and so forth, I had been around the boxing business all my life. At the time I was writing *On the Waterfront* I was the first boxing editor of *Sports Illustrated* and I was actually managing a boxer, so I have hung around with and actually worked with fighters, and the way they spoke and the phrases they used came very naturally to me. It was something we used to tell the fighters—to think long term."

7 Jungle Fever

In 1990 rap had a color-identity crisis. The release of Vanilla Ice's "Ice Ice Baby," sampling the catchy staccato beat of David Bowie and Queen's "Under Pressure," became to rap what Norman Mailer's "The White Negro" had been to literary polemic: a somewhat contemptible display of admiration cum envy. Vanilla Ice challenged the orthodoxy that rap was a black idiolect, and his success marked an erosion of the association of rap with the black nationalism of political hip-hop. He successfully exploited the West Coast trend of using rap to voice descriptions of ghetto life. There was something ridiculous about Vanilla Ice, a middle-class white boy rewriting his past to boast about the violence and poverty of his youth. But the public licked him up. For the big music labels he was a godsend, proof that they could turn rap into a commercial entity. MC Hammer's choreographed dancing in the video of "You Can't Touch This" was a very public display of the glossy pop-oriented approach of the major labels now infiltrating the rap arena. Meantime, Ice Cube, having split from NWA, recorded *Amerikkka's Most Wanted* with Public Enemy's in-house production group, the Bomb Squad. This was a rare collaboration between the East and West Coasts, and Ice Cube critiqued the glorification of ghetto life that he had witnessed as part of NWA (and in the process glorified the lifestyle some more). It was crews from the "CPT," the tag name for the notorious Compton district of L.A., who were at the head of a new wave of rap, their rhymes focused on drugs, materialism and the challenge of survival as a member of America's underclass. For crack had exploded across America—it was no longer seen as a problem restricted to the ghetto. In Washington, DC, Mayor Marion Barry was captured on video by the FBI smoking crack in a hotel room with a "model."* The furor over Barry's indiscretion overshadowed the arrival of David Dinkins into the New York mayoral office. One of Mayor Dinkins's first tasks was to welcome Nelson Mandela to the city. The arrival of the South African leader saw an outpouring of African-American pride.

Ghetto life, racial stereotyping and black politics would all feature

*The polite way that some newspapers referred to an old girlfriend and crack addict.

in Spike's fifth feature *Jungle Fever* (a term that Spike had heard Lisa Jones use to describe white sexual lust for black flesh). Spike insists that his interest in exploring interracial marriages was not stirred by his father's relationship with Susan Kaplan: "Interracial relationships have always been a big thing in movies, all the way back to *Birth of a Nation.*" The most infamous of these were Sidney Poitier and Katharine Houghton announcing they are engaged in *Guess Who's Coming to Dinner* (1967), and football star Jim Brown's combustible clinch with Raquel Welch in *100 Rifles* (1969). Spike has fond memories of both: "Jim Brown, Sidney Poitier, they are breakthroughs. They were breaking down barriers of their time. Without Sidney, there wouldn't have been a Denzel, so there is a great gratitude. I have always appreciated Sidney Poitier. He had the weight of a race on him, and when you have those shackles on you, you have to think about not just 'What is best for me?' but 'What is best for representation of African-Americans? What will help us move forward?' And that is the same burden that Jackie Robinson and many others had in the various fields that they chose to battle in."

When Spike heard about another needless death of an African-American, he felt the burden of responsibility, as the most famous and only constantly working black director, to address the issues raised: "The germ of *Jungle Fever* was the Yusef Hawkins incident. A young Brooklyn African-American kid goes to Bensonhurst to look at a used car to buy. At the same time, a girl, to spite her boyfriend, is telling him for whatever reason, 'I'm leaving you and my black boyfriend is going to come and visit me.' So this gang of young Italian-Americans are waiting to pounce on the first black face that they see, and it happens to be Yusef Hawkins and he gets shot dead by this kid Joey Fama. So that was really the spark for the idea that I thought of for the diametrically opposed neighborhoods of Harlem and Bensonhurst. And I don't care what people say, the year *Jungle Fever* was made, 1990 — some Italian girl brings a black guy home? Maybe you can do that *now* in Bensonhurst. But back then? Hell, fucking no. *Now* these white kids are into rap, hip-hop and black culture. They weren't into it that much back then."

Spike had touched on the theme of interracial romance when Left Hand Lacey (Giancarlo Esposito) was ribbed for having a white girlfriend in *Mo' Better Blues*. It was a subject that had been plaguing the director for some time. He said, "For me, a large part of *Jungle Fever* is about sexual mythology: the mythology of a white woman being on a pedestal, the universal standard of beauty, and the mythology about the black man as sexual stud with a ten-foot dick. Buying into the

mythology is not a strong foundation for a relationship." As he had
done for *She's Gotta Have It*, Spike conducted some interviews as part
of his research into the topic. One of the people interviewed was John
Turturro, whom Spike envisaged playing a white man who falls for a
black woman. Turturro remembers, "Before there was a script Spike
interviewed me about my relationships with girls. Originally I thought
that I was going to be the main character—that's the way Spike
appraised it. To this day I still think that this would have made a better movie. I had a lot of black girls that used to like me when I was a
kid. I'd fool around with them and stuff, but I never went out with a
black girl because, with my parents, that would have been a difficult
thing. I lost my virginity to a black girl. Oops. . . . It was in my uncle's
house, east New York. And guess what? He lived in a renovated, but
not completely, Jewish synagogue—that is a New York experience.
Spike doesn't even know about that."

Once the interviews were over, the director sat down and began to
write. *Jungle Fever* kicks off with Flipper Purify making passionate
love to his wife, Drew. Their daughter sits in the next room, trying not
to listen in. Their brownstone in Harlem on the landmark block
Striver's Row is filled with good feelings and they lead an idyllic
lifestyle. Flipper is an architect who shares Spike Lee's sentiment of
giving his fellow black workers a helping hand whenever he can. His
desire to have an African-American secretary irks his bosses, and so,
mischievously, they provide their ambitious employee with an Italian-
American named Angie: the bosses taunt Flipper that to complain
would be akin to reverse discrimination. Angie works all day and in
the evening she heads back to Bensonhurst to cook for her father and
brothers. Her relationship with Paulie, who runs a coffee shop cum
convenience store, is going nowhere fast. Flipper and Angie embark
on an affair fueled by "jungle fever," but their trysts don't stay secret
for long. Flipper tells his best friend, Cyrus, who in turn tells his wife,
Vera, and it soon gets back to Drew. Angie tells her girlfriends and
they reveal all to her brother. In the resulting furor, Angie and Flipper
are thrown out of their respective homes. With the theme of the movie
seemingly established, Flipper's older brother, Gator, arrives on the
scene. He is a crack addict who feeds his need by stealing from his parents. The father is a preacher who refuses to speak to Gator because of
his addiction and, on hearing of Flipper's adulterous affair with Angie,
announces his displeasure in no uncertain terms when Angie is invited
to dinner. Meanwhile, Paulie is falling for a black woman who fre-
quents his newspaper stand. Paulie's father is also against interracial
dating. Flipper tries in vain to counsel his brother about the dangers of

Jungle Fever: Flipper (Wesley Snipes) greets new secretary Angie (Annabella Sciorra) under the smug noses of bosses Brad Dourif and Tim Robbins. (© 1990 David Lee)

crack, while his relationship with Angie falls apart. Gator is shot dead by his father. . . .

Spike was fairly certain of the actors he wanted to play the male leads. Sam Jackson for one was growing accustomed to receiving the Spike Lee phone call: "When 40 Acres first started, for us it was basically Spike Lee's summer film camp. He always called the same guys and would always have the same crews and the same actors and we would get together and it was like, 'I got some costumes, I got some film — hey, let's make a movie!' After we kind of moved on I realized that the film business was different from the way that I had viewed it as being through working with Spike." Now Spike wanted Jackson to play the crack addict Gator. Spike claims that he wasn't aware Jackson had entered a drug rehabilitation center after making *Mo' Better Blues*. The actor tells a different story: "Spike knew I was in rehab. He called me there and he asked if I still wanted to do the movie, and I said, 'I still want to do it. I'll be out by then.'"

Wesley Snipes was Spike's first choice to play Flipper. Producer Preston Holmes says Snipes was guaranteed a leading-man role after his turn in *Mo' Better*: "It was interesting to watch the making of a star in Wesley. Denzel was the star in the beginning, rightly and justifiably so, but I think everybody watching what was going on could see that Wesley had something special." Spike would cast himself as Flipper's best friend, Cyrus. Also getting the Spike Lee phone call again was Ossie Davis. He says, "Spike in a sense not only hired Ossie Davis and Ruby Dee, he also hired Ruby and Ossie. He hired the 'us-ness' of the relationships and he knew how to depend upon it, and I thought he used it well." Davis had been due to appear in *Mo' Better* before withdrawing at the last minute, and he was finding it increasingly difficult to refuse the director: "On *Do the Right Thing*, certain aspects of the production were experimental and Spike, in a sense, had to prove his point, and everybody waited until he did. Now we were a little more prepared to accept the fact that the man was a creative genius, and if he saw something, it was worth our while to see it too."

For many of the actresses, this would be their first time working with Spike. As he had done with *She's Gotta Have It*, the director gave a role to his girlfriend of the time, casting Veronica Webb as his on-screen wife. Lonette McKee, herself a daughter of a mixed-race couple, was cast as Drew. Another talent whom Spike would be credited with discovering was Halle Berry. "Robi Reed brought me to her attention," says Spike. "My biggest concern was that she looked too fine to play a five-dollar crack ho. She was saying, 'Spike, I'm telling you I can look messed up!' I didn't even know it was her the first time I saw her in costume. I'm not saying this because of anything else, but *Jungle Fever* is for me her best acting to date." Getting Halle Berry to look bad was one of the biggest problems that Ernest Dickerson faced making the film: "I had to do a lot of styling. She had to look ravaged. And she's such a beautiful lady, makeup could only do so much. It wasn't working. Ultimately I had to put a green light on her, to show how crack destroys the body." Monty Ross remembers that Berry, a little-known model, was happy to work in the down-to-earth environment that Spike had cultivated for his performers on set, a world away from the pages of *Vanity Fair*: "Back then Halle was willing to hang out in Brooklyn if that was what she needed to do. She stayed in an apartment above Spike's Joint, and we went to Ikea to get the furniture. By then word had got to Hollywood that if you are working with Spike you don't get the four-star hotel, you're definitely not pampered. Spike really wants the project to be authentic. By then this is all becoming part of the Spike Lee lore."

It was crucial that Spike find the right actress to play the first white female lead in one of his films. Robi Reed claims that nearly every white actress in New York, including Marisa Tomei, Kelly Lynch, Gina Gershon and Linda Fiorentino, auditioned for the role: "Every-

Jungle Fever: Samuel L. Jackson and Halle Berry. (© 1990 David Lee)

body wanted an opportunity to work with him. Everything he did was going to get attention, and if you had a lead in a Spike Lee movie and you were white, you probably would have every script sent to you subsequently." Annabella Sciorra, who had appeared in *Cadillac Man* and *Reversal of Fortune*, met with Spike at an Italian restaurant in Times Square: "I remember that he didn't order anything, so I didn't feel like *I* could order anything. And he was so quiet and he kept his eyes down a lot. The more introverted he got, the more shy I got. I felt like it was a disaster; I didn't say anything important. Then I went home and he called me on the phone and said, 'All right, you're Angie,' and I was like, 'Hooray!' I was so ecstatic. Though I hadn't seen the script, so I didn't really know who Angie was at that time."

Spike then had to explain to his lead actress the dynamics of the characters and the dramatic situation as he saw it. With his usual candor, Spike remarks: "Among black people, you have always heard it said that once a black man reaches a certain level, especially if you are an entertainer, you get a white trophy woman. I didn't make that up." Annabella Sciorra remembers, "At some point we discussed the characters' attraction to each other, and Spike said, 'This movie is about fear of the big black dick.' That just made me laugh—maybe there are some people out there who are afraid of Spike's dick, but I didn't understand that from the character. If I had, I would have addressed the character differently. But I was under the impression that she was falling in love with the man. He was different from what she was used to. She had these brothers who were kind of bullies and racists, and so was her dad, and she was the girl who came home from work and cooked and cleaned in her family. I think that in Flipper she saw something that she hadn't come close to before. He was educated and opening up another world for her."

The difference of interpretation caused friction on set. Monty Ross remembers Spike getting frustrated with his lead actress: "It was tough, because when it came to the love scene Anna just froze up. She made a scene the first time that we filmed her with Wesley: this black man was more of a caveman, and he just wanted to get next to this white woman. We didn't want the movie to come across as a black man just relentlessly pursuing a white woman. We wanted there to be equal passion, both people to be hungry for each other. Anna said, 'This is who I am, and I've never made love to a black man, and you know I don't know what to do.' Spike was like, 'But you're an actress, you have to act.' It was tense. . . ." First AD Randy Fletcher recalls, "We were at the architects' office, and Wesley and Annabella are supposed to do their love scene—this was during the first couple of weeks. What I think happened was that she was lying on her back and he was on top of her, and he told her to turn around. And I heard someone say, 'Cut,' and the female voice did not come from Spike. . . . Annabella wanted to talk to Spike, and if I remember correctly she almost got fired." Sciorra's memory is, "I think I called 'Cut' because Wesley took off my underwear and I didn't have anything on underneath. And to my knowledge that was not what we were doing, and I didn't have a nudity agreement with Spike and I was just about to be naked."

Like Rosie Perez before her, Sciorra had difficulties with Spike's handling of intimate scenes and is critical of his approach: "When you go into a movie, they spend all this money to coordinate fight scenes —because you can't really kill each other, you can't really hurt each other. Then you go to do love scenes, and nobody wants to talk about it, because people are afraid to reveal their sexuality. That is what happened that day. I've done love scenes since where it's talked about; it's a delicate, fragile thing and you want to convey that there are a lot of different ways that two people can make love." For Spike, this incident was a test of his filmmaking mettle and his ability to control actors: "It didn't really dawn on me that Annabella didn't know the type of film we were making until we got to that love scene. I think that when you have great actors and they believe in you, you do something and they can say, 'Wait, wait, Spike, let's not do that, let's do this.' They will look out for you because they want what's best for you too. The director always has to take the blame because you are the one who cast the film, so either you cast the wrong person or maybe if you cast the right people you didn't do a good job directing. I thought Annabella was the one. If she didn't know what she was doing, then I have to take responsibility. Maybe I thought she knew what the film was about, but she didn't. She can't be blamed. I thought that she knew; I guess she didn't."

There was one impartial witness hiding away unnoticed on the closed set: a man for whom sneaking into the shooting of Spike Lee love scenes was a work of art. Prop master Kevin Ladson recalls, "I was hiding under one of the tables and I was so giddy. They had to redo the scene—Spike didn't like the energy. And I think Wesley came in a little tipsy and it just set it off and we had to do it again, and everybody was in a big funk. I'm sure Wesley had liquor on his breath and he came in that day, straddling: 'Yeah, I'm doing a sex scene today.' Like, 'You better reinforce that table, put a couple of extra screws in that thing.' I thought I was going to get caught—that was the last time I sneaked into a love scene. Annabella caused a stink, and Randy got rid of everybody on the set." The scene had got out of hand and Spike had to call it a day: "What you see in the film is a reshoot because the first thing we shot was unusable. I wasn't really happy with what she was doing. It was like she hadn't read the script. I even talked to her agent and we discussed the problem. If we hadn't shot a lot of her scenes already, she might have been replaced. I was seriously contemplating it." Sciorra says that Spike agreed to do the reshoot because she complained to him: "It felt like the character was being raped, and I didn't feel that was what it was supposed to be. After we shot it, Spike called me and agreed with me."

Spike does not recall this conversation with Annabella ever taking place, but that may well have something to do with the degree to which he was preoccupied with his own problems in respect to his girlfriend Veronica Webb. Randy Fletcher, who as first AD made it his business to know the comings and goings at 40 Acres, remembers, "Boy, this is a rough one. Here's what happened. Spike was in early, always. He was sitting up in his little room one day and he called me in. 'Why didn't you tell me?' I said, 'Tell you what?' 'About Veronica,' he replied. 'I heard that she's gone to bed with a few people that we know.' I said, 'What! Spike, I have a hard enough time keeping *my* sex life and *my* relationship together. I don't care about anybody else's.' I didn't know. I had no inkling. I think all of us who are in the film business are lonely because of our work schedule and trying to find a mate who will understand that we're always gone, always working and under the gun. Trying to find the right mate, it's hard—to find someone who likes you for you and not because of your celebrity status. People want to use you. For example, they might chat to me so I can hook them up with Robi Reed, who was casting. At the time, we were doing something big, being from a minority background, making films all the time. And everybody knew that we worked with Spike Lee. I remember that scenario so clearly, because it caught me off guard."

Spike refuses to discuss Webb. But Fernando Sulichin, an Argentinian who had met Spike months before at a short film festival he had organized to celebrate twenty-five years of the New York Film School in Paris, says: "Spike loved to come to Paris to party. He is a great appreciator of music, and he loves society. He had friends in Europe. But at that time Spike was heartbroken because he had just broken up with Veronica. That affected him for a couple of years."

Then came the death threat. The crew were due to shoot night scenes in Bensonhurst, and Spike recalls, "It made the cover of the *Daily News*: 'COPS PROTECT SPIKE LEE.' We made a T-shirt out of it. There was fear that we were going there. I'm not saying that the whole neighborhood thought this, but 'All those niggers coming here to destroy our neighborhood. . . .' And once we got there, the atmosphere was chilly." Ernest Dickerson adds, "There was one location that was going to let us shoot there, and someone threw a rock through the window with a note tied to it saying, 'This is what you get working with niggers.' People were kind of expecting that our shooting in an Italian-American neighborhood was going to cause all kind of riots. They were really expecting something bad to happen. There was one night where, in anticipation of trouble, the media were out in full force, and they were reporting live from the set. But absolutely nothing happened, and it was really embarrassing for them." The incident confirmed Spike's belief about the "special relationship" between African-Americans and Italian-Americans that he had explored in *Do the Right Thing*: "I think that it's a very interesting, complicated, sometimes volatile, violent interaction over the years. That's the reason we have explored it in some of my films. I was always amazed by the similarities between African-Americans and Italian-Americans, and that's why I think we've come to blows so much—because we are so much alike."

Sciorra says of the not-so-appealing stereotypes that upset members of the Italian community: "Some of the Italian-Americans in the film are ignorant racist pigs, but that doesn't mean Spike is. I think that he shows some hidden sides to Italian-Americans, like the scenes in the candy store, talking about racism within the Italian community. Nobody ever talked about that before. I think that the same kind of thing goes on in *The Sopranos*." Spike says, "The scenes I really love were the scenes in the candy store—those guys, John Turturro, Michael Imperioli, Michael Badalucco, Nick Turturro, those scenes are amazing. I remember one line especially, where Nick Turturro says, 'My girlfriend got out of line one time, I stomped her right in the middle of her stomach.' Also including the political debate on Mayor Dinkins and Rudy Giuliani—now that was big, for New York City to have a black mayor. It's funny—in *Do the Right Thing*, Frank Sinatra's picture was burned as it was in the Wall of Fame. In *Jungle Fever* I wanted to use three Frank Sinatra songs and I had to call Tina Sinatra to ask permission. She said, 'My father wasn't happy about his picture being burned.' Oh my God, I had to beg. . . . 'I'm sorry, we also burned De Niro, Al Pacino. . . .' So finally Frank relented, and we got three great Frank Sinatra songs from one of my favorite albums, *September of My Years*."

A recurring image would play a part in a new addition to the 40 Acres lore—Spike's signature dolly-shot that saw actor and camera placed on a dolly, with the mechanism providing momentum. Similar to the disorienting feel of Harvey Keitel's drunken stupor in *Mean Streets*, it had first been used in *Mo' Better Blues*. The repeat in *Jungle Fever*, as Wesley and Spike walk down the street discussing Wesley's marital woes, was the first indication that this type of shot would become a Spike Lee signature. Ernest Dickerson says, "I know that it's definitely considered a Spike Lee signature shot. I get more questions about that than anything else. I really don't remember why we first decided to use it in *Mo' Better Blues*. Maybe it was a last-minute improvisation, and it was the only way that we could do the shot that Spike wanted." Come *Jungle Fever*, Spike wanted to reuse the shot. Similarly, he was exhibiting a penchant for having characters return to his films. The keen-eyed viewer of *Mo' Better Blues* will spot Tommy Hicks and Tracy Camila Johns in the audience at Beneath the Underdog, and others may notice that the first time we see Sam Jackson as

Madlock he is listening to "We Love Radio" ("Last on the dial but first in your hearts"). In-jokes and repeat appearances are little gimmicks that Spike loves: "We always put little things in the films that people can discover fifteen years later. A lot of people don't remember that the same cops who killed Radio Raheem in *Do the Right Thing* are the same cops who push Wesley as Flipper up against the wall in *Jungle Fever*. They come back in another film too. You can't do it all the time, but if people are memorable to me and I like 'em and it feels right for the film I'll do it. I'm not going to force-feed it. Look at Agent Flood in *25th Hour*, played by Isiah Whitlock Jr.—it's conceivable that he works in the New York City Police Department and through hard work he gets promoted to the SEC and returns to play that role in *She Hate Me*." Giancarlo Esposito, though, refused Spike's request to play Buggin Out as a homeless person in *Jungle Fever*: "So then he just played another homeless person. No big deal."

External furors, and the media's appetite for them, were detracting from what Spike saw as the central theme of *Jungle Fever*: "I just wanted to use the interracial thing as a hook. For me, the heart of the piece is the devastation of crack on families." *Do the Right Thing* had been criticized for not including references to drugs, especially as it was set in a community known for the crack dealers. At the time, Spike said that he needed to make a film solely about drugs in order to treat the subject correctly. He now adds, "I thought that *Do the Right Thing* was unjustly criticized. People would try to negate the message about dealing with racism in this country by saying, 'How come there are no drugs in the film?' I felt that instead of trying to deal with racism they wanted to deflect the discussion away from that. I found it funny, because no one was saying, 'Where are the dealers in *Wall Street*?' which Oliver Stone released around that time. People think that the proliferation of drugs is just in the African-American community. There are motherfuckers getting high everywhere. Those guys on Wall Street? Forget about it. They are the people going to Harlem to buy the stuff. When you see criticism like that, it's so blatant that they are people who are not really interested in film criticism. They just have an agenda that they are pushing. In *Jungle Fever* we wanted to show the devastation that has wiped out generations. I don't think America, still, has recovered from crack. Before, you had to have a lot of money to do cocaine, but crack is very affordable. Crack made people go crazy. When people were heroin addicts, they didn't try to hit people over the head and stuff; they just nodded out. Crack is devastating."

In trying to show this devastation, Spike created one of his most memorable scenes, the Taj Mahal sequence. Flipper goes in search of his brother Gator (Samuel L. Jackson), who has stolen a TV set from his parents (Ossie Davis and Ruby Dee) to fuel his crack habit, and finally locates him in a crack den the size of a football stadium. Ernest Dickerson remembers, "Spike wanted to show the level of craziness. A lot of that stuff was real; tons of crack vials and all types of craziness was already there. You added the extras, but a lot of that stuff is there; you just have to show the level of destruction in the community. People said it was a glorification, but for me the scene was hard to shoot and look at, because you could see the level of destruction that people lived with." Spike had a clear vision of what the den would look like: "Ernest and I decided we wanted this to be like a living hell, Dante's Inferno. Of course, there's no crack house that big; that wasn't our point. We just wanted to show, quite literally, our view of the devastation that crack has had and the souls that it has taken. Ernest came up with this idea for the sound design. Every time you hear the pipes, there's this 'Whoooosh' like their souls being sucked out of their bodies." Dickerson adds, "At that point, there was a crack epidemic in New York and I just felt that every time we saw a flame, that was a soul dying. So we wanted to have all these little flares to really just stylize it quite a bit." It was important for the scene that the right location be found, and Spike was delighted when "we found this place that used to be a grand ballroom during the Harlem renaissance, a place that Duke Ellington used to play. We just put these mattresses on the floor, and it was Dante's Inferno. And I always wanted to use Stevie Wonder's 'Living for the City' in a film, and that was the perfect opportunity to do it." For Sam Pollard, cutting the music into the scene, "it was amazing how little work I had to do in terms of cutting the sequence to make sure Stevie's music would fit to the end. It was like Spike had an internal clock that matched the music as he shot the sequence. Most times when a director wants to use a song you have to put some cuts in it to make it fit the sequence. I didn't have to, and that surprised me."

Spike says, "It was my dream to have Stevie Wonder do a soundtrack for the movie. People told me not to do it; they said it always takes him four or five years to do something. I said, 'Stevie is going to do it within the time allowed,' and he pulled through." By now Monty Ross was himself amazed at the level of fame that Spike had achieved: "It's funny about celebrity. When you reach a certain level, folks want to do things for you. I remember Stevie Wonder called my house—I don't know how he got my number—and said, 'I want you guys to come down to my concert.' The next thing I know is that I'm flying to South Carolina to see Stevie Wonder."

*

A running theme in all the families depicted in *Jungle Fever* is a generation gap in attitudes: between Angie and Mike Tucci (Frank Vincent), Paulie and Lou (Anthony Quinn), and most notably both Gator and Flipper clashing with their preacher father, the Good Reverend Doctor Purify. It's a clash Spike was all too familiar with: "Families are notorious. I'm not saying it's a black or white thing. When your parents are of a different generation, they didn't grow up with the same views, so not everybody's parents are so open-minded." Ossie Davis offers a different perspective: "My problem was on the question of the father having to kill his son." This was another occasion when Spike looked to true stories for inspiration: "It was taken from Marvin Gaye Sr. killing Marvin Gaye. I knew from the beginning that I wanted to put that in there." The scene was the toughest that Ossie would have to do for Spike: "I had to arrive at the point in my own mind and consciousness where killing him made logical sense for who my character was—a

Jungle Fever: Ossie Davis. (© 1990 David Lee)

minister and the sole representative of God to the community. Like Abraham preparing to offer up his son Isaac, I had to make sure that from my own point of view I could handle it. We have known people on the verges and the outskirts and perimeters of our own family where drugs and addictions were real problems, how sometimes the family unit was destroyed. This was, in a sense, as if it were another case of family troubles that Ruby and I had experienced in our own life, either directly or in our family situation. We went back in our minds and remembered the time when our baby daughter was found with mari-juana in her pocket, half smoked, and how we faced the situation. Spike, in a sense, took advantage of how our family had dealt with the real situation and used it, and let us use it and apply it to the scene of the film."

Spike had neither forgotten nor forgiven what he took to be the unjust criticisms of anti-Semitism leveled at his previous joint, and now wished to launch a preemptive strike on his critics, according to Sam Pollard: "In my office I have the original opening to *Jungle Fever*. It was test-screened in L.A., in New York and in Chicago. It was Spike on a crane, looking into the camera and telling the audience, 'This film is going to be about an interracial couple. All of those who think I'm anti-Semitic, you can all kiss my ass two times.' The Universal execs used the first two screenings to try to persuade Spike to cut the scene, because it was going to hurt the box office. People were saying that they wouldn't recommend the film if Spike started it off by insulting the audience, but Spike was adamant that it should stay. Finally, after the third time it's screened, he decides to take the opening off."

Nineteen ninety-one was the so-called Year of the Black Film. Almost as many films helmed by African-Americans were released within those twelve months as had been in all of the previous decade. On March 8, came Mario Van Peebles's *New Jack City*, starring Wesley Snipes, with the tagline, "They're a new breed of gangster. The new public enemy. The new family of crime." Scripted by social critic Barry Michael Cooper, who had written the introduction to the *Do the Right Thing* companion book, the film focused on the ghetto and its proliferation of drugs. The release was marred by shootings at several locations and a riot at a cin-ema in the Westwood section of L.A., yet this did not stop the movie taking in $48 million at the box office. Two weeks later the $9 million gross of Robert Townsend's *The Five Heartbeats* was small change in comparison. This was a foretaste of a trend that would see comedies such as Charles Lane's *True Identity*, Joseph B. Vasquez's lamentable *Hangin' with the Homeboys* and Bill Duke's *A Rage in Harlem* die at the box office. A $10 million gross was no longer seen as successful for a "black film." The focus of media interest was on two début films documenting the violent undertow of black urban America: Matty Rich's *Straight Out of Brooklyn*, which had premièred to much fanfare with *New Jack City* at Sundance that January, and *Boyz N the Hood*, helmed by twenty-three-year-old John Singleton, which was getting great advance notice before its summer release.

The *New York Times* made direct reference to the influence of Spike Lee's début on black film by titling a magazine article "They've Gotta Have Us: Hollywood's Black Directors." The article, replete with group photo, focused upon Spike, the Hudlin brothers, Ernest Dickerson, Mario Van Peebles, John Singleton, Charles Lane and Matty Rich. *Empire* magazine ran a profile on the perceived phenomenon entitled "Don't Believe the Hype" following a series of high-profile criminal incidents that marred the openings of Singleton's *Boyz N the Hood* and Van Peebles's *New Jack City*. The media, some of whom had been surprised that similar criminal activity did not take place when *Do the Right Thing* opened, were quick to jump on the link between black movies and real-life crime. Mario Van Peebles disputed whether any of the violence in L.A. could actually be attributed to his film, as it coincided with the release of a video showing Rodney King being beaten by several members of Los Angeles's finest. Better marketing from the film companies also revealed that 25 percent of cinema admissions in the United States were attributable to African-Americans, and it was claimed the studios were greenlighting every script from a black that passed their desk. This sounded good in media talk, but the figures tell a different story: only somewhere between twenty or thirty films—in other words, considerably less than 10 percent of total studio production output—had a "black" storyline.

Empire magazine was in no doubt that the black film "explosion" was directly attributable to Spike Lee. They even went to the lengths of asking directors Isaac Julien, Mario Van Peebles, Bill Duke, John Singleton, Joseph B. Vasquez and Matty Rich about Spike Lee's influence on their work. The almost unanimous praise was tempered by nineteen-year-old writer-director Rich, who riposted, "Don't compare me to Spike Lee. I'm more real than he is. He's a phoney. He's a middle-class third-generation college boy. With me, what you see is what you get. I'm a street kid. I think and talk street." Matty Rich and Spike Lee had gotten into a ruckus when the first-time filmmaker claimed that Spike had warned him about releasing his *Straight Out of Brooklyn* close to the release date of *Jungle Fever*, Spike's fifth feature in six years. Rich subsequently missed no opportunity to attack the older filmmaker. Looking back, Spike says, "God bless Matty Rich. I just hope he's doing well. He was just very young and ignorant about the stuff he was saying at the time. This is one of the things that is messed up now—that if black people are educated and speak correct English, they get accused of 'trying to be white,' selling out. A lot of the devaluation of education has been fuelled by this hip-hop shit, where our whole value system has been twisted—up is down, down is up—so a lot of these young kids, they equate ignorance with 'being black,' 'keeping it real.' Motherfuckers are proud to be ignorant, wear it like a badge of courage. Those comments of Matty's are that type of sick, demented, backward thinking in a nutshell. Where is Matty Rich now? Every filmmaker is going to have one film that will be from their own experience, but what happened after that? He made *Inkwell*. The young brother never honed his skills. But, as you see from his comments, that made sense. To me, he was saying, 'Why should I learn my craft? Why should I read? I'm from the streets, I'm real.' It turned out to be artistic suicide."

Jungle Fever caused Spike to have a rift with another of the black directors who had featured in the *New York Times* group photo: Charles Lane claimed that Spike's script was a rip-off of his own screenplay, *Thou Shalt Not Miscegenate*, loosely based on Lane's experience of marriage to a white woman. At the same time, the literary agency Curtis Brown was trying to sue Spike over a share of the *She's Gotta Have It* profits, claiming copyright infringement. Both claims highlighted that, in the American film industry, success is almost certain to be followed by a lawsuit.*

Jungle Fever competed in the Official Selection at Cannes, but this time out Spike was not the only black face on the Croisette. Cannes, unabashed about jumping onto any significant bandwagon, had also caught the black film bug. Poster designer Art Sims remembers, "That Cannes Festival, I had one of the best times in my life. You could make a movie about that festival. There were a number of African-American filmmakers at the festival. John Singleton's *Boyz N the Hood* was there. Madonna had a party, and Ice-T and Ice Cube had come to Cannes. It was like hip-hop and gangster rap suddenly shows up in France. Dennis Hopper saw me come into the party with a bag in my hand and he says, 'Hey, dude, just chill out, man, just relax, put your gun down there.' Spike had to jump in and say, 'He's cool, he ain't packing a gun in his hand.' Dennis Hopper thought every black guy was a gangster, he was hilarious."

---

*In this instance Spike does not recall that Lane ever followed through on his threat to sue.

The *pièce de résistance* of *Jungle Fever* was the performance of Sam
Jackson as the crack addict Gator. Cannes was in raptures at his performance. Spike was delirious: "Sam, I think that's the best he's ever
been. At Cannes they created a special award for him, because there
had never been a best supporting actor award. He was amazing. And
at the time we were shooting I didn't know that he had just got out of
rehab. I think Monty Ross knew and some other people." Sam Jackson was shocked to find out about the special award: "I called my
agent to see if I had any callbacks for auditions, and she told me that
I had received a supporting actor award at the Cannes Film Festival. I
told her that I didn't think they gave them out, then she said, 'But they
created one especially for you.' I said, 'Oh, great.' From there I got a
supporting actor award from the film critics, and there was all this talk
about what was going to happen to my career. It took me about six
months to get the award from Spike, but, you know, I finally got it. . . .
I had almost just completed doing Gator's life, as such, so it was kind
of cathartic for me to go ahead and act the role, as it signified the end
of that part of my life and allowed me to go on to the next phase of my
own life. So it was important that I embodied the character in a realistic way, instead of just a 'high' way that people see crack addicts
most of the time. I think because I had that understanding I brought a
lot that was not on the page already."

By the time Spike got back from Cannes (where black Briton Isaac
Julien had scooped the Critics' Prize for *Young Soul Rebels*), *Straight
Out of Brooklyn* had scored $2.7 million at the box office upon its
May 2 release, two weeks before *Jungle Fever* hit the screens and
went on to gross $32 million, way short of *New Jack City's* box-office
gross. Thinking back on the success of the "ghetto" drug-related
films of that year, Spike argues: "The problem for *Jungle Fever* was
that it didn't serve the media agenda to highlight the crack epidemic
over the interracial relationship—probably because they see no value
in black life anyway, and the media concentrated on the aspect that
touched upon whites. It's the same thing where somebody could write
a review of *Do the Right Thing* and lament the loss of white-owned
property, and the same review will not have one word mentioned
about the loss of life, the killing of Radio Raheem. In their value system, black life does not amount to that much." And yet Spike's trailer
and the hook for the film undoubtedly concentrated on the interracial
romance, so the media might be forgiven for the priorities they
assumed in addressing the picture.

The New York press were far more interested in the story circulat-
ing about Spike's fallouts with Annabella Sciorra. Sciorra says, "I

think the media ran away with it. They said we had such an explosive relationship on set and Spike was walking off the set or I was." Adding fuel to the fire was the rumor that Spike Lee himself did not like white women. Spike says, "That was misconstrued. I was asked, 'Are you more attracted to African-American women or white women?' I said I'm more attracted to African-American women. I don't think that that is a racist statement. I never said all white women are ugly. The question was just 'What do you prefer? What do you think is most attractive?' I was just being honest. Malcolm X, his stuff was like 'White women are the devil.' The stuff that Muhammad Ali would say was directly from the Honorable Elijah Muhammad: 'Stay away from that white woman.'" Nor, though, does Sciorra believe that Spike was seriously considering dispensing with her services: "I think we shot the love scene in the first week, so if he wanted to he had time to fire me." Could it be that Spike—who by now was saying that, along with Madonna, he was the best person in the world at marketing his own image—was purposely blowing the incident out of proportion to highlight his film? When reports of their differences broke in the media, Sciorra called up Spike to ask about the comments attributed to him: "I was devastated by it, and I still am a little bit. He kept saying, 'Oh, come on, don't believe the hype, it's just press.'"

The film received mixed reviews, many critics agreeing with John Turturro's assessment: "I think there are such fantastic things in the movie, but there's so much in it, it could be a six-hour movie. I think that Annabella's and Wesley's characters were more like mouthpieces, politically, than human beings. I'm not saying they weren't human—it just would have been more interesting concentrating on the relationship I had with Tyra Ferrell's character." But Monty Ross feels that the problem reviewers really had with the film was their unrealistic belief that all interracial couples on film should be shown to be harmonious and in love in a liberal effort to promote positive race relations. "Spike will present characters who are right in your face, not sugarcoated or fabricated cutouts. 'Here is something that is real, that really happened.' I think people felt that *Jungle Fever* should have been a little bit more loving, not so political. Of course, some fans were disillusioned, because, for example, they're in an interracial relationship and believe that love does conquer everything."

Spike had been caught out by the change in direction of black urban culture toward the more localized theme of the ghetto. John Turturro argues that the film also suffered because of a backlash against Spike in America, which Matty Rich had successfully exploited: "A lot of people were fed up with him. He would do all these interviews, be on

the cover of magazines. When you shop in stores, a lot of black people would come up to me and say, 'You're in a Spike Lee movie. Tell
him he doesn't know shit about black people. He can't speak for me.'
I'm like, 'Tell him yourself. . . .' By the end of *Jungle Fever*, Spike got
a lot of labels. But that's just part of Spike. I think he likes controversy.
He knows that controversy is good for business. But in the end, people can get tired of controversy too."

In July of that year cinema was going the way of rap, with stories
about life in South Central L.A. capturing the imagination of the
American public. *Boyz N the Hood* took $58 million. Twenty-three-
year-old John Singleton, who had once approached Spike at a *She's
Gotta Have It* screening to say that he had been inspired by him to
become a filmmaker, went on to receive a Best Director Academy
Award nomination. Spike approved Singleton's achievement: "John
went to USC, John is educated, he had formal training. I'm not trying
to say that everybody has to go to film school to be a filmmaker. Training doesn't just occur in film school—intern, shoot your own films.
But you have to learn about the craft." Spike would try to refocus
attention back on black nationalism in *Malcolm X*, but for now he
was unwilling to concede that the black population at large were
becoming less interested in the pro-black messages of political hip-
hop. Unlike De La Soul, whose second album, *De La Soul Is Dead*
(1991), saw a dramatic change in direction that unflinchingly
acknowledged the failure of their brand of happy-go-lucky rap, Spike
felt that his biopic on Malcolm X would capture the Afrocentrist
imagination just as had Nelson Mandela's visit to New York in the
run-up to *Jungle Fever*.

8 Malcolm X

The greatest miracle Christianity has achieved in America is that the black man in white Christian hands has not grown violent. It is a miracle that 22 million black people have not risen up against their oppressors—in which they would have been justified by all moral criteria, and even by the democratic tradition! It is a miracle that a nation of black people has so fervently continued to believe in a turn-the-other-cheek and heaven-for-you-after-you-die philosophy! It is a miracle that the American Black people have remained a peaceful people, while catching all the centuries of hell that they have caught, here in white man's heaven! The miracle is that the white man's puppet Negro "leaders," his preachers and the educated Negroes laden with degrees, and others who have been allowed to wax fat off their black poor brothers, have been able to hold the black masses quiet until now.

The Autobiography of Malcolm X (quote originally to be used for *Do the Right Thing*)

Denzel Washington as Malcolm X. (© 1991 David Lee)

In October 1990 Spike Lee was guest editor of *Spin* magazine. The edition included an article from playwright August Wilson, who had lately picked up his second Pulitzer Prize for *The Piano Lesson*. There was now talk of *Fences*, his earlier Pulitzer winner, being adapted to screen,* and the esteemed playwright argued in his prose that only a black director could really do justice to his work. Using similar arguments Spike denounced the decision that appointed Norman Jewison director of *Malcolm X*.

The rights to the Malcolm X story had originally been acquired from Malcolm's widow, Betty Shabazz, by Marvin Worth in 1968. Worth then produced a documentary, which was directed by Arnold Perl and nominated for an Oscar. This success encouraged Warner Bros. eventually to acquire a percentage of the rights to the story, which they shared with Worth. A feature-film project gestated under several directors before the appointment of Jewison, who had established his pedigree in handling black stars and taboo racial subject matters with *In the Heat of the Night* and *A Soldier's Story*. But Spike was irked by Warners' choice: "I didn't feel that I was the *only* director qualified to do *Malcolm X*. I just felt that it would be very hard for a white director to get the nuances of the subject. And I still think that it is very few and far between that a white director is able to get it right when they are doing African-American films." The criticism, though, had Jewison up in arms. On Canadian television he complained, "That's an apartheid statement. For an artist to say that another artist can't cope with a story because of skin color is ridiculous." Jewison, Spike and Worth met to discuss the movie. Soon after, Jewison pulled out, claiming that the new script of the film by Charles Fuller was not quite what he hoped it would be and that he had done all he could on the project. Marvin Worth would claim that he had always wanted Spike to direct the film but had offered the job to Jewison only when Spike failed to respond to a letter sent to his office.† Once the situation was resolved in his favor, Spike tried to be placatory: "[Jewison] was cool. I mean, I would like to thank Norman Jewison, because he did not have to do that. It was his film."

But not everyone thought that Spike would do a good job helming *Malcolm X*. A focus group that called itself the United Front to Preserve the Memory of Malcolm X and the Cultural Revolution opposed Lee's appointment and sent an open letter in protest. ("Our distress about Spike's making a film on Malcolm is based on our anal-

---

*Paramount Pictures had acquired the film rights for Eddie Murphy.
†Spike Lee claims that he never received this letter.

ysis of the films he has already made, their caricature of Black people's lives, their dismissal of our struggle and the implication of their description of the Black nation as a few besieged Buppies surrounded by irresponsible repressive lumpen.") Playwright Amiri Baraka was head of this group. The father of Spike's collaborator and sometime girlfriend Lisa Jones, Baraka is one of the most celebrated black authors, poets and essayists of the late twentieth century. His plays *Dutchman*, *The Slave* and *The Toilet* were favorably compared to the work of James Baldwin, Richard Wright and Langston Hughes.

Baraka's criticisms of Spike first surfaced when the director asked him to write an essay for *Five for Five*, a book that would showcase David Lee's photographs, providing a pictorial history of Spike's first five films. In chronological order, the photographs from each film are accompanied by an essay by a prominent African-American. Baraka took the commission as an opportunity to vent his frustrations at what he saw as Spike's failure to promote the (socialist) community aspects of black nationalism in favor of a (capitalist) outlook that saw salvation through personal financial gain; Baraka also observed in the films a worldview that was suitable only for a black middle class, to the detriment of the black working class. Certainly Baraka did not see Spike as having the faculties to tell the Malcolm X story. Having inspected Baraka's copy, Spike used his prerogative to pay the play-wright a $500 kill fee.* Baraka protested, to no avail, that all the essays contained some criticisms of Spike's work. Spike's counter to Baraka reflects his view that the playwright's attacks were personal: "If someone asks you to write something for their book and what you turn in is highly critical of them, you cannot be surprised if they don't want to publish it. Malcolm X belongs to everybody, and there were going to be people who felt that the film we were going to make was not going to be the authentic story of Malcolm X. What bothered me about Baraka's argument was that he was saying that the reason why this film would not be good was that I was middle class. I don't know what is more middle class than being a college professor. And I think that my first five films cover a lot of aspects of African-American society."

The arguments with Baraka put a strain on Spike's relationship with Lisa Jones, who at the time was scripting an adaptation of Toni Morrison's novel *Sula* for Spike to film. Jones says, "I didn't see it coming either. It was not like my father called me and said, 'I'm going to do this to this man and he is a very good friend of yours.' I believe

*The sum agreed to be paid if a work is not used by a publication.

Spike thought it forced me to choose more than it did; and that I would ultimately choose my father. But I felt that I could have an objective viewpoint. I was more on Spike's side—we all had Malcolm X's legacy and had a right to interpret it however we chose. The dialogue between Spike and my father was important to have, but it's hard waking up one morning and getting a call from Spike asking, 'Why didn't you tell me?' 'I didn't know,' I said. That was certainly a hard moment for our friendship. For Spike to have one of the arbiters of a certain school of black politics calling him out on whether he would be doing the right thing . . . I don't think that Spike is one who likes to be called out. I was used to having been brought up in a notorious family that lived its life in public more than private. But I guess other people in the Spike camp wondered, 'How could you be so treacherous?' I wasn't that close to my father and I wouldn't necessarily have been able to prevent it. My father represents a notion of a political activist that some people of our generation have respect for. We wanted an approval from that generation and it was hard to stomach not getting it, even if we knew that we were right. I guess Spike feared that it would turn the black community against him. There was also a concern with 'authenticity' at that point, and representing truly being black. Maybe, as Spike got further into the commercial marketplace, he thought that he would be perceived as a sellout, and he had clearly begun his career not wanting to be that."

Spike says, "I think that Baraka represents probably a *segment* of the black nationalist movement. Bobby Seale thought differently, as did Al Sharpton,* Angela Davis. . . . So I didn't feel crushed. Because Amiri Baraka is forever going to go down in history as being a proponent of the black arts movement—but we evolved. What is always upsetting to me is when people do stuff and then they don't want the generation behind them to advance it. What *we* were able to do—we were able to make money. Some people have this idea that to be a true artist you have to be a starving artist, and I saw that from my father firsthand and that's not something that I wanted. I always felt that you can be an artist and still make money. Why should the record company, the movie studios, the owner of the sports team, the publisher, make all the money off your creativity? That doesn't make sense. I think that there is a segment of people from that generation who believed if you were a black person and white people liked you, you were suspect. But one of the main

*It is no surprise that Al Sharpton, with little radical background (indeed, in 1988 the NYPD confirmed that Sharpton had been an informer for the FBI during a boxing investigation in 1983) and occasional support for Republican candidates (he endorsed New York Senator Al D'Amato's reelection bid in 1986), would side with Spike in this argument.

things that bothered me about Baraka was that I just felt he was a hyp-
ocrite. He wasn't always Amiri Baraka—there was a man named LeRoi
Jones who married a white woman and had two daughters." Amiri
Baraka eventually saw his essay criticizing Spike Lee's depiction of the
black community ("Spike Lee at the Movies") published in Black American Cinema, a volume in the American Film Institutes Readers series,
edited by Manthia Diawara and first published in 1993. Pulling no
punches, the essay makes it easy to see why Spike took offense.

The argument had descended into bickering about authenticity and
the issue of who was the most righteous brother. It would matter less
who was doing the right thing—and both sides, given the choice of
scoring points or getting to the heart of the matter, would pick the former. In this respect Spike would have done well to have taken his lead
from Nelson George's argument, made at the time Spike's Joint
opened, that whoever criticized Spike's enthusiastic capitalism had
"their head stuck in the sixties."

Another year, another season, and Michael Jordan and Mars Blackmon were shooting commercials again, this time with the aid of the
legendary Little Richard. The commercial, due to air for the first time
during the 1991 All-Star Game in Charlotte, featured Little Richard
playing a genie who grants Mars one wish. Next thing we know,
Michael Jordan is wearing Mars Blackmon's bike-messenger ensemble
and generally copying his number-one fan. Life imitated art at the
game when, in the postmatch interview, Jordan doffed an X cap of
the kind that Spike had begun designing to promote the movie. The
endorsement guaranteed that the 40 Acres Malcolm X baseball caps
became the must-have accessory of the year. Nelson George remembers, "People were flying to Spike's Joint to get the hat. At first you
could only get that hat at *that* store. It was Michael Jordan wearing it
that started it off. There was a period up until *Malcolm X* that Spike
was able to tap into the new thing going on, either through the commercials, the movies, the videos, T-shirts. . . . The whole idea of having the T-shirt line, having the clothing stores, predates Fubu, Sean
John, Phat Farm and all of that stuff. Spike had this ability to be a
heat-seeker." This was reflected in the turnover at Spike's Joint. Earl
Smith, who was now a manager at the store, remembers, "We made a
lot of money that first year. Musicians would come in, athletes, everybody. Somebody sent us a picture from a magazine in Japan and somebody was trying to set up a Spike's Joint there." So successful was the
store, Spike the entrepreneur immediately put plans in motion to open
a second store in L.A., Spike's Joint West, as soon as possible.

Spike directs Denzel Washington and Theresa Randle for *Malcolm X* while sporting one of the phenomenally successful branded caps. (© 1990 David Lee)

The success of his store, coupled to the wresting of control over
Malcolm X, only added to Spike's aura. Even Warner Bros. had to
bow to his wishes. He displayed celebrity power usually reserved for
those on Hollywood's A-list. Monty Ross says of the period, "That is
when we were at the top of the game and Spike was on all those 'Top
100 Power People' lists in Hollywood. And you start getting
limousines to pick you up."

But behind the scenes, cracks in 40 Acres began to appear. "At this
time the relationship between Spike and me starts to get strained
because we are working so much," says Monty Ross. "I have this thing
about being an African-American company: you definitely want to
have everything together. That means a whole lot of management, and
you have to start focusing on more than just the work on set; you have
to focus on the people. Also at the time we had real-estate holdings in
three or four different places and people would be calling up asking,
'Where do we send the check? Where do we pay the rent?' The staff at
40 Acres had gone from four or five to fifty. We didn't have a CEO. So
I just took it upon myself to regulate that type of stuff. You think that

you are Mom 'n' Pop and then all of a sudden you're a corporation, and people want your product from all over the world and they want to sort things out right away. We would be doing commercials and music videos in between the movies, and finally Spike calls me and says, 'You're not on set. People are asking, "Why isn't Monty on set?"' I told him, 'We have this business here, not everybody is trained. There's tons of work,' and Spike was like, 'Oh, OK, just come to set more.' It was crazy at the time. I was thinking, We gotta get help. But Spike just didn't have to think about it, because he's an entertainer and a lot of times entertainers are notorious for having a lot of businesses that they're not running well. And people kind of expect that. When you're at the top, why, you're Spike Lee—you have to make sure any type of business, whether it's large or small, is efficient.'

Malcolm Lee was to work as a production assistant on *Malcolm X*, and he remembers that the success of the caps also caused some resentment toward his cousin: "A lot of people said things like, 'Spike is bastardizing the memory of Malcolm X by commercializing him.'" The apparent cocksureness of the director also irked some: Spike appeared on *Saturday Night Live* with Chris Rock and talked up the film's Oscar chances before a roll of film had even been shot. Spike claims that he himself was taken aback at the success of the merchandising: "We had made a lot of hats before, but I can't really tell you why that one took off. I think it helped create awareness of the film. You have to realize that Warner Bros. was not spending millions and millions of dollars to advertise the film."

The relationship with Warner Bros. had got off on a bad footing as Spike fought for control of the film. The director had made three films in a row with Universal, and it was a relationship between director and studio that John Pierson believed had finally captured the holy grail for independent filmmakers: "What Spike had set up at Universal, I thought that was a model for how an independent-minded person could work with studio money. Universal would ask, 'How much do you need? Here is how much we'll give you, we'll read the script, who's in it?' And that was that, and he went off and made the movie." The trouble with this model is that while it may function if, like Woody Allen, the director steers shy of big or even medium-sized budget movies, epics are definitely out of the question. John Pierson, looking back on his enthusiasm for Spike in his book *Spike, Mike, Slackers and Dykes* (which includes the line "Spike Lee is my hero"), now argues, "If you were to ask me if I would put Spike in that same exalted position at the heart of independent film now, the answer would be no."

Warner Bros. set a budget cap of $20 million on the project. Producer Largo Entertainment initially paid $8.5 million for foreign rights, reduced to $8 million when they realized that the rights did not include South Africa, where Spike refused to release his films. Combined, the figure still fell well short of the $33 million that Spike and Jon Kilik had budgeted for the three-hour epic they planned to make. Warners' solution to the budget deficit was to ask Spike to make a shorter film, but the director was adamant that X should at least be the same length as the film Oliver Stone was making on the assassination of John F. Kennedy: "Oliver is a friend of mine and at that time he was in post-production. Warner Bros. were telling me that *JFK* was going to only be two hours long. I called Oliver and asked, 'How long is your film going to be?' He replied, 'Three hours, but don't tell Warner Bros. that I told you that.'"

Spike has an answer as to why Warner Bros. would lie to him: "Warner Bros. don't view black people as important, it's that simple." In protest the director took to calling the Warner Bros. studio lot "the plantation." Art Sims recalls, "We were leaving the Warner Bros. lot and Spike says, 'Let's go see Terry Semel.'* We got to the building and the security guard tells Spike, 'Deliveries are around the corner.' He says, 'I'm Spike Lee, I'm here to see Terry Semel.' We walk straight past Terry's secretary and she calls out, 'Spike, you can't do that.' Spike says, 'What do you mean? I'm directing a movie, I can't go see Terry Semel?'" Spike, who had given up hope of getting any more financing from Warners, was doing nothing to endear himself to his new paymasters.

Spike began tackling the script. Over the twenty years that Marvin Worth had been on the project, David Mamet, Calder Willingham, David Bradley, Charles Fuller and James Baldwin (whose script was finished by Arnold Perl) had all worked on the screenplay. Spike reviewed all the options: "When I decided to do the film, I read all the scripts and I think I made the right choice in not starting from scratch. The Arnold Perl/James Baldwin† script was the best and we just rewrote that. Denzel Washington was very involved and he did a lot of work on the script too, in helping to choose the right speeches for us to use." The big changes would come in the third act of the script, which dealt with Malcolm quitting the Nation of Islam and becoming El Hajj Malik El Shabazz after his conversion to Islam, and with his assassination.

*Co-head of the studio.
†James Baldwin was not given a screenwriting credit because his sister, who controls the Baldwin estate, petitioned the Screen Writers Guild to have it removed.

Writing the X screenplay set new challenges for the director: "It was very hard, because it's not fiction. You're dealing with someone who lived, someone who walked the earth, and you are dealing with people who know that person better than you do. You can't rewrite history, but it's not a documentary so you can use artistic license. But you cannot distort the story, and you have to be careful about leaving shit out. You have to try and pick the best moments to tell a man's story. I don't think there's a science to it; you try to make good choices and not bad ones, but you can't film somebody's life from crib to coffin. I decided not to include Dr. King. I mean, who do you get to play Dr. King? I really didn't want to get into that lookalike scenario. We already did that with Malcolm. Although I do think that far too often African-Americans have felt that they have to make a choice between Malcolm and Martin—I think that when you really do your homework, your research, you see they both wanted the same thing, which is freedom for all human beings. At the end of *Do the Right Thing*, if you look at that photo—I think that they really admired each other, even though it might have caused damage if they had said that in public."

Spike followed the lead of *The Autobiography of Malcolm X* in starting the story by showing Malcolm Little's life as a street hoodlum in Harlem during the zoot-suit era. We see Malcolm partying, stealing and wooing white girls, until his eventual arrest. Although the segment is long and colorful, the depths that Spike shows Little sinking to are not as low as those described in the book. Spike believed that Malcolm had been exaggerating the story in an effort to add dynamism and make his transformation in prison more pronounced. The biggest moment of artistic license was the creation of the character Baines, who, in the film, leads Malcolm to the Nation of Islam after he is imprisoned. The well-known reality is that Malcolm's brother Rodney first put him onto the path of Islam. Spike says that he did not have carte blanche to use Malcolm's family and, in any case, that "everybody combines characters. You can't worry about being criticized for that." Betty Shabazz was also unhappy with Spike's planned depiction of her marriage to Malcolm. Spike defended his stance: "When you do a biography, there are always going to be some blemishes that affect people close to that person. There is going to be turmoil, trials and tribulations in any marriage, especially when you are a leader of people going through a crisis and your life is in danger and your partner cannot always think about the bigger picture."

We are then led through Malcolm's life in the Nation of Islam. We see him rise through the ranks, gaining acclaim thanks to the growing crowd attending his speeches. We watch as he falls in love with Betty

Malcolm X: Spike and Denzel Washington on location for the Harlem section of the film. (© 1990 David Lee)

Shabazz and their relationship becomes strained as jealousy of Brother Malcolm's fame leads to a campaign against him within his cherished organization. The pivotal relationship in this period is that between Malcolm and the Nation of Islam leader, the Honorable Elijah Muhammad. Malcolm's sense of disillusionment with the organization starts when he hears news of the leader's adultery. It raises the tension in their relationship, until Malcolm is suspended. There is then a change of pace and aesthetics as we see Malcolm perform Hajj and have his second conversion, this time to orthodox Islam, before the watchful eyes of the FBI. Having enhanced his international standing he returns to America to launch his own movement. (It is in this period that the picture with Dr. Martin Luther King was taken.) The movie end with Malcolm being assassinated on the orders of the Nation of Islam.

Even people close to Spike were wary of how the director would depict Brother Malcolm. Ossie Davis had read the eulogy at El Hajj

Malik El Shabazz's funeral: "When Spike came to me and asked me to reprise the eulogy, I had to make the decision as to whether I wanted to let him use it. I was persuaded that I should, because whatever the film presented, whatever Spike had given us and whatever because of his youth Spike left out, I was speaking from my own knowledge of the man and the moment. I played and replayed in my mind what the real moment was, and it seems to fit well with the film. We didn't talk about my relationship with Malcolm. I think Spike stuck as close to the source available to him as he could. I don't know how I would have responded had he come to me on a personal level and said, 'Tell me about Malcolm X,' because the relationship between Malcolm, Ruby and I got to be so personal. It's like telling stories about your mother or your son—they're family issues and you just don't talk about them. So the pain Malcolm felt, the sense of betrayal he felt in his relationship with Elijah Muhammad—those things, even as I think about them now, could almost bring me to tears. The hurt he felt but did not show to the world about the abandonment, it was like, 'My God, why hast thou forsaken me?' Malcolm needed so much that Elijah Muhammad remained a divinity which Muhammad could not be, and that was part of the tragedy of Malcolm X. Spike had no access to that part of his thinking and part of his feeling, because Malcolm could not share that with everybody. But we knew. There is a spot in our dining room where he sat that day, when he came all by himself: he sat and talked, just talked, not looking for advice, not complaining, not whining, just explaining and in a way apologizing to Muhammad, with that deep, deep love."

Access to the Nation of Islam was one of the reasons that Spike pinpointed that *Malcolm X* needed to be helmed by a black director. On July 25, 1991, Spike met with Minister Louis Farrakhan, head of the Nation of Islam, at his mansion in Chicago. Farrakhan's leadership and incendiary speeches, which called for separate black states within the United States of America, attacked Jews with a virulent anti-Semitism that made him a pariah figure in the media. (He is banned from visiting Britain because the British government believes his stance would fuel racial hatred.)* His speeches, cloaked in the language of extreme black nationalism, also tapped into a black consciousness that had been exploited by political hip-hop. Farrakhan was himself born Louis Eugene Walcott and was raised in Boston, first attending an Episcopal church. In 1955, while working

---

*In 2004 Spike lamented, "They won't let Farrakhan into Britain but they will give President George W. Bush a state welcome. Where is the logic in that?"

as a calypso singer, he was recruited by Malcolm X to the Nation of Islam and so adopted the name by which the world came to know him. After Elijah Muhammad's death in 1975, the Nation split into two groups, with Farrakhan setting up a base for his followers in Chicago.

Any meeting between Farrakhan and Spike, no matter what the purpose, would fuel the same flames that had led to Spike being accused of anti-Semitism following the release of *Mo' Better Blues*. It was even (falsely) rumored that Spike had joined the Nation of Islam. He reflects: "I think the Nation of Islam have done great things for African-Americans. I'm not going to dismiss them totally because they have said things that are anti-Semitic. I told Minister Farrakhan what we were doing. I let him read the scenes involving the Honorable Elijah Muhammad because it was good, politically, to do so. I could not go into this film at war with Minister Farrakhan—that just would not have been a smart move. The minister didn't really care how we portrayed Malcolm X. His major concern was how did we portray the Honorable Elijah Muhammad."

Farrakhan recounted the Nation of Islam's version of events to Spike, claiming that Malcolm X was in love with one of the secretaries whom the Honorable Elijah Muhammad impregnated: the news of the pregnancy sparked Malcolm into a rage that ultimately resulted in his expulsion from the Nation of Islam. Furthermore, Farrakhan refused to contemplate that the assassination of Malcolm X was by members of the Nation of Islam; and he also questioned whether Malcolm X really did have a second great transformation after performing Hajj. Spike dismissed the rhetoric, in the knowledge that Farrakhan was working to his own revisionist personal agenda. Later, Farrakhan would boast that the organization had "dealt with" its own traitor.

Although Spike did not toe the Nation of Islam line in *Malcolm X*, Stanley Crouch believes that his relationship with Farrakhan undermined the whole movie: "Some of the great moments that are in *The Autobiography of Malcolm X* are not in the movie, and I think that's why. You cannot imagine a more extraordinary scene than the one in the *Autobiography* where Malcolm X goes to see the old man in Arizona and they're walking out by the pool in the mansion, and Elijah Muhammad tells him that he did impregnate the women, and did so to fulfill a prophecy. And just as Noah had to be an alcoholic, he had to do what he did. . . . That would have been a classic moment, especially with those two actors. But, you see, the Nation of Islam, they wouldn't have liked that."

Giancarlo Esposito, returning to play an assassin from Temple 25, witnessed the influence of the Nation of Islam from the moment he arrived on the set of *Malcolm X*: "I was off doing *Bob Roberts* so I couldn't make the first week of rehearsal, much to the ire of Spike. When I got to rehearsals, all of the guys who were playing assassins had been brainwashed by the Fruit of Islam. The FOI working on the set were telling all of us who were playing the assassins that the assassination of Malcolm X was an inside job: it was the FBI giving us all the wrong information. I called Spike, who told me to straighten them out. I shared my knowledge and said, 'Look, all these cats have a vested interest. Of course they are going to tell you something else about what happened to X.'"

Spike had never been under so much pressure: "I put pressure on myself. Before we even started making the film, Denzel and I were being told by black people across the country, 'Don't mess Malcolm up.'" Monty Ross adds, "We had the whole public consciousness to contend with. In people's heads you have this mythical figure, this guy who completely set things ablaze in a different way than Dr. King. You have the full consciousness of the African-American community, from the social grass roots to the highest level of folks and people at Congress. We had a groundswell of support; the people, not the figureheads, the people who really believe in what you want to do, they really came aboard." Spike tried to keep the final script under wraps. "Spike was completely secretive," remembers Delroy Lindo. "To read the script I had to go to a casting person's office and sign a nondisclosure agreement swearing me to secrecy. It was all very unusual and added to the strangeness of the situation." But the script was leaked, and Amiri Baraka got hold of a copy. As the first day of shooting neared, Baraka led protests at the five offices of 40 Acres and a Mule that had popped up all in close vicinity of the firehouse. Baraka now accused Spike of being part of a great government conspiracy to pin blame for the murder of Malcolm X on black people. Spike defends the changes he had made to the script: "We did not rewrite history. It is well documented that the assassins came from a mosque in Newark. We even put their names in the end credits. The FBI did exacerbate the situation; the job of the FBI is to go and wreak havoc, have people at each other's throats, infiltrate, to have this guy from the Black Panthers fight with the Nation of Islam."

Spike's past efforts in tackling NABET would help him as he took on one of New York's strongest unions, the Teamsters, in charge of drivers and other crew on set: "We wanted some black Teamsters," says Spike, "and the Teamsters said, 'No.' So we told them, 'We are not going to use you, and if you want to come down and discuss this with the Fruit of Islam, then you can.' So we worked it out. There is nothing to be proud of. How can you shoot *Malcolm X* and not have one black Teamster? It was a lily-white union; they had one or two African-American members. Then I heard the complaint that I do not hire white people. That is ridiculous—everything that I have ever done has a multicultural crew. We reflect the diversity of New York City." John Turturro points out, "From my experience, if you go on most productions it is predominantly white. It's not that Spike's production sets are all black—but you are going to find more black people on his production than you will on almost any other film or TV production. So what is wrong with that? That is the way it should be."

For all his attempts at securing union access for others, Spike himself had still not joined a union. "I didn't feel that I needed to join the Directors Guild. I didn't join the Writers Guild either for a while. It wasn't going to stop me making films though." But in the lead-up to *Malcom X*, Spike decided that, despite his previous bad experience with agents, it was time to acquire representation: "The reason was that I knew that there would be times when I would need someone connected on the inside to talk to these studio guys. With Bob Daly and Terry Semel at Warners, I needed somebody who would come to my defense. And it really just couldn't be a lawyer. I needed someone entrenched in the Hollywood system. That's why I decided to go with Jeff Berg, who at the time was with ICM. They had Dave Wirtschafter and were the leading agency. Later on when Dave and Jim Wyatt left ICM to head a motion-picture unit at William Morris, I left with them. It became apparent on *Malcolm X* that you need that clout sometimes. If the studio won't return my phone calls, they have to return Dave's calls, and sometimes I think a lot of these guys would rather speak to Dave than me, which is fine."

Spike had very specific ideas about casting for the film and clashed with casting director Robi Reed. She says, "I remember Spike telling me, even about actors whom he had worked with before, 'You've got to read everybody.' I don't know why he did that. I wish I had all the tapes from the auditions. Pamela Anderson read opposite Wesley Snipes for *Malcolm X*. We clashed over several choices. I felt that Drew Barrymore should have played one of Malcolm Little's girlfriends; at the time she was coming out of that young adult stage and trying to make a comeback. I felt we needed to cast younger actors. The only sure choice was Denzel as Malcolm X. Spike knew he wanted to play Shorty, but we thought about Don Cheadle. The only other actor that Spike definitely wanted was Sam Jackson."

But Jackson refused to take part and he explains that this was for one reason: "Salary dispute. Spike didn't take the rejection too well— he wasn't pleased that I did another picture. We had a phone conversation, not the most pleasant. He said what he had to say and I kind of laughed at it. He tried to explain to me that I was indebted to him in a certain kind of way, and I replied that I felt he was indebted to me in a certain kind of way: we didn't agree on that. So I said, 'That's OK, hire somebody else.' He gave us jobs every summer, he put us in the public eye in a way that might have escaped us if we continued to do theater—who knows? But we were able to give life to something that he wrote. Spike was fortunate to find a group of people like us, who were as hungry as he was. And you have to draw a line. After three or four films you have to say, 'You can at least offer me a back-end deal, especially if you're slicing your own pie as director, producer, writer, star. Come on, that's like four salaries there. And you want to pay me scale? Wait a minute now, I think I'm a better actor than you too, so let me have the role that you're doing and earn some more money myself.'" Spike counters, "I was disappointed. Instead of *X*, he did this film called *White Sands* with Mickey Rourke, which will be forgotten forever. What bothered me was not that he didn't want to do the film, but the fact that he had his agent call me. I would have preferred it if he had said, 'Look, Spike, I can't do it. I understand that you can't pay me the money I want, so I gotta do what I got to do.' Fine, but to hear that from his agent, just out of the blue . . . and it was late in the day when the agent passed on the role. When I cast Sam in *School Daze*, *Do the Right Thing*, *Mo' Better* and *Jungle Fever* I called him directly. I thought we had a relationship. I thought wrong."

Spike ran into a similar dispute with Barry Brown, whom Spike wanted to share editing duties with Sam Pollard. Brown says, "Spike and I were having an argument about money. Spike had a very definite idea of what I should make and it wasn't even what I had made working on Madonna's *Truth or Dare*. The argument came back to me that there was not enough money in the budget because they were going to have two editors. Spike had told Jon Kilik, 'Let me talk to Barry, he's my man. I'm going to work out the deal.' I was due to go to Italy and I told Spike, 'I don't ever want this to come between our friendship. Let's just decide not to work together. Let's bury this discussion right now before there's even a hint of bad feelings.' He said, 'OK, I understand that, I respect that.' So I was off the movie. Thirty minutes later

I get a call from Jon Kilik: 'This is madness, this is insane. This is not just about money, it is something else and you have to work together on this film. So what do you need to do this film?' I told him, and he said, 'OK, how long are you going to be in Italy? Because we're about to go into pre-production.'" This would be the fourth film in a row on which Spike and Kilik worked together. Many saw their relationship as the archetypal good cop/bad cop routine. Kilik argues that this is an erroneous and simplistic view of his role at 40 Acres: "I think we are both very consistent with our message. We're consistent with each other, so there's not one person saying one thing and the other saying another. I think the Barry Brown example is one where Spike might not have had time to go into detail, and I could do that in those situations a bit more easily."

Kilik's diplomacy would come in handy when Delroy Lindo, who believed he had been offered the role of West Indian Archie, discovered that he might not be on the picture. Lindo says, "I didn't have an official letter from Spike even though I had been told 'Yes.' I started getting calls from my agent saying, 'Spike Lee wants for talk to you,' but for some reason we didn't get to talk directly. Then I got a call saying, 'Spike Lee has withdrawn his offer.' I went completely apoplectic. I am a dark-skinned black man, but I turned grey. I remember getting on the phone to Jon Kilik, and Jon said, 'We thought you didn't want the part.' I said, 'What do you mean? Of course I do.' Jon said, 'I'll give Spike the message, but between you and I, I think the part has been offered to another actor.' I finally spoke to Spike on the Sunday evening—he basically tells me that the part has been offered to Sidney Poitier. Poitier was reading the script and was going to get back to them. The next day Spike called me to say, 'Allah be praised. Sidney isn't going to do it. The part is yours.'"

One of the attributes of a great coach is the ability to make your players feel wanted and part of the team. Spike looked to sport for inspiration in how to deal with his team: "The New York Yankees, the great sports dynasties—if they lose somebody they just plug somebody else in and keep going. We did fine work with Sam Jackson, but he moved on and then Delroy Lindo comes in." Spike also succeeded in making Lindo feel like he was the first choice for the role even as he was offering it to another actor. Many people, though, were of the mind-set evinced by Monty Ross—namely, that Spike had taken his eye off the ball, was beginning indeed to believe the hype about him being the central African-American figure in the entertainment industry. The feeling began to grow that one was required to answer to Spike's whim to stay on his side. Some, like Alex Steyermark, were happy to do so: "With *Malcolm X* Spike called and said, 'You know, Alex, I'm starting work on a new movie tomorrow and we are having a pre-production meeting. Would you come down?' It was a classic Spike Lee thing: he calls one night, and the next thing you know, you're working for fourteen months."

For Sam Pollard, the myth of Spike Lee, Entertainment God, was proving too much: "I was going through some mental changes, ego changes. People started to say I was Spike Lee's editor and they would be a little standoffish, which I didn't like. I felt like I had a career before I met Spike. I had a job producing a documentary in Boston and the original plan was that we would shoot this documentary whilst Spike was shooting *Malcolm*. During this time, Barry Brown would cut *Malcolm* and then, when the documentary got to the editing stage, I would hire somebody to edit and I'd come in and help Barry. I started to feel a tremendous anxiety over whether I could do both jobs. All my friends and family were telling me to forget about the documentary and go work with Spike on *Malcolm X*. About two weeks into dailies I told Spike, 'I'm going to pass on X.' Initially he tried to talk me out of it, and in my head I kind of understood that this would be the end of our relationship. I knew I could live with that. I had to explore my own creativity and I walked away from it, to the shock of my two sons, who to this day tell me, 'Dad, you made a terrible mistake.' But I had to. I felt that I did not have an identity, and a man should always be strong and have his own identity."

Spike's relationship with Ernest Dickerson had also begun to deteriorate. The DP had just completed principal photography on his directorial début feature, *Juice*. Dickerson explains, "It started during *Jungle Fever*. Spike and I started pulling away from each other. I think Spike tried to get involved in the more technical aspects of photography, and it didn't really work. We butted heads on *Jungle Fever*. It got worse on *Malcolm*. It was a dream of ours in film school to make a film about Malcolm X. I kept telling Spike, 'I want to shoot *Malcolm*,' and I was pretty much determined that after I photographed *Juice* and we were well on the way in post-production that I was going to do *Malcolm*. Spike was really generous and he made sure that I could do it: when there was a scheduling conflict, he delayed pre-production for three weeks. During the course of *Malcolm*, I found that Spike a lot of time was going right past me and setting up the shot with the crew and not talking to me about it. Sometimes, I'd arrive at the location and they'd be laying dolly tracks for shots that I would have absolutely no knowledge about. Several times, the shot being set up I didn't think was the best shot going. I would say, 'Why are you doing it here? Your better shot is down here.' Other times, Spike would be giving lighting instructions to my gaffer without talking to me about them."

As Spike recalls it, "The occasions where I went straight to the gaffer to set up a shot were when Ernest hadn't arrived on the set yet. I'm not going to sit around and wait for anybody. I arrive on the set, it's time to get busy, time to go to work." Moreover, for Spike it was natural that he would start planning for the day when Ernest, who, after all, had gone to film school to learn directing, would go off to make his own films: "I knew that I had to have a greater impact on the photography of my films. Ernest wasn't going to be a crutch for me forever. This was part of my game as a director that had to be worked on. Besides, since when does a director have to ask permission from the DP to talk to the gaffer or set up a shot? A director can't go over the head of the DP? A director is the head." Spike was top dog and, as he had done on many occasions, he was not afraid to tell people as much.

Dickerson recalls that he and Spike discussed the look of the film in pre-production. "We saw the restored version of *Lawrence of Arabia*. It was always one of our favorite films, but to see it on the big screen in 70mm for the first time really blew us away. The close-ups were so sharp, so immediate. We wanted to shoot *Malcolm X* in the same way. We knew that there was a lot of distorted history about Malcolm. We wanted people to get to know who the man really was, and we thought the best way to do that was to shoot it as a big sweeping epic. Unfortunately, it didn't work out like that; we just couldn't afford to shoot it that way. But what we did do was show people that Malcolm was a man; his life was a journey—there isn't one Malcolm, there are several." This is reflected in the movie's structure, which splits Malcolm's life into distinct stages. Spike says, "I don't view his life as three stages, but as far as the structure of the film is concerned, that is the way it worked in the storytelling." The narrative impacted on the visual style, reveals Dickerson. "Philosophically, what we talked about first was getting the feeling of the forties, that zoot-suit period. We went for a Technicolor feel and it was a little bit noirish because of the dark world that Malcolm Little was traveling in then. When he went to prison, I wanted to give him something that was really cold because all the warmth had gone from his life. It was monochromatic and balanced toward the blue side. After he met the Honorable Elijah Muhammad for the first time, that meant clarity and a sharpness of intent, so I went for a harder look. In Africa, I had a slight diffusion to show that Malcolm's attitude had started to achieve a different feel."

Due to the changes in style, fashion and hair texture, the film was

shot in three stages. One of the first shots filmed was the one that
starts the movie, and at a cost of over $1 million for twelve minutes of
film, it remains the most expensive day of filming in Spike's career.
Spike says of the necessity of blowing so much of the budget on the
opening: "We wanted to establish the world that we are in, right away.
So if you're going to spend money, let's do it right at the beginning, so
that people know it's going to be a big film, epic." It was a day that
would have tremendous resonance with Monty Ross: "From my
standpoint, it was very spiritual. You have two guys who came out of
the left field—and young African-Americans don't get a chance to tell
the nation a Hollywood story and have that much impact. For me, it
was one reason why this group had worked so well together; it just
crystallized that moment for us."

But the X shoot would become one long series of problems for the
director. A car mysteriously went out of control and crashed on set.
On one of the locations, a man fell through a floor. Another worker
was apparently thrown through a plate-glass window. Even random
events had an impact on the film. A woman who was due to work one
day as an extra on the film was mugged and murdered, and a newspaper ran an article stating that a *Malcolm X* actor had been killed. Not
long into the shoot, a news bulletin flashed up across New York's TV
screens: "Spike Lee's father arrested in heroin bust." It was not the
first time that jazz musician Bill Lee had been arrested while high on
heroin. Spike had known about his father's drug addiction for some
time, but this time the story broke because Bill Lee tried to avoid a
night in jail by telling cops that he was the father of filmmaker Spike
Lee. During the making of X, it seemed that everything that could go
wrong did go wrong. Spike had often spoken out about the danger of
drugs, and now his firsthand knowledge on the subject was being publicly revealed. Spike's brother Chris, with whom he had shared many
a highly charged moment at Madison Square Garden and who had
starred in Spike's first work with a camera, *Last Hustle in Brooklyn*,
also fell out with Spike over his addiction. Spike, who has a holier-
than-thou approach to drugs, states, "A joint has never touched these
lips." (Indeed, Cinque squirms at the thought of how Spike used to
embarrass him in front of his peers: "A lot of my friends would come
over to our house. My friends would be high, and Spike would come
in and say, 'You're high, you're wasted.'") The news of Bill's arrest
traveled through 40 Acres like Michael Jordan hurtling toward a bas-
ket. Says First AD Randy Fletcher, "I heard about Spike's father on
that night. The next morning on set Spike came up to me and asked,
'Did you hear?' I replied, 'Yes, I heard.' And I ensured that Spike only

spoke to people he wanted to that day. I did not care what happened but I was not going to let people get through to him." The set was cleared of newspapers so that Spike did not have to look at his father on the front page of the *Daily News*.

The completion-bond company, Century City California, watched in horror as the film hurtled toward the $28 million budget agreed with Warner Bros., and soon started heaping more misery and pressure onto the director. "Word came down that the bond company guy was coming in," says Kevin Ladson. "The guy [Mack Harding] wore this cowboy hat, and he would come into the prop truck, look over my shoulder and say, 'I'm the bondsman. I need to check everything here.' Every day he would come in and look over my shoulder at what we were doing. On set, Spike didn't seem to be affected by it. He kept doing his thing. Then we got word that we wouldn't be shooting in Boston, and I saw it on Spike's face: it was like he had just been beaten up." The director reveals he was trying to put on a front: "I was trying not to let it show, but I was stressed and I tried to keep it internal." He tried to concentrate on the filmmaking and left most of the discussions with Century City to his producers, Preston Holmes and Jon Kilik. Holmes reveals that the producers tried to protect Spike as much as they could: "My allegiance was to the film and to Spike, and from my point of view, the bond company's job was to jump up and down and exercise as much clout as they could, but the only real clout that the bond company had they couldn't exercise, and that was to replace the director. If you are Warner Bros. and you are making Spike Lee's *Malcolm X*, you are not bringing the film out after you've fired Spike Lee. The bond company knew this, Spike Lee knew this and just made the movie that he wanted to make. The most unfortunate consequence of that experience was that the bond company, which had been involved with bonding several of Spike's films, was the real loser in all of this. Warner Bros. got the movie they wanted, Spike got the film he wanted to make, but the bond company was on the brink before the additional overage of several million dollars. That and some other things contributed to the demise of that company."

Century City tried to persuade Spike not to go shoot in Africa and argued that the New Jersey shore in January could be used as a replacement for Mecca. When it was pointed out that in America they would have trouble finding the thousands of extras needed for the scenes, the bond company was forced to relent. Spike also had several major coups lined up: "One of my associate producers, Fernando Sulichin, was relentless. He would not take no for an answer. He went to the high Islamic court again and again, until they finally agreed to allow, for the first time, a 35mm motion-picture camera in the city of Mecca during Hajj." A concession Spike had to make was to scale down his crew to the bare minimum, and as only Muslims would be allowed to film in Mecca, he had to employ a local crew to shoot these scenes. Numbers were so tight that Randy Fletcher didn't make it onto the plane. Ruth Carter and Ernest Dickerson were among those in the crew who said that the trip to Africa was a life-changing experience for Spike. Spike says, "I remember us getting up one morning to shoot some scenes in Cairo. To see the sun rise over the pyramids and the Sphinx, that was amazing. Scientists still don't know how they were built. And those are my ancestors. It gave me a feeling of empowerment. Especially after being fed lies about the Dark Continent, Tarzan, cannibals, bones through noses, grass skirts and 'ugga-bugga.' The experience made me more knowledgeable. I think that one of the biggest things holding back America is that Americans don't travel. Only a very small percentage of Americans even have passports or speak more than one language: you have to travel. George W. Bush had never left the North American continent before he stole the election. How is that possible? Someone running for the highest office in the world?"

After leaving Egypt, Spike was due to go to South Africa in the hope of getting Nelson Mandela to appear in the film. "We were supposed to fly straight from Cairo to Johannesburg," says Spike, "but we had to land in Nairobi, Kenya, because of a bomb threat. Someone knew that we were on that plane." It surprised many that Spike, who refused to allow his films to be released in South Africa and attacked those who invested in the country in *School Daze*, would film in the country run under apartheid. In his defense he says, "I wasn't going there to get some medal from Botha. I was there to film Mandela. My heart was for the African National Congress and liberation for the people of South Africa and all the people that were in favor of the economic boycott. Mandela, the ANC, we were their guests, we were there at their invitation. It was the right move." Spike wanted the film to end in the present day to show the continuing relevance of Malcolm X. On meeting Mandela, Spike was lost for words: "It was hugely important to get Mandela. Anyone who has read his biography can see that Malcolm is a great influence, so it was a natural link. I remember sitting in a meeting with Warner Bros. in L.A., and they didn't understand why Nelson Mandela needed to be in the film. When I met him, I was in awe." Mandela refused Spike's request to say the mantra at the end of a Malcolm X speech that adorns the 40 Acres logo: "By any means necessary." "I wasn't surprised," says Spike. "I mean, it wasn't a big deal for me. I always knew that I had the footage of Malcolm, and that if this was going to jeopardize Mandela's political future in any way, who am I to tell Mandela what he can and can't do? I was just blessed that he agreed to be in the film."

John Savage, who had met Spike when doing his cameo on *Do the Right Thing*, was working with a local resistance group that, among other things, made documentaries as a contribution to the fight against apartheid. John was instrumental in getting things done for the production in South Africa, but his abiding memory of Spike's time in Africa was almost Spike's last memory: "Spike walked into a Zulu community by accident. As an American—and we have a tendency to do that—he assumed that because it was OK to film in one part of Soweto, he and his crew could go into another part. The area he ventured into was a barricaded Zulu compound. The Zulu men surrounded Spike's car because he was trespassing and they feared he might be associated with the government. For breaking protocol, you can basically be wiped out. Thank God that Spike was protected by one of my partners and friends who is a master of dealing with the protocol that a lot of tribal men have, and they quickly removed Spike from that area. On the flip side, Spike heard great music and I heard him say, 'My God, I've never heard these rhythms before.' Spike got a tremendous dose of culture here."

Also on the trip to Africa was Ralph Wiley. The writer of the book *Why Black Men Tend to Shout* initially came on set to write an article on the movie for *Premiere* magazine. His brazen attitude, self-belief and creative writing style appealed to Spike, who invited the writer to join them in Africa. Wiley picks up the story on their return to America: "Spike called me up very angry, saying, 'Jesus, I'm shocked.' I was surprised by his reaction. I don't do PR pieces, I write what I see, one side of *Rashomon*. Spike said, 'I thought I told you not to say anything about Nelson Mandela.' I told Spike, 'I didn't recall putting that in the piece, but I had to send *Premiere* magazine all my notes and they may have put that in.' I couldn't get mad at the magazine for that. He said, 'Great article.' Click. He put the phone down without uttering another word. A week later, I got the call to write the companion book, *By Any Means Necessary: The Trials and Tribulations of Making Malcolm X (While 10 Million Mother Fuckers Are Fucking with You).*" "Spike was very cooperative, fairly reasonable," Wiley recalled shortly prior to his untimely death. "He has this tendency to want to end things in this very spectacular way, in capital letters. Eventually he listens, if he respects your knowledge or whatever. If you stick to your guns long enough, he might say, 'OK, I see it.'"

The film wrapped, and the bond company and Spike began battling over the date on which a rough cut would be ready to be shown to Warner Bros. Century City was in dire financial straits and this brought its battles with Spike to an ugly head as the film was being edited. Barry Brown recollects: "We were doing a screening at Warner. Spike, I think, was already in California. I was sitting in New York, doing some fixes on the mix. The screening was also for the bond company. Mack Harding walks into the mix and hands me a letter saying, 'Cease and desist.' If I had ceased and desisted, there would not have been a screening in L.A. on Monday. I'm thinking, I could just stop and the shit will hit the fan on Monday, when I'm not in L.A. But everybody would be pissed off. *Spike* would be pissed off. I sat there for a second and then I turned to the guy and said, 'This is a closed mix, I'm going to have to ask you to leave.' And he walked out."

Fate would have it that the screening took place as the verdict in the Rodney King case was due. Spike recalls, "The first time we showed the film to Warner was the first day of the uprising in L.A., so that was very surreal. I know that they weren't even looking at the film. My white brothers and sisters were looking at their watches to get the hell out of there before these niggers come over and burn the studio down. . . . Everyone was on edge. To see a black revolutionary on film and at the same time know that L.A. is burning—I know it had an effect on them and they were scared.'

Monty Ross says that the screening was remarkably amicable: "I have to take my hat off to Terry Semel. He watched the whole four-hour-and-twenty-minute version, and then gave us some very insightful criticism. He was very calm about making the relationship work with us. The city was ablaze, there was random looting, rioting, all sorts of craziness. Terry Semel, Spike and I walked out of the screening room and Terry's assistant came up and said, 'The city is going into martial law.' At this point it was determined that the movie would be three hours and twenty minutes long. Bob Daly was like, 'What!?' But Terry Semel said, 'The city is burning down. African-Americans are up in arms, what shall we do here?' It was weird, because everything that Malcolm X stood for and spoke out against in his politics was contributing to the actual situation taking place right there in L.A. Everyone kind of looked at each other and that spiritual sense of déjà vu—or, This is the reason I was born: at this moment, to make this film."

When Spike ventures out of New York he tries to make the most of his time by being at as many engagements and meetings as possible, and the *Malcolm X* trip was no exception. Art Sims remembers that there was a radical change of plan as they left Warners that day: "Spike had to go and lecture in Orange County. There was a curfew in L.A. because of the uprising. If you were African-American and out after six o'clock, you're going to jail. Warner Bros. said, 'Spike, we can't get you to Orange County, do you want to fly by helicopter?' 'I don't fly helicopters,' replies Spike. The limousine driver wouldn't take Spike anywhere. They looked at me and said, 'Art, will you drive him?' You're talking about a black guy turning *white*. I said, 'Oh no!' Spike says, 'Where is your backbone, man?' I drove. And the traffic was so bad on the freeway it took three hours to get down the road."

The L.A. uprising was a reaction against racism that some believed fulfilled Spike's premonition of a rioting black populace at the end of *Do the Right Thing*. Certainly the turn of events in the city did not surprise the director: "I never use the word 'riot.' I always talk about the 'uprising.' Historically, we have suffered a lot because of police brutality: it happened in Malcolm's day, it happened before him and it is still happening today. It happened with Rodney King. I can't really remember when I decided to use the Rodney King footage in *Malcolm X*, but I called up the guy who caught the beating on camera. At first he gave me a hard time—eventually we agreed that we would give money to charity if he let us use the footage."

Spike now had a big problem. He had agreed to produce a three-hour-twenty-minute version of the film, but as the bond company had closed down the production he began to bankroll the movie by plowing $2 million of his $3 million salary back into *Malcolm X*. This heaped more pressure on the director, and he finally cracked at a recording session: "I picked up a chair and threw it across a room. We were waiting for something—a musician or the score had not been transposed, and the clock was running. We were on the clock. We had eighty musicians out there, just sitting there, waiting for them. It was crazy. I'm not surprised that I threw the chair. I'm surprised I didn't throw it earlier. It was my money being wasted."

With the financial screw tightened, Spike took a leaf out of *The Autobiography of Malcolm X* and began calling up prominent African-Americans, asking for donations to the cause: "Malcolm always talked about self-determination and self-reliance, and in doing this film I became a student of Malcolm. I knew Warner Bros. wasn't going to give me any money, so who was I going to turn to? It had to be prominent black people with disposable incomes who knew what the film was about and what I was trying to do, and who wouldn't miss writing that check. But I had to really deliberate on it for a while after I had the idea—I didn't call them up right away. I prayed on it for a week or so. Those were very hard calls. It wasn't chump change, either." Spike called Bill Cosby, Oprah Winfrey, Magic Johnson, Tracy Chapman, Prince, Peggy Cooper-Cafritz, Michael Jordan and Janet Jackson. A sum of $1.3 million was essential if Spike was going to finish the movie. He adds, "I don't like asking people for money. I don't like people asking *me* for money. And also I know how burdensome it is, when you're in a position like that—everybody starts asking you for money. They leech off you. This was serious business. But those giving individuals made it possible for the film to reach the theaters around the world in the way that it was intended to be played, not the truncated form that Warner Bros. and the bond company wanted. That would have been a bastardized version of the film. Then, even after we got this money, I didn't tell anybody, even Warner Bros. They probably thought that I was putting in my own money, but my money had run out. We had the idea of holding a press conference on Malcolm's birthday at the Schomburg Library in Harlem, and it was at this conference that we announced to the world where we got the money. Warner Bros. weren't happy about it because, PR-wise, they didn't look good. The next day they started to fund the movie again."

If Spike felt his problems were over when the movie wrapped, he was soon proved wrong. On the cover of *Esquire* magazine, Spike was pictured with his arms crossed and body blacked out in a classic skull-and-crossbones pose. The sensational headline to the cover story by Barbara G. Harrison was the infamous "Spike Hates Your Cracker Ass." A reading of the article shows the writer trying to expose Spike as racist, but the reader might take away the impression that Barbara Harrison was personally offended by Spike's standoffish attitude to her, seeming to believe that her liberal attitude as well as her friendship with the novelist James Baldwin would immediately make Spike like her. When Spike fails to respond as she had expected, Harrison concludes that it is because he hates all "crackers." The article left Spike depressed for days over what he saw as a miserable attack on his character. He argues that Harrison's piece "was just defamation of character. If you defame somebody's character, then what you are doing is rendered meaningless. If I do a film about racism, how do you dismiss the film? By calling me a racist. It's simple."

Nevertheless, the *Esquire* piece had done damage. Spike then created more anger when *Malcolm X* was released on November 18, 1992, and he publicly called for kids throughout America to skip school in order to see his movie. Spike argues, "Who said that the only place that you can learn is within the four walls of a school? I'm not saying that you shouldn't go to school, but there is a time and a need to leave those hallowed halls of academia and get out. Is it not true that people have class trips? You go to museums, the zoo, the park to learn about nature. Anybody who says that education only takes place within a school and not outside the walls is not very smart. In the fourth grade our teacher took us to see *Gone with the Wind* because we were studying the Civil War. So if I can go see *Gone with the Wind* in fourth grade, I definitely think that these kids today should go see *Malcolm X*. I wasn't telling people to skip school, because in actuality teachers took their classes that day when it first came out, as a class. And a lot of parents took their kids out of school and as families went to see the movie, so I don't think that it was an outlandish statement at all."

Spike was surprised that he was criticized for this rather than some of the more incendiary aspects of the film: "I thought we were going to take a lot more heat for burning the American flag. We never got any criticism for that, really. I guess the fact that the flag burned into an X got us off the hook. Maybe the film was jam-packed with too much stuff, so they really had to pick and choose what to overlook." Despite the phenomenal public awareness, *Malcolm X* took a disappointing $48 million at the box office. Nelson George argues, "The biggest tragedy of *Malcolm X* was that it takes a long time to make a movie, and I think the movie came out a year too late. There was a time when interest in Malcolm was so prevalent. When Spike got *Malcolm X* off the ground a lot of that imagery had been so saturated. The hats, the T-shirts . . . Malcolm had been sampled on a million records. That is the only thing about film as a pop-cultural enterprise: you have to be so fortunate to be ahead of the curve. I think that the movie as a pop event suffered because there was a little bit of an exhaustion with the Malcolm X thing by the time he got the movie out. Also, that is a six-year run of Spike being on the cutting edge of culture, and six years is a lot. Most people get a couple of years at best. So I think there was some exhaustion with his constant promoting, the commercials, a movie a year. There was not a lot of breathing space." Spike counters, "There was no way we could have got that film out quicker. It takes time to edit a three-hour-plus epic film. We were not going to rush that film. I personally thought Warner Bros. stopped pushing and promoting *Malcolm X* and instead went gung ho for Clint Eastwood's

Malcolm X: Malcolm counsels a Columbia undergraduate on what whites can contribute to the cause. (© 1990 David Lee)

Unforgiven, since Clint Eastwood had a long and successful relationship with the studio."

The new black talent in films was also, according to Nelson George, darkening Spike's star: "There were more black filmmakers. You had Singleton, Matty Rich, Mario Van Peebles, Charles Burnett, Julie Dash, the Hudlin brothers. Suddenly Spike is not the only game in town. The world of black film—which for a while had been centered around the yearly Spike movie: there would be a big Spike movie, a big Spike party and a big Spike controversy—that changed. Now you had black people doing pop films, gangsta films, art films . . . there were more people to pay attention to. Partly because of Spike, we no longer just had Eddie Murphy—we had Denzel Washington, Wesley Snipes, Halle Berry, Sam Jackson, Angela Bassett, Danny Glover. And it got bigger and bigger as time went on. You had a wider palette to deal with. I think also Spike's own idiosyncrasies as a filmmaker began alienating some aspects of his constituency. So you could go see *Boyz N the Hood* and it is much easier to understand what is going on at all levels, even though John Singleton was influenced by Spike. The Hughes brothers came out and I thought *Menace II Society* was one of the best films I had ever seen, just brilliantly made. There were some guys making artistic statements on the same level that Spike was doing. Because young filmmakers were dealing with more issues of street life and were a lot more accessible to a wider, younger audience, the hip-hop audience as a filmmaking audience became crystallized. You begin having stratifications of black audience in film, which had always existed: there had been jazz fans and pop. But now you had the films beginning to stratify along generational lines. Spike's audience became more of a cinephile audience, black and white. He became less connected to a younger audience that was more hip-hop oriented."

The mood of change was also affecting 40 Acres. *Malcolm X* was the project they had longed to do, but the process put strains on every relationship. Giancarlo Esposito says, "It felt like the family was broken up on *Malcolm X*—you know, money problems, people coming down to shut the movie. A movie that's shooting in many different countries and also all around the U.S.; it felt like the family was being fabricated." Spike didn't see this as a bad thing either: "Families are living organisms. They move, shift, expand, contract, multiply, divide. Why should 40 Acres be any different? People get married, have kids, get divorced and move away. One thing I never wanted was to be stagnant. If 40 Acres didn't live and breathe, it would die. Shit, we're all trying to grow."

Spike recognized that he needed a break, not because he had saturated the audience, but because of the physical exhaustion that he suffered making the movie. His cousin Malcolm Lee says, "I'm sure it took years off of his life. I didn't know the magnitude of what he was going through until now, because now I'm in the director's chair. He was under tremendous stress at the time, making this movie by hook or by crook. You have to applaud him for that, for sticking to his guns and staying true to what he wanted. I remember him telling me, 'I'm taking a break after this.' I had a feeling in the back of my mind: 'You ain't taking that long a break, because you're a workaholic.' He keeps wanting to make his product, make money, make a living, get his work out there, have a body of work. I don't think that I will ever be that driven. I'm not as passionate about directing. I'm much more of a writer. That is one thing Spike always said: 'You've got to write, write, write.' And that is the only way you can create and control your own work."

Spike acknowledges a transformation took place during the making of *Malcolm X*. But for him it was just part of growing up: "I changed over the period, but not because of how hard it was made to make the film. It had nothing to do with the hardships of the film. It was just the whole experience of being involved in the film and seeing Denzel's performance and seeing how the film affected people. Well, we went back to do a movie right away, but what I did say was that I thought that I was going to do a smaller film, not as big as *Malcolm X*. I still like doing epics. And two more that I want to make will hopefully get done: Jackie Robinson[*] and the Joe Louis/Max Schmeling project."[†]

[*]Spike had begun to pen a biopic on the first black to play in modern major league baseball, Jackie Robinson, of whom Spike says, "That is another case of someone who held the moral high ground. He was told by the owner of the Brooklyn Dodgers, Branch Rickey, to turn the other cheek, bite his lip. Abuse was heaped on him until eventually he took his shackles and he beat just about everybody else. That was stuff that killed him. Jackie was a tense competitive fighter and to hold back killed him."
[†]See Chapter 15.

9 Crooklyn

"Lady T," by Spike Lee:

It all began on September 24, 1992. Malcolm X *was a life-changing experience in more ways than one. Every year the Black Congressional Caucus takes place in Washington, DC, and is the highlight of the African-American social calendar. I was there to promote* Malcolm X; *we screened the trailer to the film. It went over like gangbusters. I was sitting with my date for the evening and I excused myself to go to the men's room. On my way, I saw a vision! The most beautiful woman I had ever laid eyes upon in all my life. She was a natural redhead with red freckles all over her gorgeous face, and her complexion was what my great-aunt sister would call "mariny" or what in today's lingo is called light-skinned. What threw me off was her dress. It was black and white, and at first I thought that she was one of the ladies serving meals. In fact, I asked her if she was working. To tell the truth, it wouldn't have made any difference to me. She said, "No." I tried to sputter out a couple of words and I went to urinate. That was it. I came back and tried to find this dream without alarming my date. I was in a tough jam. The ballroom was packed with black folks and she was not to be seen. I cursed my bad luck to the high heavens and sat glumly for the remainder of the evening.*

The evening over, heading for the exit, I was descending the escalator into the lobby when, lo and behold, the future love of my life was coming up the escalator. We smiled at each other as we passed, me going down, her going up. I was too busy at the time to think about any symbolism. I just had to talk to her. Reaching the bottom I quickly explained to my date that I had forgotten something and would be back faster than Jackie Robinson. I quickly ran up the escalator, knocking people over in the process. I did say, "Excuse me"; my mom gave me manners. I finally reached the top and didn't see her right away. I ran around in confusion. Then I saw "my waitress" from behind and I wasn't complaining. As she later told me, I rushed right up to her for a patriotic interrogation, to ask her name, then if she had a boyfriend—or, even worse, was she married? When she answered "No" to all three, I did a jig. I did a jig, because I had an opening, a chance with someone whom I had been waiting for for a while. I was dating, but this was different. I asked her for her number and she gave it to me. In that very short exchange, she told me that she was a lawyer. I did another jig—not only was this the finest, sexiest woman I had the honour of meeting and the privilege to address, she was intelligent too and went to the University of Virginia law school; no dummies get in there, especially if you're black. I said I would call her in the morning. I had to race back down the escalator before I got left. I would call "my vision" in the morning. Looking back on that eventful night, I hit the jackpot. The next morning she had a dozen roses waiting for her at work. A year later, October 2, 1993, Stevie Wonder sang "Ribbon in the Sky" at our wedding.

The lady I met that night was Tonya Linette Lewis. Now we have two children—Satchel, a girl, aged nine, and Jackson, a boy, aged seven. What's funny is that Satchel looks exactly like Tonya and Jackson looks exactly like me. How did that happen? We came together and have both of us produced our best work—our children. They are so smart, loving, caring and fun, it's scary sometimes. And I know it's a cliché as old as Moses, but time flies. Both Tonya and I know the glorious moment when both were conceived, Satchel in Boston (as much shit as I talk about Boston) and Jackson in Martha's Vineyard. Half of the stuff they say just amazes me: where and how did their (young) brains get the knowledge and wisdom to talk like they do? Again I must honor Tonya. She has been it, she got the job done. Daddy was off making movies or commercials or going to Knicks games. I'm ashamed to say on both pregnancies I left Tonya in the hospital with a newborn baby to go to a stupid-ass Knicks game. I'm not proud of it, but I did do that. And what's sad is I can't ever get that back. Before I look up they'll be in high school, then college. The regret I do have is that we didn't have any more. I don't blame Tonya a bit. She had all she could handle with me not being there. I'm blessed though; I woke up in time. I used to put cinema, even the Knicks (but play-offs only), in front of Tonya, Satchel and Jackson. Those days are long gone. Nothing is more important than them. I guess it takes some people time to wise up, and, let's face it, I was s-s-s-slow in that regard. (As we used to say growing up in Brooklyn, "I wuz re-tarted.")

Satchel and Jackson both have tons of creativity. She is going to be an actress, dancer or singer. And Jackson will direct, like his daddy. Please don't think all that creative DNA comes from me; their mother is a lawyer, novelist, TV producer and all round superwoman. Together we co-authored a children's book, Please, Baby, Please, Baby, Baby, Baby, Please, *and she has co-authored a novel,* Gotham Diaries, *with Crystal McCrary Anthony. This novel has blown up, been a great success, selling books like hot cakes and is great material for a TV series or movie.*

After my mother died of cancer at the age of forty-two, our family came apart at the seams and hasn't ever recovered. It still bothers me. Already, I've lived on this earth longer than she did. I truly believed she sacrificed everything for her five children, me, Chris, David, Joie and Cinque. If she lived, I would not be a filmmaker. That's the only way I've been able to understand, to make sense of our mother being taken away from us so young. Our mother went so quick. One day she didn't feel well and went to see her doctor. In less than two weeks I was back in New York from Morehouse College, burying my mother.

After she died, my mother would visit me in my dreams. She's stopped coming by; maybe she feels I've done OK and don't need it anymore. I do miss her.

My mother would write me every week during my first two years at Morehouse, before she got sick. I have a stack of her letters stashed away. Once I tried to read them, but it was too painful. However, one day soon I will dig these treasures out and read them to Tonya, Satchel and Jackson. They've only seen pictures of my mother, mostly at her mother's house. My grandmother, the kids' great-grandmother, Mrs. Zimmie Retha Shelton, who is ninety-eight years young, still resides in Atlanta, Georgia. She and her husband, Mr. Richard Jackson Shelton, had one child, Jacquelyn Susan Shelton. I was the first grandchild and was probably the favorite of this set of grandparents. My grandfather died when I was in high school. He worked at the post office for over fifty years. Papa, as we called him, went to Morehouse College like my father, Bill Lee, and myself. My grandmother "Mama" went to Spelman College like my mother also. Both schools are the top historical black schools, and they both met there and got married.

So that brings us to Crooklyn, *a semi-autobiographical tale of the Lee family. . . .*

As Spike's fame grew, Cinque Lee found that his own identity was crushed as a result. He even started a rock group called Spike Lee's Brother's Band, in sorry recognition that his own identity had been taken temporarily from him. Cinque says, "For some of my friends, it would make a difference. Out of the blue you would get a call that says, 'Hey, man, I got a script for your brother, can you get it to him?' I'd tell them, 'No, you would have more of a chance if you went through the regular channels.' I used to say, 'Spike thinks I'm a fuck-up,' just to get out of it. Sometimes it's a real pain in the ass being Spike's brother. The other day I went into the local Chinese restaurant and the guy behind the counter says, 'Yo! Spike Lee's brother.' I said, 'Come on, you know my name, I've been coming here for years.' Or trying to raise finance for my own films, I would be told, 'Why don't you go ask your brother?' I've got no name anymore."

The Lee family's financial struggles while Spike was growing up had a lasting impact on him: "It made me realize that the whole thing that any artist is going to face is the conflict between art and commerce. Now, would I let my family starve? No. But there are still some things that I'm not going to do. That's the balance that you have to find. My father, he made a choice." For all Spike's talk of uplifting the race and the need to be more socially aware within the black community, there is one thing that he does not hide and is unapologetic about, and that is the need to make green and be a good businessman. His commercial activities, driven by his films, looked at taking advantage of secondary markets. This is the man Lisa Jones described as having "no intention of being a poor artist."

Spike had stepped up his output as a director of commercials: spots for button-fly Levi's, a Diet Coke campaign. AT&T and ESPN had been added to his list of clients, and he appeared in a Pizza Hut ad in Japan. In the year before Stevie Wonder sang at his wedding, Spike directed the promo for Wonder's "Make Sure You're Sure," and his friendship with Prince also saw him make "Money Doesn't Matter Tonight." Perhaps the best music videos that Spike has done were completed after *Malcolm X* wrapped: Arrested Development's "Revolution" and Naughty by Nature's "Hip-Hop-Hooray." In his attempt to spread the 40 Acres mission, Spike also began working with Barry Brown on a television adaptation of *Slim's Table*, which they felt was close to being picked up by Columbia. Spike says, "Television is a great medium. Most of the stuff on it isn't that great, but we wanted to get on it back then. *Slim's Table* was something that I worked on with Brandon Tartikoff. But I've found television is just like film—when it comes down to it, you still have to deal with the gatekeepers, those one or two individuals who say we are making it or not making it."

Spike also started to executive produce other people's films. He used his relationship with Sam Kitt at Universal Studios, who would finance *Crooklyn*, in order to get things off the ground: "I wanted to do it for a long time. It's just a matter of me coming across some property that I like, filmmakers I like, and also whether studios are receptive to it. The aim was to get stuff made. There are a lot of good things to get made, I can't direct them all . . . and it's very important, because it's a chance to develop young talent, give young writers and directors a shot, whoever has a good script." The appeal of being an executive producer is described succinctly by Earl Smith: "In the beginning I think that Spike was trying to help people out, but then Spike worked out that he could make money being an 'executive producer' when he's not directing."

Spike had followed up on the now defunct 40 Acres Institute by lecturing at universities around the country. In 1991 he took a job teaching at Harvard. The appointment made national news, as the university's Henry Louis "Skip" Gates Jr.* announced, "Spike Lee is my hero." The academic describes Spike's position in American society: "He's a pop-cultural figure and I think that, in a way, he's the Jackie Robinson of the film community. He is the pioneer. Spike went in and shook up an industry that pays lip service to black people—he didn't wait for a handout. He busted his buns, made the money by hook and crook. Successful financially and successful critically. And he has been able to make the films that he's wanted to and be productive in making the films he wants to make. He seems a man who is free, a man who controls, as much as any of us can, his own destiny. That is something that all of us can admire and aspire to, particularly in the black community. I've been with Spike; people stop him in the street, they shake his hand, glad to know him, admire him." Other voices believed that Spike should have been teaching at one of his alumni schools. Spike says, "Morehouse, NYU, they never asked me to teach. It was Harvard who asked me, so I accepted."

Spike jumped at the opportunity to follow in his mother's footsteps. Gates says, "I met Spike when I did an interview with him for *Transition* magazine. Soon after that he came to Duke University to give a lecture, and Spike was very generous with his time and answered a lot of questions from the students. Then I interviewed him right after I moved from Duke to Harvard, and during the interview I asked him why he had never taught. He said that he had never been asked. I excused myself from the room and called my dean at Harvard to ask him if I was in a position to make Spike an offer. I was surprised that Spike accepted, and it made me feel like a million dollars. That was how Spike became the first person I hired in my capacity as chair of the Department of Afro-American Studies at Harvard. I explained, like I would with any new professor, that you need to have a syllabus, this is what the requirements are, you have to call the bookstore and

---

*Gates's interest in popular culture had been evident when he testified on behalf of Luther Campbell and Two Live Crew at an obscenity trial that followed the arrest of the group during a live show in 1990. Gates asserted that the music was part of an oral tradition, stretching back to the *griots* in Africa, in which society was criticized. Campbell was later acquitted.

fill out a form for books he wanted students to read. Nuts-and-bolts stuff. In a place like Harvard you don't tell teachers what to teach. I wanted him to teach something on filmmaking and something on black film, and that's what he did. His courses were enormously popular—the first day, I think two thousand people came to his class. If that's not a sign of love I don't know what is. He used to fly up from New York every Friday during the semester, which he paid for himself; he wanted to. He never missed a class. I think he saw it as part of his mission."

On Amsterdam Avenue, New York, between 156th and 157th Streets, there used to be an establishment known locally as Manny's Bar. It closed in late 2003, after years of neglect and with an increasingly aging and dwindling clientele; it is the type of bar one imagines that Shaft would have frequented in his seventies pomp. Back in the day, Duke Ellington would occasionally come in and entertain those Harlemites banned from the white bars downtown. But the roof had since collapsed, the rear entertainment room was closed off, and only a small bar was running on the day before Manny's finally locked its doors to the world for the last time. The bar smelled like it had forgotten the last time it had met cleaning detergents, and the regulars at the bar lamented into their whisky colas the destruction that drugs had wrought on the black community in Harlem. To a man, they reminisced about the good old days.

Lisa Jones speaks with a glow about the apparent golden era that was left behind once the likes of Dr. Dre took control of the rap scene: "Everyone at 40 Acres took away an almost nationalistic viewpoint out of the seventies, one that mellowed over time. It was a distinct time, with idealism based on race and exclusive community. That had to be dismantled: in this country, in this world, blacks had to do that in order to evolve. But certainly the advent of crack really upset— dismantled—any romantic notions of the black community, that we were all noble because we had been oppressed, so we would all make the right choices." The sense of disillusionment over the arrested progress of African-Americans is something that has weighed on Spike too: "Something that people know for sure, but rarely talk about, is the somewhat negative effects of integration. It really hurt black businesses and black institutions of higher learning. So you really can't say across the board that integration was a 100 percent positive thing for black people." The same might be said of small family-run businesses, increasingly being squeezed out by corporations better geared to absorb high rents and negotiate discounts to undercut competitors. But Spike's statement is a lament for the failure of the black population to "uplift the race" by supporting black business even if the fare on offer is cheaper and/or of better quality elsewhere. A sense of brotherhood was being lost. The individualism of songs such as Madonna's "Material Girl" seemed to speak more directly to American youth.

Crooklyn, set in the seventies, would allow Spike to show the idealized view that Lisa Jones reveals was prevalent at 40 Acres, and also to show, albeit in a nondidactic manner, his political outlook and vision of a more progressive black community ideal, brimful of hope. In its own way, *Crooklyn* is just as politically vibrant as Spike's earlier films, but related with a lighthearted touch. The film would signal a change in pace for a man now firmly established as an American filmmaker, no longer needing to prove his cinematic credentials with each film. It would also allow the director to reconnect with the Lee family unit— on screen, at least. *Crooklyn* tells the story of nine-year-old Troy, the only girl out of five siblings. Her father, Woody Carmichael, is a musician who's losing gigs because he refuses to play electric instruments. His lack of work impacts on the family finances, and Troy's mother, struggling to keep the family together, is forced back to work. But, though life may be hard, it is still full of joy, the children playing street games and living happily. When Troy is sent south for the summer to her aunt's house, her mother is unexpectedly taken ill and dies prematurely. The parallels with Lee's own life are clear for all to see.

The genesis of *Crooklyn* lies in Joie Lee's decision to write a script set in the seventies. Joie remembers, "The script didn't start out as a piece on our family. I was going through stuff and I was talking to Cinque about it. Cinque was saying, 'Just write it down. . . .' And that is how things germinate—Cinque and I were sharing ideas. Cinque was my muse, to be honest." But the youngest children of Bill and Jacquelyn Lee didn't tell anybody that they were writing a movie together. Cinque and Joie both harbored ambitions to be filmmakers independent of their eldest brother. "*Hot Peaches and Butter*," says Cinque. "That's what it was originally going to be called. It was Joie's idea. We drew on a lot of stuff that happened to us as kids. I guess that it was good to kind of get that out of the system—that time in our life, in the family. It was something that my sister was going to direct and I was going to produce. But we wanted to get Spike's criticism on it." Thus Cinque and Joie (so alike that Jim Jarmusch has them playing twins in one of his *Coffee and Cigarettes* segments) gave the script to their brother. Joie says, "We had thirty pages, and Cinque said that Spike told him, 'Hey, this is really good.' Spike never said anything to me. I never got any feedback. I don't know why. Maybe it was easier to tell Cinque that he really liked it, or maybe because of that he felt he'd already said it." Internally, Spike was aglow: "I was really proud," he says now, "that Cinque and Joie had come together to write this."

Nevertheless, as his failure to reveal his feelings to Joie demonstrates, Spike still found it difficult to express his emotions. Even so, James Lipton was able to bring a tear to Spike's eye on *Inside the Actors Studio* when the director talked about the struggle to get the money to finish *Malcolm X*. Spike had begun revealing sides to his character that had hitherto been hidden from public consumption. He had spoken about his family in the media and, as the Bill Lee drug arrest showed, the media sometimes removed from him the choice of whether to air the family laundry in public. Spike claims that his putting more of the spotlight on his family by making *Crooklyn* sat well with all of his brothers. Joie does not concur: "Chris wasn't happy about it. I don't think he thought it was cool at all. David—I actually wish that he had been involved. And I didn't think about David's or Chris's involvement. Chris doesn't write, but David, I feel bad about that, because after the film, he was saying, 'Do you remember this?' and things that I had forgotten. I think Chris felt exposed. And if he reads this book, I think he might feel exposed by my saying that. I don't know. Not everybody wants to be talked about. One of my uncles wasn't pleased at all. He thought that we slandered him and his wife—that was the only backlash."

David saw the *Crooklyn* script for the first time when he was asked to fill his usual role as stills photographer on the shoot. As he sat down to read, his usual sense of anticipation was muzzled by trepidation. His voice betraying his emotional attachment to the script, he says, "The toughest part of the process was reading the script, because to whatever degree, it draws from our own experiences. It was kind of reliving painful memories. That's what got me upset. It made me cry." But with a script so close to home, and Spike so proud of his family history, David suggests that Spike had no choice but to delve into his family history once he had seen the handiwork of his youngest siblings: "Only Spike could do it. I can't imagine he would have let them shop it some place else. In that sense, he wanted to exert his own control, and he did his own treatment of it. He added certain characters and changed some things." Spike insists, "I wouldn't say that I was the only director who could do this project." But he had wished to make a small film after *X*, and this script had landed in his lap.

One of the first things that Spike did, says Cinque, was to tone down the script: "The story we wrote was an R-rated version of the film that Spike made. A lot of the cursing got taken out, and the original had more of a sexual tone. Especially from the perspective of my sister—there was a lot about her character experimenting with sex. She then became younger within the film, after Spike came to the project. As a result a lot of stuff had to be cut to make it a PG-13 film. But for me, what really made the film unique was that it was told from this young black girl's viewpoint. I didn't want to change that at all." Joie watched as her film was stripped of all elements of her "deviant" behavior and became increasingly concerned with the direction that Spike was taking on the project: so much so that she decided to challenge Spike's authority. "After Cinque and I showed it to Spike, we made a contract and sold the film to him. The hardest part for me was letting it go, and I had second thoughts and I called Spike up. I said, 'You know what, Spike? I don't want you to direct it. I want to direct it.' He said, 'Too bad, go write another script, you've already sold this one.'"

The eldest brother was asserting his authority, backed by a signed legal document: it was a fait accompli. Spike had control of his family story, and it would be told in the way that he wanted it to be told. Yet the finished film would exhibit a much more democratic spirit within the "Lee" family than was being shown in its making, as many of Spike's demands are quashed by laws laid down by his mother, an authority that Spike would bow down to. A key battleground is over what to watch on television. Spike says of those scenarios, "We used to have battles because we had somewhat of a democratic system in the house as far as the TV was concerned. It would go by votes. The Knicks always played away on Friday nights and that was the same night as *The Partridge Family* and *The Brady Bunch*. David and Cinque were always the swing votes, so you'd try to make a deal with them to get their vote. Most of the time I got outvoted, so we had to watch *The Brady Bunch*." But as far as the making of *Crooklyn* was concerned, Spike, backed by his body of work and by Universal Studios, had a casting vote that counted for more than the rest of his siblings put together.

Crooklyn saw the crumbling of the fabled team that Spike had set up over his first six films. Two heavyweights left before the start of filming. First Ernest Dickerson announced his departure after seeing Spike go over him on *Malcolm X*: "Jon Kilik asked me to do *Crooklyn*; Spike didn't ask me. I remember that I read the script and I didn't think that I could do much with it. And I was looking for another project to direct. I think a part of it was being told that I had to do it for less money . . . but I think the main thing was the fact that it seemed Spike and I weren't talking to each other anymore." The resentment over money would ensure that Spike would struggle to keep actors and crew on board once they had decided they had done their time working for him for scale. Changing actors on every movie is a trick that Woody Allen—another director who pays scale—learned a long time ago. It is difficult for actors to continually amass kudos while working for the same "name" director.

Also departing the 40 Acres fold was Randy Fletcher: "I was going to start work on *Crooklyn* on the Monday, then Ernest got a big film, *Surviving the Game*. I wanted to go DGA and Spike wasn't going DGA at the time. I also knew that Ernest needed me more than Spike." After *Crooklyn* was made, Barry Brown then announced that he was quitting editing to concentrate on his directing career, as he was growing increasingly concerned that he was being looked upon as "the new Dede Allen." (The famed New York–based editor of *Little Big Man* and *Serpico* had recently relocated to L.A.)

Spike, forever looking to promote from within, surprised many in his choice of replacements. Mike Ellis stepped up to take over the reins as first AD; he was typical of the caliber of production assistants whom Spike would push through the ranks. Ellis says, "Spike wanted me to do the movie. The rest of them motherfuckers didn't. Kilik and Preston Holmes were saying, 'He's just a production assistant, a second AD at most.' Spike simply told them, 'Mike is doing the movie.'" But not all of the new starts worked out, and Spike and his new director of photography, Arthur Jaffa, were soon at loggerheads. "Mr. Jaffa had a hard road to follow," says Mike Ellis. "I love A.J. and I'm sure it was hard for him. But, then again, how many DPs had Spike worked with before? It would have been hard for *anyone*." Spike agrees: "It wasn't a good experience and I'm not going to say that it was all his fault either. It might have something to do with the fact that it was the first time that I shot something without Ernest. Saying that, we didn't click, we didn't communicate, it wasn't a good experience, and he would probably say the same thing."

In all, many of the certainties in Spike's world were falling apart just as he was getting to know Tonya Linette Lewis. Ruth Carter observed that Spike didn't seem to approach *Crooklyn* with the same gusto that he had attacked other films: "I noticed a change, in that he backed off and let the film sort of evolve. The passion wasn't necessarily as strong as it was for everything else. At our first meeting Joie and Cinque were there, and I felt that there were other people that I wanted to please on this film besides Spike. Then I found out through a friend in the movie business that Spike was getting married. My friend said, 'I went to reserve the Puck Building for my reception and missed out because Tonya got it first.' I said, 'Get out of here, Spike isn't getting married!' So I walked up to Spike on the set of *Crooklyn* and I said, 'Tell me it's not true.' He said something like, 'Don't talk about that now.' A little way down the road, weeks later, he gives me the invitation as he hands invitations out to other people."

Despite it being obvious that the film was based on the Lee family, the word on set was that *Crooklyn* was entirely fictional—so says Delroy Lindo, who starred as Woody Carmichael: "Spike made it clear fairly early on in the process that my character was not based on his father. I was thrown into a little bit of a situation because, reading the script, it was clear that this was Spike's family. But the mantra being used over and over again was 'This is not our family.' And I had to force myself to remind myself of that."

The official 40 Acres line is that this was done for legal reasons, and Spike had to change some of the real-name characters whom Joie and Cinque had used in the script. Delroy feels that this line was laid down to the actors because "it was an issue of Spike not being ready psy-

Spike and the *Crooklyn* family. (© 1993 David Lee)

chologically and emotionally to have his family history delved into as nakedly as perhaps would have been the case if he or any of the other film-makers had said, 'This is about our family.'"

Crooklyn offers a romanticized notion of the seventies: this is made clear from its opening segment, which shows children playing street games and also mirrors the opening of *Mo' Better Blues* as a mother exhorts her child to practice: "It was a way to really get the audience into the time period," says Spike. "Those games are specifically urban New York City games. A lot of them are lost forever too because children don't play like that anymore; they are too busy playing video games and being like zombies in front of their TV sets. Those games took imagination; kids used to go out on the streets and play themselves. They didn't need parental guidance to be out there."

Spike's insight into his background was a world away from the b-boy persona of Mars Blackmon: "I've never run around trying to hide from my middle-class educated background, I've never tried to dumb down and say, 'I'm from the streets, the ghetto.' Why would I want to do that? I'm never going to devalue education, the educated background that I've come from or being educated myself. It's not a negative." *Crooklyn* ends shortly after the mother's death and before the father has moved into another relationship. There is no allusion to the father having a drug problem, although this is explained away by all three Lee authors as due to the fact that "we didn't know that our father had a drug problem at the time." Indeed, *Crooklyn* has a feel-good factor about it, one that could appeal to an audience often alienated by Spike Lee. Spike took on his customary acting role, playing a neighborhood glue sniffer: "Of course there were harder drugs at the time," he recalls, "but we never saw evidence of that. So the people we had to look out for were the glue sniffers."

Some aspects of the Spike life story emerge in *Crooklyn* under different guises: "I think it was May 8, 1970. Game seven of the NBA finals between the New York Knicks and the L.A. Lakers. If the Knicks won, it would be their first championship ever. My father's lawyer, Peter Eichelberry, said that if there was a game seven, he would give me a seat. It happened to be the night that my father was giving a concert at Cami Hall. It's a small hall right across the street from Carnegie Hall. My mother said, 'You have to make a choice.' So I said, 'Well, I can always see another concert, but there is only going to be one game like this.' And I'm *still* glad that I went to see that game."

The movie reaffirms that Spike's loyalties lie firmly with his mother; but it is a reaction to his father's behavior that has truly shaped Spike's outlook as an artist. He says, "My mother was very educated. She

Spike in character as *Crooklyn*'s friendly neighborhood glue sniffer. (© 1993 David Lee)

taught English literature and also art. The film really mirrored the relationship of my mother and father, because with my father, whatever we wanted to do, it was fine with him. 'Daddy, can we jump out of the window?' 'OK, but don't hurt yourself!' Because of how my father was, my mother was put in the tough spot of being the disciplinarian all the time. When you have this imbalance, naturally the children are going to think that Mommy is going to be the bad guy and Daddy the good guy, because Daddy lets us do everything we want to do. Also my father, he never really cared about money—he always thought that it would fall out of the sky. But, of course, you have the luxury of thinking like that if you have a partner, a wife, who keeps things going. So when he was at home composing, my mother had to go back to teaching."

After *Crooklyn* wrapped, Spike and Tonya Lewis wed. The romance had taken fourteen months from first date to the exchange of rings. Tonya can happily corroborate the bulk of Spike's account of their first fortuitous meeting: "I remember he was wearing a white tuxedo. And I remember thinking his personality was so different from his public persona. And when he asked me why I didn't have a boyfriend, and I told him I hadn't met the right guy yet, he literally did a jig, a James Brown spin, he was so up and alive.

"That was a Saturday night. The next morning he called me, asked how old I was. I said, 'I'm twenty-six,' and he said, 'Oh.' I asked, 'Why? How old are you?' He said, 'Well, I'm thirty-five and I'm ready to get married.' I was like, 'OK, whatever . . .' I have to say, at that time I was dating a few other people, I wasn't thinking about getting married, and within the first week of our meeting and talking Spike mentioned several times the word 'marriage'—to the point where I had to say to him that he needed to stop. . . . I was kind of focused on my own life, and having someone like that come on so strongly, sending flowers to my office, calling me up—finally I told him, 'You can't destroy my life like this.' Also I didn't really know where he was coming from. Was this a game? Was this his line? Was this how he rolled with women? I wasn't interested in being the flavor of the moment. But I was so young, and he would invite me to come to the city and he would pay for me. The first date we had we went to Madonna's book party; she had the *Sex* book coming out. It was a Thursday night. I asked him, 'How am I going to come to New York for a party on Thursday night when I have to be at work on Friday morning?' Spike said, 'Don't worry about it, you can take the shuttle after work and then you can take the first shuttle out in the morning.' Which is what I ended up doing. And it's funny because I got to work and I was one of the first people at the office the next morning, and people had seen me on the news, walking into the book party with Spike. One of my partners said to me, 'Oh, I certainly didn't expect to see you this morning. . . .' But Spike was so ready to be in a committed relationship when we had known each other for about a week. I was like, 'Come on, let's just have a good time and get to know each other first.' We did that up until Christmas time, when I agreed to go away with him to Antigua. And I would say that it was really only seven or eight months before we got married that we were really in a committed relationship."

Ruth Carter recalls, "At the reception for the wedding I remember Spike being really happy. I was watching him on the steps before they were going to do the introduction of the wedding party. I thought, 'This is so Spike.' You're not supposed to be seen before the intro; that's the etiquette of the whole damn thing. Spike is standing on the steps looking down at everybody milling around, knowing that he's not supposed to be there. I just looked at Spike thinking, He's not about the rules."

Having addressed his difficult family history for the purposes of *Crooklyn*, Spike was now marrying and embarking on a family life of his own. His wedding signaled a new Spike Lee. Art Sims spoke for many who had known Spike over a long period when he said, "Spike always wanted to get married and have children. I think he has become more of a dad. We don't talk as much as we used to." It is a change that Mike Ellis, who remains his AD, sees as ongoing: "Everybody changes. I know that I'm different because of my children. That and more common sense . . . Spike can get what he wants out of everybody, basically, and part of that is communication. A lot of this was publicity: he was the Angry Black Man in America for years; that was his persona. Now anybody who still believes that is looking at old news; it just isn't accurate at all. But he's still upfront and confrontational and direct — oh, he's direct as fuck. And that's good."

On seeing the final product that was *Crooklyn*, Joie was pleased with the result, although there is one thing she would definitely have changed had she been directing: "I didn't like the anamorphic sequence. I mean, aesthetically, it's not something that I would have done if I had made the film." For the twenty-minute sequence when Troy visits her aunt in Alabama, Spike shot with an anamorphic lens that has the effect of squeezing and extending the length of the figures and faces in the frame once the film is projected through a non-widescreen lens. The sequence had the audience thinking that the film was out of focus, and cinemas showing *Crooklyn* were forced to put up signs stating that this elongated look was what the director intended. Spike says of his choice, "I still think that it works, but I can understand people not liking it. I really wanted to show how Troy was in a different world. It was almost like *Alice in Wonderland*."

Crooklyn was released on May 13, 1994, and took in almost $14 million at the domestic box office, just breaking even against the $14-million budget. It was a worrying sign for Spike, especially as international sales were very slow. Janet Maslin's review in the *New York Times* highlighted the surprise of the audience: "From some filmmakers, tender feelings are de rigueur; from others, they're cloying or easy. From Mr. Lee, they're nothing if not a surprise. Messy as the semiautobiographical *Crooklyn* often is, it succeeds in becoming a touching and generous family portrait, a film that exposes welcome new aspects of this director's talent. The phrase 'kinder, gentler Spike Lee' may not sit well with those who admire the filmmaker's harder edges, but it does come to mind."

One area where the film excelled was the soundtrack, of which Spike is proud: "It was the best-selling soundtrack of any of our movies. We put out two CDs and jam-packed them with the great music from the seventies. I never stopped listening to the music and it was good to put it in — it was just a matter of trying to find out the cost of the songs and whether we could afford them. That is how we made the final choice." Spike asked Q-Tip (who had first entered the main-stream working with De La Soul and then with A Tribe Called Quest) to help him: "He asked me to get a bunch of MCs from Brooklyn and he wanted me to kind of produce the record," says Q-Tip. The album would be the apex of the fledgling 40 Acres and a Mule Musicworks label.

Meantime, the first film to carry a Spike Lee executive producer credit, *Drop Squad*, was a political satire about an underground mili-tant group who kidnap African-Americans whom they consider to have sold out on their race. The slow pace of the Johnson brothers' movie did not sit well with the American public, and the film barely hit the radar on its release in late 1994.

As Spike married, 40 Acres was about to witness its biggest divorce. Monty Ross says, "By now the whole thing felt different. The people are like kids who have grown up: they know about the industry, they have made movies and they're now celebrities. Now you start to get into discussions on what size trailer people get. They need different color M&Ms. People start wanting a bigger piece of the pie. Holly-wood is wooing black filmmakers and black production staff and things of that nature. People are getting used to the good life now. This makes me start to think about my own career, and I'm thinking that I'd like to direct a movie. I imagine in my head that Spike would pro-duce my first film. And that dream never happened. At that point I had a diminished return. I thought I needed to do something. Also, I was burned out. We had so much stuff going on and people began to rely on me a whole lot. I wasn't sleeping, I had an ear infection and my stress level was high. My doctor said, 'If you keep going you are going to pop it both ends.' The relations with Spike were all work-related, trying to keep 40 Acres organized a certain way and trying to intro-duce people into the company. The relaxing time to just drink a beer, that was not happening. In hindsight, I think without those levels of intimacy you don't check in with people, and the thing just got demor-alized after that. I reached a point on some occasion when Spike said, 'I'll see you Monday,' and I said, 'I don't know.' As soon as I said that, he looked at me funny. And then I looked at him. And I just kind of walked away. . . ."

The departure of Monty Ross left the way clear for Jon Kilik to affirm his position as "Spike Lee's producer." To many in the New York film community this came as no surprise, and today Kilik and Lee are seen as peas from the same pod: not only are they similar in stature, they also share similar characteristics, both physical and mental. Unlike Ross, who was trying to juggle the many balls in the 40 Acres circus, Kilik concentrates on producing. From the get-go he kept his relationship with Spike on a strictly freelance basis. Thus, having proved his worth to Spike on *Do the Right Thing*, *Mo' Better Blues* and *Jungle Fever*, Kilik felt comfortable enough to take on work with other directors and build up his own rather impressive résumé. One of the first projects on which he worked after *Jungle Fever* was *A Bronx Tale*, the directorial début of Robert De Niro. During pre-production, De Niro invited Kilik to a reading of a script that Martin Scorsese was thinking about directing, earmarked to be De Niro's eighth collaboration with the director. This reading was to stick in Kilik's memory: "The script was *Clockers*, so I knew a little bit about the Richard Price book from that. Scorsese and De Niro decided not to do it. But the film was at Universal, where Spike and I had made *Do the Right Thing*."

Scorsese had put a lot of effort into *Clockers* and didn't want to let go completely of the project, so he spoke to Universal about the possibility of remaining on the film in an executive producer capacity. Universal, which had invested much in the project, believing Scorsese and De Niro were on board, was happy to accept the consolation prize of Scorsese working in a producing capacity once the studio realized that he had no intention of helming the movie. Scorsese then got on the phone to Spike Lee. Spike was all ears: "Martin Scorsese said that he had been working on *Clockers* with Richard Price but decided that he wanted to do *Casino* instead. He said that he wanted me to direct it and for him to produce. So I read the script and I read the novel, and I liked the novel very much."

Throughout Spike's film-school experiences, Scorsese had been a hero to him. They had first met at an NYU screening of *After Hours*, when Spike was in pre-production of *She's Gotta Have It*. Lee was

Clockers: Martin Scorsese and Spike confer. (© 1994 David Lee)

impressed with Scorsese's pleasant manner as he gave the young film-maker advice and encouragement. Once they had decided to try to collaborate the big question was whether the two directors would see eye to eye working on the same project. One person who was in no doubt was Michael Imperioli, who had appeared in *GoodFellas* shortly before taking a role in *Jungle Fever*. Comparing the two directors, he says, "I noticed more similarities than differences—in particular, in the way that they cast. The audition process was based around improvisation. Once filming starts, they both give an actor space to really let the character breathe and they're not dictatorial about what a character should do."

But once Scorsese threw himself into *Casino*, his contact with the *Clockers* film set was minimal. Kilik, who shared a producing credit with Scorsese and Lee, explains: "Spike and I had a couple of meetings with Scorsese. We had some conversations about what he and Richard Price and Robert De Niro had been thinking. It was not exactly how Spike saw it, but it gave us something to start with." Spike was indeed more taken by Price's novel than the screenplay: "The thing about the novel was that the chapters alternated between the stories of Rocco

Klein and Strike. There was one chapter on Rocco and then the next one would be about Strike. But the script by Richard Price was only about Rocco Klein. So I told Marty, 'I'm interested in doing the film, but I want to change the point of view to Strike's.'"

In Price's novel, Detective Rocco Klein is going through an existential crisis. He is having marital difficulties and struggling with fatherhood. Being one of the elder statesmen at work makes him feel out of place and he suspects that his presence is being tolerated until he retires. The only bright spot in his life is the sense of self-worth he gets from an actor who is following him around because he sees Klein as the perfect model for an upcoming movie role. None of these details are to be found in Spike's film: all that it tells us about Klein is that he smells a rat when a black man with no previous record confesses to a random murder. The story Spike tells in *Clockers* is Strike's.

A "clocker" is the lowest of the low in the hierarchy of drug dealers, out on the streets peddling narcotics to passersby: they can always be found, 24/7, doing their rounds like clockwork. Spike, having addressed the scourge of crack and its effects upon the user in *Jungle Fever*, uses *Clockers* to look at the working of the dealers. Strike is a clocker, one up from the bottom as he heads a team who work on a street corner of the Nelson Mandela Projects. He answers to Rodney, the next link in the chain. It is Rodney's fear of being arrested that Rocco Klein plays upon so as to put pressure on Strike: Klein is convinced that Strike, and not his clean-living brother, was behind the murder of a young black man at Ahab's fast-food place.

The switching of emphasis in the screenplay away from Klein did not surprise editor Sam Pollard: "Spike being the director that he is, he didn't just take Richard Price's script and shoot it. He reworked it. Spike turned it around and made it from the point of view of Strike, which really makes the film fascinating if you think about films from an anthropological perspective. This is a very powerful film about the African-American experience in the inner city and how young men struggle to negotiate life." As with *Malcolm X*, the starting point for Spike was an original book and an existing screenplay, on which he then set about putting his own stamp. Jon Kilik says, "Novels like *Clockers* and later *The 25th Hour*, although they weren't original screenplays, they became very much Spike Lee films—in both cases, I think, because the material was something that Spike knew about and could bring something to. He adapted it and molded it into something that was his own vision. His fingerprints are all over it, and it's very much a Spike Lee joint." Spike did not feel that he was adapting Price's novel; more that he was working on improving a script: "Honestly, I don't think that I've ever done an adaptation of a novel. Even *25th Hour*, that is David Benioff's script. What I did was a combination of three things: there is stuff that I liked in the book that wasn't in the script; there is stuff that I changed in the script; and there is stuff that I added."

The involvement of Price,[*] Scorsese and Universal meant that Spike would have to take a different approach from his usual one when writing this script, with decisions being made by committee rather than by Spike's force of will. "I had seen *The Wanderers* a long time ago," says Spike. "Richard Price is a great scriptwriter. He had script approval, as did Universal and Marty. Richard Price wasn't happy about the process or what I was doing. But, you know, I told him to go ahead and find someone else, because I didn't want to do a film based on Rocco Klein, a cop in a middle-aged crisis. That would have been just another cop story to me."

Spike wanted to make a commercial film that also, and perhaps more pertinently, reacted against the misdirection into which the director felt black film had stumbled. He says, "One of the main things we wanted to do with *Clockers*—and, really, it was naïve on my part—but there had been a rash of these hip-hop gangsta films, and so in my naïveté I thought that this film could end that genre altogether. It had started with *Menace II Society* and *Boyz N the Hood*, but now the stuff coming out was horrible. I said, 'Let's do something to *stop* this stuff.'" But Mekhi Phifer, the actor whom Spike discovered and cast in the role of Strike, reads a certain pomposity as well as a naïveté in Spike's claim: "That may be a personal request of his, but there is no way for anybody to command that sort of respect. Come on, man. That's like Francis Coppola saying, 'Now I've made *The Godfather*, there will be no more gangster movies.'"

In 1993 rapper Snoop Dogg was accused of possession of an unlicenced weapon and soon after of being an accessory to murder. The next year the rapper Tupac Shakur (2Pac)[†] was robbed and shot five

---

[*]Price was well versed in writing screenplays, having previously adapted his own novels *Bloodbrothers* and *The Wanderers*.

[†]By the time he was twenty, Shakur, the son of Black Panther Alice Faye Williams (Afeli Shakur), had been arrested a number of times. He turned to acting and rap, and in 1992, after he had appeared in Ernest Dickerson's *Juice*, he launched his solo rap career. The attempted murder in 1994 was rumored to be part of a feud with the Notorious B.I.G. that epitomized divisions in the East Coast and West Coast rap scenes. On September 8, Shakur was shot after watching a Mike Tyson fight and would die five days later. The Notorious B.I.G. outlived him by only six months before he himself was the victim of a drive-by murder. Both Biggie—as he was known—and Tupac would become rap heroes, immortalized after their deaths as emblems and martyrs of mid-1990s hip-hop.

times in midtown Manhattan. Tupac's death in 1994 set off a string of threats and violent encounters among rappers, producers and record promoters. Although much of the violence associated with gangsta rap was mere posturing for publicity, incidents such as Tupac's death demonstrated the gruesome results of glamorizing violence. Some years previously Tipper Gore, wife of then-Senator Al Gore, had founded the Parents Music Resource Center in disquiet about the apparent immorality of popular music, a move that would lead to an "explicit lyrics" label being put on certain albums, as well as congressional hearings on the hard-hitting lyrics and culture of gangsta rap. It was the violent dimension of the gangsta genre that Spike wanted to rail against: "I really wanted to talk about the violence. We wanted to deglamorize the violence that still exists today in hip-hop and this whole gangsta stuff. We wanted to show what these bullets and knives really did to your body. One of the things we did was to take photographs of real crime-scene murders of young black men who had been murdered by other young black men. Then we reenacted these crime-scene pictures for the opening credits, as we felt it would be disrespectful to the families of the dead to show the real bodies."

Spike was also starting to see the dangers of the *über*-masculinity of the rap scene that had once had Lisa Jones balking at the political leanings of 40 Acres. Spike's concern was coming to the fore, and this is made apparent in *Clockers* by the punctuating of the action (especially before a violent crime) by a gangsta rap video that is a long way from the consciousness-raising image rap enjoyed in its first flourish. Spike says, "There has always been a debate about rap: it can still be about positive images and that can sell records, but for the most part you have to be a gangsta rapper. That's where the real money is, and that is the stuff that record companies are going to push." In the opening sequence of the film, the young clockers are having an argument over the virtues of rap, and the positive message of Public Enemy — and, more important, the "realness" of erstwhile front man Chuck D — is put down because he "ain't shot nobody."

Spike's attack on the culture surrounding gangsta rap is countered by Mekhi Phifer: "Violence doesn't start with rap. Rap is a reflection of the violence in America; rap is not the violence in itself — people getting shot, killed and dealing drugs. Rap comments on violence like the Channel 11 news. Rap may use harsher language, because the sponsors on the Channel 11 news won't sign on if [anchor] Kaity Tong says, 'Fuck you, you piece of shit.' But it is a violent world that we live in, and rap reflects that. The same way that you can see Arnold Schwarzenegger kill a hundred people in a movie and still be elected governor of California—a rapper can do what he does. It is a source of entertainment and a reflection of what goes on in the world—at least, what people identify with." Spike answers: "How can attacking gangsta rap be naïve? Nelly's 'Tip Drill' had African-American women in an uproar. Bill Cosby has attacked gangsta rap. In the last Chris Rock HBO special, even he said that stuff is indefensible. The alibi that gangsta rap is just reflecting the world we live in is lame. In time, I feel, history will shed light on the damage these gangsta rappers have done to society."

The influence that media images might exert on impressionable youths was highlighted at this time by the accusation that there had been a number of copycat killings in France and America inspired by *Natural Born Killers*, Oliver Stone's film of a Quentin Tarantino script and, ironically, a satire on the media's fascination with and double standards over the issue of violence. Spike's view is that "people have to take responsibility for their actions. But for someone to say, 'I went out and killed somebody because I saw this movie' . . . I think it gets very dangerous to the artist, because then we wouldn't be able to do anything for fear of being sued down the line." Spike can appreciate the capacity of the audiovisual media to move people in a forceful manner —"It definitely has an effect on people: that is the power of film and television and music"—but ultimately it is the individual that must be held responsible for his own actions, whatever the social circumstances; and that, in essence, is the conundrum at the heart of *Clockers*.

Keeping to the theme of the pervasiveness of media imagery, Spike punctuates the film with an imaginative government poster campaign: "We thought about what would happen if the United States government started an ad campaign to curtail gun use. So we designed this poster of a lunch box containing an apple, a sandwich and a gun. The tag line was 'Let's stop packing.' We used that imagery throughout, even on the costumes. For example, the rapper Sticky Fingaz, who played Scientific, wears a big T-shirt with a gun on it, and at the end of the movie he gets shot with that shirt on."

Black New Yorkers are especially critical of poor political decisions on drugs partly because of what they perceive as the injustice of the so-called Rockefeller laws, first implemented by Governor Nelson Rockefeller in 1973, which hand down stiff mandatory sentences for sale or possession of comparatively small amounts of narcotics. Spike's view is: "It's crazy—whatever reason to implement the laws they had, they do not work today and they need to be overturned. It is one of the few things that I agree with Russell Simmons on." (The head of Rush Communications is accustomed to criticism from

Spike. When questioned on his relationship with the director, he sighed and asked, "So what has Spike been saying about me now?")

Another topical issue that would influence *Clockers* was AIDS. Magic Johnson's announcement on November 8, 1991, that he had tested positive for the HIV virus had led to his kick-starting a campaign to raise awareness of AIDS in America. The concern about the epidemic among the African-American community increased as news filtered through of the devastating effects the disease was having in Africa. Spike completed an ad campaign for Nelson Mandela aimed at responding to the growing problem of AIDS in America. Spike also adapted the *Clockers* script so that Errol, the enforcer in the book, carries the virus, having contracted AIDS through a blood transfusion. Spike says of the change, "Any time we can give a glimmer of attention to AIDS, a disease that is ravaging the world, we will do it. It is also important that far too often—especially among black people—we still equate AIDS entirely with homosexuality. People are getting AIDS from drugs intravenously also. And Errol was one of those guys."

Casting the picture, Spike put the call out to John Turturro: he wanted the 40 Acres stalwart to play Rocco Klein. Universal balked at the suggestion: Turturro had never "opened" a movie and was seen as way too much of a risk for a $25 million production. Spike turned to Scorsese for advice: having taken De Niro with him to work on *Casino*, the director suggested another of his own stalwarts, Harvey Keitel, then riding high from the critical acclaim for his turn as Holly Hunter's seducer in Jane Campion's *The Piano*. Universal was content to bring Keitel on board, a decision that still rankles with John Turturro: "It would have been a better movie if I played Rocco Klein and Michael Imperioli played my role." As it was, Turturro played Keitel's partner and Imperioli appeared in his third Spike Lee joint as hard-nosed detective Jo-Jo. The decision imposed on Spike was one the director would come to regret.

But a bigger problem at the outset was the casting of Strike, the young protagonist. Spike needed to find someone who could realistically portray a disaffected youth from the projects, and there was no obvious candidate. Robi Reed, who since *Malcolm X* had delegated many of the non-core casting choices to her assistant, Aisha Coley, was now persuaded by Coley to hold an open casting. (The tenacity of her protégée would not go unnoticed by Spike.) At this casting, there were lines around the block: progress was slow, applicants resigned to a three-hour wait before being given their chance. One of these was Mekhi Phifer, a kid who had grown up on the wrong side of the tracks in notorious projects in the Bronx. He

Clockers: Spike and Mekhi Phifer (Strike). (© 1994 David Lee)

remembers, "The open casting was on the radio and in the newspapers: 'Spike Lee: looking for people from the age of 17 to 23, mainly African-American.' I went down with a friend of mine and decided to give it a shot. About four weeks later, they called me back and I had to read with different cast members." In addition to Keitel and Turturro, Phifer was asked to read with Delroy Lindo, whom Spike had cast as the demonic Rodney; Isaiah Washington, who played Strike's older brother; and Regina Taylor.

Phifer believes, "I think what got me the role was me being a product of my environment. I couldn't have come out of Juilliard and got the *Clockers* role. I couldn't have lived in a posh neighbourhood and had money to go to performing-arts high schools. I was from the streets, fighting, and that energy that I brought is what got me the role." Unsurprisingly, given his relationship with Price and the way that Spike had changed the script, the director told the novice not to read the novel.

The 40 Acres head was starting to make future films part of his negotiating tool. When Barry Brown told Spike that he "did not want to edit anymore as he feared being known as an editor rather than director," Spike turned to Sam Pollard. Pollard turned him down as he himself wanted to produce more work, so Spike lured him to do *Clockers* by offering him a producing role on a documentary that he was planning on making about the 1963 Birmingham, Alabama, murders of four girls attending the Sixteenth Street Baptist Church.

The other tough choice that Spike had to make was a new cinematographer. From the experience with Arthur Jaffa, Spike knew that he "didn't want anybody who would question my decisions all the time. I wanted somebody to implement my ideas." Spike discussed with Mike Ellis the idea of using twenty-six-year-old Malik Sayeed. Sayeed was an electric on *Malcolm X* and had impressed Ellis with his speed; Ellis was equally impressed with Sayeed the DP when they worked together on music videos for "Hype" Williams. Spike decided to test out Sayeed: "I didn't know for sure, but I was willing to give him a shot." Working on commercials was a test bed that Spike turned to with all of his DPs. "I did a Kmart campaign with Roberto Prieto before *25th Hour*. Matty Libatique and I shot a TNT campaign and a music video before *She Hate Me*, so it's always good to have a trial period. They're looking at me too, so it's not all one way. We're both auditioning, I would say."

What sold Spike on Sayeed was the ambitious way that the first-time DP wanted to shoot the film. Sayeed suggested using Kodak's 5239, an Ektachrome high-speed color-reversal stock. The rarely used 5239 had been favored by news journalists in the days before videotape, but Steven Soderbergh had run into trouble when he used it to shoot a few scenes for his *The Underneath*. Sayeed now planned to use it for 75 percent of *Clockers*. *Bullitt* and *The French Connection* were his reference points. This decision was somewhat akin to a young tennis player deciding to compete in a grand-slam tournament with a wooden racket; but Spike, based on what he had seen of Sayeed at work, was happy to place his faith in the youngster.

Sam Pollard was asked to begin assembling a rough cut a couple of weeks into production. He remembers, "The stock was terrible in the beginning. The problem was that the first batch didn't have any edge-code numbers, which made it difficult for the negative masters to know where the shots were. Soderbergh had the same problem. So I had a long talk with his editor about how they used the material. Then the film had to go back to the lab. But it was scary to begin with." Kodak was so worried about what Sayeed was attempting that they sent a band of technical specialists to the set. Spike was taken by surprise: "They were talking about the negatives and how dangerous it was to shoot the film this way. They couldn't guarantee how the picture would turn out. But the technical guys at Kodak really helped us a lot."

The blame for the difficulties could not be laid on Sayeed: it was Lee who was ultimately calling the shots. The stock needed a lot of lighting and strongly picked up reds and purples. "I thought it was the right look for the film," Spike affirms. Pollard argues that Spike was trying to overcompensate for the loss of Dickerson and prove himself as a visionary filmmaker to be ranked with the likes of Oliver Stone: "This is the period when Spike started experimenting. When we started shooting stuff like the flashback scene in which Delroy is forced by Errol to make his first kill, Spike shot that 16mm; then we had to blow it up, make sure there was edge numbers on that. He started doing things with stock—now we had to be aware of the different approaches to the material, the different types of material he was using. We still have to adjust to it, because it is getting more complicated on every film, because now he uses video, film, 16mm, 35mm. . . . Part of it is the nature of how film has evolved, and it is something that Oliver Stone has been doing since *Natural Born Killers* and *JFK*."

Still, when things went wrong, Spike did not shy from laying blame on the novice: "I don't think that we had a lot of time to test, and it was hit-and-miss. The flashback where Errol holds a gun to Delroy's head, we were really unhappy with that. That was almost a reshoot because it was barely exposed, and we had spent a lot of money to light that scene. A lot of stuff was trial and error. I mean, Malik had not shot a film before." The flashback sequences were the areas that Spike experimented most with photography: one sequence, in which we see Victor working at a shop, marked the return of the anamorphic lens that had gotten him into so much trouble on *Crooklyn*.

Harvey Keitel was proving to be more than just a little difficult to work with: the actor didn't like Spike's method of shooting quickly and moving on. First AD Mike Ellis says, "Keitel was old school. He wanted to have rehearsals and know what's going on. Spike is not conventional: actors come in and go to hair and makeup, and Spike says, 'You have to do your shit over there'—rather than give explicit directions. *Clockers* had to be a little different, because Harvey was being Harvey." It was not the best time to be working with Harvey Keitel. The actor was troubled, John Turturro remembers: "He was in the middle of a divorce—maybe that had something to do with it." When Keitel was on set, there was an unusual tension that disrupted the family atmosphere Spike had spent years cultivating. "I had never worked with him before," Spike reflects, "and I guess we had to get used to each other. 'Difficult' is too harsh a term. But it does make the direc-

Clockers: Harvey Keitel as Detective Klein, John Turturro as Detective Mazilla.
(© 1994 David Lee)

tor's job harder." The relationship was not helped by a regrettable
incident during the shooting of the investigation scene, as Spike well
remembers: "We liked the stuff that Bob Richardson had been doing
with Oliver Stone, lighting from above, so we stole that. One day,
Harvey Keitel's hair caught on fire. Those lights were *hot*."

Keitel, it seemed, wanted to disassociate himself from the other
cast members and would want to direct his own performance. Prop
master Kevin Ladson remembers, "We were really smack in the
middle of projects and I don't know if he really wanted to be there.
There was one time when I got pissed when Harvey came to the set
with a gun strapped on his ankle. I said, 'You can't come to the
set strapped like this.' He looked at me as if to say, 'Man, get away
from me please.' I tell Spike that he can't come to set wearing a
fucking gun. Spike says, 'Kevin, it's all right.' You can see it if you
watch closely—it's a big bulge. It's okay, because he is playing a
police officer, but I'm giving him prop weapons, and he's there with
a real firearm."

Shooting took place in the Boerum Hill neighborhood in Brooklyn.
It was a location that Spike would take advantage of: "One day it was
raining, so we couldn't shoot what we were supposed to do and we
didn't have a cover set. So I told Mike Ellis to round up some crack-
heads and we shot them. We said, 'We'll pay you, but please do not tell

us what you are going to do with that money.' One of the ladies was pregnant—it was such a sad scene."

Spike, though, wanted the film to have more hope for African-Americans living in the projects than had Price's novel: "I felt that the book was too bleak. I'm not saying that I want to candy-coat something, but I felt that we have to leave some hope for young black men in America." Spike decided to give Strike an outside interest: "One of the most important additions I did to the script was to add his interest in trains. I had to have something, because Strike wasn't an adult yet. He's still not mature. I wanted him to have this fascination with trains and somehow work it out so that he ends up on the train at the end of the movie, trying to escape New York." Phifer recalls that the director explained to him that "it was a metaphor for Strike, loving these trains and really having the mentality to see the rest of the world very physically while kind of being mentally trapped into this world of drugs, where you stay in a perpetual cycle rather than make yourself an asset to the community."

Last of all Spike shot the scene where Strike leaves New York: "The sunset reflecting in the window, we didn't plan for that—that's where luck plays a big part in filmmaking." The director sent Ruth Carter out to get a costume that would symbolize the change in direction for Strike. Spike decided to go with his costume designer as he had something he needed to tell Carter. Carter says, "By the time we got to *Clockers*, I had started to make a lot of the costumes. Through that whole process I had one assistant, Donna Berwick, and one constant intern, and her name was Sandra Hernandez. Sandra wanted to be a script supervisor, but she came to Spike through the internship program and was assigned to my department. She hadn't worked on *Crooklyn*, because she had gotten a movie of her own. We finished *Clockers* in Santa Fe, New Mexico, and because Mekhi was having a life-changing experience during the last scene, I wanted him to have a talisman that would represent new hope. I wanted something real that was from the Indians. One day, Spike wanted to go shopping in Santa Fe, and we were in Albuquerque and I went to the Indian market-places. I remember he bought his daughter a silver spoon. And we had to meet the vans that were going to come to the location. I remember driving Spike at 100 mph as we had to get back to the location. We got there with five minutes to spare and Spike started to tell me about the next movie he was planning, *Girl 6*. He asked me, 'Who do you think should do the costume?' I said, 'Donna Berwick,' as she had been my assistant and I always thought that she would be the next person because of the way she came to me through 40 Acres. Spike said,

'Yeah, yeah, yeah. That's a good choice. What about Sandra?' I said, 'That's perfect.' And that sort of choked me up, that we together gave her a chance."

Spike was trying to let Ruth know, as gently as possible, that he wanted to use someone else for the next film. The crew that had formed the nucleus of 40 Acres had been broken, and Spike had begun to see the benefit of working with young guys who had formerly respected his work only from afar. Ruth says of Spike's position: "I guess he was making it easy for me to know, so that I wouldn't feel something was wrong and that was why Sandra was doing it, to validate the change and to make me know first so that I could welcome it even more than I did. I don't know how I would have felt if I was back in L.A. in my life and then I heard that Spike was doing a picture with Sandra instead of me. It was almost like him saying, 'I'm not switching from you; I'm opening it up for more like you. So that they can become part of it too.'"

Spike also felt that people should move on and not rely solely upon him for work. He did not want to be tied down in his choices through loyalty and friendship. Carter adds, "Spike is a very controlling guy and I think that after a while, once you've got so much experience with him, he really wants you to get outside experience besides him."

John Turturro, who had wanted to play Rocco Klein but wound up in the sidekick role, was furious when he saw the finished *Clockers*: "I was upset that I lost a lot of scenes. Spike said on *The Charlie Rose Show* that he felt 'sad.' But all my scenes had gone, *all* of them." The actor's unhappy memories of being shunted to a secondary character in *Jungle Fever* came flooding back: "But I was more disappointed with the cuts on *Jungle Fever*, because I felt that my character had a bigger canvas. With *Clockers*, the book is big, and there was a problem adapting it. Nowadays you can do it on HBO over six hours. And in that way we could have done the story more justice: it needed that much more time, because the characters are so complex in the book. Still, given the restrictions, I thought that Spike did a good job of it."

Clockers was released on September 13, 1995, to mixed reviews. The reviews that were unfavorable were generally from admirers of the book, who were annoyed that Lee had told only half the story. Yale professor Paul Gilroy went further than most in his criticism of the film when he described Spike's view of African-American neighborhoods as an "idealized and relentlessly sentimental conception." He further complained that the murderer's disastrous home life in the novel, in which he had been trapped into marriage by his girlfriend's pregnancy, had been replaced by happy families. The review in the *Washington Post* by Kevin McManus praised Lee through gritted teeth: after swiping at the "clumsy and unconvincing explanation" to the murder, he concedes: "As always, Lee fills his story with bold, vivid, glib characters who manage to be entertaining even as they flail at one another," before eventually signing off by saying, "*Clockers* is a real, wicked thrill."

David Bradley, writing in the *New York Times*, took perhaps the most implicitly critical swipe at Spike Lee three days before the film's release: "When Robert De Niro agreed to play Rocco, the film seemed destined for Oscar nominations and big box-office returns." The scarcely veiled derogation of Spike's endeavors was right at least in predicting that the box office would be dismal for *Clockers*. It returned a paltry $13 million domestic gross from a $25 million budget. This was worse news for Spike than the performance of *Crooklyn*, a film with a much smaller budget that managed almost to break even with the domestic gross. *Clockers* would eventually earn out its costs through international sales and video rentals. "I think we were very realistic with this type of life," Spike believes. "We took all the sheen off, all the gloss, the glamorization. We didn't make the guy out to be a hero. So, because there is so much money invested in that lifestyle and gangsta rap is still selling and the whole mentality is still with us, we weren't given a chance. As I said before when I used the word 'naïve,' we thought that it was going to be the final nail in the coffin for the genre." This is a view endorsed by Sam Pollard: "*Clockers* didn't make any money because, in my opinion, it's a true depiction of what is going on in the 'hood. Everybody from Mario Van Peebles to the Hughes brothers—because of the tradition, they all glamorize it. If you watch *New Jack City* or *Menace II Society*, all those films have a little glamour. This one doesn't. It *was* the nail in the coffin. But people didn't get it. They're starting to get it now."

11 *Girl 6*

Reflecting on the early days of her marriage, Mrs. Tonya Lewis Lee says: "I went through a lot of things. I'd always had my own place in the world, yet being married to Spike I just felt so much that everyone was *looking* at me. I also felt like there was a whole secret society with his friends. I'd only wanted really great things for Spike. I thought that we were going to be this dynamic couple, and I sort of expected a warm welcome. But most of the people from Spike's side of the world were not nice to me. Then, to the outer world, we would go out on the street and it would be, 'Spike! Spike!' If we were having dinner—a conversation or an argument—people would be coming up to us: there was that intrusion on privacy. And people would knock you down to get to Spike. So it was tough, trying to figure out 'Where do I really fit in here?' Then, six months after we were married, I got pregnant. And I would say that for the first five years of our marriage I was trying to figure out how to be a parent. I was raised to be the alpha woman—I was supposed to be running things, in the game, working, taking care of myself. So it was weird not to be able to do that—to have a baby and these expectations that I was supposed to be 'a housewife.' But I was going to be the best mother that I could be."

In 1995 Spike made a short film for HBO Sports about Georgetown University's head basketball coach, John Thompson. It was part of a series that Spike made for the cable channel depicting controversial African-American sporting heroes (and which had begun four years previously with Mike Tyson). Spike says, "I have a relationship with Ross Greenberg, who runs HBO Sports, and he had this show called *Real Sports*, which is hosted by Bryant Gumbel. It was a chance for me to do these mini-documentaries on people whom I admire or am interested in. With Tyson it was very much his relationship with Don King that was highlighted: we're talking about before the whole downward spiral.* . . . They were inseparable. Don King, he *is* a great character—

---

*In 1992 Mike Tyson was convicted of raping Desiree Washington, an eighteen-year-old Miss Black America contestant. He would be released in 1995 after serving three years of a six-year jail term.

let's leave out the scruples. Another one was about Curt Flood: he is the one individual responsible for these athletes, in particular baseball players, making the *obscene* amount of money that they are making now. But Flood was someone who did this as a sacrifice, one that ended his career—he never played baseball again, but he did what was right. At the time Albert Belle was a poster boy for all that's wrong with African-American athletes—belligerent, crazy, that type of stuff. We wanted to take a look at him—I never expected him to be a saint, but I just couldn't believe that he was the bogeyman that I was reading about. Finally, Georgetown has always been my college basketball team, all these great players came through, and John Thompson was there."

In 1995 Spike was also asked to join in the celebration of the centenary of cinema by making a one-minute film using the same camera and techniques that were available to the Lumière brothers when they first committed images to celluloid. Lasting one minute and six seconds, Spike's film reflected his new status as a father: he shot his attempt at getting his young daughter, Satchel, to say "Daddy" to the camera before the roll of film ran out.

Even before shooting on *Clockers* was completed, Spike was already turning his thoughts to his next feature, *Girl 6*. Since he placed cinema before family, the slowdown in output that might have been expected following the birth of his first child did not in fact materialize. But new fatherhood, coupled with the loss of Monty Ross, did lead to Spike for the first time engaging a screenwriter to flesh out one of his own ideas. The new film was to be based in and around the phone-sex industry: "I think I was introduced to Suzan-Lori Parks[*] by Lisa Jones. I'd seen a play that she wrote and I saw an exciting writer, an African-American woman playwright. I thought she would be able to write a good script. At that time I was just too busy to write it. I approached her, we talked, and then she went off and wrote it."

Casting agent Robi Reed, who had started her own family and was working more and more in her hometown of L.A., says: "*Girl 6* was offered to me, and I passed on it. I couldn't really move to New York for the time that he needed me and for the amount of money he was offering." Following in Reed's footsteps was Aisha Coley, who had cast extras on *Malcolm X* before being promoted to casting assistant

---

[*]Parks had written the plays *Imperceptible Mutabilities in the Third Kingdom, Betting on the Dust Commander, Pickling* and *The Death of the Last Black Man in the Whole Entire World*. She later won a Pulitzer Prize for her play *Topdog/Underdog*.

on *Crooklyn* and *Clockers*. Her efforts in finding an actor to play Strike had impressed the director, and Coley would hold onto the post of casting director at 40 Acres for the next decade. Coley says of casting, "Any director wants to feel that he and his actor are on the same page. And Spike is very intuitive when he meets people. He tends to be able to get a take on someone very quickly, of what they're like to work with. One undeniable thing is that he has put a lot of people on the map: actors recognize that and they are really interested in working with him." Stanley Crouch, it should be noted, dissents from this widely held view: "Without a doubt Spike Lee got a lot of actors out there—people like Bill Nunn, they were seen and he wrote good parts for them, and that was important. But he hasn't really discovered an actress of the caliber of Diane Keaton or an actor of the caliber of De Niro. Woody Allen has discovered a lot of people, so has Spielberg, Scorsese. People have come through, but it's not like people are chasing them down to be in somebody else's movies."

The scenario of *Girl 6* would unfold like so: Judy is an aspiring actress struggling to get work. We meet her, recently separated from her husband, refusing to take off her top in an audition for the hottest director in Hollywood, Quentin Tarantino. (Tarantino, his reputation enhanced by the success of *Pulp Fiction*, would play himself.) Judy's refusal to appear in the nude grates with both her manager and acting coach, who use this as an excuse to drop her from their roster. With her acting career hitting a cul-de-sac Judy tries to support herself, first by doing menial jobs, before taking a job as a phone-sex operator and being given the tag "Girl 6." But she finds herself enjoying the camaraderie of the female operators and is increasingly drawn into the world.

Harvey Weinstein's standing in the film world, like Tarantino's, went stellar after the success of *Pulp Fiction*: its $100 million gross and multiple Oscar nominations had established the Miramax chief as the kingmaker in the independent film world. He seemed to have the Midas touch when it came to midsize independent films, and so Spike turned to him after the failure of *Clockers* to set the domestic box office alight. "Originally we were supposed to do the film with Miramax. Harvey Weinstein said he was going to do it. Then at the last minute Harvey said, 'Unless you get Halle Berry to make the film, we're not going to make it.'" It was the first in a series of disagreements that would eventually lead to the director referring to the movie mogul as a "fat bastard."

Berry does actually appear in the film, making a brief appearance on

Girl 6: Theresa Randle. (© 1995 David Lee)

a news program that Girl 6 is watching about the death of a young girl in an elevator shaft. Spike says, "We didn't put Halle in to stick it to Miramax. I did that because we hadn't done a film together since *Jungle Fever.*" Spike approached Jada Pinkett before casting Theresa Randle: "Theresa did a small role in *Jungle Fever* and a small role in *Malcolm X.* I'd seen her do other stuff. There are a lot of African-American actresses out there who are very talented, but they're not often given a shot to do a lead in a film. And I was very confident in her abilities." Malcolm Lee, who was working as assistant to Spike, was not so convinced: "Theresa Randle wasn't the strongest choice on it. I think Spike gave her a little too much leeway with creating her character. I think he does that a lot of the time with his actors, wanting them to create their own space and world."

Branford Marsalis jokes, "The most Spike ever tells an actor is, 'Here's the script. Ready? Action!' I used to watch seasoned pros say, 'Spike, what is your vision?' And Spike would reply, 'I paid you good money to act, now act—*that's* my vision.'" "Now, Branford is exaggerating a little bit," Spike ripostes. "When an actor asks a question, I try to give them what they need. A lot of actors like direction. What I try to do is not *over*direct." Aisha Coley says, "My feeling is that most of the actors that I've spoken to really love working with him. Every once in a while, I think there is an actor who's maybe used to a director being more talkative or something."

Girl 6 marked the first time that Spike would work with acting coach Susan Batson. "I auditioned for *Girl 6*, for the role of the acting coach," she recalls. "If I didn't get that, it would have been a sin. Spike then had me come over to the firehouse and he said, 'I'm interested in studying acting.' I got so excited, I felt, Oh my God, this is a director who really wants to *understand* the actor's work. He took out a notebook and a pen and he said, 'OK.' I asked, 'Is *that* how you study acting?' He said, 'Yeah. Tell me—what do you do?' 'You have to come to class.' He said, 'No, no, no!' I said, 'Yes. You can work privately, but acting is about a public art form. You have to come to class and study.' He asked, 'Can't you give me a few hints?' I said, 'I'll give you a little help talking to the actors, but if you really want to learn, you'll have to come to class. You can't just sit there and theorize.' So he said he would try to come. He's never showed up. But as a result of all this, he decided to hire me as a coach to work with his actors. And he's the best director I've worked with, I feel, because he's not intimidated by my role."

Spike says, "I guess if you are secure in yourself then you're not going to mind having an acting coach around. The title we gave Susan Batson was 'technical consultant,' and she's been a great resource. She's not there to upstage me—she wants the same as what I want: what is best for the film. When I first hired her, she worked on the films with specific actors. Now she's really dealing with megastars. She still runs her classes, but she's also been in the clutches of Nicole Kidman for a while, doing films with her back-to-back." Batson says, "Most directors are very intimidated by me. They feel like you are interfering. They are constantly watching to see if you are going to change their direction of the actors. With Spike I don't have to worry about it at all. It is just, 'Susan, go in, talk to the actor,' and it makes my life easy. With Spike I've sometimes had discussions when I've felt like he's missed something that the actor needed. I would say to Spike, 'If you just said right now that this works, it's what you want, the actor will not be so frustrated.' You know, on set you're the father, you're the psychiatrist—sometimes you have to play that role. So I would say, 'Can you give the person affirmation?'" According to Mike Ellis this is not Spike's strong point. "In ten years, he has said that I've done a good job twice."

Batson also has this warning for the prospective Spike Lee actor: "I think the actor who works with Spike should know that Spike is not going to try and pull anything out of you emotionally. He'll help your choices of character and he'll help you fulfill his vision, but he is not going to bring you to a great performance. If you get a great performance with Spike, it is because you brought it to the set. He will totally and completely appreciate it, he'll love you forever and he'll keep using you. He knows when it is a great performance, he knows when the take is very good, he knows when the emotional content is there."

Girl 6 would also mark the last occasion on which Spike gave himself a prominent role in one of his own films, resolving thereafter to stick to the full-time jobs of writing and directing. Samuel L. Jackson here offers his own interpretation of the arc of Spike's acting career: "If you take it back from *She's Gotta Have It*, it's like 'The Mars Blackmon Chronicles.' And it's kind of cool if you look at it that way. First, you get introduced to Mars. Then Mars decided to stop riding a bike and goes to college: *School Daze*. Then school's out for summer and he comes home and delivers pizzas: *Do the Right Thing*. Then he drops out of school and, next thing you know, he's managing this boy band: *Mo' Better Blues*. He goes back to school and graduates, so, by the time of *Jungle Fever*, he's teaching school. *Malcolm X*? That's Mars Blackmon's grandfather. Then Mars did something bad and got fired, so by the time we get to *Crooklyn*, he is drinking 40s."[*] Jackson could easily have added that in *Girl 6* Mars is still down and out but banking on his collection of baseball memorabilia being a nest egg. Then again, like most people, Jackson probably never saw *Girl 6*.

Joie Lee will stick her neck out and defend her brother, "I think Spike is a very good actor. I really do." But Susan Batson argues that Spike does not work hard enough at the craft: "You can't really get him to sit down and do the work. So normally his performances are terrible. And I love him dearly. I think that he finds joy acting. If he would practice, he could possibly become a good actor. There is nothing he can't do, if he puts his mind to it. But you have to drop in, you have to receive the human being that you are playing, you have to really surrender a couple of things to this character—and you can't really get Spike to find that kind of focus. Mars Blackmon is one of the ones that he was able to step into and find a frame of reference that helped him."

In his review of *Girl 6* in *Rolling Stone*, Peter Travis perfectly described how Spike's standing as an actor was viewed in 1996 as opposed to 1986: "It's ironic that Lee and Tarantino both have roles in *Girl 6*. Right now they may be the most despised pseudo-actors in movies. Funny how overexposure can turn a genius into an arrogant

---

[*]This refers to the common and derogatory stereotype that lazy black American men drink 40-ounce malt liquor.

Girl 6: Quentin Tarantino. (© 1995 David Lee)

ass in the eyes of the public." When Spike needed someone to play "the hottest director in Hollywood," Tarantino, who at the time was arguing that he wanted to be an actor rather than director, seemed a natural choice: "I called him up, asked him if he wanted this part and he said yes. He wasn't getting paid, so it was a favor. Anytime somebody of that stature does a film for you for scale, it's a favor; they're not going to get rich."

Tarantino's scene starts with Theresa Randle reading a monologue used by Nola Darling in *She's Gotta Have It*. There had already been some static in the press between the two directors before they worked together on *Girl 6*. Lee had publicly criticized Tarantino for his use of the word "nigger," most notably in the "dead nigger storage" segment of *Pulp Fiction*. Lee even tailored the lines of the role to have a dig at Tarantino's claims of being the director most in tune with African-Americans; in the film Tarantino says, "It's going to be the greatest romantic African-American film ever made. Directed by me. Of course." Any animosity that Lee felt toward Tarantino was compounded on set, or so believes Mike Ellis: "Tarantino talked so loud you could hear him in Africa. He was there for three hours and that was three hours too long. All I had to say to him was: 'You have to shut up so that we can shoot the movie.' I'm not a big fan."

The release of *Jackie Brown* in 1997 would see Tarantino and Lee's argument over the use of racial slurs come to a head, and they would have a very public falling-out. When Tarantino was asked if he wanted to give his side of events for this book, he stated, "I think I've done enough to make Spike Lee famous." In an article for *Vibe* in the run-up to the release of *Kill Bill Vol. 1*, Tarantino describes how *Do the Right Thing* was one of his favorite films and he was over the moon to have the opportunity to work with Spike. This turned to dismay when Spike started slamming his films in the press. Tarantino vented his frustration that Spike did not talk privately to him about any problem rather than go directly to the press: after all, Spike had his phone number.

Spike argues, "I thought that it was important that people see what he was doing, and if it was just a conversation between me and him, that is never going to come out. If you really start to think about the scripts he wrote for *Reservoir Dogs*, *Pulp Fiction*, *True Romance* and *Natural Born Killers*, they are packed with 'nigger' references. Where does this stuff come from? Also he is going to get a whole lot of white boys hurt if they go out to school and use the word 'nigger' around black people. I remember Harvey Weinstein called me and said, 'Spike, you have to stop speaking to the press about *Jackie Brown*.' I replied, 'What are you talking about?' He said, 'You're hurting the film.' So I asked him a point-blank question: 'Would you or your brother Bob ever produce or make a film that used the word "hymie" or "kike" as many times as they use the word "nigger" in *Jackie Brown*?' He said, 'No.' At least he was honest."

It was Richard Pryor who first attempted, on his 1974 album *That Nigger's Crazy*, a popular hijacking of the demeaning connotation of the word. Kevin Ladson argues, "Tarantino overused 'nigger' in his movie, and what got me more angry was the fact that he tried to justify it by basically saying, 'I hung out with black folks when I was a kid.'" Coming to Tarantino's aid was *Jackie Brown* star and Spike alumnus Samuel L. Jackson: "I voiced my opinion because, artistically, Quentin is right. I said the same thing to the Hughes brothers when they came to me with the same bullshit about *Pulp Fiction*. How many times did we say 'nigger' in *Menace II Society*? Do we have a patent on it? It wasn't just Spike whom I was speaking out against, but anybody who tries to suppress a person's artistic bent by saying he cannot say this thing or the other. They also tried to say the same thing about Boaz Yakin and *Fresh*, and I spoke about that too. 'Who is this guy, writing a story about this young black kid?' Well, where is your story about a young black kid? Shut the fuck up and make your own movie if you don't like it." Spike responds to Sam Jackson's criticism like so: "Well, Sam and I had a disagreement. Also, I wasn't talking about

Sam; I was talking about Quentin Tarantino. I found it mildly amusing that Sam felt that he had to come to defend the 'Massa.'"

"Spike has always had little things that bother him," Jackson contends. "It's like when he had the Nike contracts and was friends with
Michael Jordan—that was like his personal territory and we weren't
supposed to tread on that. Then Spike was talking about me playing
golf and being a member of a country club. I was like, 'Come on, man,
get over it. This is part of being in L.A. and of the world.' Spike has a
big house in Martha's Vineyard. I have a house in Beverly Hills. That
doesn't make me any less the person I used to be. Now all of a sudden
I know all those guys too. But it's OK to be friends with those people
and maintain your *negritude*."

Tarantino's scene in *Girl 6* explores sexual exploitation within the
film industry: Judy's agent will tell her, "Sharon Stone spread her
legs and you see what happens." Spike states, "John [Turturro]
ad-libbed that line. No one had really heard of Sharon Stone before
Basic Instinct and she blew up when she spread her legs on film. But
actresses are asked to compromise themselves, not just from the
director but the producer too. All the time: 'Are you going to show
your tits or your ass?' They say that shit all the time. It is men making decisions. And of course they would rather have heads explode
on screen than show a penis."

Roger Ebert, often a supporter of Spike's work, took issue with
his rendering of the Tarantino scene: "What we have here is a scene
about a woman being shamed by exposing herself, and the scene is
handled so that she exposes herself. That puts Lee in the same boat
with the lecher." Tonya Lee Lewis had her own problems with the
film: "Satchel was born by the time *Girl 6* came out, and I've
always felt that *Girl 6* was Spike's way of rebelling against marriage
and children. Spike didn't tell me he was doing the film: I started
hearing about it from other people first. And I always felt that he
had a guilty conscience about it: why not tell me about it? What's
the big secret? Why am I hearing it from people who've read about
it in the paper, and I sleep with him? I felt like he was hiding something about it or he was afraid of what I was going to say. Once I
had a chance to read it, I didn't get it. First of all, I thought that the
script was so poorly developed that I did not understand the main
character, her motivation, her history. How did she get to that
place? It was like, 'Dress up a lot of pretty sexy girls and make them
talk dirty.'"

Perhaps Spike alone believed he was striking a blow for women's rights with *Girl 6*. He had previously acknowledged his failure to fully develop his female characters, and he describes Judy's drama in *Girl 6* as that of a woman "having a hard time distinguishing fiction and reality, being pulled deeper and deeper into the world of phone sex, where it is almost consuming her." But the way in which Judy becomes addicted to her work had other observers sensing that the film was rooted in Spike's own male sexual fantasy. Mrs. Lee speaks of "having this secret place that men go—that when you have the Madonna wife and child at home, then you have to secretly go off and get your primitive, instinctual sexual gratification elsewhere."

Whatever its merits, Spike visualized his fantasy/reality dialectic in three fantasy sequences where Girl 6 imagines herself living out certain iconic images from African-American film and television. Spike says, "That was an element Suzan-Lori Parks thought up. One was a take on *The Jeffersons*, another was blaxploitation films, and the third was Dorothy Dandridge's Oscar-nominated performance in *Carmen Jones*. The film is about an actress: she would have seen and been influenced by these characters growing up. I'd been thinking about blaxploitation films and those films with the super-duper black woman." These are indeed among the highlights of the film, also permitting Spike to do a turn by portraying Mr. Jefferson.

Spike's character in the movie lives in the same apartment block as Judy and warns her of the dangers of taking the "short money," the phrase he lifted from Budd Schulberg and a warning Lisa Jones says he gave to all of his own collaborators. Spike says, "I think in the end Girl 6 comes to the realization that she took the short money: thinking that somehow this occupation was going to lead her somewhere she wanted to be and that she could make the delineation without it affecting her being was not smart. But doing that type of job it would be hard for it not to affect you—physically, spiritually and emotionally."

Finally Girl 6 escapes from New York to L.A. Spike says: "Actors, eventually they all go to L.A., especially out-of-work actresses. There are certain periods of time, especially during the pilot season, when there is a complete migration to the West Coast. It's natural; L.A. is Hollywood. It is tough for actors. Unless you have that psyche where you can deal with rejection, it makes you crazy. You get very deep self-esteem issues, not just about your craft but the way you look. Am I too fat, too skinny? Is my hair too short or too long? My nose too big, too small, too wide? Am I too old? It's crazy. From a director's perspective, you cannot just exempt an actor out of hand because of the way they look, but the look entails how I envision the character. It's very hard."

Just before Girl 6 makes her move to L.A., she has a rapprochement

Girl 6: the Sid and Nancy moment. (© 1995 David Lee)

with her kleptomaniac husband, depicted in a surreal moment wherein the couple, dressed in white, kiss as phones fall from the sky. Spike conceived of the sequence as homage to a favorite movie of his: "That scene came from *Sid and Nancy*, the Alex Cox film, where Sid and Nancy are kissing and the garbage falls from the sky." The shooting of that sequence afforded Malcolm Lee a moment where he demonstrated that he was ready to graduate from being part of the crew to sitting in the cherished director's chair. "Spike was using a wide-angled lens on that scene," Malcolm recalls. "I guess he wanted to see everything. I said, 'Are you going to do a long lens too?' He was like, 'Nah.' I said, 'OK.' Then about twenty minutes later he said, 'Hey, Malik, put a 150 on there.' He didn't look at me, didn't say anything, but it seemed like I had an influence on him, and that was good enough for me."

DP Malik Sayeed was not enjoying the best of shoots. He had been shooting the male callers on high-definition video and Theresa Randle on 35mm, in a failed attempt to create a disparity that favored Randle's character. Spike recalls, "He was taking a long time to light the lead actresses. I know you want this girl to look good, but you have to light the rest of the movie too." Mike Ellis expands: "With Malik's sensibility as an artist, everything had to be perfect. This took so long that Spike did not have the time to do what he wanted to do. You can't light *Girl 6* the way you lit *Clockers*."

*

Girl 6 is littered with references to Jackie Robinson, suggestive of a difficult journey that Spike was sharing in common with his protagonist. Spike was continuing in his struggle to raise finance for a biopic that he had penned on Robinson. But studios balked at the prospective $40 million cost of the movie, especially as *Malcolm X*, *Crooklyn* and *Clockers* had not been hits. Kevin Ladson says, "We began researching it, and I guess theoretically I'm still researching that movie. I hope he gets to do it, because I know that is the one that he wants to do." Spike is still struggling to find someone to fund this period piece. It was proof, if it be needed, that Spike's star was on the wane.

Sam Pollard says that the warning signs of the film's failure were apparent before the film reached movie houses in the United States. "I thought visually Malik's work was phenomenal, and I tried things that I had never tried before editorially. I loved what we did but I never thought it worked as a film—because I thought that maybe all of us men should not have done that film. I don't really think we had a grasp of it. We screened it for Suzan-Lori Parks and I don't know whether she thought it was the film she wrote."

The film came out on March 22, 1996, two days after Spike's thirty-ninth birthday. Art Sims says, "The poster was supposed to show the different personalities of the actress all on one sheet. We had different snapshots of Theresa Randle and there was a purple phone running over them—purple because Prince had done the soundtrack." But once unveiled before the critics, *Girl 6* took something of a pounding. Spike had not helped the audience by his approach to the subject: he seemed not to like the protagonist, making it hard for viewers to identify with her plight. Another major flaw is that the middle segment of the film, focusing on the male callers, is grating and overlong. Spike says of *Girl 6*, "I think it is very experimental and, unfairly, the most underrated of all my films." Jon Kilik attributes the problem to marketing: "It was a complicated movie. It wasn't strictly a comedy or a drama, but we sold it as a comedy, which is a little bit misleading. So people saw something that didn't live up to the expectation they had." John Pierson, though, speaks for the majority of critics when he contends, "There is only one Spike Lee film that is a complete letdown, even though it has its moments: *Girl 6* is the only one of Spike's films that I think the world could live without." Nelson George adds, "I see Spike's work as being in three distinct periods: you have the films to *Malcolm X*, and then there is a middle period of *Crooklyn*, *Clockers* and *Girl 6* which is sort of dodgy—with *Girl 6* being the dodgiest."

*

The box-office failure of *Girl 6*, the departure of Monty Ross, Spike's struggle with married life and fatherhood, and the broad portfolio of 40 Acres activity—all these combined to impact negatively on 40 Acres business. Sponsors were now somewhat less keen to be associated with the Spike Lee brand. Earl Smith says: "After three years we had to close the Spike & Nike basketball camp. It got to the point where it got too big and you needed a minimum of six months to organize the event. The camp was free and I think it started to cost Spike money. The first year we had some sponsors, but because he wanted these kids to go to camp, he paid out a lot of his own money. I think one year it cost $120,000—that's a lot of money for four days. I think a lot of people in the community didn't appreciate it. Nike were a good supporter; they gave us all the equipment and teachers, but that wasn't enough. In addition, in the first year we had sponsorship from Chase Manhattan, Pepsi, some local stores. It was a three-year commitment, and the second year people got comfortable—they knew we would do it the next year, and they didn't set about trying to renegotiate contracts and get more money. Spike got tired. He is a filmmaker; he tries to start up everything, but sometimes things fall through the cracks."

Yet more time-consuming for Spike were his Spike's Joint shops in L.A. and New York. Spike argues, "Once I had a family I could not do all of the things that I was doing before." That's especially so when they're not making money. With Monty Ross no longer a buffer, problems would now always go back to Spike. Earl Smith explains the type of inane incident Spike found himself occupied by: "There was a time in the shop and a guy wanted to buy $600 worth of stuff. We packaged it all and he became annoyed when we pressed the tax button when we were ringing up and complained, 'Are you going to charge me tax?' The sales assistant replied, 'We're not charging you anything; it's the City that is charging you.' He wanted to talk to the manager. So the girls called, and I'm trying to be diplomatic at first. He says, 'I'm buying $600–700 worth of stuff, are you going to charge me tax?' I start explaining, and he says, 'I don't want that stuff. Who does Spike think he is?' I say, 'If you don't want it, you don't have to buy it, just put all the stuff back.' 'I won't put nothing back, what are you going to do, punk?' I said, 'What!? Call me punk again. I'll tell you what I'm going to do, come outside the store now.' So I went outside and was leaning on a tree, and he wouldn't come out of Spike's store. After ten minutes I go back in and say, 'Who's the punk now? And if you say something I'm going to follow you out the door.' Two weeks go by and Spike calls me: 'Come upstairs, Earl. You can't be threatening people.' I say, 'What you talking about?' He looks at me. 'Wait, let me tell you what happened. . . .' 'Earl, you can't do that. If you hit somebody, they are going to sue me.' 'Of course I wasn't going to hit him. . . .'"

Earl Smith started to work in the firehouse before Spike's Joint closed down completely, but he watched as the shops began to lose out to competitors: "We lost focus. When Spike was hands-on, there was a vision. You bring on people that supposedly know what they are doing, and we saw them trying to go and sell other people's stuff instead of focusing on developing more goods for us. Also, by now people coming from Japan are buying Sean John and they go to Macys to buy clothes endorsed by rappers."

Spike says that he finally made the decision to shut up shop because "it was just a full-time thing, retail, and I wanted to concentrate on filmmaking. It was the same thing with the music label. The record industry is crazier than the film industry, so I had to let that go. The house was being torn in all directions. The rappers that started doing clothing lines, I say more power to them. They're doing a better job than I did." Spike was even forced to reconsider his view that he was as good as Madonna at marketing himself: "I said that, but I was never trying to compete directly with Madonna. Everything she does is so well thought out and planned. Even this whole thing about her and Britney kissing, I know their records were flying off the shelf the next day. It's good to be recognized and have an iconic status, but it was never my intention to be in the public eye every minute, to have my face in the paper every day. In fact, I prefer not to be in the papers if it's not movie-related."

Following the releases of *Drop Squad* and *New Jersey Drive* Spike was happy to attach himself to an increasing number of projects as executive producer. At the *Girl 6* première, Michael Imperioli approached him: "I was working with a partner, Victor Colicchio, on a script called *Anarchy in the Bronx* and I was originally thinking about directing it. We finished the first draft and I just brought it to Spike. He read it and said, 'You should direct this and I will executive produce it.' I was pretty shocked that he had that level of interest and confidence in me. That was a big boost for me, you know, to have somebody like that behind you in that way, not as a director–actor thing anymore, but behind something that you are creating."

The regular Friday trips to Boston for teaching duties were also taking their toll on Spike. So, as his three-year contract at Harvard came up, the director began considering other options. He received a call from Mary Schmidt Campbell, the new dean at his alma mater, the

New York University Film School. She recalls: "The first time that I had lunch with him was in my office. I asked him, 'Hey, Spike, how did you like your time at NYU?' 'They tried to throw me out.' One of the things I've noticed about him is that he is a man of few words. There's an economy in his life—I think a part of it is that he's a little bit shy and another is that he husbands his resources very carefully. And one of the resources he husbands most is time. If I have a meeting with him, I know that the meeting is not going to last more than fifteen minutes. He is going to be clear in his mind what the agenda is, he is going to be right to the point. He doesn't do small talk. So I spent the rest of the lunch just talking. I basically felt like I was talking to myself. At the end of the lunch he finally looked up and said, 'So when are you going to ask me to teach?' I thought, This is like the gift from God."

The class Spike gives at NYU reflects his views on the building of a career in film. As the dean explains, "He teaches the same thing every year: the role of the director as a leadership role as well as an artistic position. Not just the art of directing but the art of managing all of those elements in the film." Like Skip Gates before her, Dean Campbell feels Spike's teaching is part of his mission: "He feels that part of what he is giving them is access. He is a very impressive teacher. I think there is something about the nature of teaching itself at its most fundamental level that appeals to him, in the same way that making his art appeals to him. I think it has to do with his sense that, in addition to the opportunity to do his work, he has a responsibility to the larger world toward the next generation and teaching is one of the tools that he can use to fulfill that responsibility. He is incredibly generous in the kind of contacts that he makes and the people that he brings into the class: he will bring in Martin Scorsese or Ang Lee or John Turturro at the drop of a hat."

12 *Get on the Bus* and *4 Little Girls*

On October 16, 1995—while Spike was at work on *Girl 6*—the Million Man March on Washington took place. The march was called by Minister Louis Farrakhan of the Nation of Islam and Reverend Benjamin Chavis Jr., former executive director of the National Association for the Advancement of Colored People (NAACP). In its conception it unabashedly aped the great 1963 March to Washington, when Dr. Martin Luther King gave his famed "I have a dream" speech. The stated aim of the 1995 gathering was a "holy day of atonement and reconciliation" for black men, and the organizers also called for marchers to register to vote: this was to be a grassroots mobilization across black religious and class lines that they hoped would draw a million black males. Those who could not attend—and women were specifically asked not to—were requested to take the day off work, in protest at the treatment of black men in America.

In a press release Farrakhan said: "We wanted to call out men to Washington to make a statement that we are ready to accept responsibility of being the heads of our households, the providers, the maintainers and the protectors of our women and children." The call evidently touched a nerve in African-American men anguished by the poverty, unemployment and crime within their communities. Debates on race had raged throughout the trial—and subsequent to the acquittal—of former running back turned actor O. J. Simpson on charges of murdering his estranged white wife, Nicole. (There were even inaccurate rumors that Simpson and his lawyer Johnnie Cochran would attend the march.) But many celebrities endorsed the event, among them Bill Cosby and baseball Hall of Famer Reggie Jackson, alongside the Reverend Jesse Jackson, Congressional Black Caucus Chairman Donald Payne, Detroit Mayor Dennis Archer, Baltimore Mayor Kurt Schmoke and the Reverend Joseph Lowery, head of the Southern Christian Leadership Conference. It was the type of event devoted to the furthering of black consciousness that Spike Lee would have been expected to attend. He says his absence was not due to filming commitments or any objection that he had to the march: "I had just had a knee operation, arthroscopic surgery, so I couldn't go."

By contrast, Ossie Davis felt that he could not attend because of his

objection to Farrakhan: "I think that the march was an acknowledg-
ment that the world had changed. A world that was created to some
degree by Malcolm was now being overtaken by another figure. . . .
Now Spike knows Minister Farrakhan, respects and admires what he
was trying to do, in a way that I could not—not because of any defect
in Farrakhan as a man or leader, but my own attachment to Malcolm
X does not allow me to be fair and logical with those who, in some
degree, are detractors. Let me explain: if I accept the pain and anguish
that Malcolm felt when he looked upon the behavior of Elijah
Muhammad, because I knew and loved Malcolm, I could not come
back and say with Louis Farrakhan that Elijah Muhammad is the
great moralist, the great spiritual leader, the great son of Allah and all
that. Yet Farrakhan has still had a positive effect on the life of the
black community, and I'm prepared—and in public have done so—to
appreciate that and to say thank you to him for that. Ruby Dee and I
sent money to pay for a bus to take people who were going to the
march. Our own son-in-law, who is a Muslim, took our daughter and
grandchildren to tap into and find the hope on the march. It is only in
the ideological areas and the basis from which all of this springs—the
basis of the black struggle—that I cannot reach out and honestly say,
'Brother Farrakhan or Minister Farrakhan, I'm affected by you and
you are the qualified leader,' et cetera, et cetera."

Indeed, the march heralded a great public debate around Farrakhan. The Anti-Defamation League of B'nai B'rith took out advertisements in national newspapers, and one of them argued, "What if
white supremacists called for a march on Washington? . . . No one
could ignore the fact that a hate-monger was the driving force behind
the march. The same is true of Minister Louis Farrakhan." Even President Clinton voiced his view, through White House spokesman Mike
McCurry, that he had "some deep reservations about the organizers of
the march, in particular Reverend Farrakhan." Farrakhan answered
his critics by revising history and claiming that he had never made
anti-Semitic statements previously attributed to him: this despite the
recorded incidents of him calling Judaism "a gutter religion" and
defending his use of the term "bloodsuckers" to describe Jews or others who open businesses in minority communities and take profits
elsewhere. In another speech he had contended, "The Jews call me
'Hitler.' Well, that's a good name. Hitler was a good man."

Orthodox Muslims decried the Nation of Islam as a sect that had
nothing to do with the teachings of the Prophet Muhammad. Farrakhan's claims were indefensible; and yet the minister skillfully played
politics for the occasion, and in the run-up to the Million Man March

he offered to have "dialogue" with his Jewish counterparts in the Anti-Defamation League, a claim that he repeated at the march before the huge crowd that had gathered (more even than the 250,000 who followed Martin Luther King): "I don't like this squabble with the members of the Jewish community. . . . Reverend Jackson has talked to the twelve presidents of Jewish organizations and perhaps, in the light of what we see today, maybe it's time to sit down and talk. Not with any preconditions. You got pain. Well, we've got pain too. You hurt. We hurt too."

Farrakhan urged his distinctive vision of black self-improvement and entrepreneurial effort by which the prejudices of whites would be refuted: "Black man, you don't have to bash white people; all we got to do is go back home and turn our communities into productive places." But he also had a message, couched in white-hot preacher rhetoric, for an entertainment industry increasingly dominated by excessive images of the supposed bounties of the gangsta lifestyle: "Every time we drive-by shoot, every time we car-jack, every time we use foul, filthy language, every time we produce culturally degenerate films and tapes, putting a string in our women's backside and parading them before the world . . . we are feeding the degenerate mind of white supremacy. . . . Clean up, black man, and the world will respect and honor you. But you have fallen down like the prodigal son and you're husking corn and feeding swine."

Haskell Wexler had made *On the Bus*, a film about a bus journey to the 1963 March to Washington, a film that Spike Lee, surprisingly, hasn't seen. Spike had no intention of making a film on Farrakhan's march until, as he recalls, "I was called up by the casting director/producer Reuben Cannon, who said, 'Me and these guys have this idea of making a film around the march and we have a writer, Reggie Bythewood.' He told me the idea: a cross-country trip on a bus from L.A. to DC, with different representations of black men."

Spike, harking back to arguments made in *The Autobiography of Malcolm X*, "just told Reuben Cannon, 'Maybe we should go for strictly African-American finance.' When you think about the principles of the Million Man March, that was right: black seed-investment for a black business. I didn't want to approach the same people who had given money to *Malcolm X*, so we made a new list. Johnnie Cochran, Reggie Bythewood, Wesley Snipes, Danny Glover and myself—we all gave money. Also, this was an investment—not a gift, like *X* was." In all, the production raised $2.5 million.

The filmmakers hoped to release the picture on the one-year

anniversary of the march. ("We thought it would clean up," says Mike Ellis.) Spike would have to work fast to meet that desired release date, and that meant commencing production before he was entirely happy with the script. "The finished film is a little too talky," Spike reflects, "but that is in the confines of the script. There was no getting around it, I knew that coming in. And that was the really hard part—how do you make this entertaining or visually interesting when the majority of the film takes place on a bus?"

Spike needed actors whom he could rely upon to spice things up and called on Roger Smith. The actor says, "It was an opportunity for me to freestyle in a certain way, to bring things to the table that weren't set in stone by the script. And it was an extraordinarily moving experience for all of us. It was done in eighteen days, and I think that was perfect—because these were characters who really didn't know each other, and I think an eight- or nine-week shoot with a big budget and hotel expenses would have been a very different film." Mike Ellis, though, almost blanches when recalling the logistical toughness of the schedule: "Eighteen days in four states—impossible. We were doing ten, eleven pages of script a day, which was great, and we got all that we needed. But if I died and went to heaven today, I would say, 'Let me in because we did *Get on the Bus*.'"

Spike also called on Ossie Davis, who retained his doubts about the ramifications of the real-life march: "What I wanted from Louis Farrakhan was that the Nation of Islam should do something that spoke eloquently to the community. If, for instance, they had set out to build a first-class university or a first-class hospital, where all the qualities of which they thought so highly were put into practice, then I would have been prepared to drop all my differences and climb aboard. But I don't believe that will happen as a result of the Million Man March. I agreed to be in the film because Spike asked me to be in it, and I loved the part of Jeremiah. It was something that I could do without waking up, and Spike let me write some of my material. It was what Jeremiah was trying to say when he was beating on the drums, about the power and the necessity of African people of the world to be proud of who they are and to accept some responsibility. Jeremiah as a character could help explain the movement and the purpose to the general African-American audiences and to the white audience too. Jeremiah could give it depth and perspective." Spike was similarly interested in this aspect of the project: "For me the interesting thing was not necessarily the destination but the journey: what happened between strangers who represented different aspects of African-American society, males who have come together and are clashing on a cross-country trip. It was very simple to decide on what they would talk about. We looked at all the issues that Farrakhan was dealing with in the black community, and it made sense that these guys would speak about that on the way to the march."

There are twenty men aboard the bus, each with a different reason for making the trip. The tour leader (Charles S. Dutton) is the referee and conductor, a stalwart veteran of the civil-rights era. Roger Smith (distinguished, as in *School Daze*, by his light complexion) is a cop from South Central L.A. A father (Thomas Jefferson Byrd) and his son (De'aundre Bonds) must travel together in handcuffs because of a court order: this both a representation of the malfeasance of the young and an obvious and acknowledged gesture to slavery. Wendell Pierce makes a cameo as a car dealer who is designated the fool of the film from the moment he gets on the bus. Through Pierce's character Spike readdressed the debate on the use of the word "nigger," now taking a dig at its increasing employment by African-Americans. Pierce's character is filled with self-hatred: "That's why he used the nigger word all the time," says Spike. Finally he is thrown off the bus by those who recognize the damage done to African-Americans by his attitude.

A UCLA film student is jokingly referred to as "Spike Lee." A homosexual couple who are venturing to the march despite Farrakhan's homophobic rhetoric are berated by other less progressive passengers on the bus. (Spike again repels the suggestion that his characters' opinions should be taken as his own: "Come on, it's not me saying it, it's the character in the movie. People who think those are my views are not

The *Get on the Bus* ensemble. (Courtesy of Spike Lee)

very smart.") An actor on the bus wonders aloud how Ice-T and other such rappers get movie roles—again, Spike has no necessary quarrel with such castings: "Sam Jackson thinks low of them. I'm not like that. Mos Def is a great actor. Q-Tip I like. I thought that Ice Cube in *Three Kings* was amazing. It all really depends on who you are talking about."

There is also a member of the Nation of Islam aboard, who doesn't say a word throughout the journey. Still, Spike doesn't avoid the debate on Farrakhan's anti-Semitism. The bus's replacement driver (Richard Belzer) is a Jewish man who eventually voices his personal concerns about Farrakhan's statements against Jews. The argument is lively, and there is a comparison made between the sixty million deaths of black slaves and the six million deaths of Jews in the Nazi camps. Spike believes the comparison was necessary here: "There have always been a lot of African-Americans who have felt that when people of Jewish persuasion talk about the Holocaust they always leave out what happened to the slaves, like it's an afterthought and the murder of six million Jews is the worst thing that ever happened in civilization. I understand, but other things have happened to other people too. It isn't really a matter of comparing numbers; what is important is the overlooking of what happened to slaves here in this country."

Given its tight schedule, *Get on the Bus* was by necessity something of a running-and-gunning production, a fact not lost upon sound mixer Tom Fleischman: "It was like a documentary. It wasn't like they spent a lot of time trying to get great sounds—they just stuck a mike out there and got what it got. And there wasn't much ADR[*] because they didn't have a budget, so we were working with tracks that weren't the best recordings and trying to get the best out of them that we could. And it took some work."

The film was completed just in time to meet its anniversary release date. Before its opening, Spike sent out checks to his investors: "We're happy to say that everybody got their initial investment back before the film even opened, and we made a small profit on it too." Ossie Davis says, "That was the most revolutionary, important thing about that film: the fact that, on the day it opened, Spike called together his investors and paid them back their money. He had pre-sold the film before it went into major distribution and, from the pre-sell, paid the investors. For a man to do that—to know *how* to do that—this is equally important to any other talent that you might

---

[*]Automated dialogue replacement.

have as a filmmaker. I think that Spike is at the top of the game. He is one of the few people who could have sat at the same table as Cecil B. De Mille, Samuel Goldwyn and Jack Warner—all those guys who invented Hollywood."

In total contrast to *Girl 6*, *Get on the Bus* opened to some of Spike Lee's best ever reviews. The few despairing comments made were about the overexposure of Spike Lee, releasing his third film within eighteen months ("a pace," said one, "that made Woody Allen look like Stanley Kubrick"). Was it audience fatigue that caused audiences to stay away from the film? Spike doesn't believe so: "I don't think Columbia really got a grasp on how to present it. It wasn't that they didn't care; it was just really mishandled." This view is shared by Roger Smith: "The film is a sorely underrated piece because it came with all that baggage—I think a lot of people thought it was a documentary."

Smith may have hit the nail on the head. One year on, a number of newspapers were reporting that there was a feeling of exasperation among African-Americans about the legacy of the Million Man March. Many of those who took to the streets of Washington now felt that it was a fleeting moment that hadn't augured the radical change that some had hoped for. Initial fears that the huge numbers at the march would propel Farrakhan to the status of a central figure in American politics had not materialized: looking back, the Million Man March may be seen as the apex of Farrakhan's career, before a speedy fall back from the mainstream toward the margins.

Self-proclaimed "King of Pop" Michael Jackson receives special thanks at the end of *Get on the Bus*. Spike had just finished making a music video for Jackson's song "They Don't Really Care About Us" from the *History* album. Spike says of Jackson, "I had a wonderful experience with him. He's a great collaborator. It's really sad what happened to him. I don't know what he ever expected to gain by having the British journalist Martin Bashir follow him around for weeks. To say on camera that you share a bed with young boys—he hung himself with that one. Did they really think that it would make people understand him more? Sell more records? He could have been more media savvy."

Given the rate at which Spike pumps out product, it was little wonder that some people thought he never shut up. As if his feature output were somehow insufficient, Spike had accepted an invitation from Jonathan Demme to work on an HBO anthology, *Subway Stories*, in which ten directors would tell a story based on New York's subway. Spike came up with a tale about an African-American and a Puerto

Rican having a boxing match on the subway, to be entitled *Niggeri-cans*. He had originally approached DP Ellen Kuras to shoot *Get on the Bus*: now he tapped her for *Niggericans*. Kuras recalls: "It was a two-day shoot, and on the first day I must admit I was a little bit nervous because I didn't know Spike and I'm used to sitting down for hours and talking to the director before the shoot. We were thrust into a situation shooting on the subway, and it was quite a challenge to do what we wanted. In addition I was working with a crew I had never worked with before. During the first couple of shots, I made a suggestion that Spike didn't take up. Then the next couple of shots were Steadicam in the subway car itself, and I just felt like I did not have a connection with him at all. So I went over to him and said, 'Hey, let's try and work this out. I'm here to do this with you, and you're here to do this with me; either we work together or we don't.' From that moment on, we were together and we have been basically together ever since." Kuras would shoot half a dozen projects for Spike over the next six years. Their creative synchronicity is considered exceptional by many in the 40 Acres community. Sam Pollard contends, "The only person who ever talked to Spike about their feelings, about how the relationship is going, is Ellen Kuras." Mike Ellis says, "I know you shouldn't have favorites, and we've had some great DPs on the sets that I've worked on, but Ellen is the best to work with."

For 40 Acres, this relationship was the one good thing to emerge from the HBO shoot: if you watch *Subway Stories* you won't see *Niggericans*. "Well," says Spike, "Jonathan Demme wanted me to cut my film as he said he wanted it to move faster. I said that I wasn't doing it, and that was it. I just found it funny that no one could tell *him* that he needed to cut *his* shit, but he could tell the other filmmakers to cut their stuff. So after I saw his piece I was like, 'Yo! Come on!'" The fledgling association sunk further in the mire as Spike mocked Demme's adaptation of Toni Morrison's *Beloved*. Then the relationship with Demme, such an early admirer of *Do the Right Thing*, got *really* bad. Spike recalls, "One time he was trying to get me to do something for Haiti and he wrote me a letter saying, 'You should be ashamed of being an African-American who stands for so-and-so.' I wrote him a letter back, it was like, 'Motherfucker, who are you? The grand White Father?' I called him every 'motherfucker' in the world, and he never replied to that letter. The first time we talked in years was at the 2004 Venice Film Festival."[*]

---

[*]Spike was on the jury and Demme's *Manchurian Candidate* was screening out of competition. Competing was Wim Wenders's *Land of Plenty*. Wenders did not complain when his film left empty-handed.

*

Spike was soon approaching Ellen Kuras with other projects: "He sent me a script that he was thinking about doing with Steve Martin. I actually thought it was really funny, but it fell through. Soon after he called me to do 4 Little Girls and I was really interested, primarily because my background is in political documentaries. It was a time when a lot of upheaval was happening in the south: there were churches that had been burned, and this was an outrage to me—I just couldn't believe this was happening in our time. I always felt that one of the reasons that I had got into filmmaking was that I wanted to use my craft to be able to say something about the human condition, however I could, in my own humble way. For me this was an opportunity to make a small contribution."

The rise of racist white groups in America's south had shot up the U.S. news agenda following the bombing of the federal building in Oklahoma City on April 19, 1995. There were also several instances of southern churches being bombed, in a manner grimly reminiscent of the murders in September 1963 in Birmingham, Alabama, of four schoolgirls attending the Sixteenth Street Baptist Church: Denise McNair, Addie Mae Collins, Cynthia Wesley and Carole Robertson.

Spike had wanted to make a documentary on the Birmingham atrocity after he had graduated from NYU Film School. He wrote Christopher McNair a letter, asking if he could make a film about the death of his daughter, but never received a response. Still, the desire remained: "It was a story that I wanted to tell, and that is not to say it has never been told before. Being the father of a young girl, I hope I never have to feel that family's emotions, with the loss of a life, particularly just the way that she was murdered. I wanted to go back and talk to the witnesses—friends and relatives who knew them, and have them speak—to really dig deep into the climate of the times."

Fame, coupled with his reputation for supporting fellow African-Americans, would finally give Spike an opportunity to make the film more than a decade later: "I was getting an award in Birmingham, Alabama. I called Chris McNair and told him I was going to be in town and that I would like to meet him and his wife, Maxine. We met and I spent the night at his home and we started talking. He was really feeling me out, and I knew that if I could get the stamp of approval from Chris McNair, such a man of stature down there—he was an elected official—then it would be very easy, or at least less difficult, to get everybody else to fall in line."

With McNair on board, Spike called Sheila Nevins, the head of the documentary division at HBO, and got the green light for funding of what would be his first feature-length documentary: "Previously I had always done small, short things. I wanted to do the feature-length form. It's a different way to tell a story. And my fiction films have helped me with my documentaries because the common denominator between the forms to me is still storytelling. There are going to be some differences, but when you really break it down, it's about storytelling."

Ellen Kuras witnessed Spike's conviction on this score, having grasped the project's brief with zeal: "I could see the connections between the recent spate of bombings and the Birmingham murders, and could see we would be able to make it contemporary. I remember a conversation I had with Spike in the car while we were going on our first scout. I was all excited about visual metaphors, going on in my typical fashion about how we could shoot this or that church, or take some archival footage. And Spike just gives me a little tiny smile and says, 'Ellen, I just want to tell the story.' I didn't try to give my opinion on what the story should be. Spike is a filmmaker: he tells stories. He gets up at four in the morning, he's always working, doing his research. I knew he would get the story down."

Spike decided that the best way to make a documentary of this ilk would be to use a bare-bones crew. It would be the one film on which he didn't use a first AD. He wanted to make the families feel as comfortable as possible in front of the camera. It was an approach that would particularly touch Ellen Kuras: "One thing that was quite revealing to me was when we went to see the McNairs. We interviewed the neighbors and we talked to the friends; it was just like my family. What I think about the difference between races is that people don't interact. I grew up in a completely white suburban neighborhood and community and I had never really had a chance to get to know anybody of color. And when I went to visit the McNairs, it was like their sister was my sister. I really felt a kindred spirit with everybody in a way that I'd never felt before on a documentary, and I was very moved by what had happened. I've been on many documentary interviews in many different situations, and the camera had always been somewhat of a go-between for feeling real emotion with the people while you are shooting. But with Maxine McNair I just broke down. I was so upset, I could hardly look through the camera. The story became more and more powerful as we interviewed more and more people, even though I wasn't sure how we would put the whole thing together to tell the story."

Happily, that aspect of the production would solve itself, as Spike had a debt of service to repay Sam Pollard for his agreeing to work on

Spike on location for 4 *Little Girls*, Ellen Kuras at the camera. (© 1996 David Lee)

Clockers. Pollard describes how he got his producing credit on the film: "Basically it was to help with the conception of the structure, to edit it. I went down to Birmingham on the first shoot, and as we're setting up to shoot the first interviews I was behind Spike as he was asking the questions. Between takes I would lean forward, and Spike would say, 'What did you think?' I would say, 'That wasn't bad, maybe you should ask this?' At first I didn't think Spike was a very good interviewer. I thought, He's not getting emotion out of the people. I was wrong. When I watched the dailies I realized that one thing about being a good interviewer is not always how you ask the questions but if the person who asked you the question touched you. Everybody Spike interviewed, they all opened up to him. The only exception was George Wallace, because he had an agenda. . . . But they trusted him, who he was resonated with them, and they opened up. We spent a lot of time screening all of the dailies together. We would come to 40 Acres at 7 a.m., because I was teaching then, and we would spend three hours a day screening dailies for two weeks straight. We talked, selected all the material that we liked, and I started working on the structure in the editing room. Spike was asking if he needed narration and what the structure should be. I basically said the structure should be that there are parallels—the family, the history of the community—and then they come together on the explosion."

The film opens with Joan Baez singing "Birmingham Sunday,"

Richard Fariña's haunting lament of the devastating incident, over a series of still photographs that really do speak a thousand words. "A lot of times when you see still photographs in documentary, they're so perfunctory that you don't really pay attention to them," says Ellen Kuras. "Spike and I discussed how to make the stills come to life, so that they would be more of a discovery and provide something revealing to the audience. I shot them with different types of lens, with Super-8, reversal, black-and-white, cross-processing—all sorts of things. I was even able to try and take it one step further by taking the archival footage and colorizing it in a way that would make it stand out and be more exciting to look at."

The story of 4 *Little Girls* is told by a series of witnesses, from the families and friends of the victims to surviving activists and informed commentators. Most fascinating are the viewpoints of those in power at the time, including the Princeton-educated counsel for the man accused of the bombings, who tries to give a reasoned defense of Bull Connor's use of water cannon on a group of children, and a stricken George Wallace. The former governor ridiculously tries to defend himself by calling in his personal assistant and "best friend," Eddie Holcey, who happens to be African-American, to appear before Spike's camera. Sam Pollard says of the bizarre footage, "A lot of people think Spike ambushed George Wallace, but it's not the case. That's who this man was." As Spike watched George Wallace attempt a more sophisticated exploitation of African-Americans than he had previously been notorious for, it brought home once more that many things had not moved forward following the struggles of the civil-rights movement.

HBO were so pleased with 4 *Little Girls* that they decided to screen the film in a New York cinema on July 13, 1997, thus readying it for submission to be eligible for the Academy Awards in the Documentary Feature category. The reviews were unanimous in their view that 40 Acres had created a fabulous and intriguing documentary, and the film played all around America in the following months. Come Oscar night on March 23, 1998, 4 *Little Girls* had already picked up a clutch of awards and was the clear favorite for the big trophy. Sam Pollard remembers, "We all thought we were going to win the Oscar. The night before we received a black filmmakers' award. I was there with Spike, our wives were all there, and Spike had given me a silver dollar as a good-luck charm for the next night that I put in my tuxedo. At the Oscars we are sitting there—and all awards ceremonies are pretty boring, but, you know, the anticipation builds up and gets to you. And it reached a furor as Robert De Niro is calling out the nominations. And they gave it to the Holocaust film. We left. We did not stay to the end. I was pissed off. I could not take it. As Spike said on the 4 *Little Girls* DVD, "If there's one thing you can bet the bank on, if there is a Holocaust film in the Academy Awards you are not going to win." We didn't say much to each other; we just went to dinner at Denzel Washington's restaurant. 'We wuz robbed'—I think Spike said that."

"I knew we were going to lose the same minute the nominations were announced," says Spike. "The producer of the Holocaust film was a rabbi. Documentary films on the Holocaust are a cottage industry unto themselves." The winner was Mark Jonathan Harris's documentary *The Long Way Home*, which tells of the struggles of European Jews to survive in the aftermath of World War II up to the advent of the state of Israel. Undoubtedly the Academy's voters had a recent history of responding strongly to films treating the Nazi genocide; for Susan Batson the injustice was simply on the merits of the respective films. She says, "I really am so angry that he didn't win the Academy Award for 4 *Little Girls*—I thought that was exquisite work. I feel that he struck a tone with it that was so surprising, and I have a feeling that it came out of him, because he has a little girl. It was so intimate and so rich and so powerful that I'm very touched by that film, and by him."

The experience of making the film had a profound effect on Spike: "That is the type of film that affected me just like *Malcolm X* did. When you get to meet the African-Americans from a much older generation, you would think that somehow they would be full of hatred and bitterness. But they weren't. These are people who lost their daughters. But they were very philosophical. Of course, they had many years to live with this pain, but it is something that never goes away. They are going to take that to their grave—and Alpha Robertson did when she passed away in 2002."

Stanley Crouch believes that 4 *Little Girls* marked a major development in the work of its maker: "I think he was baptized by those parents when he made 4 *Little Girls*. I thought that it woke him up as a man. I think then that he stopped being like a sullen adolescent college boy who made movies and had these trickle-down black nationalist ideas. I think that when you grow up in the environment that he grew up in in Brooklyn, where there is all of this crude hostility and third-rate black nationalist bullshit—and the most that has happened to the people there is that they might have been harassed by the police—and then to see the extraordinary humanity of these people who actually had their children blown up, it makes you seem small. It was their humility in saying, 'I know that I was bitten but that is not a good

enough excuse to get down on all fours and start barking like a dog.'
His work changes dramatically after that, so I think it had an effect on
him, being around them. I think he started to go in the direction of
becoming a major film director."

The director also announced that he was merging his talents with
DDB Needham to form an advertising agency called Spike/DDB that
aimed to tap into the "urban" market. Hip-hop was now America's
best-selling music genre, and corporations were seeing inner-city
youths as fashion leaders and a lucrative market. Spike had demonstrated with his Nike and Levi's spots that he was adept at exploiting
the market, and the venture would allow him to take more artistic
control of his work: "When I do commercials, I know that it is the
client's word that counts at the end: they present you with the idea,
the storyboards are there, and you just execute it. I really wanted
to have more of a hold on the creative thing. Keith Rhinehart, chair-
person of DDB, approached me. They gave me the start-up money and
they also gave me a foothold and connection to the clients already in
their stable. I'm not there day-to-day, but as far as the work goes, I
have to approve all of it. For the most part I've directed all the spots.
Much credit has to go to Dana Wade, who cracks the whip under me
and the creative director Desmond Hall." Spike would own 51 percent
of the company to boot and it would provide a lucrative additional
revenue stream for him.

Spike, still only forty, was already being viewed as an elder states-
man. Even as his box-office receipts shrank and he was beginning to
struggle for the attention spans of youth culture, significant elders
were beginning to reevaluate his work. This was a man who had
finally shaken off his Mars Blackmon image.

Completing 4 *Little Girls*, forming Spike/DDB, shooting commercials, making music videos for Bruce Hornsby, Chaka Khan and Curtis Mayfield, the birth of his son, Jackson, teaching at NYU . . . such a schedule would keep most people more than occupied in the course of a single year. But Spike even doubled up on the little leisure time that he took in watching the Knicks by now writing a screenplay (and publishing a separate book) on basketball. Amusingly, Spike still believes that "being married and having kids means that I can't do as much as I did before." But in 1998 he was displaying no sense of career fatigue: and it is a testament to the smooth-running machine he had established since the breakthrough of *She's Gotta Have It* that he was able to move so effortlessly from one project to another. He had also become expert, somewhat in the style of Andy Warhol, at delegating tasks and overseeing productions on which he gave a final seal of approval.

The basketball book was entitled *The Best Seat in the House*, in honor of Spike's coveted courtside seats at the Knicks. The cover of the book has Spike sitting on a chair with his Nike trainers flashing before us. Within its pages Spike writes of Nike's chief executive Phil Knight: "We have become friends over the years: he is a nice guy if a little strange, revels in being an outcast, an underdog." But Spike's business association with Nike would raise some unavoidable questions related to the company's contracting out of production to factories in China, Vietnam and Indonesia that employed sweatshop labor.

Phil Knight argues, "Spike has become very closely associated with Nike in the sense that now, whenever controversy comes up, they ask him questions and he has to respond. It bothers us the way we get characterized sometimes by the media. Then it further bothers me when they ask people like Spike and Michael Jordan, neither one of whom has actually been to the factories, to comment. It's whatever can get a headline, and something related to celebrity makes it a much bigger issue. Both of them have handled themselves brilliantly when asked that. I don't like the fact that they are asked, though."

Spike treads carefully in his comments on Nike: on the issue of sweatshops he has consistently toed the Nike line, including the initial placement of blame upon the local manufacturers. As the facts have become more widely known about the vile conditions and the meager wages in the factories, Phil Knight has been forced to back-track. He put the following public-relations spin on the affair: "Some of the things you have done, you realize that you've screwed up. But you just try to do better all the time. We are making some progress." So it's unsurprising to hear Spike Lee say, "When it first came out, they were guilty. That was indefensible. Nike has become aware of that and Phil Knight has done a lot to try and rectify all that stuff." And yet, if Spike really believed that the exploitation of child labor and of minori-ties was indefensible, surely it would be expected that he would be calling for the boycott of Nike? It seems that Spike's love of basketball and his respect for business have wrought a certain kind of havoc upon his beliefs.

To write *The Best Seat in the House* Spike once again called up Ralph Wiley, the *Sports Illustrated* columnist and co-author of the *Malcolm X* companion. Wiley remembers, "The publisher was Crown and they wanted Spike to do a basketball book on how he's a fan at all these Knick games. We didn't want to do an autobiography, and yet it had to be autobiographical. So we start talking, and he tells me about going to these Knicks games with 'his brother,' and I know his brothers Cinque and David, who work with him. But then he was mentioning Chris, his brother who used to go to the Knicks games with him. Chris was a bike messenger. And, clearly, I saw that this was Mars Blackmon. Mars ended up being Spike's homage, his tribute, to his brother, this way-ward brother Chris—who still may be wayward but made his way into his art. Immediately I knew that this is the basis that we jump off of. But it was difficult; Spike was sensitive to that. He would ask, 'Why do we have to do this?' But because I felt this was the essence, he went along with it. I find it very appealing, this integrity of his to say, 'OK, this is the right thing to do, go ahead and do it.' On *Best Seat in the House*, the whole Chris thing was hard. I made the mistake of asking his wife whether she had met Chris, and she was like, 'I ain't ever met Chris.' Spike was upset but he got over it. I said, 'Look, Spike, you asked me to do the book.' And he smiled."

Working with Spike has a serious downside, says David Lee: "It per-meates my dream life that I'm constantly being tortured on set by Spike. I'm sure the others, the ADs and the PAs, must hear Spike's voice in their sleep too, because everybody jumps. It's almost like a joke: you hear Spike yell and it's time to hit the deck. When Spike has a certain tone of voice, there might be like collateral damage or something." David is ruefully amused about the power relations implied: "Forty-three years old and I'm still like one of his younger brothers that he has got to occasionally reprimand. But to me it's part of his personality; he is the archetypal or stereotypical elder brother—so opinionated and self-assured and stubborn, and really good at giving demands—and it serves him perfectly well as a director."

Cinque also goes against the general view that Spike had become less tempestuous over the years: "I don't think Spike has mellowed out at all. He would never blow up as a kid. He is angrier now. Maybe he is not angry in his films, but he can get pissed more than he used to get." Someone who felt Spike's voice was less heard on his films than it ought to be was his wife, Tonya. Since they had married Spike had not written an original screenplay, and as Tonya reflects, 'It felt like it was a long time from *Do the Right Thing, Mo' Better* and *Jungle Fever*, and I personally wanted to bear witness to that aesthetic again. I wanted to hear from him in his work, his own voice, and I kind of felt like I wasn't alone in that—that his audience too would really respond to it."

For ten years Spike had dreamed of making a sports movie: realizing that he needed a box-office hit before he could find sufficient funds to make *Jackie Robinson*, he set about writing a contemporary basketball story. His courtside spat with Reggie Miller of the Indiana Pacers, one that critics claimed spurred the player into demolishing the Knicks' play-off hopes in 1994, made front-page news and ensured that Spike was the celebrity basketball fan par excellence, his association with the Knicks rivaling that of Jack Nicholson's courtside loyalty to the L.A. Lakers. His new script was called *He Got Game*, a term of admiration applied to adept basketball players from Spike's Brooklyn courts.

Spike hoped to avoid the traps into which he felt most sports films fell. He argues, "The best sports film ever was *Raging Bull*. The other film I love is a documentary, *Hoop Dreams*. Most sports films are horrible, because athletes, they are real. And the key to sports is that the game is so dramatic, and you can't re-create that. One way that you can get around it is by not having the film come down to the big game at the end, the big finale. That is so corny. Also I hate when people make things about professional sports and know that they have had to come up with fake names and fake uniforms. We wanted to look at the underbelly—that is what's interesting. *He Got Game* really talks about the athletic prowess of Jesus Shuttlesworth, the number-one high-school player of the nation, number one out of five hundred *thousand* kids who play varsity basketball. What we were really trying to do was show the whole hypocrisy of the NCAA, how they really pimp what they call 'student athletes.' They make all the money and they give these guys a stipend, saying they gave them free tuition; that's not enough, not with all the money that they are making. If you are a highly recruited football or basketball player and you can generate some money for the schools, they will go all out to make sure that you will come to their school. To get these young black men they give them a car, money, throw in some jewelery and they let them know that there is white pussy for them too. If you are the top high-school player in the nation, they will be throwing you the panties."

The debate over student athletes, education and professionalism that has raged for years exploded again in 2003, when Lebron James, an outstanding forward at St. Vincent–St. Mary High School in Akron, Ohio, and Carmelo Anthony opted out of college and decided to sign with the NBA immediately out of high school. The rules had been changed only a few years previously to permit student athletes to test their potential value in the NBA draft without losing their amateur status. The trail taken by Lebron James and Carmelo Anthony had been blazed in the late 1990s by high-school phenomenon Kevin Garnett, now one of the league's premier players. The legendary Cuban boxer Felix Savon refused a $10 million payday to turn professional and fight Mike Tyson, arguing, "Who needs $10 million when you have ten million Cubans who love you?" This is not a view endorsed by Spike Lee, who became one of the main proponents arguing that Lebron should turn professional. Lebron's decision brought the side benefit of a $100 million endorsement contract from Nike, run by Spike's friend Phil Knight. "We liked everything we'd seen about him," says Knight. "His work ethic, his habits and his intelligence. He was the high-school player of the year and everybody wanted him. We weren't highest bidder but we had to bid pretty big to get him. The Michael Jordan sports endorsement has been the most successful of any sports endorsement ever; Tiger Woods is another one that has been very, very successful. So with people like Lebron, we look at that, it means something."

Spike Lee says, "I don't know how you tell someone that you should go to college. Forget about his NBA contract—Nike was going to pay him $100 million. The soccer player Freddy Adu who signed for DC United, he is just fourteen years old. The girl who wrote the script *Thirteen*,[*] she was thirteen when she wrote it. I think people are really getting hip to all these institutions making money and trying to keep these kids amateur, like there is a great aura about amateur status.

[*]Nikki Reed.

They're not amateur in business, because they're making all the money off of you and the kids are not getting anything. The universities and colleges don't care about those guys being educated, especially African-American athletes—they are discouraged from taking the classes and told to concentrate on sport."

He Got Game suggests that where there is business there is likely to be corruption. The film starts off in prison, as Jesus Shuttlesworth's father, Jake, is offered an incentive by the state governor, through a prison officer intermediary: he will regain his liberty if, in the course of a week's parole, he can persuade his gifted son to sign up with his alma mater, Big State University. Several colleges are coveting the young talent and he is due to make his final decision in seven days. Jake has been imprisoned for murdering his wife in a violent feud, and naturally Jesus Junior hates his father. Jesus (named after Earl "Black Jesus" Monroe, one of Spike's favorite players after Walt Frazier) also resents Jake for burdening him with this name. Jesus and his sister have been brought up by their uncle Bubba, but Jesus, because of his basketball talent, is able to take advantage of some gray areas in the regulations to start supporting his sister and himself on his own.

Spike uses the ticking-clock plot structure ("We had to have some way of getting him out of prison, and I don't think it's that far-fetched") to anchor a story that raises a recurring theme in his work: that of parents trying to push their children into careers: "You always have this dynamic where the father thinks that he could have got into the pros, but something happened that killed his dream—because he got married or injured. So what is the next thing that he has to do? Well, he has a son, so he has to guide his son to be the great athlete that he wasn't."

"I sent Denzel the script on a humbug," Spike recalls, "not really expecting that he was going to gravitate to it, because Jake was kind of a shady guy, and up to that point in his young career Denzel hadn't done those types of roles before. But he said, 'Let's do it.'" Thereafter Spike was determined to cast a basketball star as Jesus so as to bestow authenticity on his work: "I just felt that it was imperative—that if Jesus Shuttlesworth was going to be the best high-school player in America, there were no actors who could fake that. So we had young pro athletes come in and audition, and I warned them, 'If you get the part, you are going to have to rehearse for seven or eight weeks before we start shooting.' That's a big commitment, because these guys bust their asses in the regular season, and when the season ends, they just want to go home and chill, let their bodies recover. But not only were they going to have to start rehearsing as soon as the season ended, the film wouldn't end until the day before they had to report back to training camp. Not too many guys wanted to do that, and I understood it. But then Ray Allen of the Milwaukee Bucks walked in; he had a great smile, and he was eager to work."

Acting coach Susan Batson had been doubting the wisdom of Spike's insistence on hiring a nonprofessional, and she saw similar doubts nesting in the director before Ray Allen's emergence: "Denzel said, 'No,' Ray couldn't possibly do it. But I think Spike had confidence in his own eye, and when he found Ray, he only needed me to say 'Yeah.' He only needed confirmation. You cannot influence Spike; he is connected to some kind of truth in himself, and that is his guidance."

Next up, Spike began to hunt for actresses. He needed someone to play Jesus's childhood sweetheart, LaLa Bonilla. "The thing I like about *He Got Game* is that everyone is dirty," says Spike of a film that he feels is one of his best. "But at least LaLa's honest. She tells Jesus she's not foolish enough to think that they will still be together after he goes away to college. So she ends up wanting to get something for herself. For me, Rosario Dawson was the whole film *Kids*, and I thought that she would make a great LaLa. She was from the Lower East Side too, and she has a great look." "I imagined Spike to be a bit of a terror," says Dawson, who turned eighteen as she was cast. "I knew that there were difficulties with him and working with women, and I was kind of curious about that. But in the end he just kept on pushing me—he pushes people because he sees their potential and he expects them to go there. He is like, 'Why are you holding back?' And he really just gave me confidence, because he'd say, 'I'm not worried about you, just do your job.' We'd shoot a scene and then he'd say, 'OK, print,' while I'm like, 'Argh! How was it?' But he'd just put his thumb up and walk away. And you're just touched that he has given you that much of a gesture."

Actress, model and vocalist Milla Jovovich was chosen to play Denzel's love interest, hooker Dakota Burns. "I'd always wanted to work with Spike," Jovovich asserts. "To me he was one of the most influential directors of my generation. When *Do the Right Thing* came out I was thirteen years old: my friends and I got the soundtrack and went to see the movie, and that was like 'our film' for ages. He represented everything that was cool and free. The reaction to Spike Lee in my head was the same as people have to Eminem today. People were really up in arms about everything Spike was doing. So as young people we were completely inspired by that, because that's what you love as a teenager—people telling the truth and not being scared to ruffle feathers doing it."

He Got Game: Ray Allen and Rosario Dawson. (© 1997 David Lee)

Both young actresses found a certain hilarity in Spike's head-principal demeanor on set. Says Jovovich, "My sense of humor is very much about calling people exactly in the moment, and because Spike is so straight-faced and deadpan it was very easy to make fun of him. I think that it might have gotten his goat a little bit." Dawson weighs in, "Spike is a control freak. My parents say he has a Napoleon complex. And my mom is six feet tall and my dad is six three. They would come on set and stare down at him, and he'd be like, 'Yes, can I do something for you?' And I love that."

Cleveland Browns legend Jim Brown, an icon of an earlier generation, was also working with Spike for the first time: "I used to watch him sometimes doing interviews on TV and I recognized that he was very conscious about black people participating in the industry and the history of black people in this country—and that he was a proponent of equal rights for everybody. When I met him, I complimented him on his attitude toward African-Americans and his films being films that had a lot of racial content but were really about people. I also told him that he was young and some of the things that he said about black history weren't necessarily so. . . . And the interesting thing about him was that he accepted my attitude toward him. So I liked him right away."

With the cast in place, the crew went to Brooklyn's southernmost tip to shoot: "Coney Island is a great basketball hotbed," says Spike. "It's where Lincoln High School is. Stephon Marbury of the Knicks went there, his cousin Sebastian Telfair too. They've always had great ballers in Coney Island." Setting the film there also meant that he could consult Earl Smith for advice in what was Smith's backyard: "They shot in the projects that I grew up in. I helped out with getting basketball players, like for the scene where they're playing in the park." Yet, as Mike Ellis confirms, the most important aspect of the location was that it allowed Spike to work using his favored method, turning New York streets into a mini-studio for the duration of a shoot: "We had the whole neighborhood. Classic Spike Lee—taking over the environment and ensuring that Plan B was close at hand so, no matter what happened, there was always something to shoot. Just look at the films—*Do the Right Thing* in one block, *Crooklyn* in one block, *He Got Game* a five-block radius of Coney Island, *Summer of Sam* three blocks in the Bronx. We've never done a film where we didn't get ahead of schedule, and that's good—so the white folks leave us alone."

Rosario Dawson waxes lyrical about Spike's depiction of the area: "Coney Island, the colors looked so beautiful. When he wanted to show how seedy and dirty it was, he did that, with the Milla and Denzel stuff. But when he wanted to show the other side, the romantic side, to give that feeling of where Jesus Shuttlesworth is from, it was gorgeous."

Aisha Coley says of the first day's filming, "That's when I realized how amazing Susan Batson was, because the difference between the before and after of Ray Allen was unbelievable." Batson herself believes that Spike refuses to compromise the momentum of the shooting day in favor of the minutiae of performance ("He'll tell you, 'You can't get it? I'll just cut it out, put the camera on the other person'") and such a straightforward approach may have been useful in handling Ray Allen. "Athletes are used to being coached," Spike reflects. "At a very early age, they get used to someone telling them what to do. That is not to say that they are going to do it any better, but they listen, athletes listen." By contrast, actor Bill Nunn was not always so happy about the conditions under which his performance as Jesus's uncle Bubba was put together: "I had a lot of things in mind for the part. Then one day Spike threw a monkey wrench at me. I wasn't planning on doing my major scene that day. I was there to do something small, and Spike said, 'We're doing the scene now,' and I just had to do it."

Malik Sayeed was back as director of photography for the film, and he and Spike once again made use of reverse stock to shoot flashback scenes depicting the Shuttlesworth family together under one roof before the tragedy of the killing of Martha Shuttlesworth, played by Lonette McKee. Also returning to the Spike fold was John Turturro as Billy Sunday, one of the coaches who tries to recruit Jesus to his school: "Spike asked me to do a couple of things. It was like a friendly gesture, a turn you do for somebody. I had fun."

On his sightseeing trip to prospective colleges Jesus is tantalized by scantily clad white girls, and Spike makes a further major play of color when a sports agent scorns Jesus's suggestion that he wants a brother to represent him. Chick Deagan (Rick Fox), who escorts Jesus around one campus, even suggests that the protégé will have an easier life with a white girlfriend. Spike says, "I've always heard black people say that they can get away with shit with white women that sisters will not go for. And I think it's appropriate that Rick's character says that in the movie. Chick is getting white girls doing his laundry, keys to daddy's car, all types of stuff. A lot of African-American athletes have these slave mentalities where it's all right to hang out and do whatever, but when it comes to finance you are going to need white people to handle your money because brothers are going to fuck it up. When we were

doing rehearsals, those guys in the film (who are all in the NBA)—
Rick Fox, John Wallace, Travis Best, Walter McCarty, Ray Allen—
they all sat around and swapped stories of their recruiting trips. If you
were a top high-school athlete, they know that they have to give you
something more than free tuition and board—you have to get somebody some perks. That stuff in the film is not made up."

He Got Game's obligatory basketball scene nevertheless comes like
a bolt from the blue when Jesus is challenged to a one-on-one by his
father. The director says of the courtside filming, "We just wanted to
show basketball in terms that was poetic, like ballet, the way they
danced—so we wanted to shoot that way." The *mano a mano* would
also be a duel between Washington the Oscar-winning actor and Allen
the thespian rookie. "Ray was intimidated by Denzel," says Spike.
"Seasoned actors are intimidated by Denzel. He had been acting since
third grade, so it is perfectly understandable for Ray Allen to feel
intimidated. But the basketball scene was one of the last that we shot,
so he was way over that intimidation."

Susan Batson notes, "The interesting thing about this was that, in
the script, the son has to beat the father, demolish him. What happened when we shot it was that Denzel came out and was able to hit
some baskets." Spike concurs: "They were playing hard. Denzel
started throwing up some lucky shit that was going in, and Ray
started getting mad. But Denzel was saying, 'Look, I know the script

He Got Game: the climactic Allen–Washington courtside duel. (© 1997 David
Lee)

says that I'm going to lose fifteen to nothing—*fuck* what the script says, I'm not getting shut out, I'm not going to be no doughnut.' And I told him, 'Play. . . .'" As Susan Batson saw it, "I was shocked, because Ray—who was twenty years younger and up against Denzel the actor—looked like he had never played a game of basketball in his life. I turned to Spike and said, 'Cut!' and he said, 'No.' He was sitting there watching, until it finally got ridiculous and then he cut. So I went up to Ray and said, 'Do I have to teach you basketball? What in the hell is going on?' And Ray looked down on me and said, 'Susan, Denzel got game.' I said, 'Denzel got game? Are you crazy? He ain't got game, he's just acting his buns off and you're believing him.' Denzel, he couldn't walk the next day, but his commitment to 'I'm going to play basketball' came forward that day and it was amazing."

Though in life Spike would back the pragmatic and lucrative professional choice of Lebron James, *He Got Game* ends with Jesus choosing to go to the school that his father wants him to, so rejecting the riches on offer to him at the time. "That was about the love for his father," Spike asserts. "He is trying to build back their relationship. But his father had to end up back in jail—it would have made it too Hollywood, too saccharine to end up any other way."

The soundtrack to *He Got Game* would prove one of the finest to grace a Spike Lee joint. Music supervisor Alex Steyermark says, "Spike uses music in very unexpected ways. It is really bold: if I have to pick a quality that I've learned from Spike, it is that I've learned to be bold. Go for it, visually, stylistically, musically. He likes bringing different cultural elements in music. And only Spike would bring together Aaron Copland and Public Enemy. But they are both quintessentially American music icons: Copland, from Brooklyn, the quintessential American classical composer, and Public Enemy are the equivalent to hip-hop."

"I've always loved Copland's music," says Spike. "It is definitely American. And basketball, even though it's played the world over now, is very American. You always hear 'Fanfare for the Common Man' in commercials—people who don't even know who Aaron Copland is still know his stuff. I just felt that juxtaposing Aaron Copland with Public Enemy would be a good mix, and it came off. I had the blessings of the Copland estate, so I had all of his recorded music, and I picked out the stuff that I liked and tried to match it up with the picture. And Public Enemy did such a great job on *Do the Right Thing* and Chuck D is a big basketball fan, so it was good to come back together."

*

So, having persuaded her husband to bring back his own voice, was Tonya Lee pleased with the results? "*He Got Game*, it wasn't exactly on the button. I was happy he did it. In some ways, I did feel his voice. But I took real issue with that LaLa character and we had real debates about her. I just felt there wasn't that much exploration of her— granted, she wasn't the main character, but I think that you should know all of your characters. But here she was, this girl who was trying to break off a piece of somebody else's success, and I was really frustrated because I didn't really understand why she was that way." Spike answers, "There are women who want a 'baller,' plain and simple. To me LaLa is a very well developed character. That's who these women are who go after these 'ballers,' and they start in high school." Developed or not, LaLa struck a chord with audiences, as Rosario Dawson can attest: "Spike says all the time he gets a bombardment of basketball players who are like, 'I wanna meet LaLa.' And he has the audacity to ask me, 'Do people still call you LaLa?' I hear people call out, 'LaLa, how you doing? You got a man? You married? You want to fuck?' I don't understand, because if you think that I'm that character, why would you want to date me? LaLa is cutthroat."

Spike was himself familiar with people wanting a piece of him, and indeed this tendency was about to force him to move from his beloved Brooklyn. "People were ringing our doorbell every hour of the night," remembers Tonya, "asking for a job, a hook-up, anything. 'Here is a script, can I have a job? Can you give this to Spike?' It was an issue of quality of life, in particular for me and my children. I couldn't live in a place where the neighborhood felt they could ring our doorbell. The last straw came for me when I was at home by myself, four in the morning, Satchel is six months old, and a man rings the doorbell and says, 'Someone is stealing the flowers from your window box.' I said, 'OK, thanks for letting me know.' He then rings the bell again. 'Well, you need to come out here.' And he kept ringing the bell, trying to get me to come outside. I felt really vulnerable. So I gave Spike the ultimatum."

Such had been Spike's proclamations of affection for Brooklyn that his move across the bridge to Manhattan was deemed newsworthy. But Milla Jovovich offers the following rebuke to the detractors taking the opportunity to accuse the director of being a sellout: "Spike Lee *is* Brooklyn. It doesn't really matter where he resides in that sense."

He Got Game opened on May 1, 1998, and entered the box-office charts at number one: not since his last collaboration with Denzel Washington, *Malcolm X*, had Spike had a film land on the top spot. Eugene Levy argued in *Variety*, "Lacking the moral indignation, outrage and militant politics that marked Lee's earlier work, this vibrantly colorful film is a tad too soft at the center, and arguably the director's most mainstream movie." But reviews were generally favorable, the critics united in agreement over the Aaron Copland score. Bruce Diones of *The New Yorker* stated, "The film is gorgeously shot (slow-motion basketballs spin in the air like Kubrick's spaceships), and the majestic Aaron Copland score helps some of the images to soar."

Stanley Crouch believed that *He Got Game* confirmed his impressions of first seeing *4 Little Girls*: "I thought it was a hell of a movie. The basic thing with Spike Lee is you've always got the ever-present potential for a kind of adolescent quality—the rock'n'roll position that is always available, the hostile entertainer: 'Part of my entertaining you is I'm going to say "Fuck you,"' so you actually come to be entertained by that. I think he largely suppressed that in *He Got Game*. He may have grown out of it. To a certain extent, the human reality is that you can't divide the world on the basis of ethnicity because it does not have anything to do with the souls of people: everybody has at some point to set aside their ethnicity to find out what their soul is. But black women destroyed *He Got Game*. All over the country they were saying, 'Denzel, you said you wouldn't!' All these black women outraged that their Denzel was in a love scene with a white woman." The "white woman" in question, Milla Jovovich, says, "I think that Denzel knew—but none of the rest of us really knew—what kind of reaction that was going to get from black women

He Got Game: Milla Jovovich and Denzel Washington. (© 1997 David Lee)

all around America. But Spike is always starting trouble. That's Spike. And I think that it hit a raw nerve for black women." In complete contrast to *Jungle Fever*, where Spike had overplayed the interracial relationship in the publicity for the film, the director was unconcerned by this aspect of *He Got Game*: "You have a man who's been in prison and she is a prostitute and she is next door—this was not an issue."

New York actor Ed Norton, who had recently been nominated for an Oscar for his performance in *Primal Fear*, was downbeat about the general response to *He Got Game*. "I first met Spike because I wrote him a letter about *He Got Game*. I wrote to Spike and Denzel. I felt it was like a stylistic masterpiece, such a great American film, and a deeply American film. It really rolled around in these hugely American questions: the examination of fathers and sons, rage and money, and the whole matrix of money and sports and fame, the way that the American value system has everybody in a twist about how they are going to get on the gravy train. But every review I read of the movie was so literal, it quibbled with the reality of certain things. The film was in no way literal; it was such an epic poem, the whole thing was stylistically heightened. You have this hero, moving on an almost Homeric journey through these moral sirens. The guy saying, 'This watch, this car, this house,' and the colleges offering him women and fame, and his uncle wanting cars, and his girlfriends wanting a piece of him. It was so beautiful, so technically audacious, and people treated it in such an absurdly banal way—I thought that it was another one that people really missed the boat on."

Something that at the time did capture the imagination of predominantly black audiences was Kevin Rodney Sullivan's black romantic comedy *How Stella Got Her Groove Back*. Starring Angela Bassett as a forty-something woman who falls for the dashing Taye Diggs while on vacation in Jamaica, the film took a whopping $38 million at the box office following its summer 1998 release. Soon 40 Acres would itself take advantage of this new subgenre in movies—the black romantic comedy.

Spike was moving from one job to another with such alacrity that not even those closest to him could keep track of all his activity. His brother David reflects, "There is this whole other person who you find out information about thirdhand. One of the weirdest moments was when I was just reading the newspaper one day and I saw Spike was in Italy with Luciano Pavarotti. I didn't even know he'd left the *country*. But there it was, he was in Italy with the Three Tenors. I *still* don't know what that was." In fact, filming the Three Tenors for PBS was a display of intent by Spike: he still hoped to move 40 Acres into the lucrative television production market.

To this end Spike further agreed to film a one-man Broadway show by his friend the actor John Leguizamo: "I'd seen *Freak* before," says Spike, "and I'm a big Leguizamo fan." But filming a stage piece posed a fresh set of directorial problems for Spike: "I was talking to the cameramen over a headset because I was in a control room with monitors in front of me. But I didn't want to do anything that was going to get in the way of John's performance: we just wanted to show his talent and try to transfer that to the tape. So it was a matter of having our cameras in the right places and in communication with each other too. We recorded the show in front of a live audience on two performances. After the first show everybody reviewed it together, we talked, and then we rectified our mistakes the second time." Barry Brown would cut the film so that each of the numerous characters that Leguizamo assumed throughout his show were viewed from a different perspective. The success of the collaboration led to Spike asking the Hispanic Leguizamo to take a lead role—that of an Italian-American—in the next feature film he had decided to shoot, *Summer of Sam*: "There was concern from Michael Imperioli that John wasn't Italian-American. That was a big concern with his accent. But in directing him I wasn't going to say, 'Talk like Vinny from the Bronx.'"

Summer of Sam constituted the latest version of the *Anarchy in the Bronx* script that Michael Imperioli had first presented to Spike at the *Girl 6* première. "We took it to certain companies with Spike," says Imperioli. "It was rough going, as it often is for first-time directors. My partner, Victor Colicchio, and I, we did more drafts and the scope of the movie kept on getting bigger: it went from this small neighborhood character study to a story of New York City at the time of the Son of Sam killings. I began to feel the movie got a little too big in scope for me to tackle as a first-time director. Around that point Spike said he wanted to direct it, that he had nothing on his slate for that summer. He had seen every draft and been involved in it, so we said, 'OK.' He then took our last draft and he did a shooting script, adding some other elements to the story."

The heart of the narrative remained the same. Imperioli explains how the idea came to fruition: "My partner had a friend who was a punk rocker in 1977. Victor himself was in a punk band at the time and this guy he knew was pretty much beaten up by people in his neighborhood, who considered him a suspect for the Son of Sam murders. That was amazing to me, because a cousin of *mine* was almost beaten to death by people who were from his neighborhood who thought *he* was the killer. So Victor's acquaintance was the basis for the character of Richie, played by Adrien Brody. Richie is like a freak

Summer of Sam: Adrien Brody as Richie. (© 1998 David Lee)

to the people whom he grew up with, Italian guys who hang out on the
street corner. He's a punk and he dances in a gay emporium—to them,
those are the most base kinds of things you can do. Then the second
main character, Vinny, was based on someone I knew, mixed with a
composite of people my partner had knowledge of. On the surface
Vinny really fits into that neighborhood: he's handsome, a good
dancer, a good dresser, the ladies all love him, he's a man's man. Yet he
has this side that really is kind of hurtful and incapable of loving, and
it ruins his marriage. Whereas Richie, the guy people think is a demon,
is capable of love."

Spike was enamored by the story: "One of the things that I loved
about the script was that it showed you human nature: when something bad happens, there has to be a sacrificial lamb. A mob mentality
takes over. And a mob don't give a motherfuck about 'Guilty' or 'Not
guilty': they just need somebody's neck wrung for that bloodlust to be
quenched. So Richie has to be the Son of Sam, because he's a punk and
wears his hair long and his sexual preference is shaky and he hangs out
in the Village. There's four good enough reasons for him to be Son of
Sam. And if he's not? We don't like the fuck anyway, so it doesn't matter if we kill him. That's the mentality. I had input on the script but I
didn't want to rewrite it—there were just some other things that I
wanted to push the button on. The original script never left the Bronx,
but I wanted to incorporate other parts of New York City."

Michael Imperioli's credits on the picture would contract yet further: "Originally I was going to play Richie, but then I was contracted
to *The Sopranos* and that summer of 1998 we shot the first season of
the show, so I wasn't even able to be around that much." Imperioli
makes the briefest of cameos; Adrien Brody was cast as Richie, with
Jennifer Esposito as his love interest, Ruby. Mira Sorvino, Oscar-
winner for *Mighty Aphrodite*, took the role of Vinny's exasperated
wife, Dionna. Sorvino had just ended a relationship with Spike's newly
acquired nemesis Quentin Tarantino. "Mira came with a reputation of
being a hard actress," says Spike. "I didn't see it. She was great."

Spike's film would begin and end with to-camera addresses by Jimmy
Breslin, the *New York Daily News* journalist with whom David
Berkowitz corresponded while he was preying on canoodling couples
in parked cars. Spike says, "By letting Jimmy give an overview we
wanted to show that really this is a historic piece, not something made
up. This shit happened." Still, when it became public knowledge that
Spike Lee would be making a film set around the Son of Sam murders,
the families of Berkowitz's victims voiced concerns to the media. "It
affected the film," says Spike, "because it put us in a defensive posture

Summer of Sam: John Leguizamo as Vinny, Mira Sorvino as Dionna. (© 1998 David Lee)

even before we began shooting. News crews were showing up, and it was putting the film in a negative light. I had to start doing interviews saying we're not disrespecting the victims' families. They thought the film was about David Berkowitz. But that's not the film we made. *Summer of Sam* is about the summer of 1977 in New York City, when a whole lot of different things were happening. We never heard a complaint from the families again after the film was in cinemas."

The year that Spike Lee decided to become a filmmaker, 1977, was thus a pivotal moment for the director. For the young Michael Imperioli, it was an equally impressionable period: "That summer is emblazoned on my memory. I was twelve years old, so just old enough to really be affected by it. I was a Yankees fan. I love the New York movies of that era, like *Taxi Driver*. And I really like the music from the time—I'm a huge fan of the CBGB period and New York punk."

Most of these were common memories for Spike, except for one: "Alex Steyermark was a great resource for me, God bless him. Thank God he loves punk, because I don't know a motherfucking thing about it. But we had to find a punk-rock band that could be the group Adrien Brody's character is in. We listened to a load of CDs and then we had to write a punk song, knowing that the lyrics would be from one of the letters from the Son of Sam." The music supervisor says,

"This was a rare instance with Spike. Usually he just knows what he wants with music. But punk was music I grew up with, that was my thing. So I put together sample CDs for Spike. Also all the references in the script were to Jimi Hendrix and I told Spike, 'If this guy was into punk he would really be more into the Who than he would be into Hendrix.' Then he went back and rewrote stuff."

Spike also sent the script to costume designer Ruth Carter, asking her —as he will often do with favored colleagues—to synopsize its story for him. "*Summer of Sam* was a period film," says Carter, "and as I had brought an Oscar nomination to 40 Acres for *Malcolm X*, another period film, I felt Spike was saying to me, 'You did good, so here's my next period thing.'" Carter was asked to work on the film, replacing Sandra Hernandez, who was aggrieved at the handling of what she took to be a demotion. Spike is unapologetic: "Why should Sandra Hernandez, because she worked on one of my films, expect to work on all of them?" The director claimed the right to hire the person he felt best fitted the job, free of obligation and no longer tied to the idea of the 40 Acres team. Giancarlo Esposito believes that Spike has grounds for such a position: "The big question Spike would always ask was, 'Are you down?' 'Giancarlo, are you down?' My answer was always 'Yes,' because I think that he is a provocative, entertaining, visionary filmmaker. Now I don't think he needs any of us."

Shooting *Summer of Sam*, Spike found himself warmly welcomed in the Bronx. First AD Mike Ellis remembers, "The community just opened up to us, so much more than if we were in Brooklyn or Manhattan. Everybody was very gracious." Spike adds, "This Italian-American neighborhood, right on the water, they welcomed us with open arms. Ladies were saying, 'Spike, come over to our house for lunch, we'll make you some good Italian food.' It was a complete contrast to the reception that we got in Bensonhurst for *Jungle Fever*."

At sixty-six days, though, the shoot was a long one with 40 Acres for DP Ellen Kuras. *Summer of Sam* was backed by Disney, for whom Kuras had recently completed another service: "I had come off of *The Mod Squad*, where there were a lot of studio people around, wanting to exert their own control over the movie. Whereas two days later, on the set of *Summer of Sam*, it was just me and Spike. What Spike told me was that he really wanted the picture to feel hot and humid. He said, 'Take a look at *Do the Right Thing* again.' But I thought this movie had to have a different feel, a different look to it. I wanted to make the blacks more murky, because in humidity blacks are not blacks. I also discussed trying to do some of the murders with a different shutter speed, trying reversal. We had a huge crane shot as John Leguizamo drives up to the club, and the Steadicam gets off the crane and walks with him into the club. To make that shot happen with a very slow film stock would have cost a lot of money. I priced it out and then showed Spike that if we used another film stock we could get a look really close to the look he wanted for the shot and still save $20,000."

Prop man Kevin Ladson had a nightmare on the film: "Whatever could go wrong went wrong. It was a horrible experience." A day's shooting was delayed for nine hours by the wrong car being delivered to the location from Connecticut. "That was absolutely my worst day in film." With his usual candor, Mike Ellis speaks of serious problems with Adrien Brody: "I liked him for a little while, but he was just such an 'ac-tor.' On one scene he wanted to have his eye-line clear for his four pages of dialogue with Leguizamo. But he wants permission for his mother—who's a photographer—to be in the other actor's eye-line taking pictures. I'm like, 'Fuck you, what about all this actor shit?' I don't like the hypocrisy of that." Spike adds, "What bothers me most with an actor—and I'll use a sports analogy—is if you are a manager and you have a player who's more concerned about their individual stats than the goal, which is to win. And he's that type of actor. He is more concerned about how many lines do I have, how do I look, than what is necessarily best for the film."

The on-set problems with the actor were to have a decisive effect on the film. "I think that in shooting the film it was more about Adrien, but when Spike edited the film, it was more about Leguizamo," says Mike Ellis. Spike agrees: "That is something very funny about film. You can shoot a movie and then you get to the editing room, and because of the performance or whatnot, it becomes somebody else's story. When we were shooting, Adrien Brody was telling me he was the star of *The Thin Red Line*. But I guess something happened with Terrence Malick, because when I saw it, he was like an extra. When I got a Cesar award in 2002, Roman Polanski* and I talked about it also. Adrien is a good actor, but he gives the directors trouble, simple as that. I'm not trying to badmouth him, but you ask some directors who have worked with him and they will say the same thing."

As such, *Summer of Sam* would be told mostly through the character of Vinny, the young married Italian who cannot cope with monogamy. Roman Catholic Vinny (somewhat akin to one of the characters in John Leguizamo's one-man show *Freak*) is a sex addict

---

*Polanski directed Brody in *The Pianist*, for which the actor won the Best Actor Oscar.

convinced he is heading toward eternal damnation. The film starts with Vinny and Dionna dancing at a nightclub, intercut with shots suggesting they are alone. Spike says of the sequence, "Everybody has seen *Saturday Night Fever*, but we definitely did not want any Tony Manero stuff. They are dancing and they are so in love with each other that they just forget everybody, so we want to show literally that they are dancing by themselves." Vinny then sneaks off to have sex with Dionna's cousin (visiting from Italy), close to the spot where the Son of Sam is murdering another couple. Seeing the aftermath of the murder sends Vinny into a paranoid state: he now almost wants Sam to murder him in divine retribution.

The director has fond memories of a particular exchange between Mira Sorvino and John Leguizamo: "I love that scene where Mira leaves. That is all hand-held, one cut. We just rehearsed it. We just did the camera movement. I said, 'I do not want you guys to do the words. Don't do the lines; show us where you are going to go so we can get the focus marks and move the camera.' So we are ready, but we did not know that Mira was going to throw the record albums out of the window—she was throwing shit out of the window, which was great."

Dionna, recognizing that her husband is deeply unsatisfied with their sex life, attempts to spice it up. "How does he like to fuck?" she asks one of her husband's ex-girlfriends. She even accompanies him to the legendary sex club Plato's Retreat. Of the club Spike says, "I never went to Plato's Retreat. I was too young. But I had people who had been there telling me about it. We had an R-rated orgy in the film." The sexually liberated attitude of his wife sends Vinny into a further guilt-ridden flux and on the way home the couple have the first of two major bust-ups that are noticeable for the differing music accompaniments: Abba's "Dancing Queen" and Thelma Houston's "Don't Leave Me This Way." The director notes, "'Don't Leave Me This Way' was right on the money, whereas 'Dancing Queen' was a counterpoint, the total opposite of what the scene is about. But Abba would not give the song to us. I had to write them a letter and get on the phone. They thought that it would be someone poking fun, because people have definitely taken their shots at Abba over the years. I've never had this whole thing about hating disco, because for the most part when people said they hated disco, disco was a euphemism for gays, blacks and Hispanics, plus I liked disco too."

Spike wanted to tell a story that branched out from characters in a Bronx neighborhood, showing how fear gripped New York in that summer of 1977. To this end he used television footage as background exposition throughout, a device that allowed him to slip in footage of Reggie Jackson famously bringing the World Series to New York. Spike also has his swan song as an actor in a cameo role. He says, "That gave me an excuse to grow an afro."

Ultimately *Summer of Sam* was little concerned with the psychology of David Berkowitz or the efforts of law enforcement to apprehend him. Although the scenes featuring Berkowitz's killings are those where the use of reversal stock is most striking, Ellen Kuras recalls, "I was like, 'Let's abstract the killings more and more.' Because the more that the murders happen and the more and more that the press starts flushing out the stories, you realize that they become abstractions in people's minds. So in a way we were really trying to show that visually." The bizarre texture of the footage also allowed Spike to have a speaking black labrador admonishing Berkowitz (Michael Badalucco) to "Kill, kill, kill": "What we see of Berkowitz's apartment is not the real world; it's insanity. In his world, the dog told him to kill people, and that is what he did. So I didn't think it was far-fetched to have the dog speak." John Turturro remembers, "Spike wanted me to do something in that movie, but I couldn't, I needed to take a vacation with my family. So Spike said, 'Would you do the voice of the dog?' And I died laughing."

This request is a sign of a playfulness in Spike that otherwise rarely shows itself in his films or on the set. His sense of humor and cinematic references continued in the sound mix for the film. Tom Fleischman remembers, "There is a shot at the beginning that pans across Sam's apartment to rotting food on the stove. There's a sandwich, and a fly on the sandwich. All of a sudden Spike gets up and goes into the sound booth and says, 'Let me record something.' He gets in and says, 'Help me, help me,' in homage to *The Fly*. We pitched it up and made it sound like a little fly. You can hardly hear it, but it is in there."

"One of my favorite aspects of *Summer of Sam*," says Spike, "is Terence Blanchard's score. That was the first score that we did in London, at Air Studios. I think the musicians in London are great, members of the Royal Philharmonic and London Symphony Orchestra. It's cheaper than New York and L.A. too." The move to London sat well with Blanchard too: "I think it was Alex Steyermark who suggested going to London. We had a great experience. And Spike is the kind of guy who thinks, If it ain't broke don't fix it. Spike said, 'I need this score to be dark, real big.' Now that was a dark movie to work on. I had to step away from that movie a lot, working on these scenes, and it sometimes was hard for me to take it out of the realm of reality because it is a true story. You sit there and think about what these women must have been going through at a particular point in New York's history: people were

afraid of everybody, anybody who was a little different was a suspect
. . . we kind of experienced it in my generation with the sniper shootings in Washington, DC." Blanchard also encouraged Spike to use synthesized instruments on the score for the first time: "I think what Spike
wasn't into, and I'm not into, is using synthesized instruments to emulate real instruments. But when I started using pads and stuff, Spike
started to see that in some instances it was beneficial to use synthesized
sounds in addition to acoustic instruments."

Behind the scenes, the battles were not over. Ellen Kuras was
unhappy: "I flew out to L.A. to check all of the release prints, and
Kodak had changed the print stock. On *The Mod Squad* I had been
horrified by the release print: Kodak had introduced a new stock
called Vision to replace the 86 stock, and the resulting look was not
the film that I had shot. So I told Spike even before we started, 'Listen,
I know this is Disney and they have a deal with Kodak, but I'm not
printing on that new stock.' So I managed to print all of the film on the
old film stock, and when I made a print for release in Los Angeles they
said, 'You have to print on Kodak.' I said, 'Let's put the prints up side
by side and you tell me that they're the same.' And after the first reel
they said, 'All right, it's different. . . .' We ended up flashing the intra-
negative in order to get it closer. But Spike supported me all the way
through my fight with Disney. He is the type of person who takes
action right away, he does not procrastinate one iota; he will get on the
phone to whoever and start talking. The big key thing is that whenever
anything comes up, I've learned that I should let him know, no matter
what it is."

Summer of Sam received its world première at Cannes as part of the
Directors' Fortnight. "We didn't get selected for competition, but I still
wanted to go to Cannes," says Spike. "For us, Cannes has always been
a great vehicle to get awareness around the world, a great publicity
push. We've always had a great time in Cannes and there's always
been a special affinity, from *She's Gotta Have It*. There have been little things—Wim Wenders and shit—but otherwise I don't have a bad
thing to say about it." The film was soon being touted by the press as
Spike Lee's first without a predominantly African-American cast. This
one-dimensional pocketbooking of his previous oeuvre in terms of
color lit the director's ire: "Look at *Do the Right Thing*—I don't
even want to waste breath addressing stuff like that. I've been
asked by white journalists, 'How do you direct white actors?' 'Very
carefully. . . .' I mean, it is crazy." Michael Imperioli formed the same
impression from what he was reading in the press: "I think I was even
asked at the time, 'Why do you want Spike Lee to make that movie?

Shouldn't an Italian make it?' If you're making a movie about the Roman Empire should you get an Italian? Martin Scorsese made a movie about the Dalai Lama: is that wrong? Should they have got a Tibetan guy? Where do you draw that line? It becomes ridiculous at that point."

Barry Brown comments, "The criticism was based on a couple of things. One is just racism and selfishness by a white audience. I remember people would say to Spike and to me personally, right after *She's Gotta Have It* and especially after *School Daze*, 'When is Spike going to put a white person in his film?' My response was, 'Wait a second, let me get this straight. There are 300 films made every year; 299 of them are about white people—you can't give another group something? The self-centeredness is mind-boggling. Do you ever turn to one of the 299 other directors and say, "When are you going to put a black person in? When are you going to put an Asian in? Why aren't you doing that?"' And if I got mad enough, I would say, 'It is because basically you're a racist. The one black filmmaker who comes along and does anything, the first thing you want him to do is not make black films. Why? Because you have got to have 100 percent and you are not checking yourself out. Something is really, really wrong with you to ask that question.'"

Spike was increasingly of the mind that critics came to his movies with preconceptions: "Their review of my films is 'Why I Don't Like Spike Lee.' They don't review the film. After Woody Allen went through all that shit when he married his stepdaughter I decided to read every review of his next film, and there was no mention of that. Not one. Then I read my reviews. 'Why is he jumping up and down at the Knicks games?' Why aren't they able to make the distinction between the director and the film?"

Summer of Sam's U.S. première took place at the end of June 1999. "It was one of the greatest nights of my career," says Michael Imperioli. "I hadn't seen the final product until that moment. I was knocked out. It was really thrilling." Imperioli had further cause to be grateful for Spike's efforts in boosting his career: "At the end of the first season of *The Sopranos* I wrote a spec episode of the show and then I had David Chisholm, one of the creators, go see *Summer of Sam*. And that's how I got the gig writing on the show in addition to my acting role."

Summer of Sam took $8 million on its Independence Day weekend opening and eventually grossed $22 million. The reviews ranged from the glowing (Michael Wilmington in the *Chicago Tribune*) to the ho-hum (*Entertainment Weekly*'s Lisa Schwarzbaum). Stanley Crouch strikes a middling note: "*Summer of Sam* doesn't completely work, but what he was trying to do was deal with many different kinds of people—which is something that people don't often try other than on television, because American film is stuck in American fiction; there is no real conception that there is more than one ethnic group in a story. I did think that he made a mistake because, in theory, John Leguizamo should be able to play an Italian—but he seemed like a Latin guy who was surrounded by Italians, so we never bought it. It was not beyond the talented Leguizamo; I just don't think that Spike really made him do it. But I thought he had one of the most intimate scenes between two women that I've ever seen in a movie, which showed that Spike could be a great director. He has Mira Sorvino and Leguizamo's mistress talking in the bathroom, and Spike asks Sorvino to express something you almost never see in American films, which is real humility. Because she really loved this cat, whom she is trying to figure out, whom she really wants to make happy. And the way that woman says, 'Are you telling me how to fuck my husband?' and the way she nods . . . that is a profound moment for me in film. Because it wasn't trying to make fun of her and her situation."

Following the advent of Spike/DDB, the director shot an increasing number of commercials. One of the most intriguing was for the Navy Seals. Spike asked Randy Fletcher to fill in as first AD: "But I was really surprised that Spike took that job on," says Fletcher. After all, Spike once criticized Monty Ross's decision to join the army. Spike argues, "Historically the United States Navy has been the most racist of all the armed services. They came to me and said, 'Spike, we want to come into the modern world. We don't want to be the only armed services that the minorities don't want to come into.' So I did a commercial, and I had no problems with that. I was glad they came to me. It is being realistic if you say every country needs armed services. And black people have been in armed forces since . . . well, Crispus Attucks was the first person who died in the War of Independence. We have always been very patriotic. If you look at the Spanish-American War, World War I, World War II, Korean War, Vietnam, Gulf War, Iraqi War, there has been a long history of involvement. People have this backward thing of 'If you are against the war in Iraq then you are against armed forces.' That is crazy. You can be 100 percent for the soldiers but at the same time be against the war."

15 *Original Kings of Comedy, Bamboozled, A Huey P. Newton Story* and *Jim Brown*

"We started 40 Acres," states its chief executive, "thinking that we would be a group that developed a company of people in front of and behind the camera as filmmakers. What has changed is that people who started off at 40 Acres have moved on to do great things at other places. We've been a launching pad." As executive producers, 40 Acres and a Mule's box-office success rate has been as intermittent as Spike Lee's own. *Drop Squad, New Jersey Drive* and *Tales from the Hood* all failed to make a splash, and it then took the company four years to mount another production. But by this time Spike had persuaded Sam Kitt, the production executive at Universal, to come on board as head of development. Kitt got to work on three projects that would each receive theatrical release.

The small number of titles on which Spike had served as producer to that point was a surprise to Nelson George: "Despite the explosion in the early eighties and into the nineties of African-American filmmakers, we have not created producers. We have directors, we have writers, we have actors—but we don't have creative middlemen, guys with good taste who can help talent get to the next place. Whereas, in hip-hop, that is what Russell Simmons has done, what Sean 'Puffy' Combs does.* Of course, it's not like being a producer is a lot of fun; it is a lot of negotiations and a lot of tenacity. But Spike has done some of that, and Malcolm Lee's *The Best Man*, Gina Prince-Bythewood's *Love and Basketball* and Lee Davis's *3 a.m.* were all products of the fact that when motivated by a script Spike can be really useful and a great guide."

Spike decided that his cousin Malcolm was due a shot at directing his own feature. Malcolm says, "He always has a plan, even if he doesn't tell you about it. One day he said, 'Send me your short films and two of your most recent scripts.' We then met and he told me, 'Your work is good. I want to get you hooked up with my agency. I'll

---

*The business acumen of these two men, whether it be selling records, clothes or credit cards, has been phenomenal. Some have argued that it was the extravagant "playa" lifestyles of Combs and other rap moguls, such as Master P of Cash Money Records (the Cash Money Millionaires coined the term "bling bling" in 1999), that brought rap from the "gangsta" era to the decadent aesthetic of hip-hop at the turn of the century.

fly you out and you'll meet with them.' I get to the meeting and there
are five agents waiting to take me on as a client. They were like, 'Listen, Spike never recommends anybody to us; you're the first so we
knew that it warranted some attention.' I played it cool in the room,
but inside I was like, 'Holy shit, this is great: he thinks a lot of me.'
Then, when I wrote the script for *The Best Man*, he gave it to the studio that he had a deal with, before even telling me. All of a sudden I
get a call from Universal saying they want to meet me. But I think
Spike and the studio liked this script because it was commercial, it was
tight, it had a finite beginning, middle and end—there's going to be a
wedding on Sunday, the movie starts on the Friday. . . . It's a very
familiar genre, but at the same time there hadn't been any black wedding pictures done to date, so it seemed fresh." Spike felt likewise: "It
was a smart script. And I liked the way that you saw these young black
professionals in their world."

With Spike busy making *Summer of Sam* as *The Best Man* went
into pre-production, Malcolm found that "I was dealing more with
Sam Kitt than I was with Spike. Spike came to the set on the first
morning, just to say, 'Hey, good luck, call me if you need me,' and I
didn't see him for the rest of the shoot. Talked to him a couple of
times about some managerial things I wanted taken care of, and he
took care of them. But on the other hand, he is still the older cousin
and filmmaker, so he shook my cage a couple of times. Some things
we didn't see eye to eye on, and I 'won,' so to speak: ultimately as the
director it is going to be my decision, period. One time he hung up on
me. We had a dispute over some music, and I was like, 'Well, this is
what I want to do,' and he was like, 'OK, but I think you are making
a mistake.' Click. But what I appreciated about Spike's influence with
that project is that he supported me even if he disagreed. He wasn't
trying to make a Spike Lee film; he was trying to help me make a
Malcolm Lee film."

The Best Man, starring the relatively unknown Taye Diggs, Morris
Chestnut and Nia Long, opened on October 24, 1999, and bested all
expectations by going on to gross $35 million. "It begat a whole black
romantic comedy genre," claims Spike.[*] The similarly pitched *Love
and Basketball* enjoyed similar success, grossing $28 million on its
release in April 2000. The performance of the films confirmed Nelson
George's opinion that Spike was well positioned to further promote

---

[*]Although *How Stella Got Her Groove Back* was the first black rom-com to be a box-
office hit, Spike is right in the sense that *The Best Man* confirmed the genre's place in the
market.

African-American film: "*Love and Basketball* is a very fine film and made Sanaa Lathan a star. Gina Prince-Bythewood is very talented. *The Best Man* was a very commercial hit and produced a lot of talent. I hope that he does more of it, because he is really well positioned and he has such good taste and understanding of film to be that kind of figure. The problem is that it's harder to create a Russell Simmons in film; it requires you to be in L.A. and make certain alliances that are tougher for us, because L.A. is a very segregated city, classwise and racewise. But Spike as a filmmaker, he has that respect. And black film makes enough money. There comes a time in this life when you are thinking not so much about your legacy but Am I building something larger than myself? And I think Spike has done that to a great degree. Whatever criticisms I have are not of what he has done; it is just that I wish he was able to do more. Because his inspiration and the impact of his films are huge, and he's still so young, he can still do it. It's interesting, too, because I think he has had a kind of cultural rebirth. I think there was a time there that he became tired—but I feel that documentaries helped him a lot."

Spike's next project was a concert film more in the vein of *Freak* than *4 Little Girls*: a film document of a hugely successful live show entitled *The Original Kings of Comedy* which showcased four black stand-ups: D. L. Hughley, Cedric the Entertainer, Steve Harvey and Bernie Mac. The touring show had already been embraced in droves by black audiences across America, and Spike too was now poised to share in that success.

Steve Harvey relates, "The idea for the tour started with Walter Lathan. He came to each one of us and presented a proposal. And we had toured for three years before we made the movie; it was already the highest-grossing comedy tour ever. In comedic terms it wasn't just like going to see Eddie Murphy or Martin Lawrence or Richard Pryor, a single stand-up. We were four dudes who had very different takes on very different subjects. And it wasn't like a hip-hop affair; people were dressing up to come and see *Kings*. For all that, it was still kind of underground, but the word had got out in a couple of press articles and people had started to take notice of us: all of a sudden receipts were going up and people were saying, 'These guys are making a fortune.' That's when Paramount got involved, with Spike Lee. All of us jumped at the opportunity to let Spike make the film because we knew that he'd let us do our own thing. Everyone else had these ideas about how they wanted to do it. But I knew that if he came he would let us remain true."

Harvey believes that *Kings* "was an inside peek, for people who are not in the urban culture, at a lot of the ways we as a community view situations. And never before had there been such a diversified viewpoint of our culture." After attending the show a number of times, Spike was similarly struck by the demographic makeup of the audience and evolved a distinctive modus operandi for how they would be featured in his film: "We understood that the audience is a large part of the show so we had designated cameras for them. Again, we filmed two performances, and we made a rule that if we cut away to an audience member laughing, it had to be in reaction to that specific joke. We did not want to have them laugh at some shit that was recorded for something else." "I know you could say Spike's film is just their stage act," says John Pierson, "and those guys are obviously really funny, both separately and all together. But Spike really brought something to it; he was able to show the interaction between stage and audience. That's editing as well, so I'm not giving Spike solo credit, but I think the intimacy between what was happening on stage and the audience is what really makes it a fine piece of work." Indeed, many of the best moments in the film are not about the comedians at all: "Spike shot from some interesting angles," argues Steve Harvey, "and he broke up the stand-up with some behind-the-scenes stuff. That's an innovative way to do it. Every other movie of this type has just been straight stand-up."

Nevertheless, Harvey recalls some cold feet at Paramount prior to the release date: "The studios don't know our culture, they don't know what we do as stand-ups, they don't know our people. People from Hollywood didn't come out on the tour and see the reaction that people had about us. And the studio wanted to change the thing; they didn't get it. But Spike fought, fought and fought for it to be left as it was." As Spike insists, "William Goldman has one of the only true adages in film: 'No one knows anything.' Just look at the box-office results of *Original Kings of Comedy*." Steve Harvey reveals that Spike, increasingly accustomed to modest returns for his movies, played down the box-office prospects to the four comedians: "The tour had been so huge and we had high expectations. Spike had to educate me on what the expectations of the movie were. He was saying, 'Steve, we can't do a $25-million opening weekend because we're only on 800 screens.' Well, I think we opened up in 846 screens and then—to the dismay of the film people—they were stunned by how successful it was, because it was the largest per screen average ever for an August movie—almost $12,000 per screen. I think that if they had released this movie wider and not underestimated its crossover appeal it would have been even bigger. But, oh my God, did it make money: it just got up those numbers every weekend. And when the DVD came out it was the second-best seller since *Gladiator*."

As John Pierson notes, Hollywood increasingly valued directors on the basis of opening weekends and grosses: "Spike is the guy who in commercial terms has never really had a breakout hit, unless you count *The Original Kings of Comedy*. It is difficult when somebody is deciding what they can afford to give you as a budget, based on what you have returned in your last three or four films. It doesn't matter what you have done over your whole career." The success of *Original Kings* came too late to be used as leverage in Spike's negotiations for his next feature, *Bamboozled*; but this would be the film on which Spike let years of frustration in the industry boil over.

Bamboozled had been brewing for some years within Spike: "Its origin is really in one of my first films at NYU, *The Answer*, in which a young African-American screenwriter is asked to write and direct a \$50 million remake of *Birth of the Nation*. This guy sells his soul to the devil to do that film. And we intercut the film with some of the worst racist scenes from the so-called greatest film ever made. *Bamboozled* revisits that, because if you look at that character in *The Answer* and at Pierre Delacroix in *Bamboozled*, there are various similarities. And we show scenes from *Birth of a Nation* in *Bamboozled* too."

As he sat down to write, Spike began packing the script with cultural references, beginning with the title: "It comes from a Malcolm X speech, which is where I got the whole idea for the movie from— 'You've been hoodwinked, led astray, bamboozled.' But the movie's not just about black Americans; it's about people all over the world. I think we were expanding on the speech and saying, 'Don't believe everything you read or see on television. Don't be tricked, don't be hoodwinked, don't be hornswoggled. Don't be bamboozled.'"

Spike was naturally aware of the several great American movies that had previously skewered the American mass media: "I saw *Network* when it first came out, and it is a great piece of art—everything about it: Paddy Chayefsky's script, William Holden, Peter Finch, Ned Beatty, Robert Duvall, Faye Dunaway. *Network* would be a great double bill with *A Face in the Crowd*, another of the great, great films. And everything that Budd Schulberg wrote about in 1957 about the power of television—this before people even knew what television was about— happened. Budd had the crystal ball and saw that TV would rule and whoever controlled that stuff would be running things. I took another idea straight from *The Producers*: the idea that you think that you are going to do something that is going to be the worst piece of shit ever, but because the standard is so low it flies—because everything is now about the lowest common denominator."

The film would be dedicated to Budd Schulberg. Despite Spike's admiration for the screenwriter, it was Schulberg who instigated their working and personal relationship: "It began when Bert Sugar, the boxing writer, and I wrote a short treatment on Joe Louis and Max Schmeling called *The War to Come*. I sent the outline to Spike because I'd seen him at HBO dinners before the fights at the Garden, and he called right away and said, 'I really love it.' We got together and after this Spike sent me tons of material: it was prodigious—I had never seen nothing like this in my life. For about three months I did nothing but read Joe Louis. I would send things to Spike and, as he always does, he was very thorough in doing his homework. After we had absorbed all this material we sat down and planned out how to write this screenplay, and we proceeded from there. It was an unwritten rule —but it might as well have been written—that no black heavyweight could fight in the Garden and win. As we got closer to World War II and as the sense of patriotism grew in this country, Joe, despite being a Negro, actually turned into a symbol of fighting strength against fascism and was looked on as such."

Thematically, Spike was also poised to address the representation of African-Americans throughout the history of American popular culture: "The image of African-Americans has been subverted. Look at Al Jolson, look at minstrels. We have always had an impact upon American culture—I'm sorry, but white boys did not invent rock'n'roll: how could they, when we had the innovators like Louis Jordan, Chuck Berry and Little Richard? They might have taken it in another direction but Elvis Presley didn't 'invent' a motherfucking thing. The problem of black identity really goes back to what W. E. B. Du Bois said about the duality of being the descendants of slaves. Because you have the African side and the American side, and that can be and has been very schizophrenic. No matter who you are, if you don't have knowledge of self, then you are going to be lost, because you can't be somebody who you are not. That is the fundamental problem."

Bamboozled centers on Pierre Delacroix, sole black executive at TV network CNS, whose "nigger-loving" boss, Dunwitty, is frustrated over ailing ratings. Dunwitty wants Delacroix to attract an urban audience to the station. His secretary, Sloan, is skeptical when Delacroix reveals his new big idea, *Mantan's New Millennium Minstrel Show*. In fact, Delacroix hopes that the show fails, so disgusted is he with the stereotypes he routinely sees on television and how

Bamboozled: Mantan's New Millennium Minstrel Show. (© 1999 David Lee)

white the industry is. He even employs street performers Manray and Womack to be the leads in the show, rechristening them Mantan and Sleep'n Eat. The audition sees one black stereotype follow another. But the series proves a critical and commercial success, only to draw the ire of black activists and a militant group, Mau Maus. Delacroix, who first laps up the acclaim, struggles as he is criticized by his parents and Sloan, with whom he once had an affair. All that the white gatekeepers care about is the number of people watching the show. Sloan falls for Manray. Sloan's brother Big Blak Afrika, a member of the Mau Maus, decides to take retaliatory action against the racism of CNS by kidnapping the show's star and executing him live on the internet. After Manray is murdered, the members of the militant group are killed by the police, and Sloan avenges the murders by taking Delacroix's life.

Lest the audience be in any doubt, *Bamboozled* opens with Delacroix stating that this is a satire. Spike says of this component, "I gave a definition of satire because motherfuckers are stupid. When I say that, I'm talking about certain critics, not all of them. But I just wanted to state right away that this film is a satire so they could flick that switch and know. Even then, some of them still got it wrong. But I saw this done by

Hector Babenco when he made *Pixote*. It starts with Babenco looking straight into the camera telling the audience what the film is going to be about."

But both the nature of the script and Spike's recent commercial record meant that he had trouble raising the budget he wanted. Jon Kilik remembers, "We are sitting around in Spike's house one day. We had an offer that was for about half as much as we needed, and we thought about ways to cut the budget down so that we could still make the movie. Video features were something that was happening, with Lars von Trier and other European and independent filmmakers. Nobody had done it on this scale yet, but we also felt it could be something that could work on video because the story is about the television industry." Spike got on the phone to Ellen Kuras: "One night in the beginning of August, he called me at midnight and said, 'So what do you think about shooting *Bamboozled* on mini-DV?' And I said, 'I don't.' At that juncture I hadn't shot anything on video since the earliest days of my career, when I was gaining experience. So I wasn't enthusiastic about it, partially because I didn't know about it. Also, I'm a film person; I wanted to shoot in film. But we talked about it the next day, and he said, 'I really want to make this film, and the way that we can make it is in this medium.'" There would at least be a celluloid component to the piece, as Spike confirms: "Ellen and I worked out that we would shoot *Mantan's New Millennium Minstrel Show* on Super-16, because we wanted that to have a different look from the rest of the film."

Kuras set about researching the digital video (DV) format, conscious that ground was being broken for this production, and soon found some unexpected boons: "I took a look at Thomas Vinterberg's *The Celebration*, and what was striking to me in the look was that it was like a Bergman film: those guys seemed to have chosen their shots carefully and waited for the light. I wasn't going to have that luxury. I knew that it was going to be a running-and-gunning shoot from the hip. But DV enabled us to use multiple cameras, hidden cameras, to be able to put a camera on a table—and that was really exciting for both of us. Especially for Spike, because there is a lot of bulk that goes into rigging 35mm cameras, and when you want to go and have a table angle, you have to cut the table to get the camera in that spot. Not on *Bamboozled*."

Digital production as pioneered by the likes of the Danish Dogma '95 directors had already engendered sneers about "cheap film," but Spike could see a much more upbeat side to the story: "What digital has done, it has made filmmaking more democratic, in that you don't have to have millions and millions of dollars to make films." Moreover,

Digital video production on *Bamboozled*. (© 1999 David Lee)

the format sat well with the scale of his new production: "*Bamboozled*
was not meant to be an epic. It takes place in a relatively short time
frame and in the present day. And I don't think that we compromised
the intent, shape or direction of the film to shoot the film on video."

One of the first actors cast was Jada Pinkett Smith, making her comeback after the birth of two children: "Spike was the first person to bring
me back into the game. I wasn't ready to come back and work, but I did
it for Spike. He was saying, 'We only need you for a month, just give
me a month.' There was no saying 'no' to Spike. And the process
turned out to be very fast—using digital cameras, it was theater on
wheels. But the idea of *Bamboozled* I just thought was absolutely brilliant, the perfect Spike Lee project to be a part of. Spike can't call me
about no bullcrap, I don't want no black love story; it has to be something that will get people heated and has them pulling me up on the
street asking, 'Why did you do that?' And I agreed with the point of
view of how he wrote that woman. Of course, he is the filmmaker, he

Bamboozled: Damon Wayans with a rare historical piece of memorabilia. (© 1999 David Lee)

can create what he wants. I didn't agree with the point of view of *Girl 6* so I didn't participate in that project. But I agreed with the point of view in *Bamboozled*." Spike adds, "What's funny is that I wanted Will Smith to play Pierre, but he chose to do *The Legend of Bagger Vance* instead. Maybe he wanted to work with Robert Redford." Will Smith had shed his Fresh Prince image, and following the hits *Bad Boys*, *Independence Day* and *Men in Black*, had replaced Eddie Murphy as the top African-American box-office draw. Pinkett Smith claims she did not know her husband was approached. Spike smiles, "Well, I know they have a big house, I don't think it's *that* big. . . ."

For the actors who star in the *Mantan* show, Spike approached Savion Glover and Tommy Davidson: "I knew the guy had to be a tap dancer. Savion said 'Let's go' right away. He's an artist and we had talked about working before. I think that people were more surprised with what Tommy Davidson did, because he's primarily known as a comedian, but he's great in the film." Spike also got to work with another one of his heroes when he cast Paul Mooney to play Pierre's father: "Paul Mooney is one of the great comics of all time. He wrote stuff for Richard Pryor—his shit is so raw they don't know what to do with it."

"*Bamboozled* was fun to research," says Spike. "I bought a lot of Negro memorabilia. To me it is a reminder of how we were thought of —and how we are still thought of today, for all that's changed." Costume designer Ruth Carter was the immediate beneficiary of Spike's collecting habits: "Spike sent me a book with all the toys and black-faces, and I started doing the research. I realized then that this is something that we have all wanted to just sweep under the rug. But the racial stereotyping is still happening—we washed the blackface off but it is still there. You are impacted by the research and you really want to pay homage to it as well, because these were people who were feeding their families and were stars among themselves, yet they were pretending to be buffoons—Stepin Fetchit and all that."

As rehearsals commenced, Spike and Damon Wayans worked on the accent Wayans would adopt as Pierre Delacroix: "The schizophrenia of African-Americans is the gigantic flaw of Pierre Delacroix," states Spike. "It's there when his father says, 'Motherfucker, where did you get the accent from? Motherfucker, you are my son. Don't come home with that fake accent on.' But we wanted him to be one of these very affected people. I always remember how Tina Turner spent a year in London recording *Private Dancer* and when she came back she had an accent. If you live somewhere five or ten years, then you can get an accent. A year, no way." But Branford Marsalis was just one of many who felt that this aspect of Pierre's character did not work: "It was very difficult for Damon to try to invent a white voice and it comes off stilted in the performance, almost to the point of caricature."

By contrast, Delacroix's boss, Dunwitty, is a white man who wants to be black. He proudly references *Do the Right Thing* in telling Delacroix, "Look at how many niggers there are on the wall!" and goes on to assert, "Spike Lee can kiss my ass, Tarantino was right!" (Samuel L. Jackson, with whom, unlike Tarantino, Spike has had a rapprochement, says of *Bamboozled*, "It seems like Spike finally made a decision to out-'nigger' everybody in the first fifteen minutes.") The *Do the Right Thing* reference was an improvisation by actor Michael Rapaport, but the shot at Tarantino was all Spike's doing. It seems neither director could let this argument lie. "Quentin Tarantino is not the only white boy who thinks that he is black," argues Spike. "There's a legion of them. Tarantino, he actually told me to my face that he knows black people better than me and that black people relate more to his films than my films. He was serious too. We were at the Angel-ika Theater in New York and I just looked at him like he was crazy. First of all, because he knows Sam Jackson and Pam Greer and Ving Rhames? I mean, there are 35 million African-Americans, and the peo-ple he knows don't represent all. And if you think you know black people because you have seen blaxploitation films and your mother had a black boyfriend, that's crazy. I'm not saying that culture is just a particular people's own domain—it can be shared by everybody, but don't just come in claiming this and that. The difference between lik-ing a culture and appropriating a culture is how you come to it. If you come with respect and admiration, that's different than saying, 'I know this shit through and through. I know this culture better than the people who are this culture.' I have done several films dealing with Italian-Americans, but I don't come in saying that I know Italian-Americans better than Scorsese or Coppola. In the case of Michael Rapaport, he grew up in New York with black people, he likes hip-hop—it's not like he's trying to be black. He just likes this stuff. And I got love for Michael Rapaport; he's not trying to be hip, that is just the way he is and that is why I cast him."

Dunwitty does in certain instances know more about black cultural history than Delacroix, as when he asks his employee to name the cel-ebrated number 24 of the New York Giants displayed on his wall. Delacroix, no sports fan, doesn't know. "You should know who Willie Mays is," asserts Spike. "I don't care who you are!" But otherwise Spike does not miss a beat in mocking the gatekeepers of U.S. televi-sion, the very people who had failed to commission 40 Acres' innu-merable pitches. Even Delacroix has a sign saying "Idiot Box" on top of his TV set. This was another blast from the director's childhood: "My mother used to always say, 'Turn that idiot box off. I'm not going to let my children rot their brains.' That sign is reminding Pierre that the medium that he works in is ruled by the lowest common denomi-nator. I just think that it is a shame that if you look at black-themed shows—and in particular UPN, or, as they say, 'U-Pick-a-Nigger'—all those shows are broad sitcoms. It's not that much better in film."

The most conspicuous feature of *Bamboozled*'s CNS network is how white are the employees: only Delacroix and his assistant, Sloan, are black. Spike points out, "The number of African-Americans in the industry is a joke. People might think that we made that up, but no. These struggles of gainful employment are still being fought—look at the percentages of African-Americans in front of the camera, behind the camera. The figures are better than they were, but it's still not good."

The *New Millennium Minstrel Show* is so popular that even the President of the United States is shown watching it. "If the President is watching the show," says Spike, "you can say without dialogue that this is a number-one-rated show. We found footage of President Clinton watching a television screen, and he's a public figure so we just put our picture in that screen." But the brilliance of *Bamboozled*—this an extension of the view taken in *School Daze*—is that African-Americans are not immune from criticism for the continuing racial stereotyping that exists. "We weren't aiming with pistols, this was buckshot," asserts Spike. "So everybody was getting it, not just white Americans." For Jada Pinkett Smith, this was the heart of the film: "Making this movie, we were all pointing fingers at ourselves in a way. It was really an exploration of 'What do we represent in this business? Who are we? What compromises and sacrifices are we willing to make of our commitment to our higher selves and our community and our humanity? What are we doing in this industry that uplifts our community, and what are we doing that breaks it down for the sake of celebrity and money?'"

The film is punctuated with hilarious parodies of the manner in which advertisers sell products to African-American consumers, cheap alcoholic beverages and Tommy Hilfiger clothes the main targets. Spike says, "They are still selling that malt liquor, that liquid crack, predominantly to African-Americans. The adverts were part of the reason that I stated this was satire at the beginning of the movie; I mean, 'Timmy Hilnigger—so real we give you the bullet holes,' it's funny. At the time my daughter was going to the same place as his son, and one day as I dropped my daughter off Hilfiger says, 'Spike, why did you do this to me? Don't you know that I sponsor *x* amount of Martin Luther King scholarships?' I said, 'Come on, man, get out of my face.' He was the biggest fish in the pond, and when you do satire, that's who you go for." Naomi Klein's *No Logo* was a bestseller at the time and criticized Hilfiger's methods, though reading Klein's book would suggest there were bigger fish that Spike once again chose not to touch. Of course, as the proprietor of his own advertising agency, Spike was also in a sense cutting off his nose to spite his face: "Nobody knows what commercials I've directed," he states. "People in the industry do, but nobody ever asks me, 'Hey, did you direct Beyoncé in the Pepsi video?'"

The subtle casting of the insurgent group that kidnaps Mantan allowed Spike to promote his view on black culture: on show he had Mos Def, Canibus, DJ Scratch, Charlie Baltimore, muMs da Schemer, M.C. Serch—all representatives of different aspects of hip-hop: militant rap, playa rap, gangsta rap, message rap, female rappers, MCs and DJs: "I wanted to have the different genres of hip-hop. Mos Def played the

Mau Mau called Big Blak Afrika. For the show, the Alabama Porch Monkeys were played by the Roots." Spike argues, "Then you have the radical motherfuckers, and if you are not down with them, they say they'll kill you. In the film we are killing gangsta rap." Spike says of the "bling" lifestyle promoted by rappers from every record label, from Russell Simmons's Def Jam to Jay-Z's Rocafella Records and Master P's Cash Money label: "I'm not going to say that they are killing black culture, but I don't think they are elevating black culture. When your CD is entitled *Get Rich or Die Trying*,* that is not about elevation."

Spike also includes a white rapper (M.C. Serch) going by the name of 1/16th Blak whom police refuse to touch despite his cry of "I'm black, shoot me!" This was an assertion that white rappers pretending to be black were not to be taken seriously, a trend Dr. Dre flipped when he produced tracks for Eminem in 1999 that celebrated the rapper's white skin. Skip Gates says of the phenomenon: "I think it's a matter of voyeurism: these are white kids who aren't going to emulate this lifestyle, but it's like living through a keyhole and watching illicit acts and then going back to your own room. These middle-class white kids are going to go to Harvard Business School, they are not going to become thieves, hoods and rappers." Gates further contends: "There are 35 million African-Americans—so you can't ever generalize about the black community. What has happened is that the black community has been driven in two because of the class divide that resulted from affirmative action. This 'bling-bling' thing is very much with us now, but on the other hand the black middle class is larger than it has ever been—there are more black kids at NYU, UCLA, USC than ever before. And in a large and healthy middle class, people are not only thinking about being lawyers and doctors, but because of Spike Lee and those who followed Spike they are also thinking about being filmmakers. That is a good thing. Spike and his career are great motivations for people."

As *Bamboozled* reaches its conclusion, Spike cranks up the volume of the archive material showing flagrant racism on television and film: "Hopefully we gain more momentum toward the end of the film. Also we see Pierre Delacroix starting to become delusional—the Jolly

---

* 50 Cent's 2003 album. The artist celebrates his "authenticity" being proved by the number of times he has been shot. His official biography on his website rewrites the history of hip-hop, pronouncing: "More so than any other music since the blues, hip-hop is about stories. And its stories are both criminal minded and grand, making them enthralling and unbelievable, but also making them only as interesting and convincing as the teller. . . . [50 cent] is the real deal, the genuine article. He's a man of the streets, intimately familiar with its codes and its violence."

Nigger Bank [a mechanical minstrel money box] speaking to him and so on."

Mike Ellis claims that shooting digital did not make too much of a difference to the workings of the set: "Spike always uses two cameras; here we were using nine or ten, sticking cameras everywhere. It wasn't even that much faster. The misconception is, 'Video, you don't need this, you don't need that.' But that is not true; you have less latitude than film, you can't compensate for underexposing or overexposing, you still need a light—it might be a smaller light, but it's still a light, with a plug that goes to a generator." Digital video undeniably allows for more footage to be generated at lower cost, something that daunted Sam Pollard when it came to editing: "The big challenge was the amount of material. I think there are only five scenes shot with a single camera; every other scene was shot with six cameras. That was mind-boggling to me. I thought there were too many choices. That was the one time I would bitch every night at home, 'Spike is being a pain on this.' I remember showing him the first sequence with Tommy and Savion dancing, and he said, 'You cut it like television, man, too many cuts,' and internally I was furious. I thought, The reason there are too many cuts is that there are too many cameras. For the first time, the directing wasn't happening on the set, it was happening in the editing room. So this was not an easy film. And I thought that Spike felt he had something on the line here: he was more intense emotionally than on any film that I had worked on with him. There was an edge to him that he really had to make this film work, maybe because the last few films had not made any money. He was on my ass, and he even took a scene from me and gave it to Barry, which hurt me no end. I was like, 'How can Spike do this to me?'"

Barry Brown did indeed cut a small performance element of *Bamboozled*; arriving late on the project, he was stunned by what he saw in the dailies: "I went in to see this stuff not knowing anything about the scene, and I was like, 'Spike, what the fuck is this, man?' Then I read the script. If it had been absolutely anybody else, I would have walked out. 'Are you out of your mind? You expect me to do this?'" Brown liked the image quality of the rushes no better than the story they told: "I could not understand why it cost $10 million." John Pierson goes so far as to argue, "*Bamboozled* is definitely one of the top ten unpleasant digital films to watch: even though there is obviously stuff in that film that is just brilliant, it is just not worked out. Ellen Kuras did not do a good job with that." Kuras is herself unfazed: "A lot of DPs called me after *Bamboozled* because they were confronted with shooting digital. So these films were innovative, they made a mark and people took note, not only for their content but also for the visual aspects. I attribute that to the fact that Spike is someone who pushes me to explore."

Bamboozled was due for release in October 2000, less than a month after *Original Kings of Comedy* had left the auditoriums. Distributor New Line tried to run an advert in the *New York Times*: "That is what gave us the most trouble," says Spike. "The *Times* wouldn't run our ad because they said that it was too offensive. That was the point of the advert. But it was what turned off a lot of African-Americans." Art Sims says of the offending poster, "We had a pickaninny with a watermelon, and people were freaking out. To this day, I think that is our most requested poster; people just love that. Spike gave me distinctive instruction on that one: 'I want to make it like a Barnum and Bailey circus poster, but let's add the pickaninny style to it.' Originally we just had the pickaninny with the watermelon, and Spike said, 'Add some cotton, a lot of cotton. . . .' We had a meeting over at New Line Cinema. Spike was really passionate about what he wanted the campaign to be and what he thought the movie was. I knew the meeting was going to be on edge, because as soon as Spike got there, the marketing director knocked over a glass of water. Then he says, 'So, Spike, you made this movie for shock value, right?' It was like—beep!— wrong word! 'What do you mean, I did it for controversy? Blackface to sell products to black people in America—that really happened, that's true.'"

The subsequent poor critical response to *Bamboozled* had Spike lamenting, "Some people misinterpreted the film, thinking it's only about black people. *Bamboozled* is about the dehumanization and the degradation that comes via television and film." Spike was surprised at Amy Taubin's criticisms in the *Village Voice*: "Her thing was misinformed, that I cast Damon Wayans so I can get back at his brother Keenan because I didn't like *In Living Color* when it was on TV ten years ago. That is very disrespectful, to say that is how I choose my subject matter: I'm a serious motherfucking filmmaker, and I don't do films because I have a grudge against someone who did a skit on me a decade earlier. Every one of my films, if I don't feel that it is important, I'm not going to do it. Now, if you look at the body of work, you will think that *Girl 6* is not as important as *Malcolm X*. But for me to do a film it has to be a story that I want to tell."

The film underperformed at the box office, and Spike lays the blame firmly with New Line: "They didn't believe in the film, so there was no investment beyond the initial one. Of all my films, this is the one that people discover more on DVD than any other. A day does not go by when people don't come up to me and say, 'I really liked *Bamboozled*, it's my favorite Spike Lee film.' If I ask them if they saw the movie in the theater, they say, 'No, I saw it on DVD.' That is the great thing about DVDs: films have another life. Everybody thinks about that now, and we create much more material to put on the DVD. People are less willing to buy DVDs if there is no extra footage on it."

Giancarlo Esposito saw *Bamboozled* as a return to form for the director: "I don't think Spike got back to his real roots of filmmaking until *Bamboozled*. And you know, that's a long time. But I feel like *Bamboozled* was when he came back into his own; an originality that he had earlier in his career, he reconnected with it. *Bamboozled*, to me, is a brilliant film." Lisa Jones pinpoints why the film was received so badly by critics and yet loved by black viewers who later saw it: "There is a lot of distance between X and *Bamboozled*, almost ten years, and *Bamboozled* is not a story representing a great black leader: it doesn't have to be portrayed as a pure black history, subject to the criticisms of that space. It becomes a satire aimed at the white establishment, which is easier to do, and black people love you for that. It is when you get into our deities that you are treading on the sacred ground, and you have to walk carefully."

"As African-American people we are sometimes too quick to blame the white man and woman for everything," says Spike. "But we have to be held responsible for our own actions. One thing that I can't understand is that Mr. Damon Wayans can do this film and then go and do *Marci X*, the type of film of which *Bamboozled* is an indictment. One day I'm going to ask him about it."

Spike's own choices post-*Bamboozled* bore no shred of compromise. The first was a filming of his friend Roger Smith's one-man stage show *The Huey P. Newton Story*. "*Huey* was a piece I brought to Spike," says Smith. "It existed as a stage piece through more than six hundred performances. Spike came when I did it at the Public Theater and immediately started talking about how we might document it. He has always been a big supporter of my work on stage, and that work has been very political. I think that we have seen eye to eye on a lot of things in the political realm and we have been able to weave our passions together successfully in many regards." "It was a much more stylized project than *Freak*," Spike asserts. "Roger does a great show, and as with *Kings of Comedy*, we had to do something that would not get in the way of his performance but augment it. I wasn't directing the performance, I was just directing the cameras. Roger has been doing that show for years, and I told him coming in, 'What you are doing is great, wonderful, I'm not going to change a thing.'" The piece was shot by Ellen Kuras on TV-broadcast-standard DigiBeta rather than the consumer DV camera used on *Bamboozled*. "We had to split the performance in half," Kuras recalls. "Normally there is no intermission, but they had to change the tape. But generally what Spike was doing was very respectful of the original stage performance." "We shot in an old synagogue on the Lower East Side that had two levels," says Smith. "Wynn Thomas came up with an effective design of security grilling between the audience and the performers. Ellen requested that the audience come dressed in black so that they would be photographed primarily in silhouette. They were all really good ideas. The film never had a cinema release, but it's had a lot of festival and television airings. The great thing about it was that it was a way of documenting the play: I don't perform it anymore. The thing about Newton as opposed to Fidel Castro is that Huey died a pretty corpse."

Spike continued to work with Budd Schulberg on *Save Us, Joe Louis* but then almost took another boxing movie: "I met Will Smith at a hotel in L.A. to discuss directing *Ali*. We talked, but what hurt was that Will's question to me was: 'Spike, how can you expand your vision?' After that question, I knew I wasn't getting the job." John Turturro affirms, "Spike is always talking about vision and how that's the key for a director, how some people just don't have it. The worst thing you can say to him is 'No vision.'" Spike, as had become his wont, continued the fight after the movie came out: "I know several people who worked on *Ali* and they told me confidentially that the filmmakers used *Malcolm X* as the bible. One location man said that he was directed by Michael Mann to scout every location in New York that we had in our film, and he got mad when the guy kept telling him that the locations were not around anymore. But I let the work speak for itself: look at *Malcolm X* and compare it to *Ali*."*

Meanwhile, cousin Malcolm opted now to work with a studio rather than with Spike, signing up to direct *Undercover Brother* rather than a 40 Acres project about to go into pre-production. "I wasn't disappointed," says Spike. "I just knew that working with Brian Grazer would not turn out good. I knew he would not allow creative freedom to Malcolm. *Undercover Brother* was a cartoon series on the internet, completely different to what was made for the

*Budd Schulberg laments, "The box-office failure of *Ali* hurt our prospects for making *Save Us, Joe Louis*."

screen; the whole sensibility was different. The internet series is smart, satirical. And Brian Grazer, I think he often sees black people as buffoons and coons. But Malcolm is his own man." After the event, Malcolm concurred with Spike on one point: "My best directing experience was with Spike Lee."

Spike took the knocks in his stride and got to work on his next directing project, teaming up once again with HBO Sports to make a feature-length documentary entitled *Jim Brown: All American*: "I worked with Jim Brown on *He Got Game* and I've always been a big admirer of his. He is a complex man and I wanted to document the life as best you can on film. When people think of Jim Brown they think of two things: number one, that he is the greatest football player ever; and number two, they think this is a guy who threw his girlfriend off the balcony. Yet Jim is about more than athletics and his relationships: he is an activist, he is an entrepreneur, he is many, many different things, someone who refused to wear one hat. He quit the game at the top, when most athletes would have dragged on for years and years afterward. He was someone who said, 'I'm not going to let football define who I am.' He saw that he could help people more in other capacities."

"From the very beginning," Spike continues, "Jim said, 'Make the film that you want to make. I'm not going to tell you whom to talk to or furnish you with shit, just go and make the film.'" Brown recalls, "The one thing I said was that I would cooperate with him totally. I would not have any input on what he did. I'd give him all the information that I could but everything that he did would be his vision. I trusted him to at least deal with the facts. What he did had tremendous impact on the people that I run into around the country, especially poor people, especially black people. And the first thing they say to me is that they did not know all those things about me. Well, it was because you didn't do any research. So he told America things that were unknown."

Spike was ecstatic about working on a second feature-length documentary: "The great thing about doing a documentary is that if you don't know more about your subject after you have done the film, then you haven't done a very good job. *4 Little Girls* was a much harder film to do because you have to ask questions that are going to make people break down on camera. It's not something you enjoy doing, but you've got to do it to get the stuff you need. For *Jim Brown* we shot a lot more. We just tried to go out there and interview as many people as possible because you don't know where the best stuff is going to come from. I tried to emphasize that with *Jim Brown*—and this happens with all great African-American athletes—there's an assumption, fuelled by the white media, that African-American athletes are born that way, a God-given thing, that they don't spend time honing their skills but that they came out of the womb dunking or running with a football. Whereas the white athletes are portrayed as having not as much athletic skill but being very hardworking and dedicated. It is very stereotypical."

The film also takes a look at Jim Brown's acting career, which more often than not saw him play the action hero; but his clinch with Raquel Welch in *100 Rifles* was one of the groundbreaking moments in depicting love across racial boundaries on celluloid. Spike also focused on Brown's work in the African-American community. Brown says of his life story, "If I would talk about my own life, I would really talk about my community work: that is really what my life is about. My organization in the sixties was probably the most advanced economic organization that any black has ever created—the Black Economic Union, originally the Negro Industrial Union—and the concept was one that would be inspirational to the whole black community, because economic development is necessary in the advancement of a people. I don't make films, I'm not an actor; I'm an activist, I'm a community person, that is what I live off. Even when I played that is what I did, period."

Spike relates the balcony incident in all its ambiguity, yet he is very careful to show the human side of Jim Brown: the father and the man. "It was very moving for me to hear his son say, 'I can't ever remember my father hugging me,'" says Spike. "Jim, he's still relevant. That is what he always says. 'Spike, I'm sixty-seven years old, but I'm relevant. I'm still happening. I know what's out there.' He is still trying to effect social change. Jim has devoted the latter stages of his life to dealing with these misguided African-American men and this gang shit, Bloods and Crips. As for the balcony incident, I don't know what happened. I felt the fairest way was to leave it ambiguous, because Jim and Eva Marie Bohn were the only two people there. No one else was there; I wasn't. So let him tell the story and let her tell the story. You make up your mind."

Intriguingly, Nike CEO Phil Knight is thanked in the credits. Spike explains: "We went over budget and HBO said they weren't going to give me a penny more. I was incredulous: stuff goes over budget all the time. But I had nowhere to turn so I called Philip Knight, and he sent me a check. A big one." Knight was only too happy to respond: "I just thought that we ought to do it, that he has been a friend of the company. He had run into a little problem on one of his other films and I think Michael Jordan helped him out a little bit, and I had said to him at the time, 'If you'd asked me I would have helped you too.' I didn't know if it was a legitimate expense for the shareholders, so I sent it from my own pocket. That was a rare situation, you know. I'm not going to be contributing money personally to every film he makes. And I haven't seen the film yet, but I was glad to help out on it."

In December 2000 George W. Bush became President of the United States on the basis of a 5–4 decision by the U.S. Supreme Court not to order a recount in Florida. The saga of the disputed election divided America and gripped the world. In the coming months, numerous newspaper and magazine articles and books would reveal the extensive vote-rigging that took place in Florida, aimed primarily at denying African-Americans (traditionally Democrats) the chance to vote. So when Spike was approached to be part of an anthology project, *Ten Minutes Older*, which asked ten directors to make ten-minute short films, the subject matter for his film would quite literally jump from the front page.

Once again, asked to make a film in a restrictive time frame, Spike used the ticking clock to provide tension in his film, *We Wuz Robbed* (Spike taking the opportunity to use one of his favourite catchphrases as a film title): "I read the story in the *New York Times*, I think—this amazing story about how Al Gore was minutes away from giving his concession speech and how he got stopped moments before he made it. And I thought, That sounds like a movie right there. I called the people involved and then we used the incident to turn it into a re-examination of the 2000 presidential election. That includes Donna Brazile, Gore's campaign manager, giving examples of blockades being set up and black people being pulled over. It's clear that the election was rigged." George W. Bush's presence would become a feature of Spike's work in the coming years.

Of course, and amazingly, it was not even the debacle of the Florida election that would come to define the first term of the presidency of Bush the Second: "September 11, 2001, I was in Los Angeles," says Spike, "and I was up early because it was my son Jackson's first day at school. I called home to wish him luck because he was going to be away from Mommy and Daddy. Tonya told me to turn on the TV . . . I tried to get back to New York to be with my family and I had to take the train. It took three days to get back to the city."

As New York mourned the dead, the director thought up ways that he could help those most affected by the deaths and decided to auction his wife's courtside seat to Michael Jordan's first game out of retirement at Madison Square Garden. The director says, "New York City is so amazing and sometimes you think that the rest of the United States is like it, but it's not. People outside of NYC view it as not even part of America, that it's Babylon—that's really the perception of a lot of Americans from the hinterlands. This gap was definitely shortened after September 11. There was a lot of love for New York City that was not felt before: at that time everybody was a New Yorker. . . . We got a big reaction to the auction, and we had an anonymous bidder who bid $100,000 for the ticket and donated the seat to the firemen who died. And the firemen's fund chose a young girl who lost her father in the attacks to come to the game with me."

Spike was then approached to adapt a New York novel by David Benioff, *The 25th Hour.* "I got sent the script. Ed Norton got sent it at the same time. We had expressed an interest in working together over the years, and Disney said, 'If you guys want to do it, we'll do it too.'" Spike read a story about Irish-American Monty Brogan, who is on step-back.* Brogan has been given a seven-year sentence for a drug-related offense, and on his last day before he goes inside, he passes the time with his father, his Puerto Rican girlfriend, Naturelle, and his two oldest friends, stockbroker Frank and college teacher Jacob. Naturelle is suspected of having shopped her boyfriend to the feds, but that night the group visit a nightclub run by Monty's criminal associates in the Russian mafia: there he discovers that it is a member of that group who has set him up. As morning breaks, Monty goads Frank into punching him out, making him ugly in the hope that this will make him less of a sexual target in prison. He dreams of absconding as his father drives him to the state penitentiary.

The 25th Hour had taken a roundabout route to land in the hands of the 40 Acres chief, or so remembers author David Benioff: "Tobey Maguire read it and thought that he wanted to play Monty, so he optioned the book. I was hired to write the screenplay and then Maguire got the Spider-Man role, so he dropped *25th Hour.* The script was just lying around, and my agent, Todd Feldman, who also represents Spike, sent it to him. Then Spike called me up and said, 'Why don't you come to New York? I'd like to talk to you about it.' It

---

*The time given to a nonviolent first-time offender not judged to be a risk to public safety between sentencing and serving the jail sentence to put his affairs in order. This policy is explained in the book, but Spike leaves the explanatory scene out of the movie, arguing, "I did not want to spend a long time getting into the legalities, to explain just because you are arrested you can still walk around, especially if you are kind of privileged too: father is a fireman, not like he was some guy in Harlem or Bed-Stuy." The scene can be found among the deleted scenes of the DVD.

was pretty nerve-racking the first time I walked into that room with him, because I grew up in New York and he's a New York icon. Growing up, seeing Spike Lee movies, there is no doubt that he had a serious influence on me. He had been a major figure since I was fifteen. So at first it was intimidating: Spike does not waste a lot of time with a lot of small talk; he's like, 'Let's get down to business.' He'd read my novel too—I had met a bunch of people in the movie business about 25th Hour and this was the first time that I had seen the book on anyone's desk. And the pages were all dog-eared and sections were underlined. A lot of what he was saying was, 'I really liked your book and I don't understand why you weren't more faithful to it in the script.' Then he said, 'You cut out my favorite scenes!' One of which was a long cursing monologue to a mirror by Monty. Spike asked me, 'Why did you cut that?' I said I couldn't figure out how anyone could shoot it and make it dramatic. He basically said, 'Why don't you let me worry about that? You just write it.' And I did."

Spike's New York chops were a special enticement to Benioff: "The reason I was happy that Spike Lee got the job was that I really wanted it to be a real New York movie. There are so many Hollywood movies set in New York, and they don't feel like New York, because they're filmed on a studio lot or in Toronto because that's cheaper. I was really scared that some guy who had never been to Brooklyn before was going to write the screenplay, which is why I insisted on writing it myself. Then I was scared that they would get a director who had only been to New York once and stayed at the Four Seasons." Spike is, of course, only too willing to sing the praises of his home town: "If you are an L.A. filmmaker you are going to shoot on stage, but New York City has always been about being out there on the streets. From On the Waterfront to Scorsese, John Cassavetes, Sidney Lumet, Woody Allen. Because what is a better set than New York City?"

The Oscar ceremony of March 23, 2002, commenced with Tom Cruise musing rhetorically over whether such glamorous events still had a place post-9/11. But if the pre-show talk was all about downplaying the glitz, afterward it was to do with history being made, two African-American actors, Denzel Washington and Halle Berry, having picked up the respective Best Actor trophies together for the first time. On the same night Sidney Poitier was given the Academy's Lifetime Achievement Award. The event was rechristened in some quarters "the Black Oscars." Since both lead actors were Spike alumni, and Halle Berry mentioned the director in her speech, it was little surprise that Spike was asked his opinion on the changing status of African-Americans in the industry. The director shrewdly went against the grain, commenting, "Is this a signal that once and for all Hollywood is color-blind and we're all on the same playing field? I don't think so. Let's not get too hyped up. When Sidney Poitier won for *Lilies of the Field*, people probably felt the same way, and it was another forty years until Denzel won. Let's see what happens at the next few awards ceremonies before we start celebrating."

Spike had noted some of the struggles other 40 Acres graduates had endured in getting a foothold in the industry. Robi Reed, Randy Fletcher and Ruth Carter would all complain that they were now only finding jobs on "black films." Fletcher caught the mood of the trio: "I think I'm a good AD. I'm trying to let people know that I'm not just a minority AD. That was one of the reasons that I chose to do the remake of *Texas Chainsaw Massacre* rather than the better-paying *Bad Boys 2*. Because, honestly, on the set in Austin, Texas, I was the only black guy in the cast or crew." Ruth Carter, who has worked on numerous well-paying Eddie Murphy vehicles, took the job of dressing Meg Ryan in *Against the Ropes*. Spike, acknowledging the difficulties, also questions some of the compromises African-Americans are willing to make: "When people look at your résumé, they look at the quality of your films. If you've got a string of turkeys, that shit is a hindrance. I would rather be hindered by saying, 'Oh, I did *Malcolm X*, *Do the Right Thing*.'" Plans were also put in place for Spike to embark on a tour with Terence Blanchard in which the composer would conduct a live orchestra playing his scores from several of Spike's Joints, partly with the aim of showcasing the composer's talents to Hollywood studios.*

Spike and Aisha Coley began casting *25th Hour*. With Ed Norton on board when Spike took the job, Spike cast Brian Cox as Monty's father and Rosario Dawson as his girlfriend. As Monty's friends, Spike cast the relatively unknown Barry Pepper as Frank and, as Jacob, Philip Seymour Hoffman, who had been working with Ed Norton on *Red Dragon*. Norton says, "Spike and I had been saying, 'How great would Philip be for that part!' I asked Philip if he had got the script, and Philip said, 'It's a great part, but I don't really care what it is. I've been waiting for Spike Lee to call me for my whole life and I'd do any role he asked me to do.' I felt the same way." One per-

---

*Blanchard says, "Working with Spike I have had to develop this style of writing that is a little different from the Hollywood norm. It is interesting because it has hurt me, and it has helped me. It has hurt me because it has stopped me working with other Hollywood directors, because they think that I only do one thing. It has helped me in that it has really made me not afraid to use melody behind dialogue, and it has made me learn how to use my orchestrations to make space for that."

son who proved not so keen was Brittany Murphy, due to play a pupil at Hoffman's school; she was let go before pre-production. Spike says, "Brittany Murphy had to go, for showing a low level of commitment. I mean, we had a schedule, we had rehearsals, we had a read-through and she couldn't make it. Thank you, Anna Paquin, for coming in very late in the game, behind everybody else in preparation —she was a trooper."

Rosario Dawson proposes, "If you are cast in a Spike Lee joint you should be in New York preparing, regardless of whether it is two months away. I remember just a couple of weeks before we were shooting 25th Hour, I was visiting my boyfriend at the time and Spike called saying, 'What are you doing down there? Get over here. You're slacking.' But it's good because, literally, if you cannot be there for rehearsal, you are fired. You have to be there—if Denzel Washington is there, if Edward Norton is there, you should be there. And you should be there even before that, so you can watch all the films he wants you to see. And during the shooting at the weekends he has softball games with families and the cast and the crew. He is really tough on people, but he just expects you to do your job if you're hired. And if you don't, 'Don't waste my time.'"

"We had a couple of weeks where we all got together and read through the script," recalls Philip Seymour Hoffman. "There was a week where he hit on every scene and then in the second week he hit on every scene again, so you kind of worked on every scene a couple of times—more than usual on movies. You were able to talk about the scenes and give him some choices and some ideas, so when we showed up on the set I actually felt more involved already with the acting and the character than I usually am. I felt more confident about exactly what we were doing." But rehearsal for a Spike Lee joint is about more than just the scenes: it is where the director gives the actors the information that he feels they need. Ed Norton recollects, "Spike had a screening every night at 8 p.m. during rehearsals. He wants you to come watch movies, and he is looking at them for all kinds of different reasons. 'I want you to look at Midnight Cowboy again because of that sense of floating through New York in the night, the textures of it. I want to look at On the Waterfront, because that is about a character in moral crisis. I want to watch The Dead End Kids.' What does that have to do with 25th Hour? 'Well, these kids are bonded together in their childhood from their New York experience.' It is inspiring to see someone who is that passionate about movies. It affects me. When he screened Midnight Cowboy, I don't think a lot of us had seen the movie on screen for a long time, and when the lights came up at the end, Spike stood up and screeched, 'Still a motherfucker.' It was so funny."

All the advance preparation would ensure that not a moment was wasted on set, where minutes of unnecessary extra shooting can run up thousands of dollars of extra cost. *25th Hour* was financed by Disney to the tune of $15 million, 40 Acres having signed a three-picture first-look deal with the mouse house. While Spike was filming *25th Hour*, Martin Scorsese was putting the finishing touches to *Gangs of New York*, financed with a $100 million budget from Disney subsidiary Miramax. "I think it gets under Spike's skin a little bit that other movies will get so much more money to work with," says Ed Norton. "I'm not totally of the same mind with that, because we're not in the business of investing money in movies, and I'm glad that I'm not, and I'm sure that he's glad that he is not. But people make those decisions based on a set of formulas and business models that I don't really want to get involved in. I think you have to be careful as an artist, and this is where Spike is impressive in his execution but irritated in principle. I don't think that you can expect people to give you a lot of money for a movie. You have no fundamental entitlement to $50 million, especially if the movies you're making ain't making that much back. I think that what is great about Spike is that he may look at people and say, 'Why does that piece of shit get a $50 million budget and lose money?' but he takes, say, the $15 million that he gets for *25th Hour* and he gets so much more out of it. He takes personal responsibility for making his days, and that's impressive to me."

The major changes that Spike brought to Benioff's novel concerned the recent atrocity inflicted on New York. He says, "The novel took place before 9/11, and it was simple: we felt that in shooting a film like this in New York City, so close to what happened on 9/11, in being responsible filmmakers we had to reflect that in the film. Ed Norton and I both felt that we could comment on post–9/11 New York City. So New York City became even more of a character in the film, even though it was a wounded New York City with people trying to cope with their own particular lives. No matter what New Yorkers do, it is really in the back of their minds thinking about the planes that went into those towers. I tried to keep that in the back of my mind. I thought the best thing to do was make Monty Brogan's father a fireman and have Barry Pepper's apartment overlooking the building site at the World Trade Center. Then you go down the line: father is a fireman, he owns a bar, OK, so let's put up a shrine for the firemen. At that time Americans wanted blood; you saw the 'Bin Laden: Wanted Dead or Alive' T-shirts everywhere, and worse. But 9/11 was not the reason that I decided to make *25th Hour*. I didn't make it to show the pain of New York City, because you have to tell the story. The backdrop of 9/11 was something that we felt could help tell the story."

Philip Seymour Hoffman felt the resonance of the script: "Spike doesn't screw around; he addresses the here and now in New York, and that is what he does in *25th Hour* in a way that I think really took people by surprise. Spike really attacked the issue of 9/11 in this story and linked the story with the city, acknowledging that something awful had happened; life was going to change, it wasn't going to be the same for Monty Brogan or for the city. As a New Yorker I appreciate it, because I think he is right; he is being honest about the state of the city at that time. I think that he does capture that right-after-9/11 feeling in a great way. It still has that wonderful Spike Lee touch that addresses New York City in the way that New York City is, and it is ultimately very moving and makes you proud to live here." "New York is a great city," Spike affirms, "and what the city is made up of is its people. A line in the apartment overlooking the World Trade Center site is very important when Jacob asks Frank, 'Are you going to move?' and Frank says, 'Fuck that. Bin Laden can drop another one.' That's not really Frank talking—that is the line of eight million New Yorkers saying, 'We're staying here.'"

The opening credits establish the post-9/11 feel of the film as we see a plane flying past a Manhattan skyline. "We always try to utilize the opening-credit sequence as a space to get the audience's minds right to the film that is about to follow," says Spike. "This credit sequence shows the Twin Towers light mural which they had in NYC a little while after September 11. I thought, We have got to use that. The plane flying through the shot, that was luck; we were just pointing a camera when it happened. The good stuff, the magical stuff, you can't control. But half of filmmaking is luck. You just make your own luck. The cameras were rolling; we weren't fucking around holding our dicks, we were working."

The Irish bar owned by Monty Brogan's father is adorned with pictures of deceased New York firefighters. It is here, in the midst of a heated dinner-table argument, that Monty stomps off to the bathroom and regurgitates the furious, racist monologue that Spike insisted David Benioff put back into the screenplay. "I think it's probably the most memorable scene in the movie," Benioff concedes. "Certainly, when people talk to me about it, it's the scene which comes up most often. And, of course, it's a bit of a Spike Lee trademark: there's a similar scene in *Do the Right Thing*." For Spike this was not foremost a self-homage: "I knew we needed something right there to show the mental state of Monty Brogan. 'What have I just done, Lord, what have I just done?' But we had fun with that sequence. In *Do the Right Thing* there were fifteen Puerto Ricans in a car and in *25th Hour* there are twenty-two. I had to make it worse. But what really makes it worse is that we never saw fifteen Puerto Ricans in the car, but in *25th Hour* whatever Edward says you see, so you see the Puerto Ricans grabbing up all the space in the car."

"What was great about it is that it didn't even feel imposed, even though it was such a quintessential Spike cinema moment," says Ed Norton. "You look at it on the page and you think maybe this is too interior, but Spike takes it and explodes it into a great piece of visual cinema. You could think, The issues of race, are they as provocative as they were when he first started working? And you think, Probably not, and that's a good thing. But on the other hand, the trailer for *25th Hour* had come out, not even the film, and I got a letter—anonymous, of course—from some couple in Virginia or Maryland, basically saying, 'We loved your movies and thought they were great, and now we see you in this trailer kissing a black girl. How can you do that? We're never going to watch your movies again.'"

The production of *25th Hour* moved along smoothly and affably, though Mike Ellis was nevertheless awaiting one inevitable moment: "Spike will blow up at least once on set so that everybody will hear it. You can't second-guess when. A lot of times when he is upset it's just him at the monitor, muttering under his breath. But when shit is hap-

The cast and crew of *25th Hour*. (© 2001 David Lee)

pening, I'm sitting next to Spike, so I know. On 25th Hour we were doing a scene in this little bar where Rosario Dawson comes in and meets Barry Pepper and Philip Seymour Hoffman. And Barry said, 'I want to try something different, I think I would be like. . . .' Spike, after a fashion, said, 'Look, we don't need ten million motherfucking directors on this set. This is what we are going to do.' I mean, he blew up as much as he blows up. But Edward was laughing. And I knew it had to happen some time."

Barry Brown remembers that Spike asked him to take a new approach to the editing of this film: "I don't think that you could help but be influenced by MTV. If you look at a lot of the things that I cut for Spike, things don't languish, there's a pace that stays quick pretty much throughout. But on 25th Hour, Spike asked me to let the scenes breathe." Sam Pollard, still smarting from the Bamboozled experience, was nevertheless lured back into the fold to cut a couple of sequences: "I cut the scene when Monty and Naturelle are sitting on the stoop and I cut the big fight scene. I thought Spike was really doing me a big favor, because they paid me great money, but Barry could have done it without me really. Maybe he was feeling generous, you know. He's not a guy who is not open with his emotions, but he'll do some stuff where you say, 'Oh, I guess he is being nice.'"

Recording the score in London, Spike and Terence Blanchard incorporated Northumbrian pipes and set about incorporating Irish and Islamic traditions. Blanchard says, "Spike told me he wanted post–September 11 New York to be another character in the film, so my whole intention was to not let you forget that while you are watching this film. In the music I think Spike was trying to make a statement about America—all too often Islamic music and Irish music have been associated with just certain sections of American life, and I guess he was trying to say, 'All of this is America.'"

At the eleventh hour Spike was tinkering. "The most nerve-racking moment in the whole process was toward the end," says Benioff. "Spike was doing ADR work with Brian Cox, recording his voice-over for the final sequence of the movie, and he called and said, 'I've got five minutes of good footage of the desert but I've only got four minutes of voice-over. I need another page.' I said, 'OK, let me get to that in, like, a week?' He said, 'No, no, I got Cox in the studio right now. I need it in an hour.' At this point I felt that I knew the character well enough to write his thoughts and not spend too much time pondering it. But there wasn't time to panic."

The voice-over occurs in a fantasy sequence that sees Brogan contemplate what life could be like if he absconded as he is being driven to jail. There is a moment of doubt: will the character do so? Ed Norton recalls, "One of the things that I love about Spike was the way he dealt with the question of how are we going to perceive this ending. Should it be left uncertain? Did he turn and escape or did he go to jail? Spike was immediately definitive on that: he said that there is no reason to make this movie if he does not go to jail in the end. 'No, he's going down. He going to the hoosegow, he's going to the hoosegow.' This whole movie is about the consequence of choices. And yet there are lots of interesting moral questions in it. Are his friends responsible to him? Should they have said something? Are they complicit because they did not say something? Is he a victim of draconian drug laws? Or is this the choice he made to traffic in people's misery?"

The reviews for 25th Hour ran the gamut from Mick LaSalle in the San Francisco Chronicle stating that it is "a film of sadness and power, the first great twenty-first-century movie about a twenty-first-century subject," to Richard Corliss arguing that "it is pretty lethargic stuff." It is a film that has divided critics into two camps: those mesmerized by Lee's paean to New York and those believing that he was just rehearsing well-versed themes. Undoubtedly, it is Spike's most accessible movie since Crooklyn. David Denby declared in The New Yorker, "It captures the city's bitter, wire-taut mood after September 11th, and I hope that Disney finds some way to bring this acrid and brilliant little picture to the large audience it deserves." The lament was voiced because 25th Hour was released on December 22, 2002, on five screens, in order to qualify for the Oscars and avoid the dates allotted to such contenders as Gangs of New York and the monolithic The Two Towers, part two of the Lord of the Rings trilogy.

It was a situation that frustrated Ed Norton, who argues, "On the whole I think the critical reaction was very positive, almost universally so. The only thing I felt was unfortunate was that the studio released it at the wrong time, even though this release date had grown out of something really positive. Mike Eisner had told his employees, 'I really want some Oscar-caliber films,' so he had almost given his staff a mandate to go and find some films to campaign for Oscars for. Mike Eisner loved it, and it was almost like they got so focused on the mission of 'We want to have a movie for Oscar time' that they did not look up and say, 'OK, it is December already, the horses are in the gate. If you're taking an aim at that in the award season, the five leading runners are already picked. You can't take a little movie like this and slip it out in the last week of December and expect it to punch into that equation.' I think that was a big mistake. I think they should have held this movie, taken it to Cannes, somewhere it would have been really appreciated, and put it out maybe in the quiet period in the spring. Within the community of filmmakers, I have not been involved in a movie that I've had so many movie people come up to me and say that that was one of their favorite movies in the last five years. I think that it was deeply appreciated there. It was just a lousy release strategy—really kind of too bad."

Another explanation for the film's failure to earn more than $13 million at the domestic box office can be found in the lethargy of audiences toward the phenomenal output of the director, which leaves even some of Spike's most avid supporters struggling to keep up. John Pierson comments, "Now I'm going to admit something terrible, which might be a sign of how the years and the films go by: I actually have not seen 25th Hour. It came out when I was away, and when I came back I just never quite got around to catching up. So I'm a movie behind for the first time in my life."

As Spike went around America and Europe promoting the film, he used the platform afforded him to become one of the most vociferous opponents of the impending war in Iraq. Live on British TV, once the war had started, he openly demanded, "Where are the weapons of mass destruction?" He also argues, "What I do find interesting, and this is one of the things I try to show in the film, is how Bush was trying to get everyone to forget about Bin Laden—because they cannot find him—and make believe he never existed by replacing him with Saddam Hussein. Bush does not understand that the true source of American might is not its military strength but the way in which it can influence people's minds through culture."

Also released at the end of 2002 was a children's book that Spike co-wrote with his wife, named after Mars Blackmon's catchphrase, *Please, Baby, Please, Baby, Baby, Baby, Please*. Spike says, "It was my wife's idea to do the book and also to pick that phrase for the title. She was very shrewd and insightful. I would never have thought of writing a children's book, and the way that it is used in the book is genius. The book is really based on our bringing up the two kids, and they like the book a lot and that makes me feel good. Having kids has changed my mind-set but it has not affected my filmmaking yet. That's what I keep telling Tonya—I know I have children but it does not mean I'm going to make children's films. The only film they've seen of mine is *Crooklyn*."

With Jackson Lee getting older, Tonya began to act on her desire to do more creative work, as she no longer wished to pursue a law career. The book was part of that process: "It was my idea and essentially I wrote the book. Spike was excited about that and supportive of it, but it was my project and happily so. In some ways I guess that people were always looking at me as 'the wife.' The thing is that, after a while, they get to know me and my work and then it is no longer about Spike. I had been working at Nickleodeon and I then persuaded them to make an animated short of the book. Spike did not have anything to do with that other than the voice-over. I was directing him on that, and Spike can be so contrary when he wants to be. The first time Spike read it he destroyed it: there was no realization that it is a children's book and you are reading this to kids. He was just so funny and wrong that we had to go back to re-record it, and I was feeding him the lines, trying to give him the tone and the rhythm. Afterward he told me, 'You're not supposed to feed your actors lines.' I said, 'I understand but clearly, dear, you needed some help.'"

Spike's abilities were being more appreciated by Mary Campbell at Tisch,* where he had recently received a promotion. The dean says, "He came up here one year and said, 'We seem to be having less and less African-American students. What's happening?' So we had a meeting of graduate students and Spike came, and I asked, 'What can I do to make sure that this school continues to have diversification?' They all said we need to go down to the historically black colleges and recruit.† Spike said, 'If you do that, I will go.' And he did. And I thought, Gosh, he is really committed to this place. If he were shooting in California, he would take five students with him to intern. He was doing all kinds of things. And I thought, Why don't we just formalize it? We were changing the chair at the time, and I had joked, 'Why don't I give you the chair?' and he said, 'No, not yet.' I thought he was certainly doing enough to be artistic director, so we put things down on a piece of paper, and he agreed to it. Now I really feel when I pick up the phone and say, 'I'd like for you to do the introduction for the Showtime film we did based on remembrances of 9/11,' I *should* be asking him, as he is the artistic director of the department. It certainly empowered me to find opportunities for him to do more things. It seemed like the more that we expanded his role, the more he did for the school."

Spike was also given an honorary degree by Princeton University. His talent as a filmmaker was also receiving the highest honors in Europe. In France he received the Cesar award for his collective oeuvre and in Britain he received the BAFTA Lifetime Achievement Award

*The School of the Arts at New York University was renamed the Tisch School of the Arts after Preston Robert Tisch donated a huge sum of money in 1982.
†Spike went to Morehouse (where he is on the board of trustees) and Howard on these recruitment trips.

from Sir Richard Attenborough. As Spike reveals, old grievances were raised by the esteemed British knight: "I'd never met the man before. I wasn't going to bring *Cry Freedom* up. It wasn't about being gung ho or you're right and I'm wrong; he brought it up. Sir Richard had his view and said that Mandela liked it and the film was important in helping bring an end to apartheid, and I had my view. There is still a mutual respect. It's just disheartening to see, when you know what the true story is and you see it turned into something else. It is bollocks."

Mars Blackmon also came out of retirement to produce one final commercial with Michael Jordan to commemorate the basketball star's definitive retirement from the game. This, coupled with the life-time achievement awards that celebrated his oeuvre, would normally be a great time to end a story, but then again, Spike has never been one for safe, unambiguous endings. . . .

In May 2003 TNT, a subsidiary of Viacom, announced that it was changing the name of a channel aimed at young teenage males (with programs of *Jackass*-style humor) to Spike TV. The announcement was countered by an affidavit from Spike Lee, protesting that his own brand was being infringed by such an action. The story made front-page news, and Spike found himself an underdog in this corporate clash: "You have to be particular where you fight your battles, and it's no fun being David going up against Goliath. You might have the strongest case, but these corporations, their pockets are endless, and if they wish to they can keep a case going for years and years—you'll go to the poorhouse in the meantime. Viacom were pulling out all the stops. But I didn't understand why they would choose that name. They lost millions just because they had a launch date they were working to, and spent all this money on promotions, but they were in limbo once the case started."

Column inches in the mainstream media were filled with commentators either lauding the director for his convictions or laughing at his over-self-aggrandizement. Legal minds, meanwhile, were occupied with the complexities of the case. Spike asserts, "My complaint was not that they wanted to use the word 'Spike'; it was the combination of 'Spike' and 'TV' that I was complaining about. Even after the publicity surrounding the case there is still a perception that I have something to do with the channel. There are a lot of Spikes in the entertainment business: Spike Jonze, a very fine filmmaker. But most people don't know what Spike Jonze looks like. People don't realize that I'm a brand, and all the goodwill that I have invested in it can be contaminated by 'Spike TV.'"

Having enjoyed a good relationship with Edward Norton on *25th Hour*, Spike called on the actor to contribute to the affidavit: "I know how he feels about big business, so he said, 'Fine.' My wife, Tonya, was very, very helpful throughout this process." Tonya employed her jurisprudential knowledge to aid her husband: "Although I would say that I think it's good that he stood up for what he believed in, I do wish that he could pull back and protect himself a little bit more. I had an ongoing relationship with Viacom myself. I've worked with the same people that started Spike TV and I worked with them while the dispute was going on." "What people fail to realize," says Spike, "is that every decision made on the case we won—six or seven New York State judges ruled in our favor. But Johnnie Cochran, whom I hired to represent me, got the word that we should settle, so Tonya and I conferred with Johnnie, and that is what we did." It should be said that the decisions that Spike won were in relation to whether there was a case for Viacom to answer. And clearly it would have been harsh to say that an industry figure of Spike's stature, owning an advertising company at work in the same medium by the name of Spike/DDB, had no right to argue his case before a full hearing. Crunch time came when Viacom attempted to get Spike to put $13 million aside so that he could pay damages if he lost. It was a risk Spike was not so willing to take, hence the settlement. Although its terms are wrapped in a nondisclosure agreement, they were more than just financial: "One of the things that came out of the settlement was that my wife got some money that she was able to put into a mini-series she produced in 2004, *Miracle's Boys*, which is from an award-winning novel by Jacqueline Woodson. So that turned out good. And I directed the first episode, and the sixth and final episode."

Of the experience of working with the company he took to court, Spike reflects: "Viacom owns Paramount, VH-1, Comedy Central, MTV, Nickleodeon and much more—so you are going to work with them if you're a filmmaker. They are too big. I mean, I made *Original Kings of Comedy* at Paramount, and there are good people I have worked with. With the Viacom network, it's the guys who run the thing whom I had the problem with. But for me to say, 'I'll never do anything again for Viacom,' that would not work."

In 2003, 40 Acres got a TV project off the ground for the first time, some reward for Spike's long endeavors in that line: "I am much more persistent when it comes to TV, because I have some credibility in film but I've never done a big television series before, and TV is even more restrictive than film in the ways that you see black people. But Sam Kitt had met a young writer, Alex Tse, who wrote a script called *87 Fleer*. They had this idea about Chinese and African-American gangs in San Francisco, and Showtime wanted a series made from this idea." The plan was for Spike to shoot a pilot and hand over the reins to other directors once Showtime decided on how many episodes to commission. Preston Holmes was asked to work as a producer on the project: "It was the first time that Spike had done any long-form shooting in California. It was interesting to work with him again after about ten years because I love Spike's passion about what he does—this is a man who loves movies and who I think is most happy when he is shooting and editing. If anything his passion is even more intense than I recall. He is older, of course, but instead of slowing down he seems to have picked up the pace. While we were doing the Showtime piece he was doing concerts across the country where Terence Blanchard was performing the music to Spike's films. That was just amazing to me."

"It was fun to shoot in San Francisco," says Holmes. "We had a great crew, mainly from feature films; a wonderful cinematographer, César Charlone, nominated for an Oscar for *City of God*. We had to fight for César because he hadn't worked in the States, didn't have a crew. 'Can he speak English?'—all of that. They hadn't even heard of *City of God* at Showtime." *Sucker Free City*, as the show was christened, follows three characters, one white, one black and one Chinese, who become embroiled with one another through girls and crimes ranging from bootlegging to murder in a run-down neighborhood in San Francisco. "Each city has its own rhythm and its own attributes," says Spike, "and San Francisco is a great city. I don't know if there is actual static between black and Chinese gangs there, but I had to highlight it because it was in the script."

Casting director Aisha Coley had taken a job at Fox but recommended Kim Coleman to Spike: "You never forget that person who gave you that first break, someone who has been as loyal as he has been, and you obviously don't want to leave somebody like that hanging." Spike auditioned Anthony Mackie for the role of K-Luv after seeing him on Broadway and in *8 Mile*. Mackie says, "Spike wasn't what I expected. He didn't walk around with any airs. He's always on set, doesn't have a trailer—you get directors who aren't half as talented or well-known as he is and they go sit in their trailer all day. Whereas with Spike if I had a question from the acting aspect all the way to the production aspect he was willing to sit down and talk to me about it."

Spike's relationship to the rising generations came to the attention of his sister, Joie, as she visited the *Sucker Free City* set: "One of the young actors said to me, 'Oh, I really enjoyed you in your brother's earlier work.' I was like, 'What!?' I just hadn't heard that before—hadn't thought of myself as the older generation. But younger people don't always know what Spike did, what he pioneered. Recently I was in the neighborhood, walking around, and there were these teenagers bothering someone's dog behind a fence, so I made a comment. Then they started coming after me: 'Hey, that's Spike Lee's sister! Your brother's films suck, he's nowhere near as good as John Singleton!' I said, 'You guys are so fucking ignorant, you don't even know what you are talking about.' They don't know that Spike opened the doors for everyone else. Then they talked about putting a cap in my ass. . . . So not everyone likes Spike, I know that—I hear it, believe me."

Ultimately the experience of working on *Sucker Free City* left a sour taste for Spike: "The only reason that I did it was because Showtime said that they wanted a series, but now it has gone from a series to a miniseries to four hours, and now it's down to a two-hour film. Everybody involved in this did it thinking that it would be at the very least a miniseries. Showtime can do what they want, but if you had told me from the beginning that it was a one-off, I would have said, 'No.' I think that if it ever gets seen it will be enjoyed. But I didn't enjoy working with Showtime at all. I got the cut I wanted; they just had their own different way of working which I thought, sometimes, was detrimental to the film. The guy I had a relationship with at Showtime, he left—and any time there is a regime change, it's not good. For me Showtime are small potatoes compared to HBO; there is a reason why HBO won all those Emmys." *Sucker Free City* would eventually play at the Toronto Film Festival in October 2004 as a one-off Spike Lee project: "They called me and asked me if they could do it. I said, 'Go ahead.' But they wouldn't even pay for a print."

Mercifully, Spike moved swiftly into pre-production on his next feature film, *She Hate Me*. "I co-wrote it with Michael Genet, a fine young playwright who had a small part in *25th Hour*. I had an idea that Michael put in story form and wrote the first draft, then I wrote my draft. The genesis was Enron, Halliburton, Tyco, WorldCom—all those companies who display greed at its utmost. It's not the government that runs things in America, it's corporations. They have billions of dollars, they pay lobbyists so they can change laws to maximize their profits. The guy that runs Clear Channel is one of the biggest contributors to the Bush campaign. Clear Channel is a company that now owns every other radio station in America, and before Bush came into office there was a limit on how many media outlets you could own. When Bush got elected, he relaxed that law. This guy bought up all the stations. This stuff works hand in hand. You don't have to look too hard to look at the connection between big business and George W. Bush. The Bushes are oil barons. Just look at what Michael Moore does so wonderfully in *Fahrenheit 9/11*: he shows the relationship between the Bush family and the Bin Laden family. Bush is there for Big Business, and they are going to try and do everything to keep him in there. So if we can get a couple of shots in, we are going to do that.

Let me give you another example. What company got an $8 billion contract in Iraq without a bid? Halliburton. And the White House says that there is no connection between Dick Cheney being the Vice-President of the United States and him being the former president of Halliburton. So you have this great big story about the moral and ethical decline of corporations. And when people think of corporations they imagine this big behemoth, this monster, so we wanted to have one individual in conflict with their own ethics, morals and scruples. The moral debate then goes deeper for this character, John Henry Armstrong, because he is offered a deal to impregnate women for cash incentives. It's not simply the fact that these women are lesbians. The women could have been heterosexual—he's trying to deal with the fact that he brought nineteen kids into the world. And the fact that he signed a donor-waiver agreement, that's inconsequential—he is still the father of those nineteen kids."

"Spike brought me in," recalls Michael Genet, "and he said, 'Have you heard there is a significant portion of the lesbian community who want to become mothers and they use turkey basters to get pregnant?' I had heard nothing of this phenomenon, and I'm thinking, Oh my God, is he going to want to do this as a movie? Because this is definitely going to be another controversial Spike Lee joint. And he said, 'I don't know what the story is, but that interests me.' I said, 'OK, let me go off and see if I can come up with a story for you.' He was pleased with the work I did, and what Spike does, which is real smart, is he takes that and then does the rest of the writing to turn it into a Spike Lee movie that has his stamp on it. But he had so much stuff that he wanted in this script, like wanting to see Frank Wills,* that a couple of times I was like, 'Just slow down. I mean, how are we going to fit all this into a two-hour movie?'"

One of the things that Spike wanted to see was a reflection of the changing notion of family: "I'll give you a story: Satchel, who is nine, and Jackson, who is seven, a couple of years ago they came to me and my wife and said, 'Daddy, we have a kid in our class who has two daddies and another who has two mommies.' So Tonya and I told our children to sit down and we went into an explanation of this. Once we had finished with our speech, our children looked at us and said, 'Does that mean they're gay?' So kids are exposed to a lot. A seven-year-old today knows what I knew when I was twenty. We live in a different world, and my wife and I are trying to teach our kids that they have to be open and treat those kids with same-sex parents like everyone else."

*The security guard who called the police when he noticed a break-in at Watergate.

Producer Fernando Sulichin described how it is becoming increasingly difficult to raise funds for an independent Spike Lee joint: "In *She Hate Me*, there is an actor called Jamel Debbouze and an actress called Monica Bellucci. African-American films historically don't perform well in Europe. And Spike's films are mostly aimed for the American market. However, Spike could not get the financing from America so he needed Europe. I said, 'Listen, you need to help me out. You need to put in a couple of Europeans so I can at least attract financiers.' But it's hard to be an independent filmmaker because studios are run by secretaries who have no clue what a good film is. How can they relate to someone who wants to make a story about Joe Louis written by Budd Schulberg?"

For Spike it is a problem that is still about more than just money, something he wanted to address in *She Hate Me*: "Hollywood is still in the business of stereotypical images, not just of African-Americans. We still have stereotypes of homosexuals, Latinos, lesbians, women . . . and I don't think it's going to change until people of color get in those lofty positions of the gatekeepers. The only reason that I've been able to break the mold is because I have been able to do films that don't cost a lot of money. The average cost of a Hollywood film today is $50 million. This is just to make them, I'm not talking about prints and advertising. *25th Hour* cost $15 million, *Bamboozled* cost $10 million, that's the world I'm operating in. These films don't cost a lot of money. *She Hate Me* was $8 million."

Moreover, Spike was still able to attract a stellar cast: "The gatekeepers and I were so impressed with Anthony Mackie's work on *Sucker Free City*. I knew we were going to do *She Hate Me* right afterward and I gave him the script and said, 'Let's go.' For the part of Fatima, one time it was going to be Thandie Newton, Halle Berry . . . In fact, I had given the role to Nia Long, but right before we started rehearsal we had philosophical differences so a change had to be made. That is how we got to Kerry Washington, whom I'd seen in a lot of independent films, and she is wonderful in this film. Then we had Monica Bellucci, Woody Harrelson, Brian Dennehy, Ellen Barkin, my main man John Turturro, Jim Brown—and the new people, Dania Ramirez and Q-Tip."

Kerry Washington's description of her last-minute audition sounds like a sequence from *Girl 6*: "He pushed the bar, he tested my limits in the audition. He had me kiss another woman. He wanted to see how comfortable I was with my own sexuality, with my ability to do that— after I read some scenes with Anthony Mackie—because I think he really wanted to test whether I'd be able to take on the responsibility of this role. Spike didn't try to make me feel comfortable; he is not a director who's invested in coddling his actors at all."

When Danny Aiello pulled out of a role as a *Godfather*-type mafia boss a week before production, Spike put out a call to John Turturro: "I told Spike, 'I'm too young to play Bellucci's father, let me be her uncle or something.' But then I figured it was a comedy anyway. Then I called him back. I had second thoughts. Eventually I said, 'All right, but I'll wear dark sunglasses, OK?' It was a real pain in the ass. I was doing two other jobs at the same time, but I did it for Spike. And it was like, 'Now you owe me one, you bastard. You're going to write me a good part one of these days, no more cameos'—otherwise I'm going to his head with a frying pan." Rosario Dawson, however, could not be massaged into a change of prior commitments: "I was supposed to work on *She Hate Me* and it got pushed back and then I got a part in Oliver Stone's *Alexander*. Spike was like, 'You could do that movie any time.' I said, 'I don't think I can do that 400 B.C. epic just any time. I'm not being disloyal. I know that I was able to get in that room and get this part because of the risk you took in casting me and letting me do my thing. So I'm hoping that you're happy for me, and not just being like, "Bitch, you left."'"

Shooting was pushed back to October 2003, the start of the semester that Spike teaches at NYU. Dean Campbell reveals the lengths that Spike went to in order to keep his obligation to his pupils: "He's usually tried to arrange his teaching schedule so that he's not shooting at the same time. We had thirty-five students in the third-year class, and he invited all of them, if they wanted to, to have an internship on *She Hate Me*. Twenty-nine wanted internships, and he signed them all up and placed them in various departments. The other six accompanied him on the set during the class time. So in fact they got hands-on experience working on a professional set."

It was not just young students to whom Spike was offering lessons. "Spike creates an environment on his sets that encourages creative artists to explore their own talents," says Lonette McKee. "Spike enjoys mentoring and nurturing other talented people. And somehow his success gives all of us permission to dream loftier dreams. *She Hate Me* was the fourth film I had done for Spike, and we had worked together on my music CD, which he executive produced. He was always right there on set, watching everything and orchestrating his vision beautifully. I definitely came away with priceless information and understanding of how to get films off the page and onto the screen."

Spike himself will no longer champion a solidarity in black film, not when the product has been, in his eyes, increasingly coarsened. *Soul*

Plane was a 2004 hit penned by Chuck Wilson, who received his first break as an intern on *Crooklyn*: "We have to understand the stereotypes, we can't keep those stereotypes going. So when African-American filmmakers make a film like *Soul Plane* and then say, 'It's just a comedy, just a movie,' these are people who don't really know the history of the negative portrayal of African-Americans in film and television. All along I've been blasting that film, saying it's nothing but buffoonery and coonery. So they ask Snoop Dogg about it and he said, 'How can Spike Lee talk? Those films *School Daze* and *Do the Right Thing* are nothing but stereotypes. And now he has made this film *25th Hour*, he should just be quiet.' Sometimes you can let people hang themselves."

Spike, aware that he has himself fallen short in his depiction of female characters in the past, employed a "female sexuality expert" to help the actors prepare for their roles. Kerry Washington says of the classes that took place over a two-week period, "The lesbian boot camp was like training. Basically we had a woman, Tristan Taormino, who is a lesbian sexuality expert, come in and talk to us about different aspects of lesbian life, from cultural identity to sex to anything you can possibly ask. She brought in guest speakers. It was great, it was fun. This process was for us to have assistance in building the full identity of our characters."

"*Sucker Free City* had been much more open and improvisational, everybody really collaborating to make the project," says Anthony Mackie. "There he was an actor's director. For *She Hate Me* he was a director's director. He knew the movie and the story that he wanted to tell, and he was very deliberate and controlled about not stepping over the lines of that." Spike employed hot young DP Matty Libatique, best known for his work for Darren Aronofsky on *Pi* and *Requiem for a Dream*, and who had just finished working on *Never Die Alone* for Ernest Dickerson. Libatique says, "Spike set up almost every shot. At times when I voiced my opinion Spike was responsive, so that collaboration was working, but I respected him so much. Not only is he the director, he's fucking Spike Lee."

Spike says of his own on-set demeanor: "My visual sense is now much better. When Ernest and I did films together, his visual sense was years ahead of mine. I let him do everything. I woke up one day, probably around *Jungle Fever*, *Malcolm X*—that's when I said, 'Ernest is not going to be around forever, what's going to happen then?' That's when I started going to the woodshed, as far as being a well-rounded director, not relying totally on the DP for placement of camera and choice of lens and all of that stuff. It was about being more active, thinking about stuff in pre-production, trying to visualize in my head what it is that I want. It was very easy not to do when Ernest was there. It was easy to give him an idea and let him run with it. But what you want to achieve in each film is to utilize your skills and the tools you have in hand to benefit the story. What can I use to tell this story the best way? Everything is for the telling of the story."

For *She Hate Me*, Spike made a call to prop master Kevin Ladson, out of favor since relations were strained five years earlier on *Summer of Sam*: "I said, 'OK, finally I'll get a chance to talk to Spike. I kept a journal, I can explain to him what was going on then.' So I show up at his house. I'm ready to talk, I whip out the journal with highlights in it, and he says, 'Man, put that away. Do you want to work on the film? Let's just start from scratch.' And that was it. It was one of the most wonderful times I've had working with Spike. Even before we started, he did a TNT spot and I was just having a good time working on that too. Spike was in a good mood and we were talking, and I just said, 'Spike, it's good to be back home.' And that's the first time—after all this reaction I've been seeking—that he looked like he had a tear in his eye. He gave me this big old hug and he wouldn't let go."

She Hate Me was rejected by Cannes in 2004, so denying Spike the chance to serve up his latest before jury president Quentin Tarantino. "I heard somewhere Tarantino was not the first choice," Spike muses, "but Warren Beatty didn't want to be away from his kids and Jack Nicholson isn't missing no play-off games." That July, the movie would barely open at the box office. Critics were unanimous in their derision. Lesbian groups were offended. Perhaps Spike Lee should have shown his wife, Tonya, the product earlier in the day: "I think that Spike puts himself so deeply in his work in ways that he does not even understand. I think that there is so much of him that he doesn't even see it. We had a deep discussion with *She Hate Me*, because I had only seen it when I went to the première, the first time that had happened with any of his work. After seeing it, I was like, 'OK, now I understand, I see.' He was like, 'What are you talking about?'"

But as *She Hate Me* was getting panned and Mike Tyson's latest comeback was derailed by Danny Williams, Tonya was receiving wide acclaim for her début novel, co-written with Crystal McCrary Anthony. *Gotham Diaries* tells the story of high-society African-Americans in Manhattan. Spike says of his wife's success, "This is something that she has had within her all along. But you have to be encouraged, and she was pushed in another direction by her parents, who were business people. She had to be a lawyer, a CEO or a doctor; those were her choices. Her father was huge, the treasurer of Philip Morris, and for a black man to have done that at the time was remarkable. As with Tonya's sister Tracy, it was a path that they were expected to follow. Tonya has always told me that she wanted to do something creative. The thing about *Gotham Diaries* is that they went about it in a roundabout way: they first went to HBO to do it as a series; HBO wasn't buying. Here is a great lesson: they turned a negative into a positive; instead of saying, 'Scrap it,' they said, 'Why don't we make it a novel?' So they wrote a *New York Times* bestseller, a summer read on all the beaches. And I hope they will get their original wish and it will be a TV series."

Spike himself returned to television in the summer of 2004 for work on *Miracle's Boys*, the TV series produced by Tonya and the first long-form project Spike would direct outside of the 40 Acres aegis. But Spike's adventures in television are set to continue, with plans afoot for a series based on *He Got Game*.* "It is very interesting that there is a controversy happening now on college campuses," Spike reflects. "One particular school, the University of Colorado, women are coming out of the woodwork now and saying that they were raped during these recruitment parties. And they were citing Jesus Shuttlesworth, his recruitment trip in the movie, going to the school and meeting two naked ladies."

The lack of box office for *She Hate Me* was another setback in Spike's ambitions to get *Save Us, Joe Louis*, *The Jackie Robinson Story* and *Spike Lee's Huckleberry Finn* off the ground. *She's Gotta Have It* producer John Pierson says of Spike's steadfast refusal to change method, "Sam Kitt is a really good friend of mine, and he has run the company for a long time now. Spike is not going to listen to him, Spike is not going to listen to *anybody* fundamentally when it comes to certain things. We don't need some heavy-handed Harvey Weinstein type person to overinterfere with Spike. But there are just some things that if more of his films had, it would obviously be an improvement. Endings have traditionally been bad. I'm not even going to say he needs better endings; if more of the films *had* endings, that would be a start."

The ambiguities at the end of his first five films, and in particular the quotes at the end of *Do the Right Thing*, come to mind. The utilization of Malcolm X's justification for violence after Dr. King's call for peaceful resistance would irk many, especially as Spike would throw

---

*Ralph Wiley, who had worked on a *Huckleberry Finn* script with Spike, was penning this project until his unexpected death in the summer of 2004.

the question "What do you think?" back at reporters who asked him what his position was. Edward Norton feels that Spike is unfairly criticized: "Spike brings you into a story and forces you to swirl around in the questions that the characters are experiencing. He doesn't spoonfeed you at the end. People get confused in the short term. When a movie literally says, in a voice-over at the end, 'I know now that my father was a good man and everything is OK,' it helps the critic feel smart because all the subtext has been explained by the film itself, so they don't have to do all that much original thought. But if a movie asks questions they think it's confused and dogmatic."

Spike suggests that his endings are actually born out of faith in the audience: "There are certain things that I want the audience to do when it comes to the endings of my films. More often than not, I let the audience do some work."

Nelson George notes that the ambiguity in structure occurs in more than just the endings: "Ultimately he's an auteur. A lot of other people used to say to me, 'How come Spike doesn't collaborate with a screenwriter?' They always thought from a classic point of view that his films were problematic, especially his endings. But Spike said to me, 'I don't believe in Hollywood script structure.' For an American audience, your rhythms are used to being given to you in a certain way, then paying off in a certain way. So much is setup and payoff, conflict and resolution. Spike consistently goes against that: he defies expectation, he has multiple endings, he does not always pick up threads, some threads are just essays in the middle of the film. And I think that ultimately his style of filmmaking is best suited to that. I don't think as an artist he is comfortable working in the confines of a traditional screenplay. Every time he is given one, he Spikes it."

Philip Seymour Hoffman adds, "He can make any film that he wants to make. Spike Lee could have a totally different career; he could easily be a top dog commercial Hollywood filmmaker. His dictionary, thesaurus and vocabulary of filmmaking is vast. I don't find him trying to make pieces of entertainment or something just to be highly commercial or successful; he is just constantly making films that he needs to make." Yet John Turturro agrees with the common complaint made by critics that the numerous tangents in Spike's joints veer too far from the central stories: "This is part of every creative person's problem, that you don't trust how good something is, to say, 'You know what? Less can be more.' With Spike I think that he hasn't had someone tell him sometimes that his work is so good. I always tell him when he asks me, 'Cut it, make it shorter, shorter, shorter.'"

The experimental narrative structure of his films is not always appreciated "because Spike has got a big mouth," voices Ed Norton. "Sometimes, I don't think that Spike is his own best advocate. I've told him that. 'You should let me talk about your movies, because I talk about them much better than you do.' He comes off as much more angry. People associate Spike sometimes with an angry righteousness and urgency that I don't think his films have. I don't feel his films are angry at all. They are very compassionate." John Turturro was in partial agreement with Norton: "Ed likes to talk a lot. I'm not saying that in a negative way. I don't think that he has done enough work with Spike to articulate Spike. But I do think Ed has a point. I told Spike early on, 'You shouldn't talk to 'em that much. Let your work do the talking.' I'm a big believer in that." As is Spike's wife, Tonya: "I wish Spike would not talk to the press so often and I try desperately sometimes to talk to him about it, because I think he hurts himself often by saying what he thinks. Why does he have to be the person to stand up? I don't think that is even where his power is, and it is not going to do much to change things; it is only going to adversely affect him. But I think that it is also a learning process for him. I'm not sure that he has really thought about the effect that it has on his career."

In regards to the media, Spike is largely unapologetic: "I regret some of the things that I've said in the heat of the moment. But I think that a lot of times they are lazy, and laziness just boxes people in. It's just plain laziness to say this person is this and this person is that, without any effort to try and dig deeper and touch more than the surface." It is this cantankerous nature that appeals to Jada Pinkett Smith: "You either like Spike Lee or you don't like Spike Lee; there is no gray area when you are dealing with him or his projects. You are always clear where he stands: he is black or he is white. Most people try to fiddle around their truth. You might not agree with his truth but at least you know what it is."

Yet it's entirely plausible to argue that Spike's greatest achievements have not been behind the camera. "Spike taught me to be sensitive: he inspired me to be more conscientious about our people and using and working and hiring our people," says Art Sims. The inspiration that Spike has provided to students and young African-Americans in particular is immeasurable; and despite having worked in movies for two decades he retains a certain cachet. Dr. Herb Eichelberger says of his latest charges, "The students are still really excited about him. They pick up equipment and ask, 'Did Spike use this?' They often come up to me, particularly women, and say, 'I'm going to be better than

Spike.' I tell them how he formed 40 Acres and how you have to have friends around you to do that."

Ernest Dickerson says of his school chum, "Spike fought hard to try and keep the integrity of his films, and I think that is what every film-maker should try to do. Someone once asked Spike, 'Who is your girl-friend?' and he said, 'Suzy Cinema,' and it is true. Randy Fletcher and I talk about how it would be great if we could just do one more film for old times' sake. I'd think about it seriously because we had good times and I think it might be fun to try to do it again."

Q-Tip says of Spike's position in African-American film, "He is its pulse, its heart, its plasma, its skeleton, its flesh, its skin and, you know, painfully for Spike, he is its sensibility and intelligence as well. Which is why he makes the films and the choices that he makes. He wants to have something with some substance. I think that is a lot for one man to be. I don't think that he asked for it, but it is his birthright." Mary Schmidt Campbell elaborates, "This is a man who says some things that nobody else says in our culture. It may be uncomfortable or sometimes may embarrass us, but he says them any-way. For that reason you can go to his body of work and you can dis-cover all kinds of things about your life, culture, sex, gender, because he has not shied away from even the most difficult subjects." Roger Smith says that this has become about more than one man: "I hope that the body of work continues to grow, not simply through Spike, but all the people who have had an opportunity to work with Spike. He has literally changed the complexion of American film-making, and whenever I go work with other people, it becomes painfully apparent what Spike has achieved."

For some, there still remain several caveats when talking about his body of work. "I still don't think he's hit his masterpiece," said Ralph Wiley. "I really don't. That is the great thing about it. Some people you think of—say, Coppola—you feel like that is it for him, it is all down-hill from here. With Spike there is still something left." Stanley Crouch says of the desire for Spike to outdo himself: "Any movie he makes I'll go see, because you never know, he might make that masterpiece, then he might make a string of them after that. I've thought about it and believe he needs to get somebody who is smart and whose opinion he trusts to look at these movies with him, to help him avoid certain traps he falls in."

Ed Norton argues that such a view fails to acknowledge the great films already in Spike's portfolio: "It's not that Spike doesn't get his due. There is a generation of people, my generation, who have a very different feeling and relationship with Spike's films than the sort of baby boomer generation of critics who have been writing about them. It is no coincidence that when Criterion released *Do the Right Thing* on DVD it was snapped up by every person under the age of thirty-five because that is one of the defining films of our lives. So is *Malcolm X*. To me, he is our generation's Woody Allen and he is appreciated as such. If you look at Scorsese's career, Spike's is in a very similar arc. At the moment he is where Scorsese was before *GoodFellas*, acknowledged by the generation that came of age with him as a master craftsman, as one of the great virtuoso stylists, one of the really original voices, one of the people who is sticking in a fork and looking at the really dysfunctional things of our generation's times. You know, in the same way that *Taxi Driver* was for that post-Vietnam generation, *Do the Right Thing* and these movies are for us. Spike is not going to get his full due until the generation that was most impacted by his movies becomes the mainstream adult generation."

"I think the most important thing that Spike did," says Lisa Jones, "was that he decided that he did not want to be just an artist, he wanted to create a legacy in a particular industry, and that was huge—because he didn't just make a film or two: he has a whole oeuvre. He didn't get jobs just for himself; he allowed a whole generation of young people access to the industry. I think that that is his major contribution. Spike really got in there and said, 'This is not going to be just about me, it is going to be about changing the industry.'"

And the person closest to Spike, his wife, Tonya, adds, "Spike has always wanted to make money with his films. I don't think that Spike was ever the artist who was going to create art, just to do it and to get it out there. Spike has hustled every film that he has made, and worked hard to hustle so that his films can make money. It is funny that people have this image of what they want Spike to be. I just know that Spike wants to make movies, probably until he can't breathe anymore."

Epilogue

Dear Satchel and Jackson,

Daddy began making films before you were born. And although you've seen my commercials and music videos, of my eighteen feature films you've only seen one (because of the "adult" material)—*Crooklyn*. I just can't wait until the both of you get older and we can sit down along with Mommy and have marathon movie sessions. I can't wait to see what your intelligent minds will say about the many different films and subject matters. I already know what your mother feels, but I want to know what you feel. What will be your favorite? What film will you HATE? What film will you ask me, "Daddy, why in the hell did you make that?" Whatever it is, I want to know. I want to sit down with the both of you and talk for hours. You can help your father. Hurry and grow up.

Love,
Daddy

Acknowledgments

From the moment that I approached Spike Lee with the idea for this book, he has been the most fabulous interviewee, critic and host. The welcome I received into the 40 Acres family will stay with me forever.

To all those who agreed to be interviewed, I hope that the reading will be half as rewarding and enriching an experience as it was to converse with you. Sadly, both Ralph Wiley and Ossie Davis passed away before publication, and praise be to Allah for letting me be blessed by their wisdom. My thoughts remain with their families and friends. I also thank all the assistants, agents and managers who helped make these interviews happen.

There are three people without whom this book would not have been possible, who were always supportive, understanding and able to proffer astute opinion whenever and wherever it was needed: Richard T. Kelly, the Alan Shearer behind the book—editor, talisman, but above all my friend; Jason Lampkin, who selflessly went beyond the call of duty in ensuring my time in New York was happy and productive; and Alex Holroyd, my first and best reader, of whom there is little that I can write that could relay the extent of my gratitude.

There are several people working at Faber & Faber, my British publisher, whom I would like to salute for their endeavors: Kate Ward, Ian Bahrami, Bomi Odufunade and Camilla Smallwood. For their hospitality and welcome in New York City, Ben "Monk" Jorgensen, Cordelia Stephens, Tatyana Chiporoukha and Michelle Peltier.

Big respect to my understanding friends and colleagues at lafamiglia: Jesse Lawrence, Cristian Solimeno and Bruce Melhuish. That sentiment also goes out to Alessandro Grandesso at Circuittooff and David McManus.

Last, and most important, I would like to thank my parents, who have always encouraged and supported all my endeavors, even when they knew I was being foolhardy. Their attitude, values and ability to overcome life's travails have been inspirational. I will always be your loving son.

—Kaleem

Appendix

November 29, 2004

From the very start, one of the goals at 40 Acres and a Mule was to demystify the whole filmmaking process. We wanted filmmaking to be accessible. It is a craft that can, with serious study, be learned like anything else. We wanted people of color (male and female) to pursue careers in film, not only in front of the camera but, even more important, behind it. With this charge, 40 Acres had to tangle, battle and finally negotiate with the lily-white trade unions to open up their ranks.

What follows is what we hope is a complete list of all the filmmakers, all the actors who got their start under the 40 Acres banner. This roster is perhaps one of the greatest accomplishments of the 40 Acres and a Mule legacy.

We apologize to anybody whom we overlooked; and I would like especially to thank "Big Mike" Ellis.

Spike Lee
Brooklyn, New York
By Any Means Necessary
YA DIG SHO-NUFF

Directors
Ernest Dickerson
Malcolm Lee
Lee Davis
Malik Sayeed
Jeff Byrd
Abdul Abbott
Cinque Lee
Millicent Shelton
Darnell Martin
Maurice Marable
Dave Meyers

Production
Caryn E. Campbell
Angela Quilles
Susan Fowler
Desiree Jellerette
Sherri Snead
Debra Jeffreys
Paulette Clark
John Murchison
Colin Cumberbatch
Liz Wade

Wardrobe
Sandi Figueroa
Askia Jacob
Paul Simmons Jr.

Accounting
Eric Oden
Darryl Smith
Carmen Hernandez

Sfx
Steve Kirshoff
Willie Caban

Script
Shari Carpenter
Andrea Greer-
  Crawford

Costume Designers
Ruth Carter
Karen Perry
Donna Berwick
Sandra Hernandez
Tracey White
Barbara Chenault
Emilio Sosa
Danielle Hollowell
Dana Campbell
Rita McGhee

Casting
Robi Reed
Aisha Coley
Winsome Sinclaire
Andrea Reed
Tracy Moore-Marable
Tuffy Questell
Tracy Vilar
Kim Coleman
Traci Runcie

DPs
Ernest Dickerson
Arthur Jaffa
Larry Banks
Henry Adebonojo
Malik Sayeed
Ellen Kuras
César Charlone
Rodrigo Prieto
Matty Libatique
Cliff Charles
Kerwin Devonish
Phil Oetiker
Leslie Saltus

Editors
Barry Brown
Sam Pollard
Leander T. Sales
Greg Speed
Kim Chisolm
Jeff Cooper
Geeta Gandbhir

*Production
  Designers* ·
Wynn Thomas
Ina Mayhew
Ted Glass
Ron Norsworthy
Bruton Jones

*Art Dept.
  Coordinator*
Erik Knight

Screenwriters
Chuck Wilson
Joie Lee
Cinque Lee
Malcolm Lee
Lee Davis
Michael Genet
David Benioff
Suzan-Lori Parks
Eric Daniel

Producers/UPMs
Monty Ross
Jon Kilik
Preston Holmes
Brent Owens
Butch Robinson
Marcus Turner
Gingi Rochelle
Abdur Rahman

Hair and Makeup
Larry Cherry
Anita Gibson
Ellie Winslow
Mary Cooke
Matiki Anoff
Cliff Booker
Marjorie Durand

ADs
Randy Fletcher
H. H. Cooper
Dale Pierce-Neilson
Mike Ellis
Michael "Boogie"
  Pinckney
Tracy Hinds
Van Hayden
Sarah Gyllenstierna

Prop Masters
Kevin Ladson
Paul Weathered

Props
Jann McClary
Victor Littlejohn
Adrienne Anderson

Grips
Lamont Cawford
Robert Woods
Tony Arnaud
Terrance Burke
Lois Thompson

Construction
Martin Bernstein

Lead Man
Scott Rosenstock

Scenic Charge
Jeff Glave
Sound
Abdul Abbott
Rosa Howell-
   Thornhill
Larry Decarmine

Teamsters
Kenny Gaskins
Telly Davis
Donny Thompson

Gaffers
Charles Houston

Christian Epps
Visual Efx
Randy Balsmeyer

Stills
David Lee

Stunts
Jeff Ward
Manny Siverio

Locations
George Norfleet
Charlynn Hopkins
Al Valentine

Joe White

Parking
Eddie Joe
Jean Sassine

Composers
Bill Lee
Terence Blanchard
Ricky Gordon

Music Supervision
Alex Steyermark
Barry Cole

Talent
Tracy Camila Johns (Nola Darling, *She's Gotta Have It*, 1986)
Joie Lee (Clorinda Bradford, *She's Gotta Have It*, 1986)
S. Epatha Merkerson (Doctor Jamison, *She's Gotta Have It*, 1986)
Raye Dowell (Opal Gilstrap, *She's Gotta Have It*, 1986)
Jasmine Guy (Dina, *School Daze*, 1988)
Darryl Bell (Big Brother X-Ray Vision, *School Daze*, 1988)
Roger Guenveur Smith (Yoda, *School Daze*, 1988)
Kyme (Rachel Meadows, *School Daze*, 1988)
Martin Lawrence (Cee, *Do the Right Thing*, 1989)
Rosie Perez (Tina, *Do the Right Thing*, 1989)
Leonard Thomas (Big Brother Gen. George Patton, *Do the Right
   Thing*, 1989)
Cynda Williams (Clarke Betancourt, *Mo' Better Blues*, 1990)
Nick Turturro (Josh Flatbush, *Mo' Better Blues*, 1990)
Halle Berry (Vivian, *Jungle Fever*, 1991)
Mekhi Phifer (Strike, *Clockers*, 1995)
Thomas Jefferson Byrd (Errol Barnes, *Clockers*, 1995)
Gretchen Mol (Girl #12, *Girl 6*, 1996)
Dania Ramirez (Alex Guerrero, *She Hate Me*, 2004)
[N.B.: Robin Harris appeared as Bartender at Sam's in *I'm Gonna
   Get You Sucka* (1988), his only credit prior to Sweet Dick Willie
   in *Do the Right Thing* (1989); Bill Nunn has an uncredited role in
   Sharky's Machine (1981), his sole appearance prior to Grady in
   School Daze (1988).]

Blessings

I dedicate this book to the four most influential people in my life. I can plainly state it is not a coincidence that they all happen to be African-American women (well, one is a little too young — let's call her a young woman). They are Mrs. Zimmie Shelton, my maternal grandmother; Ms. Jacquelyn Shelton Lee, my beloved mother; Ms. Tonya Lewis Lee, my dear wife; and Ms. Satchel Lewis Lee, the first child and only daughter of Tonya and I.

All of these strong African-American women have made me a better human being. All have made me question, reach, strive, create, and drive for more than I ever knew that I had in myself. There is a lineage here, a trait that embodies the best there is in the makeup of the African-American family. I call it the backbone.

Thank you, Mama, for your blessings, for putting your first grandchild through Morehouse College and New York University Graduate Film School. Thank you, Mommy, for your blessings. You along with Daddy exposed me to the world of the Arts at a very young age. Thank you for staying with me 24-7 when I was at a critical stage in my life, a time when I was lost, I didn't know who I was or who I could be. Thank you, Tonya, for your laser-hot honesty. Thank you for your blessing of LOVE and AFFIRMATION. I used to be skeptical about affairs of the heart until I met you, but never again. I do and always will believe the Higher Being brought our spirits together. And thank you to Satchel. Thank you for your blessings, you and your brother Jackson have made my life a joyous celebration. I LOVE Y'ALL TO DEATH.

Spike

Index

A Note on the Author

Kaleem Aftab is a freelance writer and a director of the TV and film production house la famiglia (www.lafamiglia.tv). He writes mainly for the *Independent*, *Hotdog*, BBC Collective and *The List*. He resides in London and parties everywhere else.